'Ubuntu is an inspiring memoir about an extraordinary journey taken by an exceptional woman. Heather Ellis writes about her most daring adventures and deepest struggles with humour, heart, guts and grace. I was enthralled by every page.' –Cheryl Strayed, author of *Wild*

'Most of us wouldn't take a motorcycle solo through Africa. Or remember much about what we were saying, smelling, believing or hoping twenty years ago. Heather Ellis did that, and has written a remarkable book about it too. She tells her story vividly and honestly, taking us through fields, national parks, into towns and down red-mud tracks, meeting other travellers and working with locals, eating rice and fish, honing her self-belief and increasing our respect for her with every day on the road. This is a really fascinating and compelling tale, told well. For anyone who has ever doubted themselves, *Ubuntu* has a message: there is a way through, down a road you haven't travelled yet.' – Kate Holden, author of *In Her Skin*

'No two big journeys are alike, and Heather Ellis' could not have been more different to mine, but certain fundamental similarities seem to unite us all, from the prosaic –'My bike was dangerously overloaded' – to the sublime awakenings that such journeys engender. Hers was a great adventure into the soul of Africa, a thrilling story of endurance and self-discovery, told with care, intelligence and deep humanity. It is beautifully written and a pleasure to read. So read it.' –Ted Simon, author of *Jupiter's Travels*

'Ever wondered what your life would look like if you chose to trust rather than fear? Heather Ellis does just this as she rides a motorbike across Africa. She discovers a land torn apart by war and poverty but also a land rich in beauty and kindness. Reading this book is challenging and inspiring. Heather's journey will stay with you long after you finish her story.' –Maggie Mackellar, author of *When It Rains & How to Get There*

UBUNTU

ONE WOMAN'S MOTORCYCLE ODYSSEY ACROSS AFRICA

HEATHER ELLIS

NERO

Published by Nero,
an imprint of Schwartz Publishing Pty Ltd
Level 1, 221 Drummond Street
Carlton VIC 3053, Australia
enquiries@blackincbooks.com
www.nerobooks.com

National Library of Australia Cataloguing-in-Publication entry:
    Ellis, Heather, author.
    Ubuntu : one woman's motorcycle odyssey across Africa / Heather Ellis.
    9781863958202 (paperback)
    9781925203882 (ebook)
    Ellis, Heather–Travel–Africa. Motorcycle touring–Africa.
    Africa–Description and travel. Africa–Social life and customs.
    916.0433

Cover design by Peter Long
Cover photograph by Heather Ellis
Text design and typesetting by Tristan Main
Quote p.ix copyright © Desmond M. Tutu
Map p.x by Mapping Specialists, Ltd.

For
my parents, Kitty and John Ellis,
my children, Ethan, Morgan and Ashton
and
the people of Africa

As I travelled through Africa on a motorcycle, writing became my friend – my travelling companion with whom I shared my experiences as I lived a thousand lifetimes every day. These diaries, filled with my thoughts and conversations, helped me write this book. The rest came from my memories, researched facts and my own interpretation of events. To preserve anonymity, I have changed the names and identifying details of some of the people in this book. While not all the people I met on my travels and all my experiences were included, these omissions were only due to space limitations and the trajectory of the story.

I wrote the first draft in 1996 when events were still fresh. I did not complete the final draft until 2015. While the events, characters and conversations remain the same, I have the advantage of time to understand what it all meant: all those coincidences, chance encounters and the constant accuracy of my intuition. But the distance of time has also allowed the book to tell its own story. And that story is *Ubuntu*.

Heather Ellis, 2016

www.heather-ellis.com

One of the sayings in our country is *ubuntu* – the essence of being human. Ubuntu speaks particularly about the fact that you can't exist as a human being in isolation. It speaks about our interconnectedness. You can't be human all by yourself, and when you have this quality – *ubuntu* – you are known for your generosity. We think of ourselves far too frequently as just individuals, separated from one another, whereas you are connected and what you do affects the whole world. When you do well, it spreads out; it is for the whole of humanity.

Desmond Tutu

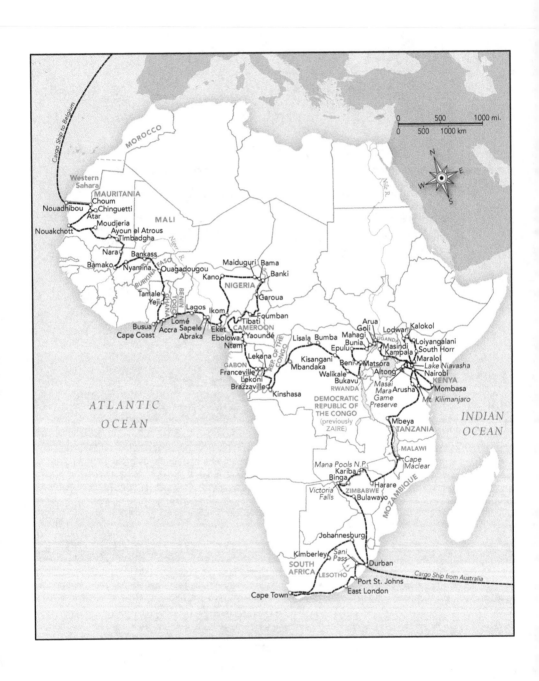

Cargo Ship to Belgium

MOROCCO

0   500   1000 mi.
0 500 1000 km

N
W   E
S

Western
Sahara
MAURITANIA
Choum
Nouadhibou   Chinguetti
Atar
Moudjeria
Nouakchott   Ayoun el Atrous
Timbadgha
MALI
Nara
Bankass
Bamako   Nyamina
Timbadgha
BURKINA FASO
Ouagadougou   Maiduguri Bama
Kano   Banki
Tamale   BENIN   NIGERIA
Yeji   TOGO
Lagos   Garoua
GHANA   Ikom
Busua   Lomé   Foumban
Cape Coast   Accra Sapele   Eket   Tibati
Abraka   Ebolowa   CAMEROON
Ntem   Yaoundé   Arua Lodwar   Kalokol
Lekana   Lisala Bumba   Goli   Loiyangalani
Kisangani   Mahagi   UGANDA   South Horr
GABON   Mbandaka   Bunia   Masindi Kampala   Maralol
Franceville   Epulu   Beni   Matsora   Lake Niavasha
Lekoni   Walikale   Altong   Nairobi
Brazzaville   Bukavu   KENYA
Kinshasa   RWANDA   Masai   Arusha   Mombasa
DEMOCRATIC   Mara   Mt. Kilimanjaro
REPUBLIC OF   Game
THE CONGO   Preserve
(previously   Mbeya
ZAIRE)   TANZANIA
REP. OF THE CONGO
MALAWI
Cape
Maclear
Mana Pools N.P.
Kariba
Binga   Harare
Victoria   ZIMBABWE   MOZAMBIQUE
Falls   Bulawayo

ATLANTIC
OCEAN

INDIAN
OCEAN

Nile R.

Niger R.

Johannesburg

Kimberley   Sani
Pass   Durban
SOUTH
AFRICA   LESOTHO
Cargo Ship from Australia
Cape Town   Port St. Johns
East London

PART THREE
CONGO TO MAURITANIA

PROLOGUE

I was eight years old when I first rode a motorcycle. It was on Ingomar Station, an 1800-square-kilometre sheep property near Coober Pedy in outback South Australia. My ten-year-old brother and I lived there with my aunt and uncle, while my parents mined opal a day's drive into the desert. With our cousins – three girls, just a few years apart – we rode Honda Z50cc mini bikes. We lived on those dirt bikes: on weekends, after school and even during playtime, when we escaped from the school ground in a cloud of dust. During shearing season we mustered sheep on our little motorbikes through mulga scrub, spinifex and fine red sand – the same riding conditions I'd encounter in Africa as a young woman twenty years later.

I was a strong child. I looked like a boy. I had fine sandy-blonde hair which my mother kept short because she said 'it would thicken it up'. My cousins, with sun-kissed locks trailing down their backs, teased me incessantly. I spoke with a lisp and was teased for that too. Alone and left out, I befriended three Aboriginal girls, daughters of the station workers. They wore faded floral dresses with frayed hems and carried digging sticks. I wore shorts and a T-shirt, cast-offs from my cousins. Together we'd walk barefoot into the mulga scrub near the homestead to dig for yams. We'd chew on the water-laden tubers, spitting out the grit as we sat amongst our rabbit-warren-like excavation in the red sand. Or I'd join them to dig fat white witchetty

1

grubs out from under the roots of the mulga trees, screwing up my face every time one of them popped one into their mouth as if it were a strawberry plucked plump and ripe from a vine. They'd laugh, and our giggles joined the happy chirping of the small birds that darted amongst the scrub.

During school holidays, my brother and I went to the diggings, to stay with our parents in their caravan on the opal fields. As they mined, we'd wander into the desert in search of opal floaters – broken bits of white rock that indicated where a seam had pushed up deep from underground. In the stillness, I felt something strangely comforting, as though I too was part of that vast expanse.

After two years in Coober Pedy, when my parents had mined enough opal to buy a house with a pool, a new car and a colour TV (the first in our street in 1974), we moved to suburban Townsville, in Queensland. Motorcycles and the sense of connection I felt with the Aboriginal girls and to the desert were gone from my life – shelved to emerge years later. I turned to books and discovered Africa. I read on the school bus, in the library during recess, in the classroom with the book hidden under my desk, and at night when my parents thought I was sleeping. I started with Robert Ruark's *Something of Value* and while the bloodthirsty account of Kenya's Mau Mau uprising against British rule both mesmerised and horrified me, his descriptions of Africa and its people fostered in me a longing to go there. Ruark was quickly followed by most of Wilbur Smith, starting with the *The Sunbird*.

As I grew older, I drifted away from my dream to travel to Africa. After high school, I followed my parents to the Northern Territory, where my father had recently started work as an operator at the Ranger uranium mine on the fringes of the Kakadu national park. I worked there, all up, for nine years, living in the nearby township of Jabiru alongside my three-hundred-plus colleagues. I got my start as a receptionist, but soon transferred to the better-paid position of stores clerk in the supply department. In 1983, I resigned to backpack through Europe, but returned to the mine two years later to work as a tour guide and, finally, as a radiation safety technician.

Living in a small mining town with just about everything within walking distance and a free bus service to the mine, there was no real need for a car, so the obvious choice for transport was a motorcycle. When I first moved to Jabiru after high school, my father assured the local police sergeant, who he was mates with, that I could ride a bike, and I was issued with a motorcycle licence on the spot. My first bike was a little Honda XL185, ideal for exploring Kakadu's wild places.

After nearly six years working at the mine, I was twenty-eight years old and yearned for change. My restlessness ate away at me; I felt as though my life would only begin once I'd left the isolation of the mine and its small town. My backpacking trip had given me a taste of adventure, and I wanted more. But I had no ideas, no plans, no dreams of any substance – until a sudden moment of illumination on a Sunday afternoon.

I was drinking beers with friends at a barbecue when, for no apparent reason, I blurted out: 'I'm going to ride a motorcycle through Africa.' As I recall, motorcycle travel was not a topic of our idle chat as we sat on eskies and plastic chairs in a friend's backyard. I couldn't believe the words had come from me. But the idea felt like it had been there all along, lying dormant for years, waiting for this moment. I sat stunned and speechless, as if some otherworldly force had gripped me by the shoulders and said: 'You *need* to do this.' In that instant, time stood still. It was only a brief pause, but it was long enough for me to notice. And while my drinking buddies quickly forgot my momentary lapse of reason, I did not. I could think of nothing else: the idea both frightened and enlivened me. But at the same time, I also felt in complete balance, as though I had known all along that this was my life's purpose.

Days later, although my friends and work colleagues responded with a barrage of doubts, the idea had not died. Instead, it had grown in strength and, like a tiny living thing, I held it close and nurtured it.

In those first days and weeks, I had a lucid dream of flying over the Indian Ocean. With my arms outstretched, I skimmed above the waves until I hovered over the docks of Durban in South Africa. My motorcycle

3

was on the deck of a ship and, after it was unloaded, I rode fast and confidently over Africa's desert plains. The dream reassured me that my idea was true and solid, and that I was on the right track.

The planning began. I told my parents, on a visit to their banana farm in north Queensland where they'd moved from Jabiru several years earlier. With slow deliberateness, I explained that their only daughter would soon ride a motorcycle alone through Africa. They understood immediately that I would do it, and that none of their objections would sway me. My father hid his worry behind humour and mumbled something about me ending up in a cooking pot. I told them not to worry. I would be okay. I could not explain why, but I knew I was meant to do this.

PART ONE

KAKADU TO KENYA

1

IT STARTED WITH A KICK...
AUSTRALIA TO SOUTH AFRICA

I rode on a dirt track fringed by two-metre-tall spear grass the colour of golden wheat ready for harvest. It would soon be flattened by the knock 'em down rains signalling the start of the wet season in the Northern Territory. My motorcycle was a Yamaha TT600 built for extreme off-road riding. I'd bought it in Darwin a week earlier, following advice from my motorcycle-riding workmates about what motorcycle I should take to Africa. They had all said: 'Nothing is as tough as the TT600.'

It was my rostered day off and the first chance I'd had to take my new motorcycle off-road through a stretch of muddy swamp, down a gully and over a section of rocks that littered the track – similar conditions to what I'd encounter in Africa. An hour after I began, I reached a gorge of monsoon rainforest at the base of the Arnhem Land escarpment. It was a majestic place where a 500-kilometre-long escarpment rose up 200 metres from an ancient seabed, now the Kakadu wetlands. Leaving my bike, I hiked to a spring-fed rock pool and glided silently through water made cold and dark by its depth. Chilled, I lay on a ledge to warm my body. I felt at home. As if I belonged. As if this secret place embraced me – protected me, spoke to me. Looking up, I saw that dark clouds had gathered above me. I quickly climbed down from the ledge, swam back across the pool and trekked down the gorge to my motorcycle. Before I headed home, I stopped to stare in awe at the place where the track ran parallel to the escarpment. Against a backdrop of gunmetal grey clouds, the late afternoon sun illuminated the reddish-brown stains that ran down the cliffs, as if a prehistoric serpent had perished on its summit, plucked from the sea below by a giant pterosaur.

Towering above me was a sheer wall of sandstone. I rode towards it, leaving my bike at the base of the cliff and scrambling over truck-sized boulders to reach a ledge. I stood breathless and sweaty in the humid summer heat and gazed out over Kakadu. It was a giant patchwork of brown and black where the wetlands had shrunk and controlled burns had left the land bare, but the rains would soon return and it would be alive and green once more. I leaned against the smooth rock. It felt cool through the thin cotton of my shirt and I pressed my body against the ancient stone, as if it radiated a hidden energy as old as the Dreamtime. I asked for its blessing: for it to empower and protect me on the journey ahead. I did this without thinking; my actions were an instinctive response to the feeling of the stone.

I would never have dreamed of doing anything like this until recently. Previously, I'd given no thought to the meaning of things, to this ancient land or to the earth's hidden energies – other than the radiation levels detected by my monitoring instruments at the mine. And the connection that I had made with the desert and its people as a child in outback Australia had faded. But since that moment at the barbecue nearly nine months earlier, everything had changed. Now, as I looked up, the cliff towering over me, I intuitively felt some kind of ever-so-slight mysterious force – a primordial energy that permeated everything.

The storm clouds grew blacker and heavier. I climbed down from the ledge and scrambled over the boulders. Behind me, the rain fell in great sheets. I reached my motorcycle as the first heavy drops stung my back and arms. Water gushed down the track, and where it crossed a gully it was a raging torrent. I had no choice but to ride across; if I hesitated the torrent would soon be too deep and I would be trapped until the waters receded hours later. I rode through, water lapping at the muffler. I reached the other side, the bike climbed out and I opened the throttle for home.

On that solo ride into one of Kakadu's secret places something happened – an awakening of sorts. I felt it as a heightened sense of aliveness. This awareness was physical, but my mind could not grasp what it meant.

Something else remarkable happened on that daring ride. In our shared adventure, in our shared moment of vulnerability in the rising flood waters, I no longer saw my motorcycle as a pile of nuts and bolts, plastic and steel. It, too, seemed different – as though it radiated its own aura. From that day on, I affectionately referred to it simply as the TT.

*

The Yamaha TT600 is pure enduro, a big bore single-cylinder thumper of a motorcycle with a deep, almost primeval sound that says power and strength. No terrain can beat this bike, even when loaded with nearly a hundred kilograms of luggage, tools and spares. And all this can easily be removed and then, at just over 120 kilograms, the bike is light enough to be ferried across a river on a canoe or lifted onto the back of a truck.

When I collected the TT in Darwin, it started with the first kick. While this is expected for a new motorcycle, it was quite an achievement for me, as I stood at a slight 165 centimetres and when I sat on the bike there was a good amount of space between the ground and my feet. I could only kick-start it by standing on the foot pegs, the bike on its side-stand. Realistically, I should have chosen the TT350 model. It was lower and lighter, so it would have been easier to ride, and it was still almost as powerful as the TT600. But I didn't question my choice, because the TT600 felt right, just like the idea to travel across Africa did.

I solved the problem of the TT's height by trimming more than half of the foam from the seat. When riding on long stretches of tarmac, to prevent 'numb bum', I would sit on an air-inflated wine-cask bladder placed under a piece of thick, woolly sheepskin. With the press of a finger, the bladder could be easily deflated when I needed to stop and touch the ground on tippy toes.

Next was the dilemma of how I would carry my mountain of gear. But this, too, was easily overcome, as right there on the Yamaha shop floor was a set of suitcase-shaped thick leather pannier bags and a heavy steel frame. With some minor modifications they would fit the TT. They cost $500 and belonged to a Swiss motorcyclist who'd ended his ride around Australia just days before.

This was the first of many coincidences that unfolded soon after the idea of my ride had burst into my life. In the beginning I shrugged these off as just good luck, but as each day passed, little, almost indiscernible, things happened at every turn. I was on the cusp of a new life and tingling with expectation, and in this heightened state of awareness I began to notice these subtle hints of synchronicity.

A few weeks after I purchased the TT, a motorcycle traveller knocked on my door. It was a hot, humid afternoon when he arrived dusty, sweaty and pink-faced from riding on the dirt roads through Kakadu. He was a short man – shorter than me – and about thirty, I guessed. When some local townspeople visiting Darwin came across him, they told him he simply must visit me.

'Hello. I am Rolf. I come from Germany. Your friends tell me you want to travel Africa by motorcycle. It is very tough,' he said with a stern gaze through little round glasses, his head tilted upwards.

So size doesn't matter when it comes to motorcycle travel, I thought as I smiled down at him.

Rolf told me he had ridden from North to South Africa and was now riding through outback Australia on his Yamaha XT600 Tenere.

When I showed him the TT with its leather panniers, he said, 'These will not do. No, no, the thieves will steal all your belongings. No, you must have metal panniers. Much stronger,' he insisted, emphasising that great planning and specialised equipment was required to undertake such an expedition. 'And this *motorrad*. With all your things, it is much too heavy.

What you do when you fall? You will not lift it.'

But I would no more trade the TT for something more suitable than if I were a mother and it was my child.

'Yes, on your trial run, you will see this bike will not do,' Rolf added, shaking his head with disapproval over my poor choice.

'Trial run?' I stammered. I'd never considered doing a trial run but it made sense and I made a mental note to include this in my planning. A one-week ride to Uluru, the ancient monolith rising up out of Australia's red centre, would be perfect.

But I never did that trial run. With all the planning, I just forgot about it.

'The roads in Africa have much bumps. You must wear a kidney belt to stop the vibration damaging the little tube attached to your kidneys. This belt holds everything in place and protects your back and insides when you have a fall,' he said, holding up a wide black belt with Velcro straps. 'This is very important. You will be many hours every day on your bike.'

'Yes. Thank you,' I said, and dutifully added kidney belt to the list in my 'Africa planning' notebook.

Rolf's arrival may have seemed more of a hindrance than a help, and not *that* unlikely an occurence. After all, I lived on the fringe of Kakadu, a must-see on any trip around Australia. But I viewed his visit as another sign. It was 1992 and well before access to instant information via the internet. Until the moment when Rolf appeared on my doorstep, all I knew of motorcycle travel was what I'd read in Ted Simon's classic motorcycle travel book *Jupiter's Travels*. (A mine worker had given me a dog-eared copy of Ted's book when word of my ride spread.) Like a sponge, I soaked up Rolf's travel advice: some I took on board, some I discarded.

'Do not trust the Africans. To them you are "business",' he said when he moved on from Jabiru a few days later. But as I stood watching him ride away, I felt no truth in his parting words.

Nevertheless, most of Rolf's advice did seem invaluable and I began making a long list of all the motorcycle spares, camping equipment, first-aid supplies, documents, vaccinations and visas I would need. I fitted a twenty-one-litre Acerbis plastic petrol tank to the TT to give me a range of 400 kilometres plus fifty on reserve. I bolted a set of metal Barkbusters hand guards to the handlebars to protect my hands, clutch and brake levers. I designed modifications for my motorcycle: a front rack, a toolbox and a solid steel barrier to protect the engine from falls. I then headed to the mine's welding workshop with my designs and made a cash deal with a welder on nightshift.

As much as those early days of planning were driven by my obsession with the ride, I was not immune to niggling doubts. *What if your bike breaks down? What will you do if you're attacked? You can't go alone. What about a travelling companion?* All of these questions were put to me once word of my plans spread amongst friends and colleagues. And as the chorus of doubters grew louder, so too did my own misgivings. Riding a motorcycle through Africa alone meant confronting a plethora of possible dangers, and there were also practicalities to consider. The inside of a motorcycle engine remained a complete mystery to me, and mechanical breakdowns worried me more than the remote possibility of rape, mugging or murder. Fear set in and now I not only wanted a travelling companion, I wanted one who could fix motorcycles.

When Rolf and I had discussed my lack of mechanical aptitude and the pros and cons of travelling companions, he had assured me I was still better off on my own. 'Do not worry about your bike. It is new. It will not break down if you change the oil and do your maintenance,' he said. 'There are so many people travelling Africa by motorbike and they will help you. Some you may travel with for a time, but you will find travelling alone is very good,' he added.

But despite Rolf's assurances, it was with great relief that, two months before departure, I found a travelling companion.

Dan worked as an operator at the mine and had grown up riding and repairing dirt bikes. He was tall and gangly with shoulder-length, sandy-brown hair that hung over his face, which he'd flip back with a toss of his head to reveal an easy *hey man, be cool* smile. Dan had been at that Sunday afternoon barbecue and had said, 'Hey, that's a beaut idea.' He, too, was in his late twenties, but looked more at home on a surfboard than travelling Africa by motorcycle. While we mixed in the same group of friends, we'd only ever exchanged a few words. But I reasoned our common desire to explore and experience Africa was all that was needed to make our travelling partnership work.

Dan's motorcycle was a Honda XR600 – the main off-road competitor of the Yamaha TT600. It meant we could not share spare parts, and it also proved to be a dark omen symbolising the incompatibilities between us that soon began to emerge. We spoke little during the weeks leading up to our departure, but Dan agreed, in his casual, laidback way, with my rough plan, mapped out over many months working nightshift. The ride would take a year or two: neither of us was on a time limit. First we'd ride down to Perth, from where we'd take a cargo ship to Durban. We would ride around South Africa and then head north into Zimbabwe and quickly cross Mozambique, which had only recently emerged from a sixteen-year civil war, to Malawi. In Tanzania and Kenya we'd visit the game parks and maybe climb a mountain or two. After that, the idea was to ride west into Uganda and Zaire (renamed the Democratic Republic of the Congo in 1997), then up through West Africa and into North Africa to Morocco. We were both undecided about the ride home, but by then my funds would be low and I planned to head to London and get a job to finance the second leg of my world motorcycle odyssey.

*

On Sunday, 7 February 1993, the morning after our farewell party at the local pub, Dan and I rode away from our friends, our lives and our well-paid jobs for our first stop, Perth. By chance, it was a year almost to the day since I'd blurted out the idea of doing this ride. As rain fell over Kakadu, I gripped the TT's handlebars and tensed my body against the impact of a heavy wet-season downpour.

My motorcycle was dangerously overloaded. Most of the equipment stuffed into the two leather panniers and Gearsack bag on the seat behind me was for the TT and for camping. But I'd also packed a lot of unnecessary equipment, things that were classified as 'might need'. These impractical things included a heavy cotton string hammock, and scuba fins, mask and snorkel for the coral reefs fringing the glorious golden sand beaches along Africa's east coast. I also carried Lonely Planet's *Africa* guidebook – a weighty tome affectionately known amongst travellers in Africa as the 'Bible' – and several novels, including Robert Pirsig's *Zen and the Art of Motorcycle Maintenance*, which seemed an appropriate read for the start of this ride.

In the early days of planning I had sent off requests for sponsorship to Yamaha, Tsubaki and Mobil. My letter to Mobil was an afterthought, prompted by a conversation with the driver of a Mobil fuel truck on a delivery to the mine. He'd taken more than a passing interest in the map of Africa spread out on a benchtop in the security gatehouse where I was working nightshift. (A few months earlier the mine had retrenched nearly half its workforce and my job as radiation safety technician had been amalgamated with that of security guard.)

'You should get Mobil to sponsor you. They're all over the world,' he said.

So I wrote to the Mobil office in Darwin and promptly received a letter of introduction. My priceless letter advised: *Heather Ellis is a motorcycle enthusiast travelling the world, and as part of her expedition is trialling exclusively Mobil lubricants, but particularly Mobil 1. Heather would appreciate any form of assistance that can be provided.*

I also wrote to Japanese chain manufacturer Tsubaki and they supplied me with four motorcycle chains. I gave two to Dan and I carried two myself, which weighed heavily in my panniers. Yamaha also responded to my request for spare parts. It was a heavy load to lug through Africa, but at the time I was sure I'd need most of it. To honour this sponsorship, I dutifully plastered the TT with sponsors' stickers and promised to write magazine articles and contact local media.

I packed the bare minimum of clothes, most of which I wore at any one time. My riding outfit consisted of my lace-up steel-capped work boots, black jeans, a Gore-Tex motorcycle jacket and a short-sleeved denim shirt. The rest of my wardrobe, along with underwear and socks, comprised a polar-fleece jacket, a long-sleeved shirt, black leggings (which doubled as thermals), a swimsuit, a sarong, thongs, canvas shoes and a sun hat. I packed wet weather pants, a sleeping bag, a Thermarest mattress, a water filter, a small cooking pot, and lots of little plastic containers filled with sugar, tea, coffee, milk powder, spices and salt. My first-aid kit was packed with medicines to treat common infections, bandages in case of injury and ointments to treat festering wounds.

I did not pack condoms. Somewhat naively, I figured I'd avoid any risk of catching HIV by remaining celibate in Africa. In the months leading up to departure, however, as if to rid my body of any residual cravings, I took several casual lovers. I was possessed by a physical, almost primal, urge for sex. With no misguided thoughts of romantic love, I indulged in liberating sex like nothing I'd ever experienced. The kind of sex filled with passion and lust and waves of orgasmic pleasure; this was sex for sex's sake. My promiscuity was very out of character, as I'd remained mostly single for the past six years, with just the occasional boyfriend. Even though we'd all been scared by the 'Grim Reaper', an HIV/AIDS awareness campaign that burst onto Australian television screens in 1987, there was no talk of safe sex with these partners. We all thought that in our isolation we were protected from the outside world. Besides, in our small-town ignorance, we all thought that HIV happened only to gays and drug users, not heterosexuals having a bit of orgasmic fun.

But mining towns, filled with single people who holiday in South-East Asia and transient workers from everywhere, are far from safe from sexually transmitted diseases. When rumour spread that one of us had tested positive to HIV, panic gripped the town. The person diagnosed left within days and we all lined up to be tested. Given the all clear, I vowed never again to have unprotected sex. But the vows were short-lived and the Grim Reaper was soon a distant memory.

With the wet-season downpour behind us, I settled into Day One of the ride and, for the first time, I started to notice things – the sort of things that are obvious when riding a motorcycle. I breathed in the smell of recently rained-on earth mixed with the scented leaves of eucalyptus. Even over the rhythmic thump of the bike's engine, I could hear the constant shrill of a billion cicadas. Spear grass grew tall and I rode down a tunnel of iridescent green. The road opened to floodplains, lush with the thick growth of wild grasses, only to close in again to dense woodland where shrubs hugged the smooth tarmac. The TT purred like it would go forever and I relaxed into the feeling of riding on a road that only went forward. It was the freedom of a journey by motorcycle. It was the freedom to live with no time limits, no commitments and no responsibilities, other than to the road ahead and what I would find there.

*

We were two weeks into our pseudo trial-run before Africa, and 1000 kilometres from Perth, when we pulled up late one afternoon at a scenic lookout. It was barely a low hill but its summit offered an endless view over a rocky desert dotted with grey salt-bush. Not even the persistent little black flies seeking my salty wetness could distract me for those first few moments.

'Massive, isn't it?' I said to Dan as I gazed across an endless desert that stretched beyond the horizon, thousands of miles across Australia.

Dan stood in silence several metres away, his back slightly turned as if to tell the world we were complete strangers. Things had gotten steadily worse between us since leaving Kakadu, to the point that we now only spoke in clipped sentences and mumbled grunts. Sometimes we camped, and in those long uncomfortable hours before sleep, Dan busied himself collecting wood for a fire while plugged into his Walkman and I sat with the TT as if it were my only friend in all the world, checking it for loose nuts and bolts and any emerging problems. To cut down on weight, we had agreed to carry only one tent. While it was large enough to give us space to sleep, Dan at one end and I pressed up against the other, the space was not enough to deflect the tension. So mostly we stayed at backpacker hostels, sharing eight-bed dorms with others. With long-legged Scandinavians and big-breasted Poms around, I understood that Dan didn't want me to cramp his style and I kept my distance. But I felt as though this avoidance just looked odd to the backpackers, and it made me feel even lonelier.

'We're different people. We don't click. That's just the way it is,' Dan said when I reached out to him over breakfast at a hostel one morning, in a futile attempt to put an end to the tension between us.

'But we're travelling together,' I pleaded as he pushed back his chair with a loud scrape on the timber floor, leaving me alone with my tea and toast.

Where had the high gone? Where was that reassuring force that had sustained me throughout the year of planning?

I knew my fears were pathetic and filled with self-doubt borne from Dan's persistent disregard of me. I'd never been treated this way by anyone and felt confused as to the cause. Was it my fault? There was no reason to blame myself, but I did, and the more I tried to make things right – to make our travelling partnership work – the more Dan retreated from me.

As I looked out at the desert, Dan's words played over and over in my head: *We don't click. That's just the way it is.* I realised suddenly how right he was and how blind I'd been not to see it. I recalled my relief when he said he'd do this ride with me. But I knew now I had ignored the warning signs out of my own buried insecurities because deep down I was afraid to travel alone. Dan never looked me in the eye when we spoke and I had always felt an uncomfortable energy between us, as though we were two magnets with like poles facing, naturally repelling each other. We were simply not of the same tribe. We had no spirit of kinship with which to grow and learn from the experiences and discoveries that we'd find in Africa. This realisation both shocked and liberated me because I under-stood I was not the problem. I realised then that I had no choice but to stop pushing for a resolution. Instead, I'd let things be, and go back to what I'd done over the past year: take one step at a time and let things fall naturally into place. Maybe, I thought, as our journey progressed Dan and I would find a faint level of compatibility – but I knew this was wishful thinking born out of my own fears.

'We've got to get moving,' Dan said as he waved angrily at the flies. I turned away from the view of the desert and got back on the TT to follow his trail of dust to the highway and the turn-off to Monkey Mia.

Dan was still seething from the argument we'd had earlier when we pulled up for fuel at a roadhouse. He had wanted to reach Perth quickly by riding on the highway and saving his motorcycle and his money for Africa. I, however, could not curtail my enthusiasm to explore and had insisted we take a detour to visit Monkey Mia and its dolphins. Dan had finally relented. This 300-kilometre round-trip detour allowed our paths to cross with two seasoned motorcycle travellers, a couple from Denmark about the same age as us. He rode a Honda XR600 (the same bike as Dan); she a Yamaha XT400. He had shaggy brown hair and a bristly face with a permanent grin that comes from knowing life is to be lived as one great adventure. She was lean with platinum blonde hair plaited like rope, and walked with the strength and confidence of a woman who had conquered her fears. We shook hands as though we were long-lost friends – such is the understanding, the camaraderie, that comes with motorcycles, and even more so amongst motorcycle travellers.

Gladis and Anders were near the end of their trip and would be returning to Denmark from Perth. Their travel advice helped cull a little of my mountain of gear: a candle lamp, two of my three novels (not *Zen*), and a camping spade. But I refused to ditch my scuba fins, mask and snorkel, or my hammock. Dan relented and culled his stack of cassette tapes. Instead of pub meals with a couple of beers and game of pool, we followed their example and cut our costs by making our own food: a lunch of bread, salami, cheese, cucumber and tomatoes eaten under the shade of a tree, or a rice and vegetable curry cooked on a campfire or in a communal hostel kitchen.

We rode the last stretch to Perth together, following the tracks that hugged the coast, and I welcomed their easy nature and good humour, which deflected the tension between Dan and me.

Once we arrived in Perth, there was little time to dwell on this tension, as we had two weeks before the ten-day voyage across the Indian Ocean to Durban. Our days were filled with last-minute preparations. There were vaccinations (yellow fever, cholera, hepatitis and typhoid), a dental check-up, and more gear to buy. I purchased a Nikon SLR camera and more first-aid supplies. There was the complicated and expensive process of a Carnet de Passage to organise. This important document was the passport to import and export a vehicle into another country without paying duty. Without it, we would not be riding our motorcycles through many of Africa's nations.

I handed over the $7500 as a security deposit to the Royal Automobile Club of Western Australia, which would be returned once I reached Europe, where a carnet was not needed. My money rapidly dwindled to just $2500, which had to last the next four months, until late July, when my bank balance would be topped up with a tax return of over $4000. I carried US$1000, half in cash and half in travellers' cheques. When this ran out, I could access more through my American Express card at their branches in most of Africa's capital cities. I'd also given my mother authority to access my bank account to pay for these Amex withdrawals.

At first our list of necessary preparations seemed insurmountable, but each tiny step brought us closer to departure. When it was time to say goodbye to Gladis and Anders, my embrace was filled with gratitude for their advice and friendship at a time when I was feeling so alone. Our motorcycles were loaded onto the container ship to be stored in an engine room. To stop them rusting from salt air during the ten-day voyage, each was sprayed liberally with the water-displacing spray WD40, and wrapped tightly in clear plastic.

The ship was 200 metres long with twenty-five crew, plus five passengers including Dan and myself. Diana, a South African retiree, and her German shepherd, who was too old to travel by plane, were returning to Durban after a long visit with her daughter in Perth. Nathan, 'the Onion Man' from Tasmania, a tall freckle-faced youth fresh from university with a shock of ginger hair, was responsible for the refrigeration of thirty containers of onions bound for England. And Jim, a retired merchant seaman from Perth hunched over with age and arthritis, just wanted to be at sea again.

Dan and I shared the owners' cabin. We both breathed an audible sigh when we saw it had two separate rooms, as we each craved privacy and space from the ever-present negative energy between us. During the crossing we kept to ourselves, only seeing each other at meal times, or passing on deck or in the cabin, when we exchanged a mumbled greeting. I spent my days reading *Zen* and lifting weights in the ship's gym, a small room just below deck. When I started planning the trip, I quickly realised I would need strength to ride a fully loaded motorcycle weighing in at 200 kilograms. There was no gym at the mine township, but the police had allowed me to use theirs at their station, and over the past year my body had become a powerhouse of strength, with muscles like hardened steel.

As passengers we were treated as honoured guests, dining with the captain and his officers at a long table set with plates and cutlery, with five courses for both lunch and dinner. Meals were always accompanied by endless carafes of red wine and freshly baked crusty rolls. Dessert was fresh fruit followed by strong black coffee and the chef's home-made lemon liqueur.

After a few days at sea the crew befriended us, and some nights we'd be invited back to a cabin to drink their duty-free booze. On one such evening, Dan and Nathan called it a night, but I stayed to finish a bottle of bourbon with one of the crew. After living in the Northern Territory for nine years, I'd become firmly entrenched in the Top End 'drink til ya drop' lifestyle. Many times I had crawled and staggered back to my one-room unit alone after a night of heavy drinking.

'I'll go now,' I slurred as I stood, then banged head-first into the door before pulling it open to stagger towards the three flights of narrow stairs to my cabin near the bridge. It was a full moon and the seas were calm. Hands reached for me. 'I help you,' a voice whispered and a strong arm circled my waist as I was led along the walkway to the ship's bow. I was gently pushed, or maybe I fell, on hard, cold metal. Hands pulled at my leggings. Even in my bourbon-fuelled drunken stupor, I realised two very important things. Through my careless actions, a mix of naivety and trust, I'd placed myself in a dangerous situation. And half the ship's crew were probably watching with high-powered night-vision sea binoculars from the bridge.

I mustered super-human strength, pushed him away and stood up, almost toppling over but gripping a railing to regain my balance. Placing one hand over the other on the railings, I slowly inched my way back along the narrow walkway to my cabin, where a third very important thing dawned on me: I was no longer in a small, isolated mining town where there was always someone to watch over me.

Mostly, though, as we crossed the Indian Ocean, the seas were calm and the ship rose and fell with the enormous roll of the waves. I sat at the very tip of the bow, where the crew had welded railings, and as I dangled my legs over the edge, I ran my fingers through my hair. It protruded just a few centimetres from my head, as I'd lined up earlier that morning with the rest of the crew for a haircut from the radio operator who acted as the ship's barber. I sat there, feeling both invincible and insignificant as I watched dolphins leap and glide as they played in the bow wave far below. I'd just finished reading *Zen and the Art of Motorcycle Maintenance*, which has nothing to do with fixing bikes but everything to do with the idea of *Quality*, which is also what is needed if mechanical repairs are to last. I'd struggled to understand Pirsig's theory. Just when I was sure I'd grasped it, my thoughts became scrambled and I'd start the process of, 'If this means that, then that means this' all over again. But on that tenth day, as Durban appeared on the horizon and I sat mesmerised by the dolphins as they swam and leapt with great skill, I intuitively felt that *Quality* lay at the very heart of all things. Had the dolphins done the best they could do? Had they, over millions of years, strived for *Quality* and I now witnessed their evolutionary reward? Maybe, like the dolphins, I too had done the very best I could and made an idea become reality, my commitment helping everything to fall into place. I was here, sitting on the bow of a container ship, dolphins leaping beneath me, with Africa on the horizon. My idea was no longer a string of words that I'd casually blurted out to friends. I'd taken that first step and I was now moving forward, as if driven by some hidden force that nothing could stop.

2

THE DAWN OF UNITY
SOUTH AFRICA

Once our ship docked in Durban, we rode no further than a youth hostel in the city centre. Each afternoon we strolled to the mall to drink beers and watch the promenade of tourists. The ship would be in port for a week loading and unloading cargo, and most evenings some of the off-duty crew joined us as the sun cast long, golden shadows across the Indian Ocean. A few beers with them would usually end at a bar open till the early hours.

A week went by and my agitation grew: this was not the Africa I yearned for. I consoled myself with the excuse that to avoid the risk of becoming road carnage, it was best we stay in Durban until after the Easter long weekend. The hostel's staff had repeatedly warned us about South Africa's notoriously bad drivers.

While Dan slept, I walked for miles each morning along the golden sands of Durban's beachfront. The council authorities kept most of it clean of the black sludge left behind by the container ships, and the sand was only spoiled at the far reaches.

I found myself walking there on my twenty-ninth birthday, feeling like I had nothing to celebrate and no one to celebrate it with. I reached an abandoned jetty, its pillars thickly encrusted with barnacles. An elderly

African man sat alone fishing with a hand line. He was withered by age and sun and had a wise, Yoda-like face.

'Catch any fish?' I asked and leaned to peer inside his plastic bucket.

'The sea is not so good today,' he said and waved a leathery hand for me to sit beside him. 'Where you from? Not South Africa,' he said with a frown and I got the feeling that a white woman striking up a casual conversation with a black man was not normally done here.

'Australia,' I responded, dangling my legs over the side of the jetty as he did. 'It's my birthday today. I'm twenty-nine,' I gushed like a small child wanting to share my special news.

'Well, well. Happy birthday,' he grinned. 'You are so far from your family. Do not tell me you are alone here in Africa?' he asked, his toothless grin gone, replaced with a frown.

'No, I'm with a friend. We're both on motorcycles,' I said, but instead of lightness and expectation, my words were filled with sadness. 'We will ride all the way to North Africa. It's true!' I added with a sudden defensive perkiness as I interpreted his look of surprise as disbelief.

'I believe you, I can see you will do it, but you have a problem with your husband,' he said, his black eyes piercing into my soul like long tentacles probing for the truth.

'Dan. My *husband*? No. We are just friends. But I don't think he holds the same desire to travel Africa as I do,' I said, letting the words spill out as though I were confiding in an old friend.

'Maybe he is afraid. You are a woman and do not see the dangers. But this Dan, he is a man. He see the bad. He must protect. A woman does not see the world the same way as a man. If any bad thing should happen to you, he will be blamed. It is a heavy burden for a man to look after his woman,' he said.

'I am *not* his woman. We are travelling companions. That's all,' I replied, a little annoyed that he didn't get it.

'It does not matter. You are still a woman and he is still a man,' he said, and gave a quick jerk of the line as a fish nibbled the bait. 'Maybe this journey is not for him. Be patient. You are new to Africa.'

As he pulled in the fishing line, I looked out over the sea. It was choppy with white caps under a cloudless blue sky. If what this old man said was true, I didn't need to be held back by another's fears when I had enough of my own. We sat in silence, and as the old man re-baited the hook, I considered the source of the tension between Dan and me from a different point of view. While I had accepted we didn't click, I suddenly wondered if he was also filled with resentment against me because he saw me as the cause of him giving up his job, his friends, and possibly his life? Was the old man right and this journey was not for Dan? Had he convinced himself otherwise, just as I had convinced myself we would make suitable travelling companions?

'Do not swim in this sea, it is full of sharks,' said the old man, startling me from my thoughts as he threw out his fishing line.

I gasped. In those first few days in Durban, when we'd joined the crew from the cargo ship drinking beers and shooters in smoke-filled bars until the early hours, I *had* swum in this sea. On one of those nights, I'd needed fresh air and had escaped the press of sweaty bodies and thick cigarette smoke on the arm of a merchant seaman, who'd led me to the beach. I stripped to my bra and pants to swim waist deep in the gentle surf, ignorant of the threat that lurked just offshore. I'd also been oblivious to the threat on the beach, where meaty hairy hands reached for my body which I'd so casually, so naively, stripped to my underwear. Once again, booze had made me careless, and in my drunkenness I was unaware of my vulnerability until the cold sea sobered me. It was another lesson and this time I vowed to heed it.

'I'm going now,' I said and held out my hand to the old man. His skin was rough, but his touch warm.

That evening Dan and I sat alone in the hostel dining room. We drank beers and ate pizza and he wished me a happy birthday. I felt light-hearted, the happiest I'd felt in days. It was as if the words of the old man had pushed away the black cloud that hung over me and the sun shone again to bathe me in rays of confidence.

'I want to leave tomorrow,' I said with conviction as I looked for possible routes to Cape Town outlined on the Michelin map of southern Africa spread on the table between us.

'No worries,' Dan croaked, as though unfamiliar with speech, and I realised it was the first time we'd had an actual conversation, or at least the beginning of one, in several days. When I returned from my walks he was often gone from the hostel and did not return until after I was asleep at night in the dorm we shared.

'I was thinking, we could ride across Lesotho to reach Cape Town instead of the boring stretch of highway,' I said moving the map towards him.

'Sounds good,' he replied and so it was settled, the next morning, on Good Friday, against all the warnings about atrociously bad drivers during the Easter holiday weekend, we would venture into Africa.

*

Traffic sped past with no regard for speed limits or road rules as we rode away from Durban towards the mountain-top country of Lesotho. We would ride up the notorious Sani Pass, a nine-kilometre gravel track of hairpin turns covered in shards of loose rock that heads up over the northern Lesotho mountain range. There had been horrific vehicle accidents on this back road into Lesotho, a land-locked country surrounded by a slowly collapsing apartheid regime. But I did not know this then. I had only looked for interesting roads with many twists and turns – the tighter the better – rather than the more direct roads heading south.

Once away from the city traffic, we rode on smooth tarmac winding its way through undulating farmland to a backpackers' hostel at the bottom of the pass. There we met three dark-haired Israeli motorcycle travellers – Romie, Ari and Ariel – on their Yamaha XT500s. We'd first met them, very briefly, at the hostel in Durban. They'd spent the past week touring the Transkei coast south of Durban and, like us, they planned to detour through Lesotho on their ride to Cape Town.

The next morning we tackled the Sani Pass together. As the track climbed, we had clear views all the way to the Indian Ocean. I took quick glimpses until it became a dangerous distraction. Each hairpin bend was covered with shards of rock that moved in waves of instability as the TT powered over it with careful determination. I was grateful Dan had suggested I change the bike's gearing and helped me fit my spare 15-tooth front and 48-tooth rear sprockets to tackle the ascent. Steering the TT around each bend, steely concentration was needed to focus on the track and not the vertical drop-off that lay a few feet from my tyres.

At the top, the scenery was desolate and windswept with ragged mountain ranges in the distance. We just made the border post before it closed. Two immigration officials emerged from a hut erected out of stones and lengths of rough-cut timber. They were small, dark-skinned men, and to fend off the biting wind they wore brightly coloured blankets wrapped tightly around their shoulders and box-shaped wool hats pulled low over their ears. As they stamped our passports and carnets, we asked them to stay open a few moments longer as the three Israelis were still a short distance behind.

Just near the border post is the Sani Pass Lodge, perched on the edge of the steep Drakensberg mountain range. The Easter long weekend and an unexpected cold front saw it overcrowded with hikers, but Elizabeth, the stout African landlady who smelled of mutton stew, did her best to accommodate all who arrived wet and cold on her doorstep – hikers, four-wheel drivers, motocross riders and five foreign motorcycle travellers. Our room was no more than four walls and a cold slate floor, and cost 50 rand (US$4) each per night, but at least we had a room. The wind howled outside, blowing an icy rain against the window, which rattled relentlessly.

Over the next two days, the weather steadily deteriorated. Rain turned to snow that blanketed Lesotho and we huddled around the open fire. On Easter Monday the weather cleared, but a cold snap forecast that evening would leave the roads and the top of Sani Pass covered in ice. Riding motorcycles across this mountaintop country was now impossible. Instead, we would ride south to Cape Town via the Transkei coast and its warmth and sunshine.

The TT struggled to start in the cold, thin air. When it fired into life, I let it idle, and while it warmed, I realised how very comfortable I'd become with my motorcycle, as though it was an extension of me, and I of it. I realised that its survival lay at the heart of mine. Without the TT, there would be no ride; without it, the journey would not be the same. I felt a deep sense of appreciation for it and I had the uncanny feeling it responded, as though its sole purpose was to protect me and do all I asked of it. I trusted it implicitly and I held none of the fear on the ride down as I had on the ride up the Sani Pass – even when several times the tyres skidded on the loose rocks on a hairpin bend and I was only inches from hurtling over the edge and down into the valley far below.

When the track levelled at the bottom, we said goodbye to the Israeli boys. They would do some minor repairs to their bikes before riding to Cape Town. As like-minded souls, as motorcycle travellers, we embraced and repeated that we hoped to meet again, as they too would be heading north to Zimbabwe after Cape Town.

After the rain, snow and ice in the mountains, the Transkei coast, only 280 kilometres away, was a beacon of sun, sand and cold beer. The smooth tarmac wound through farmland and pine forests but by late afternoon we'd reached the Transkei border and the tarmac gave way to dirt and potholes.

The Transkei was one of ten homelands set up in 1959 by the white-ruled South African government to keep the black majority segregated along tribal lines – and, allegedly, to foil any chance of a national revolt. The homelands were self-governing, but were not recognised outside of South Africa. I rode past thatched huts with small crops of maize and a few scrawny goats. It was a poor substitute for the land the local people had once owned across the border – land purchased, according to many reports, at below market value by white farmers after the traditional owners had been forcibly removed by the South African government.

As daylight faded, the last of the Easter traffic sped past after a weekend on the coast. Drivers gave no room to pass as they honked their horns and passengers in the back of pickups waved angry fists at us. Clouds of dust all but obscured the narrow dirt road that wound down to the ocean and Port St Johns. I had only my dim six-volt headlight to guide me, and I hoped Dan could see the road as I followed the red glow of his tail-light through the darkness and the dust that swirled around us. When I'd bought the TT, I'd decided not to have the stator coil and wiring changed to twelve volts to give me a brighter headlight as I had figured I wouldn't be riding at night, when the risk of an accident increased ten-fold or more. It was a foolish decision that did not allow for circumstances such as the one we now found ourselves in.

Exhausted, we rode into the campsite at Port St Johns around ten p.m. As we took off our helmets, a shadowy figure approached from the darkness.

'Bloody hell! You two are fucking lucky you weren't fucking killed. Don't you know the blacks are on the rampage after some crazy white bastard shot one of their leaders?' bellowed the figure. He was a tall, thin white man with a long face, close-cropped ginger beard and an unmistakably Australian accent. He wore board shorts, a singlet and thongs, and carried a bottle of beer in each hand. He told us that Chris Hani, the leader of the South African Communist Party and a fiercely outspoken leader of the anti-apartheid movement, had been shot two days ago. This was the first we'd heard of it.

'The road *was* a little crazy,' I replied, still dazed from our near-death ride.

'Here, get this into ya. I'm Kirk,' he said and handed us the beers. I took a few swigs, the cold beer washing away the dust stuck in my throat, and as we set up the tent, Kirk told us his story.

Kirk was the campsite manager and looked about fortyish. He'd come to South Africa as a backpacker some years earlier, but had got no further than the sleepy fishing village of Port St Johns with its beach and life under palm trees, sunshine and blue skies. The campsite was his home and he earned a modest living from it, while meeting an assortment of interesting people from all over the world.

'Don't leave anything in ya tent. If ya not watching, the fuckers will take everything. Sleeping bags, mattresses, towels, the lot. Especially those fucking boots, they'll have 'em for sure,' he said, pointing to our feet. 'But ya can't blame 'em. There's no fucking jobs. Unemployment is over seventy per cent in the Transkei. There's a locker in the kitchen for ya stuff during the day.'

On this ride to Cape Town, we had found ourselves in the heart of a rapidly changing political landscape as the oppressive apartheid regime was ending in South Africa. The black majority had lived with racial segregation since 1948, when it had been implemented by the all-white Afrikaner National Party. Black people were segregated from white people in all areas of life – marriage, relationships, education, healthcare, jobs, land ownership.

We left Port St Johns two days later and while we were refuelling, an elderly African man ambled over from the shadows of a leafy tree where he'd been watching us.

'Two white men were killed here last night. Don't stop anywhere on your way out of Transkei. Just get out quick,' he warned and then moved away just as quietly as he had appeared.

We did not linger to ask questions and without a backward glance got on our bikes and did not stop until our tyres touched the smooth tarmac leading to East London and on to Cape Town. The highway was quiet, and I felt a naive sense of security until we stopped to refuel late that afternoon. The petrol attendant, a middle-aged white man in grease-stained overalls, warned that the road to Grahamstown was closed due to rioting, with petrol bombs and stones being thrown at passing vehicles.

'Just keep off the road today. They're all going crazy. The blacks take their hatred out on any white who happens to be around,' said the attendant casually, as though he'd seen it all before.

'You can't really blame them. People can only take so much,' I replied.

Over the past two days, sheltered in Port St Johns, we'd been oblivious to the chaos that had ignited following Hani's assassination. Once word of his murder spread, its impact was felt by the entire nation and rioting erupted all over South Africa, particularly on this day, the official day of Hani's mourning. Right-wing Polish immigrant Janusz Waluś was later charged with his murder, and Clive Derby-Lewis, a South African Conservative Party MP, was arrested for supplying the pistol. Both men received life in prison.

The riots, prompted by Hani's assassination, were the catalyst to end apartheid. The political parties agreed to talks, and democratic elections were held a year later. But even after just a few weeks in South Africa, I had heard many racist comments from white South Africans who spoke in bitter tones about those who threatened their sovereignty. The inequality ran so deep it was cultural, and I wondered whether this great racial divide would ever end.

We took the attendant's advice and found a hostel not far from the seafront in East London. It was comfortable and clean and there was space for our motorcycles in the foyer, but it was not friendly. The African woman at reception gave us a stern look filled with intense dislike. I wanted to show my sympathy for her pain, and the pain of millions of South Africans, but I could only manage a quietly spoken 'sorry'. She seemed to understand and told us that the following day the curfew would be lifted and it would be safe to continue our travels.

That evening, in the hostel's lounge, we watched news footage of rioting; of angry people in the major cities and towns all over South Africa. People who had lost faith that the oppression they had endured for the past forty-five years would soon be over. We phoned our parents and told them we were safe, because the news, in those last days of apartheid, was insisting to the world that South Africa was about to self-destruct in a bloodbath fuelled by racial tension.

We rode to Cape Town on sweeping bends, twists and turns, as the smooth tarmac hugged the coast. Despite this surely being one of the world's best motorcycling roads, with wild surf on one side and steep mountains on the other, the experience was lost on me as I realised we were also riding through an area populated by people who hated us based purely on our skin colour.

After seeing the sights of Cape Town, gorging on fish and chips, and climbing Table Mountain, which stood majestic and all-powerful above the city, we were eager to return to Durban to collect our spares and ride north into Zimbabwe. South Africa was too expensive for my meagre travel budget, and while Cape Town existed at a magical location at the end of Africa, it was a city of contrasts where the hunger and squalor of the shantytowns existed on the fringe of the gluttony and opulence that radiated from its centre. Despite few dogs being kept as pets, I was told the biggest selling item in the shantytown stores was canned dog food, while in Cape Town's supermarkets, it was *boerewors* (a coil of thick spicy meat sausage).

From Cape Town, the ride north took us through the twists and turns of the Swartberg Pass, a gravel road that climbed through a dry mountain range of sharp rocks and steep cliffs to an elevation of nearly 1600 metres. It gave us spectacular views over mountains and valleys, until the pass dropped to the barren plains of the Great Karoo and we followed a straight black line of tarmac into the interior towards Kimberley.

In the distance, sun glinted off metal and as the speck grew bigger, we knew it was a motorcycle. A moment later, a BMW R100GS with metal panniers pulled up where we had stopped to await its approach. It carried two riders wearing matching red, grey and black leathers. They looked out of place in Africa, as if they'd taken a wrong exit off an autobahn. They removed their silver full-faced helmets and the man, tall and gorgeously handsome with broad shoulders, reached into a side pocket of a bag and pulled out a tin of Castle beer.

'South Africa, it is wonderful place,' he crooned as he brushed matted strands of blond hair out of ice-blue eyes. He took a swig of the beer and then told us their story. He and his girlfriend were on their way to Cape Town after riding down through Africa, a journey of ten months. Travelling via West Africa to Cameroon, they'd chosen to avoid Zaire and instead had flown with their bike from Yaoundé to Nairobi.

'Why?' I asked.

'It is not possible. Zaire is very expensive. One litre of fuel is more than one US dollar and only available on black market,' he said. 'There is no law. It could be civil war at any moment. We skip it.'

'You should do the same,' his girlfriend added. 'Even in West Africa, the food is terrible, the officials are corrupt, and all the time is *donnez cadeau, donnez Bic*. Ah, I am glad we in South Africa. Here we have hot shower and good hotel.' She was stunningly beautiful, an Amazonian woman, her breasts straining at the zip of her leather jacket. Her golden-blonde hair hung in a thick plait down her back. 'The best thing to do is take the ship to Europe from Mombasa. After South Africa, we go this way back to Germany,' she told us.

'How much money did you spend?' I asked them both, not deterred from travelling all the way through.

'Nearly twenty-thousand US,' replied the gorgeous man as he crunched his empty beer can, tossing it on the ground and reaching for another.

'Twenty-thousand dollars!' I squealed.

Dan and I both looked at each other. Neither of us had that much money. We'd been told South Africa was one of the most expensive countries and we had both been looking forward to the lower prices further north.

'Well, good luck. We go to Cape Town,' said the man and beamed a brilliant smile from his unshaven face before sculling his beer.

As we watched them ride away on the long line of black tarmac, I thought of the word *ubuntu*, which I had heard from a young African woman at the hostel in Cape Town. She was athletic and strong, with short black dreadlocks. I was in the dining room early one morning, eating toast and reading my guidebook, when she sat down opposite with a mug of tea and a stack of peanut butter sandwiches.

'White woman, why you travel Africa?' she boomed. Her voice demanded my attention, as if it were the voice of one who rallies others to fight, and I thought she may have something to do with the anti-apartheid movement.

'I felt drawn here,' I replied. 'There is a kind of humanness to Africa that we don't have in the West.' My reply seemed inadequate and incomprehensible, even to me.

'*Ubuntu*,' she'd smiled knowingly, her face changing from steely anger to serene understanding in an instant. 'You will find the way of *ubuntu* as you travel Africa. The African people will help you. This is *ubuntu*. This is what we want the whites to understand. We can help each other and together we can make South Africa great. But it is very difficult.'

I later read that *ubuntu* also means the universal bond that connects all of humanity as one.

As I watched the Germans disappear, I understood they had not found *ubuntu*. Not because it was not shown to them, but because they had not opened their eyes, minds and hearts to it.

*

Ever since arriving in Africa we hadn't planned where we'd stay each night, because something invariably turned up. Dan and I never shared these thoughts, but we silently agreed to leave the progression of our day to fate. Things always worked out. Our unlikely encounters with good fortune always amazed me and each morning before we headed off into the next adventure, I'd say a silent prayer of gratitude for what would come our way.

It was cold and dark by the time we reached Kimberley and came across the Halfway House, one of its famous old hotels. The kitchen was closed so we chewed on *biltong* (strips of dried meat) sold as bar snacks as we played pool and drank our winnings in beer. In the early hours we ended up sleeping on the floor of a hotel room at the invitation of a quietly spoken white South African businessman who we'd taken turns to defeat at pool. He was on his way to Cape Town and understood we had a long journey ahead on limited funds.

As a former mine worker, I could not leave Kimberley without a visit to the Big Hole. We stood at the lookout for a bird's-eye view into its cavernous depths, which had been excavated by pick and shovel; it was reportedly the largest mine in the world dug by hand. Over 14 million carats of diamonds had been taken out of this 1.6-kilometre-wide, 215-metre-deep mine – the bottom forty metres were now filled with ground water. The Kimberley Mine Museum, laid out as a historical township near the Big Hole, was filled with mining memorabilia. I stared at an enlarged photograph of thousands of men swarming into, over and out of the huge open pit criss-crossed with lengths of wood and rope to give support. The men, from tribes all over southern Africa, worked feverishly for payment from their labour and for the reward of finding a diamond if they handed it in to the overseer – or even more if they smuggled it out to sell to an illicit buyer. Even though working conditions were harsh and thousands of men died from disease, the mine helped make many dreams come true, just as mining had done for me. These men knew living their life was far more valuable than the pursuit of more. Most only stayed long enough to earn enough money to secure their financial future: enough to purchase a gun (for hunting and a symbol of power), a few cattle and to pay a bride price.

I, too, had only stayed in mining long enough to secure my financial future. I'd bought a house, the rent now paying off the last of the mortgage while I travelled. I'd only bought it because my work colleagues had insisted that the meaning of life was a mortgage and I hadn't known any better. I was grateful for the financial reward from my well-paying job, but I was even more grateful for the opportunity that had come in the form of an idea that I believed in, and grateful that I had trusted in it enough to take that first step before I wasted too many more precious years.

3

THE TRAVELLERS' TRAIL
ZIMBABWE TO TANZANIA

As we rode through dry woodland on a straight stretch of tarmac to Victoria Falls, a bug the size of a small rodent splattered across my visor as a blob of yellow and black ooze. We'd crossed into Zimbabwe two days earlier, having collected the spare parts and tyres we'd stored at the home of a friend of a friend on Durban's outskirts. We posted our tyres by air-freight to Nairobi, and sent our spares by rail to Harare.

I was lost in thought about the travellers we'd meet at Victoria Falls that evening when the first flying beetle hit me. With a gloved hand, I carefully wiped away its remains, trying not to smudge my visor as I swerved to avoid impact with another bug. Victoria Falls is one of those places where travellers congregate, and I had especially hoped we'd meet other motorcycle riders. I craved the easy laughs and the sense of togetherness I'd felt with the Danish couple on the ride to Perth, and with the three dark-haired Israeli boys at the top of the Sani Pass. We all shared the same sense of freedom, as well as the hardships that came with motorcycle travel. When I was with these people, I felt happy, confident and so sure of myself. Even the tension between Dan and me seemed diminished. Most motorcycle travellers in Africa begin their ride in Europe, travelling south through either Tunisia or Egypt, and I looked forward to hearing their tales of adventure and advice for the road ahead. The past two weeks on the road with Dan had been the loneliest so far and now, more than ever, I needed the company of like-minded souls.

While Dan and I had reached a kind of unspoken mutual understanding and travelled together rather well with regards to day-to-day decisions, we still had no words to share. No thoughts, churned up by the hours spent on the road, to discuss. Through habit, I had grown to accept the uncomfortable aura between us. Each morning, I was always keen to pack and be on the road, as it was only then that I could relax and lose myself in the freedom of riding my motorcycle as the miles slipped away beneath its tyres.

I continued to wonder why we both endured the tension. I could not answer for Dan; but for me, even though I tried to convince myself otherwise, I knew his constant disregard had slowly peeled away my self-confidence to the point that I now lacked the courage to move away from the negativity. So I endured it, not unlike a wife may endure years in a loveless marriage. Her life may not be so bad, may even be comfortable, and she is afraid of the unknown, of the uncertainty of finding happiness or being worse off than she already is, so she stays. This was how I felt, and while Dan and I were not married, not even in a relationship – indeed, not even in a friendship – it seemed I continued our travel partnership for the same reasons. I knew this tension would eat away at us until we could endure it no more and we would finally find relief and go our separate ways. It was not a matter of if, but when. My greatest fear was that when the inevitable happened, I would not be capable of travelling alone. Each day, as this moment grew closer, so too did my fear of its imminent approach. I was consumed by a sense of dread. I hated this feeling, as it subsumed the strong, determined young woman who'd got the idea to ride a motorcycle through Africa and believed in it as though nothing but death would stop her. Now, during those hours on the road, cocooned inside my helmet, I imagined all the bad things that could happen as though they already had.

What if the bike broke down? What if I had an accident? But I was not even giving myself a chance, I argued, as I tried to quell my mind, which raced with multitudes of horrendous scenarios. Why could I not believe that the coincidences and chance encounters would continue to unfold as if the universe or God or something was giving me a helping hand? Why couldn't I take that first step again, as I had done to make the ride happen in the first place?

Throughout South Africa, despite having the freedom of motorcycles, we had ridden on a well-worn backpackers' trail. Zimbabwe was no different. Victoria Falls, where the sleepy Zambezi River is 1700 metres wide and plunges a hundred metres into a narrow chasm, is well-established on the travellers' trail of southern and eastern Africa. Here on the border of Zimbabwe and Zambia, all manner of businesses catered to the adventurous spirit. There was no shortage of things to do, from white-water rafting and micro-light flying to sunset booze cruises and horseback game-viewing safaris.

As our motorcycles rumbled through the gates of the Victoria Falls campsite, I looked ahead for others like us. The grounds were crowded with overland truck tours, 4×4s – mostly Land Rovers, South African tourists I guessed – and the multi-coloured tents of backpackers. We spotted three motorcycles, all Yamaha XT600s, parked in the shade of a cluster of stunted, bushy trees. Next to the bikes and their tents, three men sat drinking beers. We rode over and I hit the kill switch, stopping the TT's engine and allowing myself to hear the thundering of the falls that sounded no more than a stone's throw away. Two of the bikes had fixed metal panniers and were easily identifiable as German (Germans always had fixed metal panniers), and the other motorcycle – rusted, beat up, with bald tyres and no panniers – belonged to a smallish unshaven young man with matted brown hair who looked to be in his early twenties. He sat with slumped shoulders and looked like he was homeless and in need of a good meal and a wash. He said hello and his accent pegged him as South African.

The two Germans told us they had ridden down through North and West Africa, across Zaire to Kenya, and were on their way to Cape Town. We told them about the German couple we'd met near Kimberley; yes, they'd met them too. I asked them about travelling through Zaire.

'The only problem with Zaire is the mud and the immigration official at Bondo. He rip everybody off,' said the tall, thin German, slightly bald except for a few tufts of brown hair. I guessed he was about fortyish. His friend looked the same age, but was a little shorter, and I thought they might be brothers, though I later learnt they weren't. 'You go through after December, you have no problem, no mud then,' the taller one said, his hazel eyes glinting with a cheeky sense of adventure.

The South African said he hoped to ride to Nairobi but was unsure he would make it without a carnet and very little money.

'I make it this far. I am still riding my motorcycle. This is *lekker* for me,' he said, spreading his arms and turning his palms skyward as though offering his humble thanks to the God of Travellers, or whatever it was that kept a watchful eye on us.

This trio had been at Victoria Falls for the past week but would move on in the next day or two. I looked around the large, open campsite with its perfectly placed clusters of shade trees. It sat in the middle of the town, close to shops, bars and the mighty Victoria Falls. What pressing need could there be to leave? For the Germans, their motorcycle travels through Africa were nearly over so they were in no hurry to leave this idyllic place.

But two days later they did move on. The Germans headed south, while the South African rode north to Kenya through Zambia.

'Zaire is good place. It is real Africa, do it,' said the shorter of the two Germans before they rode out of the campsite.

After I'd said goodbye to the Germans and the South African, I joined Dan at the campsite of a group of about a dozen Australian and New Zealand backpackers. They suggested we accompany them on a boat trip along Lake Kariba to Mana Pools National Park and camp on the banks of the Zambezi River, where the game, mostly elephants and hyenas, were free to roam around us. They'd met a white Zimbabwean who offered a budget tour of the park in his campervan. We'd leave our motorcycles at a hotel outside the park and spend a few days of early-morning walking safaris (no guide needed), sunset game-viewing from the roof of his camper, and afternoon canoeing on the Zambezi – with hippos, if we carelessly ventured too far from the shore. Our journey would begin at Binga, where we would take the mail boat for the three-day trip on the 250-kilometre-long lake to Kariba, where a gigantic dam built across the Zambezi River harnesses hydro-electric power.

Mana Pools lived up to all my expectations and we had several near-death encounters with game: an angry bull elephant mock-charged us one morning; our Zimbabwean guide found himself being stalked by a pride of lions as we hid behind a thicket of bushes; and the canoe I was in with three others drifted too far from the shallows and hippos surfaced all around us. But unhurt, we left Zimbabwe and rode north to Malawi, crossing Mozambique on a highway cleared of landmines following the end of a civil war.

Malawi was the halfway point on the travellers' trail of East Africa, and the township of Cape Maclear on the 580-kilometre-long Lake Malawi was its epicentre. Backpackers and those from overland tours, as well as overlanders in 4×4s and motorcycle travellers, stopped at this giant inland sea at the southern end of the rift valley. The lake is seventy-five kilometres at its widest point and 700 metres at its deepest. Gentle surf breaks on beaches of fine golden sand and the clear waters are abundant with fish. Cape Maclear attracts divers and backpackers seeking cheap scuba courses or cheap marijuana in the form of Malawi Gold. Aptly named, Malawi Gold is the gold standard of marijuana and is apparently much sought after for its potency – its long-lasting psychoactive effects were just as appealing to visitors as the cheap diving.

We rode into this backpackers' haven just after the sun had set, as a huge orange orb beyond the calm waters of the lake. This small township was made up of thatched huts dotted with a few low cement buildings haphazardly knocked together to accommodate the needs of those wanting a bed, a cold beer, a hot meal or a learn-to-dive course.

Emmanuel's Campsite, at the far northern end of the township, was preferred by motorcyclists. Once I got used to the persistent calls of '*How about BBQ? How about spliff? How about washing?*', life at Emmanuel's was comfortable, in a warm and fuzzy kind of way.

A fence provided privacy from the hustlers, who viewed all travellers as 'business'. A thatched shelter on the beach provided shade, and also doubled as the campsite's lounge and dining room. All our meals – mostly salad, chips, and fish cooked on an open fire – were eaten there. I spent hours sharing tales of adventure with travellers from all over the world. We snacked on pineapples and pawpaws – sweet and juicy with the flavour that only comes from just-picked, naturally ripened fruit – purchased from the local kids who called out to us from an imaginary no-go line that Emmanuel had drawn in the sand for the comfort of his guests. I still had the heavy string hammock, and it more than justified its weight, as next to our tent were two trees perfectly spaced for it to be strung up. The hammock became a much sought-after spot in the shade where one could be gently swayed by a cool breeze blown in across the lake. Everybody was happy, the travellers because we could relax and the locals because they could earn a living.

I had heard about people staying at Cape Maclear for weeks, with those weeks drifting into months. We had also planned to stay a week or two as, after all, there was no schedule. We were free to go anywhere we wanted, anytime. But events made the decision for us when Dan crashed his motorcycle riding into Monkey Bay to buy supplies at its supermarket. The day after his accident, he agreed to have his wrist X-rayed at the hospital in Mangochi, which involved a one-hour, bone-jarring ride as my pillion on the TT. His wrist had a hairline fracture, but the hospital was out of plaster. The doctor advised he continue to strap it with the two sticks we'd used as improvised splints and the elasticised bandage from my first-aid kit. The bruising and grazes on Dan's fractured right wrist – his throttle wrist – forced us to stay another three weeks at Cape Maclear.

Emmanuel's Campsite got busier and busier by the day, peaking at twenty multi-coloured tents and twelve motorcycle travellers. Only at Cape Maclear would you see so many in the same place at the same time. It was here that I met Leo and Myles, both from Melbourne. Over three years, they had ridden their Yamaha XT600 Tenere motorcycles through Asia, the Middle East, Europe and down through Africa. After a rest at Emmanuel's, they would ride to South Africa and then board a cargo ship from Durban across to Perth just as we had done.

In this pair of unlikely travelling companions I found an understanding ear, and they nodded knowingly when I opened up about the lack of compatibility between Dan and me.

'We can't stand each other either,' said Leo. He was a smallish dark-haired man about thirtyish with boyish good looks. 'He does his thing and I do mine. Before I got here, the last time I saw Myles was in Nairobi and before that Cairo. The next time will be at Vic Falls.'

'Fuck off, mate. You'll be lucky if you see me again when we make it home,' said Myles, who was about the same age but gangly and scruffy with thinning brown hair and a quick wit that matched Leo's. 'I can't stand that bastard either. We went our own way when we reached Europe. I reckon if we spend any more than an hour together, we'll kill each other,' Myles grinned. 'Travelling companions are overrated. You're better off travelling alone. Best thing we did was doing our own thing.'

'But how come you're both here together?' I asked, puzzled, but I knew the answer because even though they professed to detest each other, they still shared a camaraderie that Dan and I never would.

'Just another of those chance meetings,' Leo replied. 'Funny thing. It happens all the time. I reckon Myles is stalking me.'

'Best thing you can do is talk it out then go your own way. Your trip won't be anything until you do that,' Myles said and looked me straight in the eye as though he knew exactly the turmoil that festered inside me.

'Yes, I know. I reckon we'll go as far as Nairobi. We share a lot of gear. I need to get my own tent, petrol stove and a heap of tools,' I said, deflecting the conversation to the more practical aspects of our travelling partnership to avoid picking at the emotional stuff, which sat raw and painful just under the surface.

'You'll know when the time is right,' said Leo.

42

'Yes, it'll reach the point when you won't fucking stand the sight of each other and doing your own thing will bring the greatest relief,' said Myles, giving Leo a friendly pat on the back. 'Isn't that right, mate?'

'Fuck off,' Leo replied and we all laughed. They with a shared acceptance of their incompatible travelling partnership and I because they filled me with confidence for the time that fast approached when I'd travel alone.

Motorcycle travel transcends all cultures, genders, ages and physical disabilities. The other motorcycle travellers at Emmanuel's were Bernard the German, on a Suzuki DR650; Swiss guys Philippe and Yvan, also on DR650s; and Gary, another Australian, on a Suzuki GSXR 750 road bike. There was also a Japanese couple, Atsuko and Heroaki, on Honda CT110 'postie' motorcycles. Heroaki had an artificial leg. They had ridden all the way down through the Sahara, West Africa and across Zaire and each carried a twenty-litre jerry to give their little bikes a range of 1000 kilometres. A few days later, it was a welcome surprise to see the Israeli boys, Romie and Ari, ride into the campsite. After selling his motorcycle, Ariel had returned to Israel from South Africa to do his mandatory military service.

While I enjoyed the conversations with the steady stream of new faces that drifted in and out of Emmanuel's, I craved physical activity. I'd become a little bored with spending my days under the thatched beach shelter with the overlanders and an assortment of backpackers passing around yet another spliff. One day, as I gazed out at the lake, I realised that I could easily swim the kilometre to Thumbi Island using my dive fins, which were still strapped to the handlebars of the TT. This small rocky outcrop offshore from the campsite was surrounded by clear water that teemed with fish. My swim became a daily routine that toned my muscles and kept me strong and ready for the ride ahead.

Dan's wrist healed, his grazes stopped festering, and finally it was time to leave the warm embrace of Cape Maclear. Romie and Ari joined us for the ride up to the Tanzania border. From there, they would ride back to South Africa, to sell their bikes and return to Israel.

We rode on to Mbeya, an easy ride before nightfall. It was hard to believe things were so different only a short distance away in Malawi, which did not enjoy the same economic benefits. Here in resource-rich Tanzania, we rode on smooth tarmac across an undulating landscape devoid of the poorly constructed thatched mud huts that were common-place back in Malawi. Mbeya was a provincial township with low cement buildings lining streets that bustled with people, traffic, street vendors and a few goats feeding on the scraps of paper that littered the ground.

We found a local hotel with a basic room. It had a restaurant that over-looked the town's busy bus depot and we ordered a meal of chicken, chips and gravy. While we waited, we drank cold beers in silence, watching the rush of people moving to and from the buses which pulled up and drove away in clouds of black smoke. Over the past month we had always been in the company of so many other motorcycle travellers coming and going from Cape Maclear that Dan and I had found no reason to communicate. At Mbeya, though, it was back to that uncomfortable feeling from which neither of us could escape. We had not yet spoken about the route we would take to Nairobi, but before leaving Tanzania we both wanted to visit the Ngorongoro Conservation Area and its deep crater teeming with wild-life. I was keen to get off the beaten track, and especially off the 'travellers' trail'. Since Zimbabwe, I'd felt an impenetrable divide had grown between me and Africa – I was in it, but I was not part of it. Secretly, my prefer-ence was to take the back roads through Maasai lands, but as we waited for our meal, I agreed with Dan that it was best we stay on the tarmac to avoid further injury to his still-fragile wrist. Although he didn't tell me, I knew it still pained him, and riding over a potholed dirt road would be agony. Our food arrived and we ate in silence.

The following morning we headed north on smooth tarmac, passing through dry savannah and the lands of the Maasai. The plains of brown grasses gave way to sparse woodland dotted with baobab trees. Maasai men herding cattle stood staring at us as we passed. When we stopped at the towns for fuel or to eat spicy grilled meat cooked fresh by the side of the road, groups of Maasai youth adorned with brilliantly coloured neck and arm beads surrounded us to inspect the two travellers on motorcycles. These proud young men were very striking, with their hair entwined with ochre rope and lengths of bright-red cloth draped across their lean, muscular bodies. They seemed to radiate an inner beauty that touched all who came near them. I felt a strange kind of uncontrollable happiness well up inside me from these brief encounters with the Maasai, who valued their traditional life and shunned Western influence.

It was a warm afternoon and I rode wearing only a T-shirt, enjoying the cool breeze through the thin cotton. As I overtook an overcrowded old bus with many broken windows, the few passengers standing on the rear step cheered me on. They stretched out their hands and I returned the gesture, lightly touching the tips of one man's fingers. We both laughed with exhilaration and I opened the throttle, the bus disappearing behind me.

In the last of the fading light, I pulled over to where a village hugged the main road and waited for Dan. It had everything we needed – a guesthouse, food stalls to buy our dinner and a bar with cold beers. It was nearly dark and I was determined to keep the promise to myself and to the TT that I would never again ride at night with only the faint glow of the six-volt headlight to light my way. Dan pulled up beside me and I suggested we stop there for the night.

'There's a sort of major town only twenty kilometres further on. We can get some decent food and a shower,' he replied. 'I read about it last night in the Bible.'

I reached into my Gearsack for the Lonely Planet guidebook. I now considered this weighty tome both a blessing and a curse. While it was helpful in capital cities to find embassies for visas, its recommendations of places to stay and eat meant that we were caught on the travellers' trail of East Africa with no escape.

The Good Book confirmed there was, in fact, a hotel catering for backpackers up ahead with steaks, hot showers and cold beers. I reluctantly got back on the TT and rode slowly into the darkness.

A common sight on Africa's roads was broken-down trucks. One was parked up ahead and I approached it with caution, as a large group of onlookers were milling around. Just as I was about to pass, a man walked in front of me, and then stopped in stunned amazement. I braked but did not swerve, as I anticipated he would surely jump to the left or right to avoid impact. But no, he just stood there and then went flying as I hit him. I went down and the TT slid along the road.

Wasting no time, I limped over to my bike, yelling at the confused people to help me move it before it was mangled under the tyres of the next speeding truck. With the TT safely dragged out of danger, I looked for the man. He was sitting stunned next to the broken-down truck. I held out my hand to help him stand up. It appeared his injuries were only minor: a few grazes and bruising. My shoulder ached and my elbow was badly grazed, due to not wearing my motorcycle jacket. I would also be limping for the next few days, as my right knee had taken a bad knock. Worse, I would not be able to kick-start the TT.

As Dan pulled up beside me, the injured man demanded he pay compensation. Dan handed over 500 shillings, about US$1. The man looked at the crumpled note in disbelief and then shouted angrily at us. 'You pay more!'

The crowd moved their attention from the broken-down truck to this new commotion that had suddenly materialised out of the darkness. Dan picked up my bike and started it. Feeling the anger from the crowd as they realised we were about to do a runner, I climbed on as quickly as my injuries would allow. The people milling around us numbered about twenty and they moved in to close our escape. We both opened the throttles and the noise of two big 600cc singles made them jump back. We disappeared into the darkness just as suddenly as we had appeared. Once again I was following the faint red glow of Dan's tail-light through dust thrown up by trucks that sped past us.

This section of road was under construction: the smooth tarmac was gone. Here the road was dirt, deep wheel ruts and large potholes. After five kilometres we spotted a sheet of whitewashed iron that hung on a wire fence. In bold black letters it proclaimed Mrs Binde's Guest House. We turned off the road and followed the narrow track that led to a brick house, its blue plaster faded and flaking with age. When I stopped, my leg could not support the TT's weight and I fell in a heap at the bottom of the stairs leading to the veranda where Mrs Binde, an African woman with a commanding presence, stood with her hands on her hips and stared down at me. A crowd of children gathered, watching us wide-eyed. Dan picked up my bike for the second time that night.

'Ah, you from Australia. My husband, he work there on exchange program with mining company.' She beamed proudly when we told her our origins and that we too were mine workers. With a chubby arm, she motioned for us to come up the steps. We were seated on a threadbare couch and a teenage boy placed two cold bottles of beer on the low table in front of us. Soon afterwards, a meal of fried meat, salad and chips followed. Pain throbbed in my leg and I hoped it was only bruising and not fractured bone.

'No more riding at night,' I said and took a long swallow of the beer to wash the dust from my throat. Dan nodded in silent agreement.

It would be several days before my leg would heal. The pain was too great to kick-start the TT and this reinforced my fears of travelling alone. As we headed north, Mount Kilimanjaro loomed large and majestic, dominating the landscape. The snow-covered peak of this dormant volcano rose 5895 metres from the floor of Africa and seemed strangely out of place.

With me still stiff and sore from my crash the previous evening, we passed through Moshi and on to Arusha, where safaris to view the abundant game in the Ngorongoro Crater were big business. Competition amongst tour operators was fierce. Arusha was the starting point for safaris to the crater and Serengeti National Park, and just being in this thriving township meant we were potential customers for the touts, who earned a good commission from the tour operators. We bargained for a one-day tour for US$50 each. We left our motorcycles at the Safari Junction campsite, a few kilometres from the conservation area gate, and joined a safari in an open-top 4×4.

The Ngorongoro Crater lived up to all the expectations I'd fostered since childhood from watching wildlife television documentaries. The crater was formed when a massive volcano collapsed, leaving behind a 500-metre-high unbroken rim, eighteen kilometres across. The abundant game of every description and a lake filled with a sea of pink flamingos was, unfortunately, set against a backdrop of 4×4s filled with camera-clicking tourists.

We arrived in Nairobi on a Friday afternoon and settled into Mama Roche's, a campsite set up by an elderly Polish woman in her suburban yard and popular with overland 4×4s and motorcycle travellers. First thing Monday, we rode out to Nairobi Airport to collect the motorcycle tyres that we'd sent from Durban three months earlier. We paid a tout a small sum to deal with the customs officials, but despite our tyres being within sight behind the wire-mesh fence, our paperwork needed several more stamps before they were released to us.

It was a warm, sunny day, the sky cloudless and clear blue and Dan and I ate fried chicken and chips at a cafe near the customs building, which was closed for lunch till two p.m. We sat at a white plastic table shaded by a sun umbrella. It was eerily quiet; there were no other diners outside. With no other distractions there was no avoiding our unspoken thoughts as we were both aware that Nairobi was the end of the road for us as travelling companions.

'So what now?' I asked, speaking to the top of Dan's head as he fumbled with an empty Coke bottle, rotating it over and over with his long fingers as though he'd find the answer hidden within the opaque glass. We both knew what I meant and I waited for him to speak. I did not expect an outpouring of emotion, as our conversations still only extended to a few words.

'I'm Africa'd out,' Dan mumbled through a long fringe of brown hair that covered most of his face.

Africa'd out. It was a term I'd heard often from the backpackers on the travellers' trail. Even though his response was expected, the words still startled me. The moment of reckoning I always knew would come, but ignored, was here.

'I'm going to ride over to Uganda to visit the gorillas with Justin and Paula and the Germans. You can come along too if you like,' he added, the

invitation falling away to be almost inaudible. We'd met the German couple, who'd driven overland through Egypt from Europe, when we arrived
at Mama's, and Dan had hit it off with them immediately. Justin and Paula,
the Australian backpackers whom we'd met at Vic Falls back in April, were
also camped at Mama's.

'Then I'll take a ship from Mombasa to Europe,' he said as he continued fumbling with the Coke bottle.

'I'm not *leaving*,' I replied so forcefully that it surprised us both, and
his head snapped up to look at me. His face was lined and his eyes tired:
he seemed old beyond his years. I'd never noticed before; but then we'd
never really looked eye to eye, not for more than a few seconds anyway.

'I've had enough,' he grumbled and I knew he didn't just mean he'd had
enough of Africa. 'From Europe, I'll ride home through the Middle East
and India. I'll be back by Christmas,' he said, sounding a bit more upbeat
with the thought of seeing family and friends again. 'You do whatever you
want,' he added, and turned his attention back to the Coke bottle.

'Africa is just beginning for me. I *can't* leave now,' I said, so confidently
that the words didn't sound like they came from me. Over the past five
months, I'd been weighed down by so much self-doubt fuelled by his indifference to me that it had almost crushed me. But Dan's decision to leave
freed me and I felt the confident young woman who'd spoken those fate-
ful words at that Sunday afternoon barbecue slowly re-emerge.

'I want to ride north to Lake Turkana first. I'll cross Uganda on my
way to Zaire. I'll see the gorillas there. No point going through Uganda
twice,' I added. He was not the only one who had secretly made plans.

'You're bloody mad going into Zaire alone. You'll get yourself fucking
killed,' he said and looked me in the eye again as though I were a strange,
demented creature not of this world.

'I want to see Zaire. It's what I *want* to do. It's been part of this trip
from the very beginning' I replied and smiled at the memory of those early
days of planning. But I think, by the way Dan just shook his head, that he
misinterpreted my smile as a deranged grin, which I'm sure confirmed his

thoughts about my growing insanity. I was about to say more but there was no point, because he would not understand that I knew I was meant to make this journey; that I knew I would be okay. I was no longer afraid. I was done with self-doubt and in its place was an enormous sense of relief. I thought of Leo and Myles and how they'd told me this was how I'd feel. I smiled with a sense that the natural order of things had fallen back into place and I would travel alone, as it was always intended I should. And Dan would embark on his own journey, as it was always intended he should.

'Well, let's get the fuck out of here. Customs should be open by now,' Dan said, and with a few strides of his long legs he was at his bike, pulling on his helmet and gloves.

4

ALONE
MAASAI MARA TO LAKE NAIVASHA

'Take care of yourself,' Dan said, placing a hand on my shoulder as if I were his little sister and he was reluctant to let me go alone into the world.

'I'll be fine,' I replied, looking away as I felt the beginning of tears. Despite all our incompatibilities and all the tension between us, we'd shared the bond of a common journey. We'd left our sheltered mining town because we both knew there was much more to life than the routine where today was the same as yesterday had been and as tomorrow would be. We'd gone in search of adventure and in Africa we'd found it. But, I was discovering, there was also something else to be found. Something mysterious that I could feel, as though I'd walked into a vacant room and sensed someone was standing in the shadows hidden from my view. I could not grasp the meaning of this feeling. I was not yet capable of understanding what it meant, but nonetheless, I knew something was there.

'Don't do anything fucking stupid,' he said and wrapped his long arms around me. I hugged him back.

'You better go. They're waiting.' I sniffed and wiped away a tear that I'd failed to control as I looked towards the Germans' Bedford van idling on the side of the road in front of Mama's. 'See you back in Oz,' I said as he strapped on his helmet and got on his bike. I squeezed his arm to show

51

I did care. To show that there were no bad feelings between us. He nodded, kick-started his bike and then disappeared into Nairobi's chaotic traffic following the Bedford van.

'Heeda, come drink tea,' Mama Roche called as I closed the heavy steel gates behind me. She sat on the front porch of her rundown weatherboard bungalow, which was painted a deep bottle-green.

Mama was a short buxom woman with a mop of curly white hair and thick glasses. She'd first opened her leafy suburban backyard in Nairobi to travellers in 1971. She'd invited several to stay with her after finding them camped in a city park and warned them of robbers with knives. Thanks to that long-ago act of goodwill, Mama Roche was blessed with a profitable backpacker business.

Behind the high brick walls and formidable steel gates, Mama's yard was dotted with brightly coloured tents, and washing was strung across the shrubbery. Her three old dogs, who did a fair job of keeping the thieves from scaling her fence, snarled at me as I walked past. Mama had done the same when Dan and I had first ridden through those gates nearly a week earlier.

'Camping, seventy shilling. No tent here. No touch dog. Wolfy, he bite,' she had barked. But despite this fierce first impression, this old Polish woman now mothered me like a stray. As a young woman, she too had found herself alone in Africa, when she'd arrived here after World War II. With her husband dead and children gone from Africa, she lived alone surrounded by travellers.

'I never see a girl travel alone on a motorbike,' Mama said, as she poured tea into a fine china cup with saucer and offered me a custard-cream biscuit. But her attempt to boost my confidence had little effect, as the reality that I was alone in Africa now hit me, and I could only think of the things that might go wrong. On her porch I was safe, but soon I would venture into the world that existed beyond her steel gates, where people lived by their wits and there was no one to watch over me.

My plans were not fixed on any one route in particular; I just knew I would eventually ride across Zaire, then west and north, to the top of

Africa. But before leaving East Africa, I wanted to take a detour to Lake Turkana and Sibiloi National Park in northern Kenya, where the fossilised footprints of our ancestors remain embedded. I felt innately drawn to this particular spot, as if something very important about our existence would be revealed to me there. There was no foundation to this drive. I had never studied palaeontology. Nonetheless, I could not ignore the pull. I did not question the practicalities of this 1600-kilometre round-trip from Nairobi. Instead, I responded entirely to an instinctive urge. With my pilgrimage complete, I reasoned, I would return to Nairobi and be ready – spiritually, mentally and physically – to ride alone into Africa's dark heart.

While my plans weren't ruled by time limits, my schedule was ruled by the weather. I needed to cross Zaire and its unsealed roads in the dry season which began in December, when the huge bog-holes would be passable. But other than this small restriction, I was free to ride when and where I pleased. This ride was not about reaching the top of Africa to say *I've done it*; it was more a meander, as I let my intuition lead me to something yet to be revealed. Ultimately, I would arrive in London. I'd already heard from the Brits I'd met that good money could be made in London as a motorcycle courier. As soon as I'd heard that, I knew immediately it was for me – or more to the point, for 'us'. A job like that would keep the TT and me together, and would provide the means to top up my travelling funds for the ride home on a route yet to be decided – most likely via Europe, Russia, Central Asia, China and South East Asia. These were vague plans, so far into the future I gave them little real thought. I had more immediate plans to worry about.

As I prepared for the ride to northern Kenya, each day rolled into the next and my pile of replaced equipment steadily grew. To start travelling again, I needed to restock all the equipment that Dan had been carrying. This included a tent, tools, an air pump and a puncture-repair kit. I tried not to think about how I would manage the first time I had a flat tyre or if my motorcycle broke down.

The backpackers and overlanders who moved continuously through

Mama's enlightened me on the art of theft deception. I now carried my camera in a hessian bag secured with rope as a drawstring. It looked like I was carrying nothing of value, perhaps a few potatoes purchased at the local market. But inside was a Nikon SLR with 70–200mm zoom lens, in a padded camera case. My passport, documents, slide film and US$1000 in travellers' cheques, recently purchased at the American Express office in Nairobi, were securely locked in a heavy-duty plastic Pelican case purchased in Perth. This was even more securely locked to the TT and hidden inside a ten-litre plastic jerry. I had cut the bottom out of it and slipped it over the case and then covered it in hessian. The Pelican case looked like it was concealing something of value; if I didn't disguise it, I would be an easy target for thieves and corrupt officials, especially at the armed roadblocks when I crossed Zaire. The rest of my money, US$500 in cash, was hidden on me inside the zipper of my leather belt. As I travelled cheap, eating at roadside cafes and either camping for free in villages or staying at local hotels costing on average US$1 per night, my expenses ran to about US$10 per day. When this money ran out, I'd access more via an American Express card with payments made through my bank account in Australia, which was boosted with the recent deposit of a $4700 tax return.

On the day I left Nairobi, Mama Roche gave me a motherly hug. 'When you come back, we drink beers at Everest,' she said. I nodded nervously, my thoughts focused on the traffic that roared and honked beyond her gate. I'd left some of my gear with her, and would collect it in a month, after my ride to the Maasai Mara and Lake Turkana.

I kick-started the TT and steered it into the street, my heart pounding as I gripped the handlebars and wove through traffic that obeyed its own rules: he who is bigger wins. Trucks had right of way, *matatus* came next, then cars and lastly motorcycles – although the TT, being bigger than the other bikes, came somewhere between the two. Then I was clear and with Nairobi's chaotic traffic behind me, I leaned back and enjoyed an easy ride along smooth tarmac as I headed towards Maasai Mara. I'd arranged to camp with a Danish couple I'd met at Mama's. They'd hired a 4×4 and invited me on a day's game drive as motorcycles were forbidden in the game parks. We'd arranged to meet at the Fig Tree campsite near Talek Gate, on the far northern reaches of the game reserve.

It was only 280 kilometres to Fig Tree and I stopped at Narok, the last town before Maasai Mara, to buy supplies of fresh fruit and vegetables at a local market. After leaving this small dusty town on the fringe of the Mara, the tarmac ended and I rode on dirt tracks covered in fine bulldust that at times felt like I was riding through knee-deep talcum powder. As the TT bounded over the bumps, which hid enormous potholes, its shock absorber easily cushioned the impact. It was a slow ride until I reached the flatness of a vast dry grassy plain that disappeared into the distance. Here the road ended to be replaced with a maze of two-wheel tracks leading to nowhere in particular. I stopped, at a complete loss over which to follow. Hearing a distant rumble, I turned and an ageing truck slowly crawled its way towards me.

'Hello. Which way to Talek Gate?' I shouted over the noise of the diesel engine when the truck pulled up in a cloud of dust.

'You follow me to Aitong. Only one road from there,' the Kenyan driver yelled back, a warm smile breaking across his round face as he acknowledged my task ahead. 'Long journey,' he said, 'Very good.' And with that, the truck lunged forward as he shifted into gear with a loud crunch of metal.

The truck was loaded with bags of maize flour and several youths were perched on top. They motioned for me to be quick or else be left behind. I kick-started the bike and the boys stared with gaping mouths as they heard the unmistakably powerful sound of the TT firing into life. They cheered as my quick acceleration left the truck still crunching its way through second gear. I rode on ahead to avoid its dust and stopped when I reached a low rise. Below, on the dry dusty plains dotted with flat-top acacia, was a small village of mud, thatch and corrugated-iron buildings. I waited for the truck and then rode beside it into Aitong. I waved my thanks and the driver waved back, then pointed to the only road across the expanse of brown. It led to Talek Gate.

My map showed it was about forty kilometres to Fig Tree Camp. With an hour of daylight left and in the coolness of late afternoon, I enjoyed the easy ride across the Mara plains. I rode past herds of wildebeest, zebra, hartebeest and impala. I stopped to watch a group of eight giraffes silhouetted against the setting sun. I had never thought I would see so many animals outside the reserve, but it was not fenced, so the animals moved about freely. I passed groups of Maasai youth wandering along the road as they herded goats back to the safety of their *manyattas*. These collections of mud-and-thatch huts, enclosed by an impenetrable thicket fence, were home to extended families all across the Mara plains. They stopped to stare at the *mzungu* on a motorbike and I waved back.

Just as the last of the day's light faded from the sky, I arrived at Fig Tree. The track in from the turn-off just before Talek Gate was wet and boggy, but somehow I made it without dropping the TT. Fig Tree turned out to be a tented lodge for wealthy tourists. When the Danes and I had planned our rendezvous, we'd mistakenly thought Fig Tree was the public campsite near Talek Gate. They had not arrived and it was unlikely they would find their way, as there were no signs on any of the tracks that criss-crossed over the plains.

'No camping allowed,' the neatly dressed Kenyan man told me when I asked at reception. 'This is not that sort of place and there are wild animals. You'll have to go back to the public campsite,' he said with a clipped British accent cultivated to reflect a bygone colonial era.

Behind me, a group of Japanese stood patiently waiting to be allocated their rooms. I was covered in dust and my boots and jeans were caked in mud up to my knees.

'Well, I cannot ride out on that muddy track at night,' I said firmly. 'I have no headlight.' It was a fact. My six-volt headlight was not much better than a torch.

The Kenyan in his immaculate colonial uniform of black slacks, vest, bow tie and crisp white shirt, looked at me and sighed.

'I've arranged to meet my friends here at Fig Tree,' I pleaded. 'We thought this was the public campsite – it was an honest mistake. I have no choice. I must camp here tonight. I won't bother anyone and I will be gone at first light.'

'Totally out of the question,' he said, tapping a pen on the counter impatiently.

I stepped aside, not wanting to upset him further. I could also feel the annoyance of the travel-worn Japanese. They had probably caught a night flight from Tokyo and come directly from Nairobi airport.

At nearly US$50, paying for accommodation in a *banda* – a luxury tent – was not an option that I could afford. The cheaper I travelled, the further I travelled. Giving in too easily and paying for things like accommodation when ordinarily I paid very little would see my money dwindle fast. I had been in Africa long enough to understand that US$50 had a far greater value here. It represented several tanks of petrol, several meals, a few beers and several nights camping or accommodation at local hotels. No, I would not part with US$50 when I could sleep for free in my tent.

'Okay. I'll leave,' I said as I quickly weighed up my best option. I would ride back along the road a short distance and then pitch my tent. I reasoned I'd still be close enough to the lodge to be out of harm's way of lions on the hunt or scavenging hyenas or elephants stepping on my tent, or any of the other wild animals that frequented these parts. The lodge would think I had left; being out of sight, I would be comfortably out of mind.

As I turned, I bumped into a tired American in his late fifties with thinning grey hair, dressed in khaki. 'Hi. I see you have a problem. I have a spare room in my *banda*,' he said, introducing himself as Jim. He was the lodge's balloon pilot and once he'd collected his passenger list for the morning, I followed him, feeling as though I was not the first stray traveller to turn up at Fig Tree.

With the day's mud and dust washed off, I pulled on my only decent clothes, a blue long-sleeved shirt and black leggings, and black canvas shoes. My mud-encrusted jeans, boots and bike jacket were piled neatly in a corner by the door where they could do little damage.

Jim was at the bar, and as I sat down he ordered us beers and dinner. Two large plates piled with beef stew, boiled potatoes and fried eggplant were brought out. Jim told me he had worked at resorts for the wealthy in exotic locations all over the world but had finally settled in Kenya. Here on the Mara, a ride in a hot-air balloon was sold as a 'must do' experience and many of the lodges and luxury camps dotted along the boundary of the game reserve offered balloon safaris.

After the meal I followed Jim to the staff canteen, an old corrugated-iron shed. He bought a crate of beer and handed out warm bottles of Tusker to the off-duty Kenyan staff, a group of three men and two women. We sat on empty beer crates on the bare earth. It was a warm night and the insects buzzed around the dull glow of the single lightbulb, and I thought of how events had unfolded. Here I was with a bed to sleep in, a belly full of food and a beer to wash away the day's dust and worries. I'd started the morning nervous and scared, asking myself why I was here in Africa, completely out of my depth, but in the space of less than ten hours, my perspective had changed entirely. There was no need to worry, as all I needed had been provided. Even my own apprehension had not stopped events unfolding in my favour. I finished my beer and Jim handed me another.

'Cheers,' I said, and as our bottles clinked, I made a deal with myself that from this point on I would have faith that all would be okay, that things would work out – it had happened for me on this day, so why wouldn't it happen again tomorrow and again the day after that?

*

Two enormous balloons filled the dry, brown landscape with colour as the first rays of sun tinged everything orange the following morning. Jim had woken me early with a soft tap-tap on the door and I'd quickly pulled on my muddy clothes and boots, praying that one of the passengers would sleep in or feel too ill to float silently over the Maasai Mara. But to my great disappointment all were accounted for. It was August and still peak tourist season. Jim said he was sorry and I thanked him for his generous hospitality. The Kenyan workers called and I climbed in the back of the old Land Rover for the short ride back to the lodge.

'You wait one, maybe two days. You get to go up in balloon,' one of them said as I stared at the huge multi-coloured balloons that drifted silently above us and out over the plains.

'Thank you,' I said. 'But I must move on.'

The four men nodded their understanding and said goodbye. I packed the TT and in full daylight easily rode out on the muddy road and found the track to the public campsite near Talek Gate. About a dozen tents were scattered along an area on the banks of the Talek River, which was the northern boundary of the Maasai Mara. I rode slowly past each tent as I searched for the Danes. They were not there. It was seven a.m. and I needed to get to the main gate if I was going to hitch a lift with one of the tourist vehicles heading into the park.

'No problem, we'll get you a lift,' a khaki-clad Kenyan park ranger said when I told him I wanted to visit the game reserve. After I parked the TT near the high mesh fence, he and his colleague stopped the first minibus full of tourists and asked if there was room for one more. They were Spanish and spoke very little English. John, the Kenyan driver and tour guide, indicated I should join him in the front passenger seat. The Spanish had their own guide and so John was free to quietly tell me about the animals and their habits. He stopped a short distance from where a pride of lions was feeding on a wildebeest, the morning's kill. Vultures, perched on the branches of a spindly tree, waited patiently for their turn at the carcass.

'They won't move in until the head vulture does,' John said as the lions, their swollen bellies filled with fresh meat, slowly ambled away. The ugliest and biggest of the vultures glided effortlessly down to land beside the remains. He hopped a few steps and then buried his beak and long scrawny neck deep into the carcass to feast on the intestines. Beside him the other birds landed and fought amongst themselves as they tore what bits of meat were left from the bones.

At the invitation of the Spanish, I was treated to two days of game-viewing, and as they were also staying at the public campsite, they insisted

I join them for meals. The Spanish showered me with hospitality, which meant so much more to me than a free tour and free food. Their kindness reinforced my faith that the world is a good, warm and friendly place. The last remnants of my fears were all but gone.

As I rode away from the Mara, I stopped many times on the plains just to listen to the herds of wildebeest mooing and watch the calves running and bucking as they played. I was captivated, and each time I stopped, I was reluctant to start the bike and break the feeling of harmony. There was just the wildermess, me, and the TT, and I was grateful that it allowed me this contact. I could smell the dust. I could feel the breeze that cooled and energised me. Up ahead a storm brewed, the clouds were black and heavy and the wind was charged with the storm that was heading my way.

I pulled off the road and quickly got out my groundsheet to cover myself and the TT and waited for the downpour. The rain would soon fall in great torrents and turn the hard-packed dirt to black slippery mud. Within a few minutes, a group of Maasai youths spotted me.

'Do you speak English?' I asked the boys who stood in a neat semi-circle around me. They were *moran*, the teenage boys who herd the family's goats and cattle and have begun the initiation towards manhood. They stared at me in silent non-comprehension, then a smaller boy aged about ten years was pushed to the front.

'You cannot stay here,' he said with an authority that was beyond his years. 'It is very dangerous. Elephant killed a man here.'

I looked around and noticed the broken branches of the trees and the fresh elephant droppings that littered the nearby dry creek bed. A trail of devastation lay along its banks. The trees had literally been torn to pieces.

The boy insisted I follow them back to their *manyatta*. 'It is safe there,' he said.

'I am just waiting for the storm to pass,' I said and pointed at the black clouds that were about to burst above us. A few large drops hit my face as I looked up, and the *moran* boys quickly headed back to their *manyatta*. One remained. He was a young man aged about twenty or maybe younger and I felt that he did not want to leave me alone in an area where a man had so recently been killed by an elephant. He stood beside my motorcycle, oblivious to the raindrops hitting his bare arms and strong shoulders. I motioned for him to join me under the groundsheet I'd strung up. I held one corner and I gave the other to him.

The storm lasted about half an hour. We watched the rain fall over the plains in great sheets of water. Neither of us spoke, as we did not know each other's language. When the storm passed, he left as silently as he had arrived. The boys returned and helped me pack my groundsheet. As I had not eaten my supplies of food – a loaf of bread, some bananas, a few carrots, a cabbage and an onion – I gave it all to the boys. They quickly ate the bread and the bananas and waved me farewell as I rode towards the village of Aitong, where I found a room in a crumbling mud-brick house that doubled as a local hotel.

*

The black soil had dried out and in the coolness of the morning, under a clear blue sky, I rode away from Aitong. The TT's engine made a steady thump-thump as it cruised across the Mara plains on a dirt road that was smooth and straight. Impala fed on the sides, bounding away as I approached. Maasai boys, herding cattle and goats, waved as I passed. It was all too perfect. Slowly my speed increased.

When the road changed to bulldust, I hardly noticed. My mind was elsewhere. I'd forgotten about the potholes that lay hidden. Cruising at about sixty kilometres per hour, I hit one and ploughed through the bulldust as though I'd fallen into a vat of talcum powder. I went flying over the handlebars, the TT airborne behind me. When we both came to a stop I stood up, covered from head to toe in a layer of fine brown dust. The top of my leg and shoulder hurt, but nothing was broken. I dusted myself off and walked over to the bike, lifted it upright and checked for damage. The powdery dust had saved us both. The front carrier frame was bent and the pannier frame was pushed in against the rear tyre, but there was no serious damage.

Then my whole body started shaking. I sat down and a few moments later a Maasai boy aged about ten sat down beside me. He'd been herding the family's goats and had seen my fall. With a great waving of his arms, he demonstrated how I and my motorcycle had tumbled through the air. It must have been an impressive sight, I thought as he excitedly re-enacted my crash.

It was not long before a 4×4 heading to the Maasai Mara stopped beside me. I asked the Kenyan driver if he had a steel bar to lever the pannier frame away from the back wheel.

'It is not good to ride so fast on this road. Many big holes under the dust,' he advised as he leaned on the iron bar to straighten the frame.

'Yes, I know. I've learnt my lesson,' I said.

The bike was undamaged and started first kick. Except for a slight twisting of the front forks, nothing mechanical was broken. I waved to the boy, and as I rode slowly towards Narok, I said sorry to the TT and patted its petrol tank. Through my careless inattention, I had nearly failed it and myself.

I rode into the small town of Narok about an hour later. Not only was there a welding workshop but it also doubled as a Yamaha motorcycle dealer. The mechanic straightened the front forks and welded the pannier frame. There were no cracks in the bike's frame; the leather panniers had taken the impact. The levers were protected by the metal Barkbusters bolted to the handlebars. The repairs took under an hour and cost 900 shillings, about US$15.

I rode slowly away from Narok with great caution over the potholed tarmac as I headed north for the two-hour ride to Lake Naivasha, where I'd stay at Fisherman's Camp. I arrived late in the afternoon and rode into a grassy campsite deserted of other campers and overland travellers. I set up my tent overlooking the lake, under one of the enormous flat-top acacia trees dotted throughout the campsite. After washing away the fine dust under a cold shower, too tired to eat and too sore to move my bruised body, I fell into an exhausted sleep.

I woke early to a cacophony of birdsong from the shrubs that hugged the lake-shore and from the acacias shading my tent. Still sore from my crash, I spent the day washing the TT, checking for any further damage and writing my diary. In the late afternoon, as I drank a cold Tusker beer purchased from the camp kiosk, I heard the familiar sound of a motor-cycle and waved to its rider. An overloaded Suzuki FX200 trail bike pulled up beside me. The rider dismounted and removed her helmet to reveal a waif of a Japanese girl in her early twenties with a perfect peachy complexion.

'So I am not the only crazy woman riding a motorcycle through Africa,' I said. 'Hi, I'm Heather.'

'Kon'nichiwa. I am Kaoru,' she said giving me a brilliant smile. She told me she'd arrived in Kenya two days earlier, and had left Nairobi only that morning – this was her very first day of travelling by motorcycle. She'd shipped the bike from Japan to Mombasa and taken a flight to Nairobi.

'I can't believe I meet you,' Kaoru gushed over and over again. With each shake of her head, her sleek black hair glinted with a bluish sheen in the afternoon light.

I noticed how small and delicate she was; it seemed impossible she had the strength to ride a motorcycle at all. I offered her my second beer and went to buy two more as she set up her tent. Later, we cooked a meal of rice and vegetables flavoured with chicken stock powder and exchanged stories of how we came to be in Africa.

'In Japan, we work all our life. Never have adventure. Just work, work. Small holiday. But I not do this. Never,' she said with stern determination as she crossed her arms in defiance of a system that shunned individual-ism. 'I very unhappy. Very sad. I have my motorbike in Japan and one day I say I will ride through Africa. It is crazy idea. But I do it,' Kaoru said, her face radiant with her achievement and the memory of her light-bulb moment.

'The same thing happened to me,' I smiled and recounted my story.

'This is so amazing. I am here in Africa,' she said, her words bubbling with effervescence.

'I know,' I said, and we both giggled like two children who had done something really mischievous and gotten away with it.

With the campsite almost deserted, it was quiet and as darkness fell the hippos ventured away from the lake to feed on the grass around our tents. Kaoru's excitability was infectious and as we watched by torchlight from a safe distance, the world through her eyes and giggles was the most wonderful, amazing place.

The following afternoon we rode to Elsamere for high tea in the manicured gardens overlooking Lake Naivasha. Elsamere was the former home of George and Joy Adamson, the big cat conservationists. Joy was the author of *Born Free*, the story of orphaned lion cub Elsa, raised by the Adamsons and successfully released into the wild. Kaoru and I gorged on freshly baked scones and cakes and sipped tea from fine china, all for 150 shillings, with the proceeds going to wildlife conservation around Lake Naivasha. After our third plate of scones, chocolate cake and jam tarts we reclined on the cushioned chairs shaded by tall flat-top acacias, where black and white colobus monkeys played amongst the branches and took great delight peeing on unsuspecting tourists. We made sure to sit at a safe distance. Elsamere was a genteel experience – a relic from east Africa's bygone colonial era – and was likely to be our last. The next day we'd return to Africa proper: to potholed roads; ramshackle villages; and meals of *ugali* (stiff maize porridge), beef stew and steamed cabbage. There'd be no chocolate cake or scones, but I wouldn't want it any other way. Even so, Elsamere was a very nice interlude.

I woke early the next morning and packed the TT for the ride north to Lake Turkana. Each item, by now, had found its own special place, just as water finds its level. Tools and spares were at the bottom of the right-hand pannier, while my petrol stove, utensils, food, more spares, first-aid kit and sleeping bag were packed in the left-hand side. Everything else went in the Gearsack that sat on the seat behind me. My tent was strapped to the handlebars and a ten-litre water container was strapped to the rack in front of the headlight. It was empty, but I'd fill it when crossing long stretches of dry country just in case I broke down and was stuck for hours if not a day or two. My spare ten-litre jerry for petrol, four litres of Mobil oil and the disguised Pelican box with all my valuables were strapped to the rear rack behind the Gearsack. This order created a sense of harmony, as the remnants of my fear still niggled away inside me. Fear of the unknown, despite all the evidence that said there was nothing to fear. While no harm had come to me, I could not push away entirely thoughts that I might not be so lucky on the next road I travelled. My weapon against this doubt was to focus on everything with a step-by-step approach. The fact was that each time I packed my bike, each time I rode forward on a road littered with potholes and rocks, my strength and skills grew and so too did my confidence.

When I'd finished packing, I drank sweet black tea and ate a breakfast of bread and bananas as I watched Kaoru pack her motorcycle for her ride down to South Africa. A backpack and a few plastic boxes were tied with bungee cords to the back of her bike. Her spare oil, camping mattress and sleeping bag were all shoved under a bungee net that covered the lot. As yet she had not experienced thieves or rough, potholed roads and I helped her rearrange the load to make it a little more secure. After South Africa, Kaoru told me she would ride through Namibia, Angola, Zaire and West Africa and I advised her to never leave her bike and gear unattended.

'People are poor and you can't blame them if you leave it for the taking,' I said.

Before I rode north and she south, we rode together as far as Nakuru, an hour's ride from the campsite at Lake Naivasha. Here we shared a lunch of chicken, salad and chips followed by large bowls of chocolate ice-cream.

'Are you scared?' I asked Kaoru as we both spooned ice-cream into our mouths, savouring the sweet chocolatey indulgence.

'Yes,' she said, but very faintly, as though admitting it would somehow weaken her resolve. She was so beautiful, so small and fragile. I wondered what the Africans would make of her.

'I am too, but just a little,' I said. 'With each day it does get better. So far nothing bad has happened to me, so I just say to myself: Why be afraid, there's no reason to be afraid. In Cape Town, this African woman told me I'd find *ubuntu*. It means we are all connected, that we are one and we need to help each other. And so far she's been right. Everyone I've met has been good and kind,' I said and noticed Kaoru was nodding her head in complete agreement, as if the past two days we'd spent together was proof enough.

With our feasting over, Kaoru and I stood next to our bikes in the warm sunshine.

'*Arigato.* I so pleased I meet you,' she said.

'Me too,' I replied and we embraced, promising to stay in touch. Despite our fears, we shared the same innocence and belief that the world was a kind and good place. Our paths had been destined to cross at Lake Naivasha. It was a chance meeting that gave each of us the reassurance we so needed in those early days of going it alone.

5

SHOW OF STRENGTH
SOUTH HORR, NORTHERN KENYA

As day changed to late afternoon, the intense heat gave way to a cool breeze and it was another of those times when I wished the road would go forever as I travelled north towards Lake Turkana. A smooth dirt road cut through scrubland dotted with flat-top acacia and I was grateful it was freshly graded with no bone-jarring corrugations. That night I would stop in Maralal, a small town in the heart of the Samburu district. I rode past manyattas with Samburu men in warrior garb armed with long spears and bead-adorned women carrying wood piled high on their heads.

The graded section of road went for only a few kilometres, then deteriorated into potholes, which I avoided as best I could until my rear tyre began to drift. At first I didn't know what was wrong, but it soon became apparent: I had a puncture. I parked off the road, near a spindly tree and shade, as I knew this would take some time to fix. I lifted the Gearsack off the back of the bike and placed my tools neatly on the ground before laying the TT unceremoniously on its side to rest on the panniers. This positioned the rear wheel off the ground where it could easily be removed after undoing the centre bolt.

Before leaving Australia, I'd practised fixing a flat. It was one of the things I did over and over again – but that had been months ago. Alone under the tree, I struggled to lever the tyre off the rim. I needed strength to make a gap with the screwdriver with one hand and push the lever between the tyre and the rim with the other. The more I struggled, the more I panicked. The sun cast long shadows and it would soon be dark. In desperation, I threw the tyre levers at the bike.

'Fuck you!' I yelled, then held my head with blackened hands.

'Hello. You have problem,' said a deep voice behind me.

It was so unexpected that I fell on my bottom from where I was squatting on my haunches. Staring down at me were two Samburu men dressed in tribal red and ochre robes. They both carried spears and the taut muscles of their bare shoulders glistened with the setting sun.

'You need help,' one of them said and leaned close to look at the rear wheel lying on the stony ground.

'Flat tyre,' I said and retrieved the tyre levers I had discarded so angrily a moment before. 'I must get this in here.' I poked at the spot between the tyre and the rim then handed him the lever.

With the screwdriver, I gently pushed down on the rubber, and he easily slipped the lever into the gap.

'Thank you,' I said as I removed the tube and prepared it for the glue and patch.

A nail had punctured the tyre, one of many that rattled from the wood crates on the back of trucks carrying supplies north.

'Where you go?' the other man asked as he squatted beside his friend.

'Maralal and then Lake Turkana,' I said and pointed to the side cover and the roughly drawn world map of my route from Australia.

'Long journey,' the first said and the other nodded in agreement.

They talked amongst themselves with nods and the occasional sideways glance at me, which I interpreted as a mix of disbelief and respect. My perception of their good intent was felt as a physical thing, like an ever-so-slight pressure forced through the air, and I breathed it in.

'Do you know Lake Turkana?' I asked. 'I'm going there to see the fossils of our first footprints,' I said and pointed to their feet.

The two men looked at their feet and then at me, confused. I hoped I had not insulted them.

'Big crocodiles in lake,' one of them said.

They watched intrigued as I pushed the tube with its new patch back into the tyre. Moments before, I'd been a hopeless fool stuck in open scrub with a flat tyre that I could not fix and now I was like an old pro. I reached for the foot pump and once the tyre was inflated, the two men helped me lift the TT upright. I knelt to gather my things, and when I stood they had disappeared into the scrub as silently as they had appeared. I smiled at how things had worked out: help had miraculously arrived just at the very moment I needed it.

It was almost dark by the time I rode into Maralal. With its dusty streets lined with single-storey, crumbling cement-block buildings, Maralal was the last frontier before the desert to the north. It was the last town where I could stock up on food and petrol. Maralal was also where the Samburu from these villages came to trade, see friends and have a few beers. People from all the tribes wandered about the town, their traditional dress identifying their origin. I found a guesthouse amongst the many that lined the main street. A room with an electric light, somewhere safe to lock the TT and hot water cost sixty shillings (about US$1).

After a shower, I wandered to the nearby Buffalo Bar and sat outside with a cold beer. As I reclined on an old but comfortable lounge chair covered in faded red fabric, a group of teenage boys ambled over to join me. They hoped to make a sale but I had no money for brass snake bracelets, and when they could see their efforts were wasted they packed away their curios and settled down to talk. I asked about road conditions and Lake Turkana.

'You will see very big fish. More than one hundred kilos,' one said.

'Do not swim in the lake. The crocodiles are bigger and they will eat you,' said another.

*

After leaving Maralal, the recently graded road soon deteriorated and was littered with rocks and potholes, which I dodged to avoid another puncture. As I approached the village of Baragoi, a horde of teenage boys ran after me, each holding a bottle of Coke. The main business here was selling Coke to the mzungus who passed on their way to Lake Turkana. The rough roads and distance kept most tourists away, but those who made the effort mostly travelled on overland truck tours or 4×4 safaris and eight to twenty thirsty passengers from one of these vehicles was good business. Competition was fierce. With a trail of Coke boys behind me, I stopped at a shop with a lean-to veranda where I could rest in the shade.

I didn't even bother to ask about a cold Coke, but the boy who handed me the thick opaque bottle had done his best to cool it with wet hessian.

'Business quiet?' I asked as I paid the boy.

'Yer, no truck for a few days,' he said and traced a finger over the map on the bike's side cover.

'Any motorcycles been through?' I asked.

'No, you only one for weeks,' he said, moving his head from side to side in disbelief.

Another youth pushed his way to the front of the group that milled around me.

'I have been in Baragoi long time. I never see woman alone on big motorbike. You are the first, very good,' he said.

'I'm sure I won't be the last,' I replied.

It felt good to have their respect at this early stage of riding solo. In just one week of riding alone, I had blossomed with self-assurance like a withered flower that had come back to life after a long spell without water. This person was so far removed from the woman from those first months of this ride that I hardly recognised her. That person had clung to the safe sanctuary, albeit one filled with tension, of travelling with another. But as I entered the unknown, I felt intensely alive, as though all my senses were working together at a heightened level of awareness.

I finished the Coke and handed the bottle back to the boy. I checked the oil, as the engine now used about 600ml every thousand kilometres or so, which was not good. But the engine had not lost compression and as long as I kept the oil topped up, no damage would be done. I was grateful for the four litres of oil given to me by Mobil Kenya in Nairobi when I produced my letter of introduction from Mobil Australia.

'You buy tobacco for the elders,' the boy said and told me it would be a welcome gift for the people who lived near the lake.

The other boys sat in the shade next to the TT ready for the next tourist, which might be later today, tomorrow or perhaps the following day.

'Okay,' I said. 'What about petrol?' I wanted to buy a few litres to top up the tank, as I'd been warned there was no fuel after this village.

The boy indicated I should follow him and he ran on ahead to one of the Indian-owned shops at the back of the main street. The fuel was hand-pumped from a rusty 44-gallon drum into a large metal jug. At forty-seven shillings a litre, it was double the price I'd paid in Maralal.

After Baragoi, the flat expanse of desert climbed into a range of low hills and at the top I stopped to stare at a vast flat sandy plain, with ragged mountains as a distant backdrop. In the late afternoon the heat haze coloured the mountains in purple hues. I was completely mesmerised and struggled to move, but it would soon be dark. I rode on to South Horr, a small Samburu village nestled in the Horr Valley next to a mountain stream that flowed down from Mount Nyiru. Shaded by large leafy trees, the campsite was just before the village. There was only one small A-frame orange and brown tent next to the stream, which babbled gently over the rocks. I did a double-take, as the tent looked just like mine. I'd purchased the same tent of dubious quality from an English couple who'd reached the end of their backpacking travels in Africa. A slender young woman with long, brown hair that fell in spirals around her shoulders crawled out.

'Hi, I'm Molly,' she said in an unmistakable Australian accent. 'I've been camped here a week. I started out with a Kenyan boy I met in Wamba. We hitched lifts and then walked from Maralal to South Horr. There's hardly any bloody traffic on that road. Hey, do you want to climb Mount Nyiru with me? I'm leaving tomorrow morning.' Her green eyes sparkled like a child about to embark on some grand mythical adventure conjured by an overactive imagination.

'Yeah, sure,' I said as I gazed up at the mountain that towered above the campsite. 'Why not. What happened to your Kenyan friend?' I asked as I looked around.

'He's not interested in climbing mountains and when a truck passed by yesterday, he got a lift back to Wamba,' she explained and picked up a few sticks from the pile beside her tent to light the evening's cooking fire.

As the flames danced high into the night, we ate rice and vegetables flavoured with chicken stock powder, a meal that was very unimaginative but tasty, and had become my staple campfire food. Molly and I shared a similar philosophy, based on 'where thoughts go energy flows'. While it was an emerging philosophy for me, it was well embedded for Molly who bubbled with self-assurance and was completely devoid of all worry. It seemed she merely had to send out her thoughts into the ether and all would be returned just as she imagined.

Molly was an arts graduate from Sydney. She'd travelled around Kenya for a month. She travelled light and described herself as a minimalist who saw no reason for possessions. 'We are only here for such a brief time and it is our experiences that we will take with us, not our things,' she said, rolling a joint and offering it to me.

'No thanks. I don't really smoke. I had a bad experience in Malawi after eating banana cake made with Malawi Gold,' I said and felt a little queasy as she lit the joint and I smelt the pungent smoke. Molly nodded as she inhaled.

After a long moment of silence, she took her gaze away from the flames and looked at me. 'I knew you'd turn up,' she said with a mischievous smile. 'I didn't want to climb the mountain on my own.'

The campsite's Samburu watchman, James, was to be our guide to climb Mount Nyiru. He was just a little taller than Molly and me, but with strong wiry arms and broad shoulders, the muscles well defined even under the faded black cotton of his threadbare T-shirt. He spoke more than a few words of English and had a warm, saintly smile.

It took a full day to reach the 2700-metre summit. James walked fast in bare feet. Molly and I found the going tough, but our pride would not let us complain. Near the summit, we passed an old *manyatta*, its roof partially collapsed. It was used by the Samburu *moran*, the teenage boys and young men who graze cattle and goats on the lush grasses high on the mountain. The *moran* spend weeks or months living alone off what nature provides. It is a time to learn self-reliance and it also keeps them out of trouble and away from the girls in the valley below.

'This is the time for the *moran* to grow. These boys reach manhood knowing their cattle and how to look after them. The married men stay in the village and look after their wives, and make more babies,' James explained as we walked.

The summit was a large flat area of solid granite, a perfect vantage point to admire the view out over the Horr Valley and across the plains of northern Kenya. James pointed out the mountains he had climbed searching for amber and sapphires. A cold wind blew across the mountain and we shivered as we prepared our meal of rice, potatoes, tomatoes and onions, flavoured with chicken stock powder. James struggled to start the fire in the strong wind that whistled across the bare rock. Molly and I huddled close to form a windbreak so there would be enough heat to cook our food.

The cold howling wind meant the three of us hardly slept, and at first light we packed the tent and ambled down the mountain, the walk warming our chilled bodies. James pointed out the plants and herbs used for food and medicine; most were for treating malaria. It made me wonder about its prevalence in the area, as I'd read there was only minimal risk in the north. To give my body a break from Lariam, the malaria prophylactic – a drug that can play tricks on the mind with vivid hallucinations – I'd stopped taking it the week before. I was only carrying a six-month supply of Lariam and reasoned that if I was not in a malaria area, why take it?

As we walked, we had time to stare in awe at the trees that grew tall and majestic. Grey spidery lichen hung from the branches and a thick green moss covered the trunks. James trimmed toothbrushes for us from the supple branches of a shrub. The antiseptic properties in the sap killed the bacteria as the chewed fibres cleaned our teeth.

We stopped often to rest, not so much because we needed to, but rather to admire the views out over the Horr valley below and to watch colourful birds dart amongst the bushes and trees that towered above us. The mountain had an abundance of wild flowers; rich purples, oranges and bright yellows gave off the strongest, sweetest perfume. At a stand of shrubs densely covered with bright orange flowers, wild bees buzzed with a feverish frenzy as they fed on the nectar. It was a sign a hive was near and we watched the trail of bees disappear into the thick branch of a tree too high for us to climb.

We arrived back at the campsite mid-afternoon. During the last hour of our walk, I had begun to feel feverish and weak. It took all my effort to push the TT from the forest station office to where we were camped about fifty metres away. I'd left it there so the ranger on duty could keep a close eye on it. For this security I paid him 100 shillings (about US$1.50) and he looked a little overwhelmed when I handed him the money. My bike was very special, I told him, and he just looked at the notes and nodded. We each paid James 300 shillings (about US$4), as we'd agreed.

I was now shaking with fever and did not have the strength to set up my tent. James helped and hit the tent pegs into the hard ground. I crawled inside and spent the next three days sweating and shivering, aching all over with a headache that threatened to split my skull. These were all the symptoms of malaria. I treated myself with Chloroquine, which the Italians had given me on the cargo ship. I hardly moved from my tent. My body was wracked with fever, and diarrhoea ran out of me as a smelly brown liquid; I had no choice but to wash myself in the creek. I had been drinking this water and wondered how many other people upstream also used it as both toilet and kitchen. From then on, I boiled all the water I drank and hoped the villagers downstream did the same.

Molly cared for me during these feverish days, feeding me on sweet black tea and dry toast. On the fourth day, the fever subsided: the medication had killed the malaria parasite. It was also time for Molly to return to Nairobi and we embraced and hoped that fate would bring the two of us together again at some point in the future. I sat on one of the large boulders next to the creek and watched her walk to the road. Her brown hair shone like burnt gold in the morning sun. She wore a white singlet and dark green velvet pants hugged her slim legs and hips. She carried a small canvas backpack with her tent and an old grey blanket strapped to it. Her shoes were sandals made from old car-tyre rubber. As I watched her, a truck pulled up, probably the only one all day, and she climbed in and a moment later was gone.

I was alone in the shaded campground but it was not long before James, the village children tending the goats, and the women heading out for the day to collect wood stopped to check on me. Word had spread I'd been sick with malaria.

That little campsite with its shade trees, the Samburu people who casually wandered by, the gentle song of birds and the trickle of water over the rocks was a tranquil, peaceful place. In this calmness, I let the sun warm my body and felt a deep sense of timelessness, as though nothing else really mattered but being and belonging to the earth.

Still very weak, I washed my clothes and then packed the TT with as much as I could, as I planned to leave the next morning. At noon, I walked a kilometre along the track that followed the creek to South Horr to buy fresh vegetables from the Catholic mission. I craved fresh food and the vitamins and life-force this would give me to reenergise my body. I had not eaten anything but campfire-toasted stale bread for the past three days; my hunger was a good sign that I was on the way to recovery.

The mission was run by Spanish nuns, who sold me a handful of oranges, spinach and tomatoes and said I could help myself to the basil, oregano and thyme growing in the rich red soil.

It took me forever to walk back to the campsite. Earlier that morning I'd felt well enough, but now I was exhausted. I could only walk about fifty metres before I had to rest. When I got back to my tent, I crawled inside and fell into an exhausted sleep, only waking late that afternoon. I cooked a meal of pasta and a sauce made with tomatoes, spinach and fresh herbs. As I ate, I realised I could not ride over the rocky road to Lake Turkana the next day. It was another two days before I regained enough strength to leave.

As I packed the last of my things, James, the women and children stood around me waiting to say goodbye.

'Here is the *panga*,' said James, handing me a large knife in a stiff cow-hide sheath. I pulled it from its sheath to feel the sharp blade. When I'd seen James clearing the overgrown track with a *panga* during our mountain hike, I'd asked him to make me one so that I could show I was not to be messed with. He agreed and his price was 200 shillings.

'It is very sharp. Be careful how you use it,' he said as I handed him the notes and slipped the *panga* under the straps that secured my tent across the handlebars.

'Your enemies will see the *panga* and know you will fight them,' he said as he nodded his approval at where I'd placed it.

'No, I won't be fighting anyone. But hopefully they will see it and leave me alone,' I laughed, but I sounded nervous.

'You do not have to fight. You just need to show you can fight. Strength also comes from here,' he said and lightly touched my head with his index finger. 'You are a strong woman but you must stand tall like a man. Your enemies will know you have the strength to fight back. Nobody will attack you if you are strong. Do not show fear. Then you will be lost,' he added.

The *panga*, resting for all to see, also gave the TT an added aura of indestructibility that transcended mere metal. With each passing day, my motorcycle was developing its own personality, as though it were a living, breathing thing with a sense of its own purpose.

I waved goodbye to James, the women and the children. I opened the throttle, the TT responded and we rumbled out of the campsite towards Lake Turkana.

6

THE KINDNESS OF STRANGERS
LOIYANGALANI, KENYA

As I started out on the ninety-kilometre ride from South Horr to Loiyangalani, a township with a permanent spring near Lake Turkana, I rode on a smooth two-wheel track of fine sand, packed hard by feet, hooves and tyres. I passed Samburu men and boys herding camels, cattle and goats, while women and girls gathered firewood from the acacia woodland that filled the Horr valley. This idyllic world soon deteriorated into a landscape littered with chunks of red volcanic rock. I was in no hurry, and stopped often to admire this moonscape of flat, barren nothingness. Mountain ranges shimmered purple in the distance and Mount Nyiru towered above them all. A howling wind blew across the expanse, as if God in all his fury had forsaken this place that was once the Garden of Eden.

Scientists have discovered that four and a half million years ago, this region, the northern end of Kenya's Rift Valley, ebbed and flowed between an enormous floodplain and a lake about double the size of the current Lake Turkana, which is roughly 250 kilometres long and fifteen to thirty kilometres wide. For about two million years times were good. There was plenty of fresh water and forests bearing fruits bordered the perimeter of the lake and inflowing rivers. It was a perfect world, but gradually, over the next two and a half million years, the floodplains turned to grasslands – and eventually to the desert that now lay before me. Gazing over the desert,

77

I was taken back to when our ancestors began to walk upright purely out of a need to survive. Instead of foraging in the safety of thick forests, they had to dash from one outlying cluster of trees to another, and running on two legs was surely quicker than scurrying on four. Standing upright while crossing these grasslands would also have made it easier to scan the horizon for predators. Later they began hunting game on the grasslands, and with hunting came the need to carry spears and other tools. I understood then that what lay before me was not simply our evolutionary nest. It had also been a frightening place, although walking upright had pushed us forward on our evolutionary path.

The barren plains soon ended and I struggled to steer the TT over a stony road littered with chunks of red rock. Exhausted, I stopped when I reached a low rise. Before me lay the world's largest alkaline lake, Lake Turkana – also known as the Jade Sea, due to a particular type of algae that causes the water to appear a deep turquoise when viewed from afar.

I still felt weak from the malaria and could only ride two or three kilometres before I needed to rest. I stopped where the track neared the lake, took off my jacket and walked the few steps to lie in the cool water close to the shore, keeping a watchful eye for the crocodiles I'd been warned so much about. The water was slightly salty, drinkable if need be, but I was glad I was still carrying about four litres of boiled creek water from South Horr. It would easily last the twelve kilometres to Loiyangalani.

For several kilometres, I struggled to ride over the rocks. My arms and shoulders ached with the strain. I stalled and as I lost my footing, I dropped the bike. I had no strength to lift it and, exhausted, I sat down, unable to move. This all happened about fifty metres from a group of fisherman resting under the one and only tree, a spindly thing that cast minimal shade. Without hesitation, the fishermen ran to help. After lifting my motorcycle, they ushered me towards the tree.

I sat down on one of the flat rocks, worn smooth from years of men fixing nets in the tree's small circle of shade. The fishermen were Turkana – four middle-aged men and two teenage boys, their clothing no more than rags. Years ago, before the drought, fishing would have been considered below their warrior status, as a tribe's value was determined by the number of cattle and goats it possessed, but in times of hunger everyone adapts in order to survive. One of the men stirred a blackened pot of red kidney beans and maize kernels (relief food donated to the drought-stricken region), and spooned some into a bowl, handing it to me while the others continued to repair the net. The food was bland and the beans tough, but it filled my stomach and restored my strength. The boys could speak some English and I asked about their fishing. Their catch was the huge Nile perch that the boys in Maralal had told me about.

'We have Nile perch in Australia but it is called barramundi,' I said and explained that its skin was very strong, like leather, and was used to make handbags, wallets and clothes. One of the boys translated and the men all laughed at the preposterousness of such a thing. They then walked with me to the TT and waited to make sure I made it over the last rocky section. Overwhelmed with gratitude for their help, I gave the fisherman the tobacco from Baragoi. For them the tobacco was a rare luxury and I wanted to repay their kindness. Their look of sheer pleasure told me they were pleased with my gift.

'Rocks not so big,' one of the boys said and pointed up ahead where the road dipped and then went over a slight rise.

The boy was right and the large chunks of rock soon gave way to smaller ones. From there it was an easy ride for the last eight kilometres to Loiyangalani.

This desert township had once been on the lake but was now about a kilometre from the shore, as Lake Turkana had been receding by up to thirty centimetres a year. Water was lost through evaporation and irrigation from the Omo River in Ethiopia. This river was the lake's main source of water, as rainfall was less than 200 millimetres per year and inflows from the Turkwel and Kerio rivers were dependant on seasonal rain. Plans by the Ethiopian government to dam the Omo for hydroelectric power had campaigners predicting the lake would eventually dry up, bringing devastation to all who called the region home. But of more immediate concern was the drought that had gripped northern Kenya since 1975. The earth was bare and dry, baked by a hot, relentless sun. Almost the entire population of the town was made up of Turkana, Borana and Gabbra tribespeople. They'd moved in from the desert and their little domed huts fringed the town. To survive, they had no choice but to live there while they waited for the next ration of relief food – maize, beans, cooking oil and nutrient-enriched milk powder. A few people owned boats and ate fish but most did not have money to buy fish, let alone a boat.

Children chased after me and people waved for me to stop as I rode through Loiyangalani, which comprised several iron-roofed mud-brick shacks lining a dusty road. I stopped outside the Cold Drink Hotel.

'They did have a fridge but it stopped working years ago,' said a teen-age boy, his dark skin smooth and radiant, slightly lighter than the other boys. He was Ethiopian or Somali. He stood next to me as though he had appointed himself my minder.

According to my guidebook, there were two options for cheap accommodation: this local hotel or a campsite near the overpriced Oasis Lodge just out of town. With few travellers making it this far north, I'd likely be on my own at the campsite. Here I'd have the company of the locals.

I walked into the main room of the shack that served as a hotel. It was furnished with a few wooden tables and chairs made from rough-cut timber. The boy reached behind the makeshift bar and handed me a warm bottle of Coke, telling me I'd find Mama, the owner, out the back. As I walked into the yard of hard-packed sand, I saw a stout African woman stirring a large fire-blackened pot over hot coals; evidently, this was the hotel's kitchen. I asked about a room and followed her to an iron-roofed mud-brick shack with a narrow veranda enclosed with wire mesh. Inside was one large room devoid of furniture and with no windows other than a few gaps along a wall where it joined the roof. It was sixty shillings and I would be sleeping on my Thermarest and sleeping bag, with the TT secure outside on the enclosed veranda.

I'd arrived too late for bathing at the town's permanent spring, which was open at set times for women and then for men. Instead, I washed off the day's dirt and sweat with a cup and bucket in the wash room, a flimsy wooden structure with no floor other than two large stones for my feet. Later, Mama led me to the lounge room, which doubled as the dining room. It was narrow and furnished with a low coffee table, a threadbare red velvet couch and two single matching lounge chairs. A kerosene lamp hung from the low ceiling. I shuffled between the furniture to sit at the end of the couch and wait for dinner.

A moment later I was joined by three others, who introduced themselves as Sharif, Abdersak and Kadil – the last the boy who'd earlier appointed himself my minder. They were all from Somalia and were all related to Mama in one way or another. Sharif was in his late thirties, but could have been older. He was a short man of slim build, with wiry black hair that gave him a decidedly shifty appearance. He worked as a mechanic at the Oasis Lodge, which catered for fly-in tourists on fishing trips. He asked about my plans.

'I want to ride to Sibiloi National Park to walk in our first footsteps, and to see the fossils,' I said excitedly. Along with the fossilised footprints, I was also interested in the fossilised remains of mammoths and the trunks of giant trees.

'You will not find the road. It is not marked and is very sandy. You will need a guide or you must follow one of the 4×4s taking tourists to the area. Do not go alone,' he said, looking at me with a raised wiry eyebrow. 'I just finish my contract with the lodge and have no more work,' he added, and I got the uncomfortable feeling that I had suddenly become 'business'.

'The road to Sibiloi goes through a dangerous area,' he went on. 'The bandits are armed with AK47s. They must protect what little grass is left for their animals. I know this area well. I know the tribes and where to find water.'

As I sipped *tangawizi*, a delicious sweet ginger tea, Mama brought in plates of chapatti and a goat-meat stew. A bowl and jug of water were passed around and we each washed our hands. Abdersak, a gangly youth aged about twenty with the harmonious aura of one who is close to God, told me he lived in North Horr but was here to teach the local children the Koran.

'Your room is usually the classroom. But we are happy to sit outside on your veranda,' he said with a politeness that was genuine.

'Yes, of course,' I said, feeling bad that I'd taken over their classroom.

'You pay for the room. Mama let us use it when there are no guests,' he said to explain the arrangement.

Kadil, who had a permanent grin, told me that Mama was his aunt and he helped out at the hotel in return for meals and a place to sleep.

'Why you go to Sibiloi?' he asked. 'It is far and very sandy. It is dangerous in the desert. There are lions and they will eat you,' he added.

But I knew there were few lions outside game parks and reserves in Africa, as they'd been hunted or shot long ago by villagers and tribespeople protecting their livestock.

'I want to walk where we first walked,' I said, and he looked at me quizzically.

'It is very difficult to do this,' he replied.

'Going to Sibiloi is my pilgrimage. Like a religion,' I added, trying to explain why I felt compelled to go, a deep yearning that was impossible to ignore. 'Sibiloi is our birthplace. Where we evolved from apes,' I said and left it at that to avoid confusing him.

'You must visit the El Molo then. It is very close for you on your motorbike. They live the old ways,' he said cheerfully, as though this would be an adequate substitute for a reckless venture into the desert to Sibiloi.

Numbering only about three hundred people, the El Molo lived in two villages on the lake about ten kilometres to the north. I'd read in my guidebook that this was an over-commercialised experience and an invasion of privacy for the El Molo, who endured a constant stream of tourists wanting to wander around the village of one of Africa's smallest tribes. However, tourists were good business and the fees they paid helped support the entire village, alongside the fish they caught in the lake.

'There is a Turkana boy. He speaks English and El Molo. I bring him here in the morning,' Kadil added with a satisfied smile.

*

I was sipping my first glass of *tangawizi* the next morning when Kadil arrived with a Turkana boy named Fred. I quickly realised that my silence in response to the suggestion the previous night had been interpreted as acceptance and the deal done.

'You leave now before the day is too hot,' Kadil said.

Fred was a slender, shy boy aged about fifteen who beamed broadly, not believing his luck, when Kadil told him he would ride with me on the big motorbike to one of the two El Molo villages. I had no plans for the day and Kadil advised me that Fred did not want any payment, just the opportunity to practise his English.

'When he is older, he wants to work for the lodge but he must first speak good English,' Kadil explained.

I could not deny Fred the chance to practise his English nor the opportunity for a ride on the TT, as he stared at it with a look of sheer amazement and joy.

The road north was all hard-packed dirt across a flat plain. Fred directed me past the first El Molo village and on to the next sandy bay, where I parked the bike a short walk from a collection of dome huts made from tightly woven palm fronds and anything else that could be found in the surrounding desert. A horde of about twenty children ran out to meet us and I expected them to pester me for pens and sweets, as they were surely familiar with tourists. But they did not and I wondered if this was all part of good tourist relations to counteract the bad press about them in the guidebook.

Fred led the way to the chief's hut. He went in and I waited outside, along with about half the village, who stood motionless beside me. They wore reddish-brown bits of cloth or grubby Western clothes turned the same earthy tone as the ground. The girls also wore necklaces of mostly red and yellow beads. The older they were, the more strands they wore.

'It is 600 shillings (about US$7) for the crocodile hunt, including a camera permit,' Fred said, returning from the hut after speaking at length with the chief.

'Crocodile hunt?' I said, bemused, not sure how all this had come about. The chief looked happy to have my business and beamed a wide, toothless smile from a wrinkled face. After nine years in Kakadu, I'd seen my fair share of crocodiles fishing on billabongs in dinghies with work mates. I expected that, just like their counterparts in northern Australia, these crocs would be shy but cunning creatures that would dart off into the water long before a spear could penetrate a thick, scaly hide. But a moonlit walk along the shores of the lake would be a surreal experience so I shook hands with the chief to seal the deal and Fred told him we would be back late that afternoon.

During the heat of the day nobody moved in Loiyangalani. With the Koran lessons finished, it was quiet on the veranda and I lay in my room dozing. To get some relief from the dry heat, I made frequent trips to the wash room, where I poured cups of water over myself, still fully clothed in T-shirt and sarong. Late that afternoon, as a cool breeze blew in from across the lake, Fred returned and we went back to the El Molo village to hunt crocodiles.

After I pitched my tent on the rocky ground, Fred and I strolled amongst the dome huts and along the lake shore. The children had lost interest in me, as their evening meal was now far more important. Fred talked about the El Molo and about the drought. He pointed out how far the water had receded: a small stone church now sat a kilometre away. I asked about Mount Kulal, the mountain with the clouds hovering around its peak, in the distance. At a height of 2300 metres, it enjoyed frequent rainfall and its summit was lush and green.

'The Catholic Mission grows all kinds of fruit and vegetables there,' Fred said.

'Does it?' I replied, the seed of an idea forming as I gazed longingly up at the mountain.

We were invited to join the chief and his family for the evening meal and I was given a mug of milky tea made from fish-flavoured water. The El Molo cart all their fresh water in drums by donkey cart from the spring at Loiyangalani and none of this precious water was wasted, not even the water used to boil the fish. This in particular, actually, since it contained all those nourishing juices. Not realising, at first, that the tea contained boiled fish water, I took a large gulp and nearly threw up. I handed the mug back to the chief, who handed it to one of the grubby kids who took a drink and passed it on, and a moment later it was finished. A plate with boiled Nile perch, kidney beans and maize kernels was placed on the ground. The chief picked out the fatty globules, offering me the calorie-rich delicacy. The El Molo, like the Aboriginal people of Kakadu, value fish fat; for thousands of years Aboriginal people have highlighted the globules in their X-ray-style rock paintings. I took a small portion and, to be polite, forced myself to eat it. With the appetiser done with, we then ate with our fingers, peeling sections of the white fish off the bones. It was delicious.

Later in the evening, before the moon rose, Fred and I followed a group of six men carrying spears and harpoons across a narrow sandbar that separated a lagoon from the lake. As the full moon began to cast long rays of light across the water and on the beach up ahead, the crocodile hunters lost their element of surprise.

'The children want to sing and dance for you,' Fred said when we returned to the village a half hour later.

On cue, two smaller children clasped my hands and sat me down near one of the dome huts. The harmonising of the children's voices resonated in the still night, and it felt as though the essence of Africa flowed through their singing. I asked Fred the meaning of the words.

'They sing Christian songs,' he replied from where he was sitting beside me, his arms clasped around his legs as he swayed to the rhythm.

The children sang and sang but it was late and the adults complained about the noise, yelling at us words that I assumed meant 'keep it down', so we moved to the outer edge of the village, where I sat leaning against a dome hut, the younger children huddled close to me. But the singing was a disturbance here too and an old man leapt out of the hut and chased us away with a stick. Fred, the children and I all laughed hysterically as we ran to the lake shore, far enough away not to disturb the sleeping adults. The older girls stood in a line and sang under a moon that shone with the brightness of daylight. The *moran* boys, the young warriors, soon joined them but they no longer sang Christian songs. I did not need Fred to translate. These songs were about love and bravery and as they jumped in unison on the hard-packed sand, their voices carried them to a distant past.

I thought of my own past, of my mother and father back in Australia, where they grew bananas in the tropical north. I'd been away for nearly six months and kept in regular contact by sending a letter home every week without fail and phoning at least once a month. I knew my mother worried about me, but even though I was alone I did not feel lonely or homesick. Whenever I spoke with her, I reassured her that I was okay. 'The people here are good to me,' I'd say. But her perception of Africa was fuelled by news reports of wars and massacres, of famine and disaster.

This was not my reality as I sat with Fred and the children. Africa was like one village, and no matter where I was, there was always someone to share kind words or a meal. I thought again of the South African lady at the hostel in Cape Town who'd told me I'd find *ubuntu* as I travelled Africa. A little girl aged about seven smiled up at me and I smiled back as we shared a moment of understanding that transcended culture and language, on a night when everything was in alignment: the rays of moonlight, the gentle ever-so-slight breeze blown in across the lake, the harmonies of the singing, the pounding of feet on the hard-packed sand – all seemed to energise the moment.

I was grateful for my brief glimpse of El Molo life and grateful that I was not treated as a tourist, even though my visit was no different to that of others. Fred and I left soon after sunrise and I promised to return the following afternoon with some fruit from Mount Kulal in exchange for fish. My seed of an idea had blossomed. I had seen no fresh fruit and vegetables in any of the stalls in Loiyangalani and I was sure many of the El Molo children had never seen anything like an orange. Fred told me the trucks delivered fresh fruit and vegetables twice a week. It probably went to the mission and the lodge, and what was left for purchase would be very expensive for the local people.

Loiyangalani got its fresh water from a spring hidden amongst a cluster of palm trees. It overflowed to run as a trickle through the town and across the backyard of Cold Drink Hotel to disappear into the dry, sandy ground on the town's outskirts. The spring was why Loiyangalani existed, its name in Samburu meaning 'place of many trees'. As mentioned, bathing was allowed at a set time each afternoon, and when it was the women's turn to wash I would go with them, walking through the palms to the secluded pool to soak in the cool, crystal-clear water.

Near her outdoor kitchen with its blackened pots, Mama grew a few tomato plants, but with a constant supply of spring water there was potential for so much more. Instead, I saw women queue all day outside the mission compound as they waited their turn to enter and receive a ration of food for their family. They waited hours in the hot sun, as the few trees that offered minimal shade were too far from the gate. To wait in the shade would mean they would lose their place in the queue. Hundreds of women and their children waited this way.

It was Sunday and after a breakfast of salted fried goat-meat and pancakes, with nothing better to do, I joined the tribespeople coming from all directions and filing towards the Catholic Mission and its large church that sat with a commanding presence on a low hill. With its high brick walls and steep roof, it stood truly magnificent on the town's fringe, where it overlooked the dilapidated buildings and clusters of thatched dome huts. There was standing room only and people were crowded at every narrow window. I walked up the steps to stand before the large double doors, not knowing whether I should go in or stand outside with the steadily growing crowd. Two women took my arms as they walked into the church and led me to a pew a few rows back from the altar.

People from each of the tribes were there, identified by their different elaborate neck rings, coloured strands of beads, stretched earlobes and ochre robes. Other than the silver-haired Father, a tall, thin man of about sixty, I was the only white person. I had not intended to be so right amongst it all.

The Father raised his hand and pointed to my side of the church and the women stood and began to sing. When they sat down, the other side took the lead like a well-choreographed performance. Their voices were clear and strong and filled the church to float to the ceiling and out through the narrow windows. Their harmonising moved through the people who were pressed against every opening, hoping to get a glimpse of the magic inside.

The Father spoke and, abruptly, the singing stopped. After his sermon, we all stood and about two hundred people filed forward, one after the other, for the Eucharist. A woman beside me pushed me forward with subtle encouragement to follow the others. I was not a Catholic, but I had no choice but to take the bread. When all were done, the singing resumed until the Father signalled the end of the service. For a few moments, there was silence and no one moved as we sat absorbing the last vibrations from the singing that seemed to resonate as a distant echo inside the church. I felt united with all those around me, as though we'd shared something deeply spiritual that was bigger and bolder than the religious conviction that comes with Sunday mass. Then everyone stood up, as if privy to an unspoken command, and the church emptied as suddenly as it had filled.

*

It was accepted that I would eat all my meals with Sharif, Abdersak and Kadil in the tiny lounge room. I looked forward to these meals with the Somalis, as they spoke English well enough to answer my questions about the Turkana area and its tribes, but Sharif only wanted to talk about the sapphires he'd found in the ironstone country near the lake.

'This area is on the way to Sibiloi,' Sharif said leaning forward, his eyes open wide as he stared at me intently so he would not lose my attention.

'Three years ago, tribesmen found sapphires there. They showed them to me and we returned and we found more. I took these to Nairobi and was paid US$700. It is a short detour from the road and the stones are easy to find. I do not have a vehicle to go back, but with your motorbike it will be very easy,' he confided as he plotted his grand scheme.

'I have no interest in fossicking. But maybe we can do a deal and I can take this detour in return for you guiding me to Sibiloi,' I said, raising an eyebrow questioningly.

'I will do this. It is settled. We will find many sapphires and make much money,' he replied and leaned back on the couch with a smug, satisfied grin. 'I finish my work at the lodge tomorrow. We leave the next day, early before it is hot. We will be at the sapphires before midday. You will see,' he said confidently.

I asked Sharif about the village of Gatab on Mount Kulal, as I planned to ride to the summit early the next morning.

'I want to take oranges to the El Molo,' I said and recounted my night on the edge of the lake when the children sang and the *moran* danced with the girls.

'The road is no problem for the motorbike,' said Sharif with disinterest as he inspected his nails and chewed off any that were too long.

After I'd emptied the panniers and Gearsack, with the intention of filling my bags with as much fruit and vegetables from the mission garden as I could carry, I left at sunrise for the 120-kilometre ride to Gatab. To reach the turn-off, I rode back towards South Horr for sixty kilometres and over the same hell road I'd battled two days earlier. Without the weight of my luggage, the TT bounced over the rocks smoothly and I was soon riding up the narrow dirt track to the summit of Mount Kulal, which was shrouded in a permanent mist. Long tendrils of grey lichen hung from the trees and the grass grew thick and lush in the red soil. The change was dramatic; one moment I was riding through dry scrub and the next green farmland. Timber and mud-brick huts were scattered about the summit, which covered only a few square kilometres before the terrain abruptly became desert again.

I stopped to ask directions to the mission garden from a young Kenyan man walking towards Gatab. He was dressed in army fatigues. He introduced himself as David, and told me he was the local policeman. He offered to join me, so I moved the Gearsack to the back rack to make room for him on the TT.

Before entering the garden, we walked to a vantage point that afforded clear views out over the lake. It looked every bit the Jade Sea, as it stretched far to the north. David pointed out the path going down the mountain to Loiyangalani, a two-day walk. The line of dry scrub was only a stone's throw from where we stood.

David called to the gardener and we waited at the gate. A fence made of bits of chicken wire, sticks and old iron circled a half acre of fertile land that was a virtual Garden of Eden. An elderly man with a stiff leg limped towards us and David told him that I wanted to buy fruit and vegetables for the children of Loiyangalani and the El Molo.

'You can fill your bags,' David said.

While in the garden, I was allowed to eat as much as I could and I devoured juicy ripe raspberries in seconds. I paid 200 shillings (US$3) for fruit and vegetables that filled my pannier bags and Gearsack. The gardener counted my purchases: eighty oranges at one shilling each, a large bundle of spinach, three cabbages, a lettuce, a good two kilos of cherry tomatoes, several cucumbers, and two lemons to go with the fish I'd trade with the El Molo. As I stuffed it all in my bags, David looked at me in disbelief, but I assured him I would be able to ride my motorcycle back down the mountain.

Before leaving Gatab, I rode on a narrow walking track to reach a group of mud-brick huts that overlooked the lake. One served food and the 'Special of the Day' was a large plate of goat and vegetable stew served with rice. As I ate, three local men joined me. From a piece of dirty cloth tied with string, each showed me their collection of amber, uncut sapphires and other coloured gemstones they'd found in the surrounding hills.

'Only twenty dollar for each stone. Very cheap,' one of them said.

'Very beautiful,' I replied. 'But I have no money to spend on gemstones. My journey is long.' They nodded and gently rewrapped their precious stones.

On my way down the mountain I rode with the greatest of care, not wanting to drop the TT and squash the oranges I carried in each pannier. On one hairpin turn, the bike went over and I don't know how, but I managed to lift it and then kick-start it while coasting down the steep track before I reached the next tight bend. As I rode my heavily laden bike over the roughest of rocky roads at the hottest time of the day, I kept thinking I must have totally lost my mind. But when I reached Cold Drink Hotel and saw the look of appreciation on Mama's face for the vegetables, and more than twenty children gorging on oranges that burst with juicy sweetness, it was well worth the ordeal.

In the coolness of late afternoon, I took a large bundle of spinach and a pannier full of oranges (keeping a few for the ride to Sibiloi) to the El Molo in exchange for some fish. I'm sure they never expected me to keep my promise. The chief bellowed a few words and a moment later a hessian bag heavy with fish was brought over and I selected four pan-sized Nile perch.

A short time later, at the back of the hotel, I filleted three of the fish in front of an audience of children who looked perplexed at my wastefulness. I gave the other fish, along with the heads and carcasses, to Mama, and asked if she would fry the fillets for our dinner. This would be a farewell dinner of pan-fried fish, chips and salad, before I left Loiyangalani with Sharif early the following morning. In exchange for the detour to search for sapphires, he had agreed to waive his US$150 fee to guide me to Sibiloi National Park where I would, at last, get to walk in the first footsteps of our ancestors.

7

LOST
LAKE TURKANA, NORTHERN KENYA

As Sharif and I prepared to leave for Sibiloi National Park, a group of grubby children and passers-by stood outside Cold Drink Hotel to wish us well for our expedition into the desert.

The detour to search for sapphires, Sharif assured me, was fifty kilometres, and we would return to Loiyangalani in three days. I packed enough supplies for a five-day trip that would cover about 400 kilometres, including Sharif's detour. I carried eleven litres of water, flour, rice, milk powder, a tin of golden syrup, two tins of tuna, a few carrots and oranges, and a cabbage as well as a good amount of sugar and spices for *tangawizi* tea. I'd also topped up with fuel at the mission, the Father reluctantly selling me ten litres. I'd prattled on about the first footsteps of humans and the Garden of Eden and he'd either sold the fuel out of pity or to get rid of this insane white woman with an overzealous interest in creation. I made room for Sharif as my pillion by moving the Gearsack to the back carrier rack of the pannier frame.

After a few kilometres, as we rode along the sandy track to Allia Bay, Sharif directed me to leave it and follow the faint tyre tracks that stretched across a smooth ironstone plain. Even with all the weight on the TT, it was easy riding on the hard ground. After several kilometres, the plains ended and

I followed a narrow path made by goats that had been herded through gullies and over low hills littered with red volcanic rock. There were no roads to follow and it was obvious a vehicle had never been through the area. I wanted to give up, to go back.

'The track is there. The track is there. This is the way,' Sharif said, raising his voice to a frantic pitch and pointing ahead as the first stages of my doubt set in. I reached for my water bottle and took a long, indulgent swallow.

Why would he lie to me? I thought as I looked at him for evidence of deceit. If we became lost in the desert, he had just as much to lose as me. I looked at the goat track that crossed the shallow gully to disappear over a ridge. It was littered with large rocks.

'Sharif, you will have to walk this bit,' I said and put on my helmet. It was hard riding but I did not drop the TT as I followed the narrow track across each rocky gully.

By midday we'd arrived at a hand-dug well about three metres deep in a dry riverbed. In less than four hours, our eleven litres of water was all but gone. I looked at the shallow puddle of dirty water and climbed down the steps cut into the hard-packed sand. Brushing aside the goat droppings, I filled the containers with the muddy water. I was too hot, thirsty and exhausted to pump the dirty water through my purifier and I reasoned it would be relatively free of bacteria. Besides, the well was continually refilled by clean water that gently bubbled from the underground stream.

We rested under the shade of an acacia tree near the well and ate lunch of chapatti and chunks of goat meat sprinkled with salt. To avoid a puncture, I had left the bike in the sun well away from the acacia tree and its three-inch-long thorns that littered the ground.

'I want to go back, Sharif,' I said, determined to stick to my decision. After all, I was the one in charge of the bike and that made me in charge of this ill-planned expedition into the desert, where we could easily perish.

'There are no more gullies. From here it will be easy on the motorbike. Nothing too bad,' he said. 'Tonight we sleep at El Tokoch Well and tomorrow we reach Muda Matah Turkana Well and the sapphires. Then we follow a track that leads back to the road to Allia Bay. You will see. It is very easy for you on your bike.'

I looked at him and wanted to believe him. I did not want to give up. If we turned back, I would never get to Sibiloi. I could not wait for what might be weeks before I could follow a 4×4 laden with wealthy tourists.

Sharif was right and after leaving the well, we rode over a flat plain to follow one of the goat tracks that all headed north. It was not until late afternoon that the plain ended at a line of rocky hills and the goat track disappeared into a gully.

'We'll get through, no problem,' Sharif said with an optimism that convinced me. 'El Tokoch Well,' he said and pointed to a cluster of palm trees about three kilometres from where we stood.

Five men, about the same height as twelve-year-olds, stood staring wide-eyed as we arrived at the well. They wore ragged shorts and threadbare T-shirts the colour of dirt. A herd of about twenty goats bleated around them as the scrawny animals hustled for a space to drink from the shallow trough dug into the dirt. One man was in the well, a crater about three metres deep, and handed up a rusty tin to another, who poured the water into the trough and the goats drank greedily before the liquid soaked into the ground.

'They are Gabbra. When they heard the noise of the bike, they thought it was a helicopter from the Kenyan army on patrol,' Sharif said and laughed with the tribesmen at how they were fooled.

'They have never seen or heard a motorbike like this one. They ask if you are a man or a woman because they have never seen a woman wearing trousers. They say you look like a woman, but they are sure you are not, as you ride a big motorbike and wear men's clothing.'

I did not care what the men thought as I climbed into the shallow well, where a herdsman continued to pass up the tin. Standing shoulder to shoulder with him, I filled my bottle with the murky water and after drinking until I thought I would burst, I poured water over myself until I was soaked.

The Gabbra were one of several nomadic tribes that lived off the desert surrounding Lake Turkana, herding goats on what grass could still be found. Due to the long and unforgiving drought they competed with other tribes, the Borana and the Turkana, for these valuable grazing lands. It was an isolated region with no law and order and I was smack-bang in the middle of it with no protection other than a naive faith in the good of humanity. I felt foolish and stupid that I'd given no thought to heading off into the desert with a man of questionable credentials as a guide. As I sat exhausted under a cluster of palms on the edge of the well, the reality of my situation dawned on me, but there was nothing I could do. My survival was now in the hands of Sharif, who sat with the men, chatting without a care in the world. The banter between them was light and punctuated with laughter but it failed to reassure me that my fears were unfounded. There was no escape. I looked back towards the line of rocky hills I'd ridden through earlier and my heart sank with the thought of riding through it again. The only way was forward.

The goats continued to suck up the water as quickly as they could and then waited for more.

'One of the men will guide us to the next well. They need to find a new area to graze their goats,' Sharif called to me from where he was sitting with them several metres away.

My binoculars still hung around Sharif's neck and the men pointed to these but he refused to hand them over.

'Give them a look,' I said, too exhausted to move.

Sharif reluctantly gave the binoculars to the men and explained how to use them as each had a turn. The men talked excitedly amongst themselves and it was easy to understand their exuberance, as binoculars would allow them to keep track of their goats, spot landmarks, look for game and scan the horizon for their enemies. I watched and waited for the inevitable request.

'No, we need them to find our way,' Sharif said with firm determination, speaking to them in English when they asked, and the men nodded their understanding.

One of the men handed me a few hard reddish-brown fruit the size of chicken eggs.

'*Conie*,' Sharif said, and pointed to a cluster of palm trees where the fruit hung from it in bunches like big fat grapes.

'How do I eat it?' I asked, inspecting the rock-hard shell. Sharif selected one from the pile and pounded it against a rock to crumble the outer shell before handing it to me. I nibbled the dry fibrous husk, which tasted like burnt sugar. I later read that the palm is also called the doum palm or 'gingerbread tree'.

'*Conie* is a gift from Allah so the people of the desert do not starve. The people here do not kill their goats but they will take some blood from the neck and mix this with the *conie*. It is very good. Make you strong. The tribespeople can walk many miles just on *conie* and goat blood,' Sharif said.

'Yuck,' I said and returned to my nibbling.

'If you go many days in the desert, you will do this,' he laughed.

'I will not go many days in the desert. We will be in Allia Bay tomorrow,' I said, reminding him of the plan he'd laid out before we'd left Loiyangalani, a plan that was disappearing almost as quickly as the water soaking into the makeshift trough dug into the bare earth.

The Gabbra had finished watering their goats and herded them towards the rocky hills to graze in the coolness of the late afternoon. Before leaving, the men pointed to a low acacia tree with a wide sweeping canopy at the base of a low rocky outcrop near the well. We would sleep under it and one of the Gabbra would return early the next morning to guide us to Muda Matah Turkana Well which, Sharif assured me, we'd reach late the same day.

After clearing away the long, sharp thorns with the blunt edge of my *panga*, I rode the TT as close as possible to the tree. The spiky branches hung low, but under the canopy it opened to a protected area, large enough to stand upright. Years of casual use had left the ground smooth and a few stumps of gnarled fire-blackened wood lay in the remains of a fire in the centre.

*

As the first rays of sun filtered through the canopy, I woke to the sounds of movement, and crawled out to see a skinny little man smiling back at me. He was one of the goat herders we'd met the previous day and he would act as our guide.

'We go now while it is still cool,' Sharif said, appearing beside me.

'What is his name?' I asked, smiling at the little man, who grinned back.

'Abdup,' Sharif said and lit a cigarette.

From El Tokoch Well we followed the dry riverbed for several kilometres. Water had not flowed here for many years and the hard-packed sand made for easy riding. I carried Sharif and then Abdup, riding a kilometre and then returning for the other. When the sand became soft and their weight made riding difficult, they reluctantly walked. We decided I would stop when I found a good place to rest in the shade and cook our breakfast.

After about two kilometres, I found a shady acacia and gathered wood for a fire to cook pancakes, which we would eat with golden syrup, washed down with *tangawizi* tea. The day was already hot and the heat exhausted me. I lay in the sand and fell asleep as I waited for Sharif and Abdup to catch up.

I awoke to the sound of voices. A group of tribesmen in ragged clothes were looking down at me. Two carried AK47 machine-guns and three carried large chunks of meat impaled on their spears. The men had recently shot a *dik-dik*, a small antelope. Sharif and Abdup stood with them.

'Don't worry. They will not shoot us,' Sharif said, seeing my look of terror. 'The guns are used to protect themselves and their goats from the Turkana and the Borana. The tribes steal each other's goats and take over another tribe's grazing area by force, especially now during this drought when grass is scarce. They also shoot *dik-dik* to eat. There are many in this area,' he added.

One of the men offered us a large chunk of meat.

'I cannot eat this meat. It has not been killed by a Muslim,' Sharif said and flared his nostrils in disgust.

'Too bad, I can,' I said and asked if I could take a photo.

'No. It is illegal for them to carry guns and they do not want to be identified. The Kenyan government does not understand that guns are their only way to survive,' he said and turned to speak with the men.

'They say I can take a photo of you,' he said and one of the men with an AK47 handed it to him.

I reached into the Gearsack for my camera and gave it to Sharif, who handed me the gun. I then took delight in pretending I was a great white hunter as I posed with the TT. I handed the weapon back to Sharif, and nodded my thanks to the men.

They spoke a few more words to Sharif and then were gone. I stoked the coals so they glowed red and cooked the pancakes using my blackened pot. We would cook the meat for dinner that night.

As we ate, I told Sharif I had not felt threatened by the Gabbra armed with their AK47s. 'If they wanted to, they could have killed me and taken whatever they liked, and nobody would ever have known,' I said and shuddered with the thought.

'I told them you are here to look for new water to make more wells for their people. That you have a radio and every day you call in and if you don't the Kenyan army will search for you. I told them you are a very important person and doing great things to help their people,' he said and looked at me with a mischievous glint.

'No wonder they gave me meat,' I said.

Sharif estimated it was about another twenty kilometres to Muda Matah Turkana Well but it would take us all day to get there.

'We must go now,' he said and I looked at Abdup who fidgeted nervously beside him.

I rode on alone for two kilometres, riding fast so that the bike would not sink in the sand, and then waited for Sharif and Abdup to catch up. A couple of kilometres further, Abdup pointed away from the riverbed and out over the plains that were covered with a hard crust. Abdup rode with me first, guiding the way, and after about three kilometres I left him to return for Sharif, retracing my tyre tracks.

Since leaving Loiyangalani two days earlier we had covered only forty kilometres, and I'd used very little of the petrol in the TT's twenty-one-litre tank. But while we had ample fuel, our water would not last even a few more hours under a sun that beat down with a fierce heat. We carried eleven litres when we left El Tokoch Well, but by mid-afternoon only one litre remained between the three of us.

Abdup pointed to a valley between two low rocky hills and I sat down next to the bike. My mouth was so dry that speaking was difficult and I did not have the energy to ride any further. I felt like crying in despair. I could not go back. We could only go forward and towards the well, as it was the closest source of water.

'The well is only a few kilometres from here. We will be there soon,' Sharif assured me from where he now sat in the sliver of shade cast by a small tree.

'Good, we can drink the water,' I said and lifted the container, gulping it greedily.

I immediately felt my mouth, my whole body rehydrate. What an unbelievably good taste.

Sharif and Abdup each took a small swallow. I swished around the almost empty ten-litre container. My greed for the water had taken over and I had drunk nearly all of it. Abdup looked at me with scorn.

After the valley, the terrain opened to hard-packed ground, and I was able to easily carry Abdup and then Sharif until we reached another dry riverbed. I rode on for two kilometres and waited for them to catch up. As the sun set in the distance, the heat left the day and a cool breeze blew through the thin cotton of my sweat-stained shirt.

Sharif and Abdup walked fast towards where I rested near a cluster of palm trees waving their arms frantically.

'We've got to get away from here! We've got to run. There are Turkana bandits, about ten of them. We saw their tracks. They have just come through here on their way to the well,' Sharif said, holding both his hands to his head and pacing in small circles of panic. 'They will be camped there.'

'How far is it?' I asked.

'About three kilometres,' he replied. 'We've got to leave here now and hide. If they find Abdup, they'll slaughter him like a goat. The Turkana and Gabbra are enemies. They kill each other. It happens all the time.'

I looked at Abdup. He was shaking with fear and sat nearby crouched low under a stand of shrubs.

'They will not kill a *mzungu*. They fear this will bring the soldiers. This desert is their territory. They have their own laws. It is survival of the strongest and the AK47,' Sharif said, his voice shaky as he held his arms tightly around himself.

'We could sneak up to the well late tonight,' I said. 'Maybe the Turkana have moved on.'

'No. It is too dangerous,' he said.

'I could go alone and come back with the water,' I said, exploring all avenues to get water because at that moment nothing else mattered.

'No. If the bandits find us, they will kill us both. We stay together. You are our only protection,' he said and walked over to the bushes to hide with Abdup.

I unpacked the tent so that Abdup would be out of sight if the bandits did find us. To protect my valuables, I dug a hole and buried the Pelican case containing my money and documents in the sand and pitched the tent on top of it. I then pushed the bike far under the bushes and cut some branches with the *panga* to hide it. When I'd asked James in South Horr to make me the *panga*, it was because I wanted it to be a show of strength. I'd never thought of its practical uses, but it had already proved its value as a handy tool for both cutting branches and clearing the ground of stones and thorns. I coaxed Abdup into the tent and he crawled inside and curled into a ball at the very back. Sharif did the same. In the riverbed, we were out of the evening breeze and it was stiflingly hot, but both men covered themselves with their blankets.

Bandits or no bandits, my main concern was water; I desperately needed to drink. It was three hours since we'd shared the last of the water. My thirst was unbearable, the craving all-powerful. The only thing that mattered, even in the face of imminent danger, was water. My tongue felt swollen as though it was too large for my mouth; but despite these first signs of severe dehydration, I fell into a restless sleep and dreamed of marauding bandits. I awoke several times, believing my dreams were true.

*

'You and Abdup go to the well on the bike. Bring back water. If the Turkana are still there, tell them Abdup is your guide from Maralal,' Sharif said, shaking me awake at daylight.

Before leaving, Abdup changed into Sharif's jeans and jacket to make him look the part. In his ragged shorts and frayed T-shirt, he looked every bit a Gabbra desert man.

Abdup pointed ahead to a low mound of sand. There was no sign of the Turkana other than their footprints, which covered the ground. They had taken water and left. Like the Gabbra, they must have thought the TT a helicopter from the Kenyan army.

The well was no more than a metre deep, the sand had caved in, and only a wet patch remained. Abdup and I dug out the sand with our hands and then watched the water slowly seep through. When there was enough, we drank greedily. The murky water tasted as though it was from the purest spring. We filled the 10-litre container and my water bottle and quickly returned to Sharif, fearing the Turkana lay in wait to ambush us.

Once back at the tent, Abdup made a fire and I made pancakes. We had not eaten the night before, other than munching on half a small cabbage, more for its moisture than to satiate our hunger. Abdup roasted some of the gazelle meat. It was tender, juicy and delicious. After I packed the tent and retrieved the buried Pelican case, I rode the short distance to the well. Sharif and Abdup followed on foot.

Sharif told me the sapphires were no more than a kilometre from the riverbed on the rocky plateau above the well. We began our search. Abdup reluctantly stayed with the TT parked near the well.

'The sapphires were found here. This is my old camp,' Sharif said breathlessly, pointing at the rocky ground, sweat glistening on his face. It looked an unlikely place to camp and I could see no remnants of a fire.

But the gully we'd just hiked up from the riverbed did show all the signs of gemstones: it was littered with broken thunder-eggs, quartz crystals and poor-quality amethyst.

'I want to believe you Sharif,' I replied from where we stood on the plateau covered in red volcanic rock. I looked back over the sandy riverbeds, the distant rocky gullies and iron-stone plains we'd travelled across for the past two days. I turned and lookeds towards the north and Allia Bay. It was a vast expanse of rocky desert that appeared even more impassable than what we'd already been through. At that very moment the thing that I had suspected all along hit me with the full force of my stupidity. The sapphires were a theory, quite possibly a story from a local tribesman who'd found a few dull-coloured stones. But this realisation made no difference now. It was mid-morning and already the sun beat down with a fierce heat. We would rest in the shade and resume our search in the coolness of late afternoon.

As we walked back down the gully towards the riverbed, Sharif pointed to a large acacia gnarled with age that grew close to the well. It was a good place to camp as the tree offered plenty of shade and fallen branches for firewood – red wood that burnt slow and made good coals for roasting meat. Using the blunt edge of the *panga*, I cleared the ground of the three-inch thorns before we pushed the TT under the grand old tree.

Shrubs densely covered in small black berries lined the dry riverbed. Abdup had picked handfuls, soaking them in water to make a slightly fizzy drink that tasted like a mix of blackberry and radish.

'Abdup will leave early in the morning in darkness and return with his people. They will come back with their guns and take over this land. It has much grass for their goats,' Sharif said with the excitable energy of a boy planning a make-believe military ambush. As he outlined this new plan, he casually dismissed any chance of the Turkana returning to the well with their own guns.

As I drank the berry juice, I watched Abdup as he spoke to Sharif. His words came out in rapid bursts like a chirpy bird at daylight.

'Abdup will return with fifteen of his men and they will shoot another *dik-dik*, but they will not kill it. They will bring it to me and I will bless it, kill it and then eat it,' Sharif explained in slow gruesome detail.

'You will let an animal suffer in pain just because you want to bless it and all in the name of Allah?' I said, angry that he felt no compassion for the *dik-dik*.

'Stop this talk. You do not understand,' he said and moved away as though my presence affronted his faith.

In the coolness of the late afternoon, Sharif and I resumed our search for the sapphires. We wandered about the rocky plateau but I soon lost interest and walked to a low rise to survey the lunar-like desert landscape. The volcanic rock glowed deep reddish-brown as the sun set beyond Lake Turkana, which shimmered turquoise in the distance. I estimated we were about five kilometres from the lake and reasoned we needed to stay near it. To survive in temperatures that soared to over forty degrees Celsius we needed water, even the alkaline lake water.

We returned to our camp exhausted and empty-handed. Abdup had already started the fire and was roasting a large piece of meat impaled on a stick stuck in the ground close to the coals. When it was cooked, Abdup and I ate hungrily. I offered some to Sharif who shook his head and turned away.

'Would you rather starve?' I asked as I chewed.

'Yes, I am true Muslim,' he said.

'Sharif, surely in times of starvation, Allah will forgive. What kind of religion would allow a person to starve?' I asked, taking another mouthful of the juicy, tender meat.

'I not starve yet,' he yelled at me, annoyed that I questioned the rules of his faith.

I got up and retrieved a tin of tuna from the bike's panniers and tossed it to Sharif, which he ate with the rice he had cooked earlier.

*

In the early hours of the morning, under the cover of darkness, Abdup quietly left our camp, promising he and his men would return in two days to take possession of the surrounding land with its ample grazing for their goats. It was Father's Day and my dad would be expecting a call from me. If I died here in the desert, nobody would have any idea where to start looking; nobody knew where I was. Sharif had insisted we keep our search for the sapphires a secret. I lay in the riverbed under the shade of a leafy tree not far from the well and pondered what to do. The only relief from the heat was when I poured water over my fully clothed body; but as I lay wet in the shade this only gave short relief before the hot air dried my clothes. I reasoned no harm would be done by waiting for the Gabbra to return as they had promised.

By mid-morning of the second day, there was no sign of them. I'd eaten all the meat and Sharif had eaten the second tin of tuna. As we waited, we were slowly eating our way through all our food. Sharif had also run out of cigarettes and a look of craziness filled his beady black eyes.

'You should have brought more supplies!' he yelled as he stood staring down at me where I lay in the shade of a leafy tree near the well. He poured forth a torrent of abuse and berated the TT for its limitations in traversing the rocky terrain.

'The sapphires were your idea. I just wanted to go to Allia Bay to see the fossils,' I replied and stood up, worried what might happen next.

'The Gabbra have not returned as promised. We should leave for Allia Bay before all the food is gone,' I said and mentally calculated we could stretch the rice, flour and milk powder to three, perhaps four meals. We'd used the last of the tea and sugar that morning.

Sharif reluctantly agreed that if the Gabbra did not show, we would leave early the next morning, making a good start before it got too hot. He spoke convincingly of a road that crossed the dry river, close to the lake, a road that would take us to Allia Bay.

'We will be there by afternoon,' Sharif said, his contorted anger now replaced by anticipation. 'We will buy a goat, I will bless it and then kill it. We will eat much meat tomorrow. You will see.'

'I hope you are right,' I said, but I felt uncomfortably sure that this ordeal was far from over.

8

CHANCE ENCOUNTERS
LAKE TURKANA, NORTHERN KENYA

I sat beside my motorcycle, weak and listless, indifferent to my fate. The rear tyre was deeply bogged in the sand of yet another dry riverbed we'd crossed in our search for the road to Allia Bay. We'd left Muda Matah Turkana Well two days earlier. We'd found no sapphires and Abdup and his Gabbra herdsmen had not returned as promised. After leaving the well, I'd ridden along the dry river bed, the sand packed hard, and most of the time I could double Sharif. When we reached the lake we did not cross any type of road, nor even a faint track – though Sharif had insisted there was a road there. We had topped up our containers with the slightly salty alkaline water, then had left the lake's shores, riding inland for about five kilometres in search of the sandy 4×4 track that ran from Loiyangalani to Allia Bay, which was clearly marked on my map. From Allia Bay, Sharif assured me, I'd finally get to see the fossils, he'd get to kill a goat, we'd have a feast, and we'd be back in Loiyangalani the following afternoon – or we could pay for a ride on a fishing boat to Kalokol, a township on the opposite side of the lake where there was a tarmac road leading to Nairobi.

During those two days, as we battled heat, thirst, hunger and deep sand, I lost faith in all that I'd come to believe in. My fledgling belief that things would always work out for me was replaced by quiet acceptance that the end was near. We'd run out of food and water. We had eaten the last of the rice the night before leaving Muda Matah Turkana Well. We'd drunk the last of our water that morning and I felt as though it would not be long before we also ran out of our will to live and simply lay down, closed our eyes and died. This situation felt so close that I had the vague understanding that this is what must happen to those who perish in the desert. 'Move!' Sharif shouted and reached down to shake me awake. 'Move, we leave the bike. We walk to the lake.'

It was late afternoon and he'd caught up to where I'd bogged the TT. In this riverbed the sand was so soft, I could not double him. He grabbed me by the shoulders and pulled me to my feet, shoved an empty container in my hands and walked off. I followed one footstep at a time until, hours later in darkness, we reached the lake. I stripped to my underwear and staggered into the water, falling face first. The alkaline water hydrated me immediately. Despite its saltiness, it tasted unbelievably good and I sat with only my head above water, opened my mouth and drank and drank.

'A crocodile will very soon eat you,' Sharif called casually from where he squatted on his haunches on the shore, drinking from cupped hands.

I looked out into the darkness and imagined the hungry eyes of 40,000 crocodiles unable to believe their luck that a tasty meal had dropped into their jaws. I stood up and quickly moved to the safety of the shore.

*

It was mid-morning and I stood on the hard, black sand gently lapped by the vast inland sea. Sharif was beside me, using my binoculars to scan the horizon for fishing boats. Even he had given up on finding the road to Allia Bay and now our only hope was that rescue would come from out there on Lake Turkana. The night before, after drinking our fill, we had walked back to the TT, and early this morning we'd dug it out of the sand and I'd ridden it to the lake, doubling Sharif for part of the way, to where we now stood.

'Can I have the binoculars?' I asked Sharif and he tossed them to me.

I could feel his anger, and involuntarily took a few steps back.

'That looks like a boat,' I said and moved closer to hand him the binoculars.

'There is nothing. You see things,' he grunted and handed them back.

I scanned the lake again, straining my eyes until they hurt.

'Here,' I said, passing him the binoculars as another spasm gripped my stomach. The slightly salty water combined with the dry fibre of the *conie*, our only food for the past two days, had given us both severe diarrhoea.

Sharif took first watch and I squatted and squirted behind a clump of reeds and then returned to sit in the shade of a cluster of young *conie* palms where I'd parked the TT. I looked along the lake shore towards Allia Bay. The sand was black and hard-packed for a short distance until it gave way to swamp dotted with clumps of reeds. It was obvious that if a boat did not pass by soon I would have to leave my motorcycle and return for it by boat once we'd walked to Allia Bay.

'There's a boat. There's a boat! Quick, get to the shore,' Sharif shouted as he ran towards me.

He was right. A small fishing boat with a makeshift sail appeared as a speck on the horizon and grew bigger as it neared the shore. I grabbed my bike jacket, as I hoped the red on the shoulders and sleeves would attract attention. I picked up a long piece of driftwood and hoisted my jacket to wave it and shouted – screamed – at them to stop. Surely the fishermen could see us. Why weren't they stopping? They were not even changing direction.

'Why? You are close! Can't you see we need help?' I yelled as the boat sailed past.

'Take your clothes off. Let them see you are *mzungu*. Instead, you cover yourself. They will not come near the shore if they think you are African. They'll think you are a Borana. Borana kill Turkana fishermen all the time. It happens every day,' he said and waved his arms above his head in a mix of anger and desperation.

Sharif had already told me we could not light a fire, as the smoke would indicate Borana.

I was wearing a navy one-piece swimsuit and looked every bit the

Borana bandit from afar as my skin was tanned a dark brown.

'Please stop! Please stop!' I pleaded.

'Take your clothes off,' Sharif shouted again.

'Go. They should not see you,' I said and when he walked away, I undressed and stood naked on the shore, leaving no doubt I was *mzungu*.

The next boat was clearly visible and I waved my bike jacket vigorously.

The two boats sailed past but neared the shore about a kilometre away. I scanned ahead with the binoculars and spotted several dark shapes that appeared to move. The boats had stopped at the beach. They had seen us. We were saved. But what if they thought we were Borana and left? I quickly put on my swimsuit and bike jacket and ran over the spiky lake grass, which penetrated my bare feet with a searing pain. In places the beach gave way to swamp and I walked through it waist deep without fear of crocodiles – until I disturbed one. I stood frozen as its thick scaly tail left a large wake as it disappeared towards the lake. When it was gone, I moved quickly to reach the shore and ran on the firm black sand, pushing my legs to take longer strides.

As I approached, a group of about fifteen people, mostly men and a few women and children, stood staring at me. Three of the men walked towards me. One carried what looked to be an AK47, and he stood in front so I could see he was armed.

'*Salamu, habari*. Am I glad to see you,' I said. I was breathless and stood doubled over with a stitch. They looked at me with wide eyes.

'*In lugga on piki piki*,' I said and pointed behind me. I drew a picture of a motorcycle in the riverbed and they nodded their understanding.

I saw that the gun I had thought was an AK47 was only an ingeniously carved piece of wood with lengths of steel pipe attached to it with wire. If attacked by their enemies, this homemade replica was better than nothing. It might at least fool the bandits and give them time to escape.

One of the men bellowed something to their group and a boy ran towards me. He could speak some English.

'Hello,' he said and I told him in a gush of words how Sharif and I were lost and that we were very hungry. The men shook their heads and laughed when I told them we had only eaten *conie* for the past three days.

I walked with them to the boats, all heavily laden with dried fish. They had been away from their village for several weeks and were on their way to Kalokol, passing at that very moment when we reached the lake. This chance encounter saved our lives and I held my hands together and said thank you to the fisherman and their families, and to the universe, to God and to everything that had made our worlds collide at that very moment on that very day. An old man offered me a large piece of freshly cooked Nile perch. I peeled back the charcoaled skin to expose the thick white flesh and stuffed it hungrily into my mouth. Immediately, I felt the energy from the fish flow through me into every cell of my starving body.

'Bones, bones,' the boy said, pointing to the fish.

The fisherman indicated I get into the boat with the least amount of dried fish and we motored towards Sharif and my motorcycle.

The fishermen beached the boat and helped me push the TT to the shore. They effortlessly lifted it on top of the bundles of dried fish. Sharif negotiated a fee of 1000 shillings (US$15) for them to take us to Kalokol.

As the boat motored away from the shore, I lay back on the sacks of dried fish, staring at the sky, which glowed crimson with the last rays of sun. I had not seen the fossils of our ancestors but I had walked in their footsteps and I'd survived the desert, as they had done. I looked back towards the shore and imagined them waving to me, wishing their daughter well as I moved forward and into the next day.

The fishermen had given Sharif some rough-cut tobacco and with small pieces of newspaper he rolled us each a cigarette.

'Look, lightning, a storm,' I said and pointed to the flashes in the distance.

'No, that's just the war in Sudan,' Sharif replied and inhaled deeply on the tobacco.

'Sorry,' he added in almost a whisper.

'We're safe, that's all that matters. Thank you to Allah,' I said and leaned back as the boat glided through the calm water in the still night.

We'd come so close to losing our lives, and I glowed with a new appreciation of it. To feel the cool wind on my face, to admire the way the water reflected the last of the sun's rays, to appreciate the people who smiled back at me. My faith, which I had so quickly and easily discarded in the desert, was renewed. I made a secret promise to the universe, to God, that I would never doubt again. Events had always, in the end, unfolded in my favour, and our rescue was no different; there was no reason to think otherwise. It was a naive view, but what was the alternative? To think that bad things would happen to me? To be scared? No, I would have faith and trust and I would see where that would lead me.

*

It was still dark when we reached the other side of the lake and a beach of fine sand. We would anchor there until morning, then motor for another hour through shallow waters to Kalokol. I retrieved my sleeping bag and followed the others to the nearby dunes, which offered some protection from the wind and the sand that stung our skin. A man gave us a plate of freshly cooked fish, and Sharif and I sat huddled with my torch, picking out the bones as we ate.

By mid-afternoon the wind had dropped and the waves were calm enough to allow the boats to motor into the inlet and Kalokol. The TT was easily unloaded onto the hard-packed black sand and as I rode towards the township, Sharif pointed out a huge structure of rusting steel and sheets of corrugated iron. I pulled up and he told me it had once been a fish-freezing plant, a gift from the fishing nation of Norway. The sixty kilometres of smooth black tarmac laid across semi-arid desert to Lodwar, the nearest town with a road leading to Nairobi, was part of this generous gift. The Norwegians had discovered that Lake Turkana was teeming with fish, and there was a market for Nile perch in Nairobi. If frozen fish could be transported there, the Turkana would have a profitable business.

'What happened?' I yelled to Sharif through my helmet. The rusting bulk of the freezing plant loomed large before us.

'Too hot here. Costs too much to freeze fish. It's just a fish-drying shed now used sometimes, but the Turkana don't like to fish. If you fish, it means you have no animals and you are poor,' he replied. 'The Kenyan government also kick the Norwegians out,' Sharif added. He was referring to the events of 1990, when former Kenyan president Daniel arap Moi broke off ties with Norway, accusing the Norwegians of sheltering dissident Kenyan politicians.

The Norwegian effort to help the Turkana, while filled with good intentions, had resulted in waste of a reported US$150 million. The derelict building was a constant reminder of how international aid can easily be squandered without proper consultation and planning. Although I was all for the tarmac road.

Kalokol was home to several thousand mostly Turkana people who lived in dome huts made from palm fronds, which dotted the town's fringe like the untidy nests of some giant desert-dwelling bird. We rode down the main street on wide smooth tarmac, the best in all of Kenya. A few rundown corrugated iron shacks lined the highway. Sharif tapped my shoulder as we neared one of the shacks, a bar and restaurant. I pulled over. Once inside, I immediately ordered two beers then sat outside on the hard-packed dirt leaning against a wooden post and took a long swallow.

'There is no goat so I order chicken,' Sharif gushed as he bounded out of the shack. I handed him a bottle of cold beer.

'To our rescue,' Sharif said and we raised our bottles to salute our good fortune.

'To Allah,' I responded and gave no thought to the next second, minute or hour. I was drinking beer and I would soon be eating chicken. Nothing else really mattered.

'I go bless the chicken. Then I kill it, as there are no other Muslims to do it,' Sharif said and disappeared inside the shack.

*

Early morning light filtered through the tiny holes in the rusted tin roof like stars in the night sky. I quietly pulled on my boots as Sharif snored in the flimsy iron bed along the far wall of the narrow room we shared. It was made of rough-cut timber and through the gaps I could see the TT parked in the sandy courtyard. I stood and with the stealth of a leopard gathered my things, walked out of the room and silently pushed my motorcycle to the front of the hotel. A few dark shadowy figures ambled past.

The night before, after he'd drunk a few beers, Sharif had demanded I pay him US$150 in guide fees. He claimed to have no recollection of our agreement to waive his fee in return for the foolish detour to search for sapphires. I feared that, come morning, he would turn all who would listen against me, recruiting supporters from the Turkana locals, who, as former warriors, would surely be keen for a fight. He'd been drinking with a few of these men, who, like Sharif, had the same interest in 'doing business' at all costs.

As I pulled on my helmet, fumbling with the strap as I tightened it, and then my gloves, a small crowd of Turkana surrounded me. They'd appeared out of nowhere and their numbers steadily grew. They mumbled amongst themselves, pointing at me and the TT and I felt their tone turn angry as they realised my intention to leave.

As a boy ran inside the tin shack to wake Sharif, I started the bike, grateful it fired on the first kick. Its low, deep rumble caused the crowd to stand back and then I was gone. I opened the throttle and left all threat of danger behind as I headed south towards Nairobi.

A cool breeze blew across the lake from the east and the TT glided smoothly over the straight stretch of black tarmac to Lodwar, a sixty-kilometre ride through dry scrub dotted with scraggly trees.

*

After changing travellers' cheques at Lodwar's only bank, I decided to stay two nights in this small dusty town of low-set cement and corrugated-iron buildings. I needed to eat, and eat a lot, to regain the kilos I'd lost in the desert. My jeans, a size ten, hung loose on my hips and my sinewy arms protruded chicken-like from my sleeveless denim shirt.

I found a local hotel for US$1 per night, where I could park the TT safely inside my room out of the reach of any thieves, who, given a chance, would strip it of anything they could, right down to the nuts and bolts holding it together. My room faced a cement courtyard where there was a solitary tap and plenty of clean space to scrub and lay out clothes in the hot sun. The area doubled as the community laundry and I joined several women who were washing clothes in large, brightly coloured plastic tubs while small children darted about their feet. After the desert, my sleeping bag and my few clothes were filthy. I also washed the TT, cleaned the air filter and checked for any emerging problems. The metal clamp holding the piggyback high-pressure gas reservoir for the shock-absorber had broken and the cable joining it to the main spring had rubbed on the tyre. I'd caught it just in time and had fastened it with wire until I reached Nairobi and could replace the clamp.

After a two-day feast of fried eggs, chips, hamburgers, steak and salad, I headed towards Nairobi and, over the next 700 kilometres, I evaluated, analysed and assessed in detail what had happened in the desert: how I had nearly died, and how I felt about continuing my travels. The sane, reasonable thing might have been to cut my losses and go home, but the very thought of this filled me with dread. I could not give up, no more than I could decide to stop breathing. The only way was forward and once I reached this conclusion, I felt a great sense of expectation for the ride ahead. To continue felt so right, as though it was exactly what I should do.

I thought back to the moment when I'd first got the idea to ride a motorcycle through Africa and how I'd felt then. How obsessed I'd become and how I'd thought that only death would stop me. I had the same feeling as I rode towards Nairobi. There must be a reason for this feeling, this push, to ride on across Uganda and into Zaire, Congo and Gabon to reach West and North Africa. After a week in the desert, I felt so much more capable, both physically and psychologically; after all, if I could survive the desert, I could survive anything.

I also had an undeniable and growing awareness of something else influencing my journey. The rescue by the Turkana fishermen may very well have been just good luck, but I could not shake the feeling that it could also be another piece of evidence that there was no need to worry about a future that had not yet arrived. All would be provided. All would be okay.

I arrived in Nairobi a few days later to the welcoming arms of Mama Roche on her veranda, where we drank tea, and where, between mouthfuls of custard cream-biscuits, I told her about my desert ordeal. She oohed and aahed at all the right moments.

'You are so lucky. Your poor mother. What she think of this?' she asked as she poured more tea.

'I haven't told her,' I replied.

'So what you do now?'

'Go to the coast. I need a beach and then I want to climb Kilimanjaro. I cannot come to Africa and not climb its highest mountain,' I said.

I moved on from Mama's a few days later for a three-week meander along Kenya's coast, finally putting my fins, mask and snorkel to good use as I snorkelled the coral reefs off-shore. I hung out with an assortment of backpackers and a few motorcycle travellers, too. From the coast I headed inland and crossed into Tanzania, where I booked my Kilimanjaro climb from Marangu at the base of the mountain.

A five-day climb up this shortest and most-popular route to the 5895-metre summit cost US$300 with Alpine Tours, including a guide, a porter, a cook and all food. My hiking team was originally from Dar es Salaam. Honest, my guide, was the over-confident big brother, aged about eighteen; James, who carried my Gearsack on his head, was a gangly, shy boy of about sixteen; and Felix, our cook, was a cheeky street urchin of about twelve – far too young to be hiking up a mountain in an old pair of canvas shoes and threadbare jeans and T-shirt. He did, however, carry a quality polar fleece – a cast-off from a previous foreign hiker at the end of their Kilimanjaro trek.

Before the boys committed to the hike, I warned them I was not rich; I was on a long journey, and could only give US$10 each as a tip.

'We only get 12,000 shillings [about US$26] each from Alpine Tours.

We make our money on the tips,' Honest whined with a long face. He kicked the dirt with his boots, another hiker's cast-offs.

'I am sorry. Maybe it is best you wait for a rich hiker,' I replied and looked over at James and Felix, who stood nearby and watched us expectantly like two puppies about to be tossed a ball.

'It is quiet month. We agree,' he said, accepting that this hike would not be a good earner but I'm sure secretly hoping I'd change my mind when we returned from the summit.

It was Sunday afternoon and an hour later we followed a narrow dirt track through tropical rainforest to the first hut. It suited me, as the previous night I'd paid US$5 to camp at the nearby Babylon Lodge, and starting the hike in the afternoon meant I saved a night's camping fee. My riding gear had to double as hiking gear and I walked in my steel-capped work boots, the same ones I'd worn at the uranium mine. They were comfortable and familiar on my feet even before I started my travels and now the leather had stretched and softened to feel like a thick, sturdy outer skin. My wet-weather pants and jacket (to keep in body heat rather than keep me dry), thermals, and just about every other item from my wardrobe was packed in my Gearsack ready for the summit, when temperatures dropped to below freezing.

The first day was humid and sunny, the second cool and fresh as we reach the heath and hiked past white flowering heather trees and shrubs dotted with yellow flowers, where sunbirds darted about as they fed on the nectar. We had clear views out over Tanzania's savannah plains and I walked with three handsome young American doctors from another tour group. The doctors became my hiking companions by day, and I made up a fourth hand at poker by night. Most of the other hikers were either professionally employed as investment bankers, lawyers, doctors or engineers, or retired, and this was a holiday of a lifetime, booked through overseas tour operators. I was the only budget traveller. We all stayed in the same dormitory huts; we all ate the same porridge, soup and stew, cooked in the same huge, fire-blackened pots. But they'd paid double what I had, or even more. One hiker had paid US$700 for the same hiking experience, more than half of that booking fees paid to a foreign agent with nothing extra passed on to the Tanzanian tour operators. The guides, porters and cooks were at the bottom of the food chain and relied on generous tips to boost the pittance they received from the tour operator.

As we hiked higher, the air got thinner, and on the third day as we reached the alpine desert zone, one hiker after another – mostly fiftyish and unfit who'd thought Kilimanjaro was a leisurely stroll – fell victim to altitude sickness. Honest warned me to drink plenty of water, to walk slowly and to rest often so my body would acclimatise. While the Marangu route was shorter and easier, it also claimed the most victims, because the ascent to the summit was quicker.

'Most of these people will not make the top. But you are strong woman. You make it,' Honest grinned proudly as though he were my coach and I an elite athlete.

'This is my first mountain. Maybe I won't make it,' I replied and broke off a piece of chocolate, one of the many bars I'd bought in Mombasa, then passed it to my team as we sheltered from the biting wind behind a few boulders near the track.

Late afternoon on the third day we reached Kibo Hut. At midnight we would begin the final ascent to the summit to arrive just before sunrise – the grand climax of any mountain trek. It was below freezing and the air was so thin that climbing into the top bunk, where I cocooned myself in my sleeping bag wearing all my clothes, was an exhausting effort that left me panting for breath. After dinner of beef stew and rice, our guides advised us to sleep, as it would take six hours to walk the last 200 metres, an almost vertical hike along a zigzag track of loose stones to the summit at Gilman's Point. I lay down and tried to rest, but all I wanted to do was pee. I'd done as Honest advised and drunk lots of water, up to five litres a day, which placed an extraordinary amount of pressure on my bladder. As we waited for midnight I had to pee three times, going through the horrendous ordeal of climbing out of my warm cocoon and into the biting cold, where I had to drop my pants and squat over a hole-in-the-ground toilet. I was grateful I had not succumbed to a stomach bug.

Honest almost dragged me up the last of the zigzag path, as though we were in a race on which bets had been placed. We were the first to reach Gilman's Point, quickly followed by the three American doctors. Right on their tail was a sprightly elderly Swiss man who looked at least eighty. Their guides were still with the other members of their hiking groups. Together we sat on a large granite boulder and waited for sunrise. The sky was tinged a faint purplish pink against a backdrop of midnight blue that stretched into the blackness of outer space. We sat in silence, mesmerised, and as the earth slowly rotated on its orbit we were bathed in rays of pinkish orange light as another day dawned. From this highest of vantage points, I gazed out across all of Africa. It was vast and huge and I felt small and insignificant.

The return was a quick amble down the mountain and we arrived at Marangu village by mid-afternoon the next day. I bought the boys a lunch of goat-meat stew and beers and handed each US$10, apologising that I could not give a bigger tip.

'It is okay. You have long journey. You need your money,' Honest said. He raised his beer to wish me luck and I wished them a more generous tourist – a cashed-up American who'd give a good tip and ditch all their high-tech hiking gear, especially a pair of boots for Felix and a warm jacket for James.

By three p.m., I was headed back to Nairobi, riding on a dirt road of fine red dust and deep wheel ruts that skirted the base of Kilimanjaro. I pitched my tent in a Maasai *manyatta* that night, after asking the headman if it was okay.

'Welcome, welcome,' the old man said, but as another cramp hit my stomach, I declined the meal offered. The bug that had felled so many of the hikers on Kilimanjaro had finally got me and I started a course of Flagyl. With my roll of toilet paper and torch, I made many trips that evening to a stand of bushes near the *manyatta*, which one of the women pointed out when I asked about the *choo*. It was the one time my camping spade – culled by Anders, the Danish motorcycle traveller in Perth – would have been put to good use.

The next morning I passed through a small village and, feeling better, I stopped for a late breakfast of chapattis and goat-meat stew. No sooner had I sat down than I heard the unmistakeable rumble of motorcycles. It was Philippe and Yvan, the Swiss motorcycle travellers on Suzuki DR650s, who I'd met a lifetime ago at Cape Maclear in Malawi. Philippe was thirtyish, tall and wiry with a few tufts of wispy blonde hair framing his long narrow face. He dwarfed Yvan, who was a little bit chubby, and, with his curly blond hair and good-natured grin, looked like he'd never quite grown out of pubescence. They both embraced me, repeating over and over how this was the most amazing coincidence, and after our meal we rode on to Nairobi, to Mama Roche's, together.

We arrived late afternoon just as Mama was driving up to the Everest Hotel with three Australian men squeezed into her little hatchback. 'Welcome back. We see you soon at Everest,' Mama shouted to me as she drove out the front gate.

The three Australians, Dave, Eric and Rolf, were from Canberra and had arrived a week earlier, they told me later over beers. They'd travelled on buses, hitched lifts and walked through much of East Africa and were now resting at Mama's before heading towards Africa's dark heart. They were all tanned, with lean muscles and scruffy, light brown hair. Dressed in singlets, hiking shorts and thongs, and a 'she'll be right, mate' attitude to life, they were quintessential Aussie blokes. I hit it off with them immediately. Despite being about three years older than them, I felt as though they were my big brothers and I their little sister.

Before the ride into Zaire I needed to get another tent, as the little A-frame given to me by the English couple would be no match for equatorial rain. Two days after I arrived at Mama's from the Kilimanjaro climb, Austria's answer to Indiana Jones rode into her yard on a beaten and busted BMW R80GS. His journey was over and he would be shipping his motorcycle, complete with buffalo horns mounted on the handlebars, back to Europe. He no longer needed his three-man dome tent nor his petrol stove, but he did need some extra cash after riding down from North Africa, across the Central African Republic and Zaire. When I told him I planned to do the same, he just laughed a great raucous belly laugh.

'How much for your tent?' I asked the stocky, unshaven Austrian as he sat cleaning his fingernails with his Swiss army knife on the porch of the dormitory at the back of Mama's bungalow.

'I set up for you. You look first,' he said and grinned at me as he folded his knife and put it in a side-pocket of his khaki shorts.

Wide strips of silver duct tape ran along the entire length of the base of the tent, which had faded to a dull grey. A large patch covered the floor, and small pieces of tape sealed several smaller holes. The top cover looked brittle after too much harsh African sun.

'Thieves slashed my tent in Agadez,' he said, pointing to the length of tape. 'They stole all my clothing. And that's where my stove catch fire. Termites eat the small ones,' he replied when I asked about the tape on the floor.

'Come, I show you the operation of the stove,' he said and I followed him back to the porch. 'We leave tent for you. No more sleeping on ground. I have bed in dormitory.'

From a pannier on his motorcycle he retrieved a rusty old tin and inside, wrapped in an old trouser leg, was a petrol stove that I'm sure was of World War Two origin.

'It is Austrian make. Very good. I never have problem except one time. I have too many beers and hold it over the flame too long,' he said as he went through its igniting procedure.

'This is the quick way,' he said and poured some of the petrol from the stove onto the lid of the tin. I took a step back. He lit it and flames leapt from its surface. He held the stove over the flames to pressurise its petrol canister, forcing fuel through the jet when he opened the nozzle. Flicking the lighter, he ignited it, and the jet burnt spasmodically.

'It take a little time to get hot,' he said and I took another step back.

Soon a blue flame burnt continuously from the primitive little stove. The Austrian filled his pot, and in no time the water was boiling and he handed me a cup of sweet black coffee.

'Sixty dollars for the tent and stove,' I offered.

'They are yours. This will be the fourth trip through Africa for this stove. I buy it from another traveller,' he said grinning even more broadly than before and I knew I'd offered too much.

Now that I had a relatively waterproof tent and a petrol stove that I was assured worked most of the time, as well as my visa for Zaire, there was no reason for me to stay on at Mama's and I announced that afternoon that I'd leave the following morning.

'We have many beers at Everest tonight. This is big celebration for your farewell,' said Mama. And with Dave, Eric, Rolf, Philippe and Yvan, it certainly was. This old Polish woman's yard had been my sanctuary, my part-time home away from home over the past three months as I travelled from one end of Kenya to the other and across the middle too. I'd made many friends, because we all shared a bond of adventure, of good times and hard times. In those first days when Dan had left and I'd found myself alone and scared, Mama had taken me in like a stray and her words of encouragement, and the friendship shown to me by so many, had strengthened me.

I was such a different girl now. A confident, strong young woman with an unwavering faith in the good of people and that everything would always work out for me. It always happened this way and I believed that it would happen tomorrow and the day after that, too.

'When you come to Switzerland, come visit us,' said Philippe. Yvan nodded.

'You watch those bloody Africans. They'll rip you off first chance they get,' Dave warned with a cheeky smile.

'Be careful out there,' said Eric.

'We'll see you in Kisangani for Christmas,' Rolf added. As they too would soon travel into Zaire and planned to be in Kisangani late December, we had already arranged to celebrate the day together.

'You bet,' I replied and we all embraced.

PART TWO

UGANDA TO ZAIRE

(Zaire was renamed the Democratic Republic of the Congo in 1997)

9

FRIENDS AND ENEMIES
UGANDA

As I left the safety of Kenya behind, I entered a country still in ruin. The ride to Kampala was on a potholed road past crumbling mud huts. It had been eight years since the horrific massacre of up to 800,000 Ugandans under the rule of Idi Amin and then Apolo Milton Obote. During these years, *ubuntu* was forgotten in Uganda. The people I came across on that first day when I bought my lunch at a roadside stall were reserved and suspicious. It felt as if Uganda was shrouded in a thick blanket of both pain and poverty that only time would heal.

But as I reached Kampala, there were signs that prosperity, in the form of new buildings paid for with World Bank loans and foreign investment, was slowly returning. Nevertheless, for the poor, and even for me, everything was expensive, double the prices in Kenya. Everything, except the abundant Nile perch caught in Lake Victoria and the bananas grown in the fertile red soils I'd passed, was imported. Before I crossed the border, I'd refuelled the TT and stocked up with coffee, sugar, cooking oil and a few packets of cigarettes. I wasn't a smoker but a cigarette offered was a shared moment with another on the side of the road.

It was nearly dark when I rode into the Backpackers Hostel and Campsite, which was perched on one of Kampala's many hills on the city's outskirts. A bland cement-block building was set in a garden shaded by leafy trees and enclosed by a high brick wall. It was run by John, an Australian who'd set up the place for the overland truck tours. A truck was parked in the yard and I found space on the lawn amongst the colourful tents of its passengers, a mix of Brits, Aussies and Kiwis on a tour of East Africa. Just about every backpacker, overlander and motorcycle traveller at Mama Roche's had recommended I stay here.

Martin from Germany, on his green Kawasaki KLX650, was there. He was fresh-faced with a smattering of freckles, and looked younger than most travellers I'd come across, who were usually in their late twenties or thirties. Africa scared off most of those in their early twenties. Martin and I had first met at Mama Roche's when I returned from Lake Turkana.

The other motorcycle traveller was Ronnie, a thirtyish, short and dark-haired Scotsman riding a Yamaha XT600 Tenere. I felt I already knew this ball of energy and enthusiasm, who talked excitedly about everything: just about all the motorcycle travellers at Mama's had come across Ronnie at one stage or another on the route down from Tunisia.

After setting up my tent, I bought a dinner of steamed fish and rice from a stall outside the hostel and sat cross-legged on the lawn to eat. Martin sat with me and Ronnie joined us after attending to a blown light bulb. He'd arrived at the hostel a few weeks earlier and was earning his keep as the unpaid handyman.

'Cheers. Get this into you. You earned it. Riding with two tyres strapped to the back of your bike. You're bloody awesome,' said Ronnie, handing us each a cold beer and sitting down with us on the neatly mowed lawn.

'It was only till I got here. I'm fitting them tomorrow,' I said between mouthfuls of the delicious fish, probably caught that afternoon in nearby Lake Victoria. I'd carried the two off-road tyres from Nairobi so that not even the tiniest bit of rubber would be worn off on the tarmac. As rear tyres wear quicker than fronts, the eight-ply Michelin Desert especially had to get me all the way to Morocco before I could buy another.

'You should hang around for a few weeks,' said Ronnie. 'Help out at the HIV clinic. It's just up the road at Mengo Hospital. Things are pretty bad. Folks have no idea how many people are dying from AIDS. And they're all young men and women. They're no older than forty. They're all alone. When they get sick, their families piss off. Leave them for dead. I'm just up there chatting to them, giving them water, feeding them and cleaning them up. 'There's wee children, too. Most are orphans. They're born with it and there's nothing anyone can do.' He offered his time freely and every day faced death as a volunteer at the clinic. 'They need our help. How about it?' he asked.

'I can't. I've got to get across Zaire before the wet season,' I replied, but the truth was I knew it would destroy me to see so much suffering and death, especially to see children die. I wanted to remain oblivious because there was no hope: there were no effective medications to stop the virus killing them. These would not be discovered until late in 1995.

'What about you, Martin?' he asked.

'I want to keep moving. I don't have a lot of time left and from Cape Town I've got to get back to Germany and get a job. I can't hang around too long,' he said reluctantly and looked away from Ronnie's pleading eyes.

After I'd eaten my dinner and showered, we headed to a back-alley bar down the road from the hostel for a few more beers. I crawled into my tent around midnight. But in the early hours I woke to the strained voices of three men, Australians from the overland truck tour. Their tent was pitched a few metres from mine. The trio had been drinking in downtown Kampala and their conversation carried clearly in the still night air.

'What the fuck have I done?' the first man said.

'She was a prostitute,' said the second.

'You fucking idiot. I can't fucking believe you didn't use a fucking condom,' said the third.

Most of the travellers I'd met, whether on motorcycles or with backpacks, were men. But the danger of HIV was real for all of us, regardless of gender. Upon leaving Australia, I'd buried my sexuality deep inside me, out of harm's way. And in my naive denial, I still did not carry condoms, not even one. What would happen if I should find myself in such a situation?

After all, I was twenty-eight – in the prime of my sexuality. But since arriving in Africa nearly eight months ago, I'd never thought about sex. I had no urge. No stirrings of desire. It was as though my sexuality had been switched off. My periods had also stopped, but I wasn't concerned about this abrupt halt to my sexual desire and menstrual cycle; it suited me fine. Life was much less dangerous and messy without either, especially as there were times, stretches of two or three days, without the opportunity to wash.

As I listened to the anxious chatter of the three young men, I was reminded that our bodies have a way of overruling the mind, especially when drunk or stoned or both. Nevertheless, with the stakes so high, I found it incomprehensible that this young man had had an unguarded moment, one that may very well kill him. Africa, and especially the trucking route across southern Africa from the port of Mombasa across to Uganda and into Zaire, was a highway for HIV transmission. I, too, would be on this same highway after I crossed into Zaire from northern Uganda.

*

The next morning, I rode into town to the American Express office at the Sheraton Hotel and purchased US$2300, half in travellers' cheques and half in cash, buying up all their small denomination notes, ones and fives, which I'd need in Zaire to avoid losing out to hyper-inflation if I changed too many dollars at any one time. I would have loved to sneak in and use the Sheraton's luxurious pool, but I couldn't risk taking my eyes off my money for one second. I quickly rode back to the hostel and locked my money in the Pelican case hidden in the plastic jerry covered in hessian and then locked this back on the bike.

Late that afternoon, Martin and Ronnie watched me fit the tyres – both offered to help but I refused.

'I'll have to do it when I've got a flat and I'm on my own. This is good practice,' I said.

'Fixing a flat is one thing, but fitting a new tyre can be tricky. Better be careful you don't pinch the tube,' said Ronnie, but it was too late; the tyre was flat soon after I'd inflated it.

'Now I get to practise fixing a puncture,' I said and levered the tyre off the rim to remove the tube.

'I'd say it's a big hole by the look of how quick it went down,' said Martin.

'Have you got a spare?' asked Ronnie.

'No. But this'll be right once I've fixed it,' I replied and retrieved my puncture repair kit from a pannier.

'I wouldn't be so sure about that,' Martin commented.

'A new tube is only new till the first puncture and I'm sure I'll get heaps of punctures on the dirt roads in Zaire,' I said. A spare would only add more weight to my already overloaded motorcycle and, besides, I didn't have time to buy a new tube. I wanted to get moving first thing the following morning.

The next morning, with the TT packed, the tube patched and the tyre still inflated, I was ready to leave. Ronnie and Martin stood with me.

'This is for you. I hope you never have to use it,' Martin said and handed me a small can of pepper spray. 'There's no harm in having it,' he added.

'Just in case,' I said and popped it into a side pocket of the Gearsack, where I was sure it would be forgotten.

We all embraced and wished each other the best of luck on our journeys.

'You better visit me in Scotland. I want to know you've made it,' said Ronnie.

'Me too,' added Martin and then I was gone, riding away from Kampala and towards Zaire, where I'd cross at Goli in the north. I wanted to see a little more of Uganda than the villages that hugged the tarmac and the trucks that crossed the lower half of the country into Zaire and the mud highway to Kisangani.

There was a little more urgency to my journey now, as it was dictated by weather rather than my own meandering curiosity. The dry season in Zaire was short and the roads would turn to mud and bog-holes within months. The driest time was January; it was now late November.

But any urgency was foiled the day after I left Kampala. The next morning in Masindi, I woke to a flat rear tyre, most likely from a nail picked up the previous day. I'd camped on the lawn outside the police station, where I'd been told by the officer on duty I'd be safe. There was a hole-in-the-ground toilet out the back and a tap out the front, plus camping was free.

I pushed the TT across the potholed main street to a garage and paid the Ugandan mechanic to fix it. He used Pattex contact glue.

'Good for trucks,' he said and I bought a tube of it on his recommendation. I re-patched the tube four times that day. By the end of it, I could lever the tyre off the rim and have the tube patched in under fifteen minutes. I thought of how far I'd come since struggling with the tyre in northern Kenya, when the Samburu warriors had helped me. It was late afternoon when I finally realised that the contact glue was becoming soft from the heat of friction and the patch was letting go. Pattex worked on cooler-running truck tyres but not hotter-running motorcycle tyres.

I was heading towards Murchison Falls National Park on my way into Zaire. There was no game in the park, as the animals had been shot for meat years ago by soldiers and poachers, but I wanted to cross the Nile River near its source at Lake Albert.

Having broken all my rules about travelling at night, I found myself in darkness on a little-used back road about twenty kilometres from Bulisa, a village near the lake. The tyre was flat again even though I'd used my own glue on the previous repair. I probably hadn't cleaned the tube of the contact glue as well as I should have. I weighed my options: I could either struggle to fix the flat in the dark using my torch, or push the TT off the road and camp. As I pondered, I saw a faint light in the distance. A vehicle slowly inched its way towards me. Its headlights dipped and rose as the vehicle negotiated the deep potholes. The vehicle was a heavily loaded truck and as it neared, I heard the driver crunch through the gears until it finally pulled up beside me.

'I've got a flat tyre. Please, can I get a lift to Bulisa?' I asked the driver, who peered down as thick dust swirled around us.

He shouted a few words to the three men perched high on the load of timber planks. They jumped down and I began removing the panniers and Gearsack to make the bike lighter and easier to lift. With ropes, the men hoisted the bike and laid it on top of the load. I perched on the timber beside it and we were soon bouncing over potholes into the dark, moonless night.

Half an hour later the truck unloaded me and the TT outside the only hotel in Bulisa, a single-storey cement-block building. In the truck's head-lights, I saw its white plaster was yellowed and flaking with age.

'Thank you,' I said to the men when the bike was unloaded. I offered the driver a handful of notes. He shook his head and said something about me needing it. There had been no talk of money for the lift, which took me by surprise, as in the two days I had been there so far I had found that no one in Uganda did a kindness without demanding payment.

Four Ugandan men who looked to be in their late thirties and a boy aged about twelve emerged from the darkness. The boy could speak a lit-tle English and introduced himself as Kennedy. The others were silent but helped push my motorcycle up the low steps and through the hotel's foyer and dining room to the cement courtyard and the rooms. I was the only guest. The hotel was like most local African hotels: a bed with clean sheets in a bare room of suspect security. But the TT, once I'd removed the pan-niers, easily fitted through the narrow doorway, so it would be safe. I ordered tea and ate two bananas squashed in a small loaf of stodgy white bread I'd bought in Kampala.

*

I woke early to fix the puncture. As Kennedy watched, intrigued, I removed the patch and all remnants of the contact glue before using a new one. The patch on the puncture from fitting the new rear tyre in Kampala still held fast. The cheap watch I'd bought in Nairobi no longer worked, so I guessed at the five minutes needed for the glue to cure.

'For you, but it is no good,' I said and handed the watch to Kennedy who squatted beside me and beamed a wide smile of gratitude.

Since arriving at the hotel, I'd felt a growing sense of unease and was now distinctly aware of my vulnerability. I quickly finished refitting the tube, and as I packed the TT the four men who'd helped me the previous night watched from where they stood in front of the two exits from the courtyard. Earlier, women had casually wandered in and out of this enclosed area. Now they were gone. And the older of the men, who I guessed was about forty or maybe fifty, had yelled at the children, who had left too. My hands shook nervously as I stuffed my tools into the Gearsack. I looked up and the four men moved a little closer. My *panga* was strapped to the tent that lay across the top of the handlebars. I removed it and placed it next to my bike and thought of James from South Horr and his words about showing strength.

'You did not pay for the tea,' said the older man, who I assumed was the hotel manager.

'I'm sorry. My mistake. Is this enough?' I asked and handed him 500 shillings (about twenty cents) from the small change pouch attached to my belt. Without a word, he took the money.

'Why did you chase the kids away?' I asked, holding the tin of pepper spray in my shaking hand, grateful Martin had given it to me.

'Too many around,' he said bluntly and I noticed he was wearing the watch I'd given to Kennedy.

Another of the four men, the tallest, moved to stand next to the oldest. Both glared at me with piercing black eyes. I stood my ground, leaving no doubt that I was fully aware of their intentions. Hidden on me and my motorcycle was US$2300 and they knew it. They knew that in order to travel I must carry some money and whatever I carried was more than they would earn in four or five years.

As I finished packing, one of my gloves fell under the TT. I stood and stared at it. The oldest man took a step closer and was only a few metres away. No one moved. The other three looked tense as though preparing to pounce and I stood ready to turn into a wild cat. I played out my defence. I'd squirt the pepper spray directly into their eyes. I'd dive for the *panga* and run for the exit at the back of the courtyard. Time stood still.

But just as quickly as the men had surrounded me, the mood changed and they moved away. It was as though for an instant they were possessed by some dark force. These men would maybe have been in their twenties during the bloody years of Amin and Obote. What atrocities had they seen? What massacres had they been part of? For a moment it had felt like they were back in that savage time. But with peace had come compassion as well as rules and police. I was thankful their spirit was still true and I did not meet with a terrible, unspeakable end.

I wheeled the TT through the foyer and the men, who seconds before I was certain were my enemies, now helped push it down the low steps. As I quickly prepared to leave, Kennedy appeared beside me.

'Sorry about the watch,' I said and put my hand on his shoulder. He shrugged, clearly accepting that adults always overpower children.

'That man, he is bad man,' he said looking down and kicking the dirt with his bare feet.

In my relief to be away from Bulisa, I rode off in a trail of dust, opening the throttle to let the TT roar with all its power. The dirt road wound its way through dry scrubland and I rode fast; fear pumped through me and my hands clenched the handlebars. Even though nothing had happened, it was the first time I'd felt evil intent in Africa. I'd felt it as a physical thing that travelled in waves of vibration like a pebble dropped into a pond. The ripples were a palpable force that struck my body and washed over me and I did not need to convince myself otherwise. I wanted to be far away from its source.

I rode on a two-wheel dirt track through Murchison Falls National Park as I headed north towards Arua and the nearby border crossing into Zaire. There were no wild animals and no danger for those on motorcycles, or even people on foot, and the ranger let me through without question. I crossed the park and stopped at the Victoria Nile River, a tributary of the mighty Nile, which ran from Lake Albert. The ferry was moored and a group of youths lay in the shade of a lean-to shelter made from rough-cut timber and a few sheets of rusted corrugated iron.

'Better you wait,' one of them called out. 'Better you go with the tour vehicle this afternoon. If you go now, you must pay full cost of the ferry. It is very expensive.'

I never found out how much it was, but I believed them and headed back to a picnic shelter that overlooked the river. At one of the tables a Kenyan man was preparing lunch for the tour group the boy had mentioned. He was their cook and he told me the tour group was still at Murchison Falls, where the Victoria Nile squeezed through a narrow gorge as it made its way into Lake Albert, before flowing through Sudan and eventually becoming part of the Nile in Egypt. I parked under a tree and rested in the shade. It felt strange that I could just sit and do nothing. The rear tyre was still inflated but I kept prodding it, not entirely convinced that my patch had stuck.

When the Swedish tourists, all red-faced and sweaty, returned for lunch, I approached the leader, a round jovial man wearing checked shorts, a bright-yellow T-shirt and a wide-brimmed straw hat, and asked if I could cross with them on the ferry later that afternoon.

'Of course, of course,' he said. 'You must join us for lunch.' He put a chubby pink-skinned arm around my shoulders and led me to the picnic table under a thatched shelter.

I was seated amongst the group and a cold beer and mushroom omelette was placed on the table in front of me.

As I shovelled the omelette into my mouth, I thought of how my circumstances had done a complete U-turn in the space of a few short hours. I said a silent thank you for my good luck, or whatever else it was that had stepped in and plucked me away from trouble in the nick of time.

After lunch I returned to the TT, which was parked under a shady tree, and dozed while the Swedish tourists went on their game drive. The national park was only just recovering from the slaughter of most of its wildlife after years of civil war and, more recently, by groups of rebels. To attract foreign tourists with foreign currency, the government, with the help of international aid, had restocked the park with some game, but it would take years for the animals to breed and flourish.

At mid-afternoon, I crossed the Victoria Nile with the Swedes. I let them go ahead so the TT would not scare what few animals might be seen through the tall grass that bordered the two-wheel dirt track. I was still twenty-five kilometres from Pakwach, the township where I'd stay that night, and I estimated I had about thirty minutes of daylight. I rode in the smooth wheel ruts that crossed the undulating plains, where the grass shimmered like burnt gold in the breeze. The bike purred and I was mesmerised by this isolated expanse against a backdrop of a fiery red sun.

But perfection soon ended with the distinct wobble of the back wheel. My efforts to repair the puncture had failed. It would soon be dark and I was certain I would not be saved by a truck on this isolated stretch of dirt track. As there were no animals or people to worry about, and it would be no easy task to re-patch the tube by torchlight, I pushed the TT off the track to a clump of palms which provided some protection to hide myself and my motorcycle. I lay the TT on its side and covered it with the dry fronds that littered the ground. My water bottle was nearly empty and dinner was a few swallows of water, a couple of dry chocolate biscuits and a limp carrot forgotten in a pannier. With the bike on one side, the clump of palms on the other and the *panga* and pepper spray beside me, I soon fell asleep.

*

Snug in the soft down of my sleeping bag, I watched a fireball of orange slowly creep over the eastern horizon the next morning, savouring the moment before I got to work re-patching the rear tube.

I had taken so much care, I thought, as I peeled the old patch from the tube and began the all-too-familiar process of puncture repair. Once the tyre was fitted, I lifted the TT and was about to attempt to ride it back to the track through the clumps of tall brown grass and sand when three gangly Ugandan youths strolled past.

'Hello. Can you help me please,' I called out, waving to the boys and smiling at their dumbfounded looks as they stopped to stare.

With their help, it was easy to push the TT through the long grass and sand back to the track.

'Can you give us some money?' one of them asked.

I had no small notes and did not know what to say so I just stared at them. 'Thank you for your help,' I said to break the awkward silence.

'No problem,' they replied and went on their way. I headed towards Pakwach, where I was told I'd find a new tube in Arua, another 110 kilometres to the north. The patch I repaired that morning still held and for the first time in days I relaxed as I rode over freshly graded dirt. A brief shower of rain had settled the dust, and its smell lingered in the morning air. This far north there was no traffic and I leaned back into the Gearsack and let the TT cruise effortlessly over the undulating hills.

*

Arua was a sleepy town, its main street lined with low-set cement buildings. I stopped at an Indian-owned shop that sold auto parts and tyres and asked if they had an eighteen-inch rear motorcycle tube.

'No, we only have seventeen-inch, no eighteen-inch,' said the round-faced Indian shopkeeper.

'Shit,' I replied, cursing myself for neglecting to buy a spare in Kampala as Ronnie and Martin had advised.

'Don't worry, we get for you,' he said and called to one of the boys outside.

I sat on the step drinking a Coke while I waited. Christmas music played from the general goods shop across the dusty potholed street. Christmas already, I thought, as I heard the familiar tune of 'We Wish You a Merry Christmas'. It was so out of place and I thought of family and Christmas and home and how far away it all was. I suddenly felt homesick and so very alone in a foreign land where I knew nobody and nobody knew me. But at the same time, I also felt a rush of purpose to keep moving forward and the two feelings were so at odds with each other that I actually felt as though I was being pulled in two.

'You very lucky. This is the only one. Plenty of seventeen-inch,' said the boy, breathless from his run to bring me the tube. With a wide grin, he presented it to me as though it was the most precious thing in all the world.

'Thank you,' I said and thought of how, once again, events had transpired to solve the problems that had come my way. I paid the boy 16,000 Ugandan shillings (about US$16) and he rushed off to pay the shop owner while I packed my new tube safely into a pannier, as the rear tyre was still firm.

Arua had once boasted a large expatriate community, but these days a bed and meal could only be found at the Crena Hotel, an old timber-and-brick building with a wide veranda. A single room was 2000 shillings (US$2) and consisted of a comfortable bed with clean, crisp white sheets. There was also electricity, although only until ten p.m., when the generator was switched off. The Ugandan manager, a neatly dressed, thick-set man, continued to operate the hotel in the British tradition of its former colonial owners. Staff wore black and whites and served English meals, with roast beef on the menu that night. The only other guests were two middle-aged men: a jovial portly Kenyan in brown slacks and white-collared shirt, and a slim tallish Indian with a college-boy haircut in khaki trousers and shirt. They called me over and insisted I join them.

The Indian man was Salim, and the Kenyan was John. Salim told me he had just driven over from Mombasa with a truckload of relief food for the refugee camps at Koboko near the Sudan border. They would leave in the morning for the fifty-kilometre drive, offloading the food in a compound managed by John. They asked if I'd like to visit the camps, which were home to about 100,000 Sudanese refugees who had walked for days and weeks across the desert to flee the civil war. While the desperate plight of the refugees was hardly a tourist attraction, I was curious and so it was agreed I would follow them on the TT after breakfast.

*

After riding on a potholed dirt road that wound its way over many small hills, John and Salim travelling behind in the truck, we arrived at the compound an hour after leaving Arua the next morning. The compound was surrounded by a wall of steel panelling, and was almost empty of relief food. The sacks of beans, maize and vitamin-enriched milk powder in Salim's truck would be stockpiled here before being distributed to the international aid agencies that had temporary offices in Koboko, the small village near the camps.

'There is enough food circulating in the camps, but more is on its way from the ships docked at Mombasa,' John said and handed me a key.

I would sleep in one of three guest *bandas*, freshly painted white with blue doors and neat thatched roofs. Salim and John would sleep in the half-constructed cement-brick house.

Later, Salim and I walked towards the refugee camps, five kilometres from the compound. Several late-model white Toyota 4×4s passed us and he apologised that they didn't stop to give us a lift.

'I don't mind walking,' I said, enjoying the opportunity to stroll in the coolness of late afternoon.

'Here is one of my friends,' Salim said as a battered pickup stopped beside us and we crowded into the front.

We were dropped off at the first camp, a collection of canvas tents and blue plastic tarpaulins scattered amongst the undulating hills of dry scrub. Salim told me it was home to about 40,000 Sudanese who seemed well settled, their tents having the appearance of permanency. Free enterprise flourished and a few stalls sold cigarettes, tea, sugar and roasted peanuts. Salim bought a handful of peanuts and dished them out to the steadily growing group of grubby children who trailed behind us.

'Where do the refugees get the money to buy the goods sold at the stalls?' I asked.

'They do business and sell their ration of maize, oil and peanuts to the Ugandans, who then sell it to the relief agencies, who then give it out to the refugees, who then sell it again,' he said and pointed to a man riding a bicycle, unsteady with the weight of a large sack.

'See that sack. It may go from the refugee camp to the village three times before it is opened,' he said and performed a little pantomime of riding a bicycle up and down, the children laughing at his antics.

'Good on them. Who wants to eat maize and beans every day,' I said. 'It's much better that they can buy other things like fresh fruit, vegetables and meat.'

'And cigarettes,' Salim said with a grin. 'Some of this relief food ends up in the markets all over Uganda. The businessman knows he can buy cheap here and sell for a big profit in the city,' he added as we walked back towards the village market to buy the ingredients for the chicken curry he would cook for dinner.

As I sat with Salim and John eating the delicious spicy chicken curry, I thought of the four men at the hotel in Bulisa and how in contrast, with Salim and John, there were no such ill feelings. Even though I sat with two men whom I'd only met the day before, I did not feel threatened. Instead, I felt a sense of friendship, as though I'd known them for a lifetime.

Before I left the compound the next morning, Salim handed me a small tin. 'A present for you,' he said and I opened the tin. It was filled with about ten patches, of various large sizes, suitable for repairing punctures in truck tyres. Earlier, I'd told Salim and John about my ordeal with the punctured rear tyre and Pattex glue.

'You are both too kind, but I'll never use these,' I said picking out the two largest patches and handing them back to Salim. 'Thank you for all this,' I said glancing over at the *banda*. 'It was so wonderful to meet you.'

'We are pleased to meet you too. Good luck on your journey,' they replied and we all vigorously shook hands. Then I rode out through the double steel gates of the compound and headed back to Arua. The following day, I would cross into Zaire.

10

OLD MEETS NEW
ZAIRE

By the time I packed the TT and refuelled, it was late morning as I rode away from Arua on a narrow dirt road towards the border at Goli. It was an easy hundred-kilometre ride and I was grateful the bog-holes were dry, as a light shower would quickly turn the hard-packed brown clay to slippery mud. It was late November and my arrival coincided with the dry season, a three-month reprieve from day after day of torrential rain. From now till February there would be just a few light showers, mostly falling at night as a fine mist.

At the border after my documents were stamped by the Ugandan official, I pulled up outside the tin-roofed mud hut that served as the Zaire immigration post, and was greeted by two young men dressed in military uniform. They stamped my passport and carnet without question and welcomed me with wide grins.

'Zaire has many beautiful wonders,' said the first.

'We care very much for tourists,' said the second, spreading his arms wide as if I were about to be embraced by a whole nation.

Before signing my name in the register, I read the other entries – the names and nationalities of travellers from all over the world. Many were from Australia, New Zealand and Britain, as Goli had once been a major crossing point for the overland truck tours from London, but none had crossed since April. Even before that the entries were spasmodic, as few over-land travel companies were now prepared to take the risk of travelling through Zaire. As I held my pen poised to write my name, I hesitated for a very brief moment. Is this what I wanted to do? Travel alone into one of the most underdeveloped and lawless countries in Africa, if not the world? Did I really want to head into a country perpetually gripped by conflict and civil war? My guidebook recommended that only the most seasoned and hard-core travellers venture into Africa's interior. Was I now such a traveller?

I lowered the pen and quickly scribbled my name and nationality, as though something else had made the decision for me. I was almost at the halfway mark. This milestone would be achieved when I reached Kisangani, a city that lay deep within Zaire's rainforest, close to the equator. While I'd already come so far, I still had a long way to go, and I was fully aware of the hardships I would face. But there was no real indecisiveness on my part – just the same overpowering sense that this was the way forward that had possessed me when I'd first struck on the idea of this journey. Nothing had changed my determination.

I was not forging ahead blindly, however. I was aware of the dangers – of the armed rebels and soldiers robbing civilians because they had not been paid for months, of the poverty that caused people to lose all compassion. But this was not the Africa that was slowly revealing itself to me. So far I had always been shown *ubuntu*. Instead of harming me, people had offered help when I had asked, food when I looked like I needed it, and a safe place to sleep when I was tired. Africa had strengthened me but it had also opened my mind to consider another reality that lay just beyond my reach. I wanted to push the boundaries of reason to understand this new reality. I wanted proof that if I expected goodness from people, that is what I would receive; that if I expected the extraordinary, then my wish would be granted. As I moved forward on my journey, I wanted to prove over and over again that there was a powerful force manipulating events in my favour. And to do this I needed to go deeper and deeper into Africa, where there was no support and where I would be totally alone. After Lake Turkana, the purpose of my travels had changed. I was no longer on an adventure for the hell of it – being free, with no responsibilities, going wherever I wanted, whenever I wanted. I was now searching for this mysterious force that I sensed was there, but that had not yet fully revealed itself to me.

It was late afternoon as I rode the fourteen kilometres towards Mahagi along a narrow track fringed by grass grown tall and iridescent green from the humidity and abundant rain of the recent wet season. Mahagi was the second immigration post, as crossing into Zaire was a two-stage process. After my documents were stamped, my intention was to camp at Mahagi's Catholic mission. I hoped they would allow me to pitch my tent on a spot of lawn within their secure compound. A room at a local hotel, especially in the smaller towns, was out of the question for a single woman in Zaire. Alone, I would be an easy target for the drunk and stoned soldiers with loaded AK47s. Since government money rarely made it to the regional areas, the soldiers were forced to collect their 'wages' from the locals, business owners and the occasional hardcore traveller who passed through.

I passed thatched huts and, hearing the rumble of the TT, small children dressed in rags the same shade as the reddish-brown dirt on which they ran with bare feet, emerged like a swarm of bees.

As I approached the Mahagi immigration post, I noticed four young men leaning against a gate made of solid planks of rough-cut timber that cut across the dirt track.

'It is closed,' said one of men. 'The boss get married today. It is big wedding. You must stay here tonight.'

'Where?' I asked and they pointed to the small patch of lawn next to a double-storey red-brick building. I would be exposed to all manner of threats, the least of which was thieves. I quickly planned my escape, as I would certainly not camp there. Instead, I would ride around the building, down the low grassy bank and back onto the two-wheeled dirt track.

'Thank you,' I said, pulling on my helmet and gloves. I got back on the bike and rode slowly around the building, the men walking behind me. A moment later, I put the TT into second gear and opened the throttle, leaving them waving at me to stop.

'I'll be back in the morning. *Au revoir,*' I yelled, and rode the last four kilometres to the Mahagi township.

The Catholic mission comprised an impressive red-brick church and several low-set brick buildings. The mission compound was a world away from the poverty and decay beyond its high brick walls. I rode through the open gates and up the gravel driveway bordered by a perfectly clipped lawn to stop outside what looked to be the administration office. A short, rather round European man, with a pudding-bowl haircut and a brown robe tied with a cord at the waist, emerged as I pulled up. He did not speak and I assumed he was either on a vow of silence or could not speak a word of English, not even a simple hello.

'Can I camp here?' I asked. 'I'll be on my way early. I'll be no trouble,' I said apologetically, aware of my intrusion.

Without a word, the brother indicated I follow him. I pushed the bike over to a low-set brick building and quickly removed the Gearsack with all the things I'd need in order to wash and change into clean clothes. I followed him as he shuffled down a long stone corridor to a small room, which was bare except for a narrow single bed and a side table, both roughly cut from rainforest timber – from the trees that grew beyond the mission's high brick walls. He pointed to the washroom at the end of the corridor.

Once clean, I sat on the soft mattress covered with crisp white sheets and a grey wool blanket. A mosquito net was tied above it. As I wondered what to do next there was a gentle knock and I opened the door to the brother. I followed him and as we passed the main dining room, I caught a glimpse of a long table prepared for the evening meal. It seemed I was not permitted to eat with the brothers: instead, I was seated at a small table with a single chair in the adjoining room. An elderly African man shuffled in with a bowl of steaming vegetable soup and a thick slice of crusty white bread. It was absolutely delicious and I devoured it all in a matter of minutes. The man returned with the main course – a large plate of spaghetti bolognaise with a side dish of boiled sweet potatoes.

'Thank you,' I gushed before gobbling it all as if I had not eaten in days. In fact, it had been an easy day and I'd eaten very well over the past two days before leaving Uganda. I'd done this on purpose, to fatten myself for the lean times I fully expected lay ahead.

Was I in provincial Italy? Surely this was not Zaire. The motorcycle travellers in Nairobi had told me how difficult it would be in the heart of Africa. How terrible the food was, and especially how bad the roads were. I was yet to experience any of this hardship.

The plates were removed and a moment later, the brother re-emerged and I followed him back to my room. With a full belly, I fell into a contented sleep.

*

I woke early, just after daybreak, and had almost finished packing my things on the TT when the brother appeared beside me and beckoned me to follow him to the same small dining room, which was filled with the aroma of freshly brewed coffee. The little square table was laid with a feast of freshly baked bread, an omelette and bananas.

'Thank you,' I said and he gave me a glimmer of a smile before disappearing.

When I'd finished eating, I walked into the warm morning sunshine and, seeing one of the brothers, I asked to see the head of the mission. He pointed to a tall, thin, balding European man dressed in the same brown robes walking briskly towards the church. He stopped when I reached him.

'Thank you so much for your kind hospitality,' I said, a little breathless from my dash. 'I would like to pay something. Can I make a donation?'

'No, that is not necessary. You are welcome,' he said. I was momentarily speechless on hearing his perfect English in a world where silence ruled.

'The police post was closed yesterday and I did not stop. I will return to have my documents stamped,' I said. 'I think the police will come here looking for me.'

'Do not worry. You do not need to return. They will still be asleep after the wedding party last night,' he said. 'Good luck on your journey. God is with you,' he said, lifting his hand to give a little wave before continuing towards the church for morning mass.

'Thank you,' I said. With his reassurance, I decided to move on rather than give the police a reason to extract a bribe.

It was a two-hour ride up the mountain range to Rethy, on a hard-packed red dirt two-wheeled track, and again I thanked my lucky stars it was dry. The track curved over lush green hills and through a dark forest. In the former British colonies of East Africa I had communicated well enough in English, but from now on, with the exception of Nigeria and Ghana, I would need to speak French. The Austrian who'd sold me the tent and petrol stove had advised me that if I learnt two hundred words in any language, I'd be able to hold a simple conversation. As I rode towards Rethy, which sat perched on top of the Bleus mountain range, I practised my first ten French words, starting with numbers. I memorised these from the French phrasebook I'd bought in Nairobi. It was also reassuring to know that English words ending in the suffix 'tion' were often the same in French. At least I could ask for *direction* and *accommodation*.

It was mid-morning and the red dirt was smooth and dry as I rode through Rethy, a small village with a quaint red-brick church and several cottages clustered amongst the green hills. I stopped briefly beside the church with its commanding view over the valley far below. Dreadlocked white woolly sheep grazed on the lush grass and it was only when an elderly African man rode past on a rusty bicycle that creaked as he pedalled that I was reminded I was in the heart of Africa and not a hilltop meadow in Europe.

I moved on down the mountain. The dirt track wound its way through forest and past clusters of mud and grass-thatched huts. In the distance, dark storm clouds began to cluster and I prayed the rain would hold off or at least pass me by. But just as I neared a partially constructed red-brick building opposite a row of thatched huts, the first heavy drops began to fall. The building was a long rectangular structure with an iron roof, stone floor and archways. It looked to be the early stages of a church that had never been finished. It was another relic from the Belgians, who had been thrown out after independence in 1960. North-eastern Zaire had once had a large Belgian population, but their colonial red-brick bungalows and cottages now sat vacant and derelict.

The drops soon turned to a tropical downpour, the rain falling in great sheets that ran in torrents down the road, and I was grateful I'd found this shelter. A small group of children, their clothes no more than rags, watched me from under the flimsy thatch awnings of their huts. When the rain eased, they rushed over like hungry houseflies that had smelled a tasty treat.

'*Donnez cadeau*,' they chorused, holding out their hands in a circle around me.

'*Donnez cadeau*,' they repeated a little louder.

'I'm sorry, I don't have any gifts,' I said. They seemed convinced I was lying: surely my bags were filled with something of use to them. An older girl, aged about fifteen years, narrowed her eyes to a steely glare.

The rain fell heavier now and the road had turned from hard-packed red dirt to slippery red mud, making me grateful I'd fitted the front and rear Michelin enduro tyres, with raised 'knobby' tread pattern, in Kampala.

'*Non traction*,' I said, pointing to the road, but not one pair of eyes moved, in case they missed out on the *cadeau* they still fully expected I would produce. I weakened and opened the Gearsack, pulling out a packet of sweet biscuits I'd bought in Arua. They beamed and held out their cupped hands as I shared the treat – two biscuits each – and then scrunched the packet up to show it was empty. They devoured the biscuits in a matter of seconds and looked expectantly for more.

'*Fini,*' I said, but they weren't convinced and continued to stare as though their will alone would magically make another treat drop into their little hands.

After about thirty minutes the rain stopped and I started the TT. The children stood back and left a little opening in the circle they'd formed around me. I rode nervously out on to the slippery red mud, where the rear tyre struggled to gain traction. As I rode down the mountain I lost count of the times I lost control and fell sliding along with my motorcycle for several metres. Months of riding in Africa had made my body strong and each time I fell, I managed to lift the TT upright and get on my way again, only to skid on the next bend.

Finally, the worst of the mud over, I rode into a shantytown of rusted corrugated-iron shacks that had arisen as a result of a recent gold rush. It teemed with African men, all tall with broad shoulders and thick arms of pure muscle. Rain fell as a fine mist and I slowly manoeuvred the bike through the mass of bodies and around the heavily laden trucks. The TT's tyres were caked with mud and I skidded and landed in a heap outside a ramshackle corrugated-iron shack. It was filled with men and a few women drinking beers. They all cheered and clapped as Zairoise dance music blared loudly, adding to the craziness. The afternoon's entertainment – a tourist covered in red mud on a large, overloaded motorcycle – had arrived. Strong arms reached down and lifted me and the TT with ease. I rode a few feet only to fall again, unable to get traction. I was lifted while still on the bike, and with the engine running.

'*Merci très bien. Au revoir,*' I said loudly to be heard through my helmet and above the mayhem.

'Give money!' they shouted back and a man who stood taller than all the others raised a thick muscled forearm, shaking his fist. Another grabbed my arm as I was about to accelerate. Others yelled at him to let me go. I was surrounded by a sea of angry faces – a solid wall blocking my way. I revved the engine and with a wave of my hand, I motioned for them to step aside. Surprisingly, they obediently moved to form a long tunnel and I slip-slided through the mob. A truck passed me and several men banged on the cab from where they sat on top of the sacks.

'*Rapide, rapide,*' they yelled. I opened the throttle and they cheered as I passed.

When I arrived in Bunia an hour later, the TT and I were covered in red mud. It looked as though we'd been dipped in chocolate. I'd only ridden 150 kilometres, but I was exhausted and hungry, and I looked for a suitable hotel. The main street was lined with shops, restaurants, bars and several petrol stations, all with flaking paint that had once been white or blue or even bright pink. I reasoned that in Bunia it would be safe to stay at one of the local hotels. Besides, I did not want to travel all the way through Zaire riding from one protected mission compound to another.

I stopped outside a brightly painted blue cement building, the Hotel La Nuivette. Zairoise dance music blasted from the large open windows. Inside, several men were drinking from large bottles of beer. The watch-man, an elderly African man, directed me through the double steel gates and down the cement drive to the rooms at the back of the main bar. A young African woman wearing a tight red dress that emphasised her volup-tuous body approached me. She spoke a little English, and she told me a room cost US$3 and I could store my motorcycle in the flimsy timber stor-age shed near the gate. The night watchman would keep it safe, she said. I removed all my bags and locked the shed door with one of my padlocks.

'You change money?' she asked when we reached my room.

The hotel manager in Arua had warned me about the currency prob-lems Zaire suffered due to hyperinflation. The current notes, zaires, would soon be worthless and replaced with a new currency in an attempt to regain control. I asked the rate for old zaires.

'Twenty-five million for one dollar. How much you change?' she asked, leaning close, her cheap perfume making me gag.

'How much for one beer?' I asked.

'Twenty-five million,' she said.

'Okay. I change two dollars,' I said and she quickly whipped out a bun-dle of notes tucked into her ample bosom. The fifty million zaires would buy me a beer and a meal. I would change more in the morning for food and fuel, as the rate would only get better as everyone wanted to offload the old currency before the change.

After I'd washed off the mud under a cold shower that made me gasp, I changed into my 'going out' clothes – black leggings, a long-sleeve blue shirt and black canvas shoes – and headed to the bar. The barman opened a large bottle of Primus. I'd heard so much about this beer and it was indeed one of the best in Africa. It was another relic left by the Belgians; though fortunately the beer-brewing industry had not gone to ruin.

'What's the exchange rate?' I asked, counting out twenty-five million zaires in one million notes to pay for the beer.

'It is forty million. You change dollar?' the barman asked raising an eyebrow.

'I already changed for twenty-five million. I got ripped off,' I said and he laughed.

'You know tomorrow is last day to change,' he said. 'There is big party tonight. It is best to spend this old money. Get drunk. It is no good to keep.'

Everybody was desperate to get rid of old zaires before the change. Zaire's authoritarian president, Mobutu Sese Seko Kuku Ngebendu Wa Za Banga – which, loosely translated, means 'the almighty powerful one' – was one of the world's richest men in one of the world's poorest countries. He had introduced the new currency (the nouveau zaire) because the old money had become impractical; rather than count the money, stacks were either measured or weighed. The largest denomination note was one million, and with forty notes to the US dollar, a large wad of cash was needed to buy even the cheapest of goods. Mobutu had ordered the printing of a five-million note to pay the soldiers, but the general population doubted its authenticity and refused to accept it.

I could understand the logic behind the new currency. When inflation goes through the roof and the rate of exchange gets too high, just start again. Problem solved – except the whole country was in a state of total confusion.

As I finished my beer and was about to order a meal, two men sat down either side of me. They were tall and broad-shouldered, their tight black curls cropped short and their forearms thick and muscled. The last rays of late-afternoon light streamed through the large open windows and their dark skin glistened. One of them signalled to the barman and three bottles of Primus were placed before us. The man's massive hand gripped the bottle, making it look tiny.

'Drink,' they both said and raised their beers.

They spoke only a little English, but I understood they'd struck it lucky at the gold diggings and had much money to spend.

'Drink more beer,' the man on my left insisted.

'I want to sex with you,' said the man on my right.

'*Non, merci*,' I said and silently planned my escape as the threat of danger rolled in.

The bar was filling with men. Zairoise music pumped from two large speakers and several young women, dressed provocatively, gyrated their voluptuous bodies on the dance floor under a glitter ball. Then it dawned on me: the hotel was a brothel. I remembered the Austrian at Mama Roche's warning me that most of Zaire's local hotels doubled as brothels.

The alcohol from one and a half bottles of beer drunk on an empty stomach began to make me dizzy. The room began to spin. The woman I'd changed money with earlier tapped me on the shoulder. 'Come dance,' she said, moving her hips to the beat of the Zairoise music.

'*Toilette*,' I said and staggered a little as I got off the stool and quickly left the bar for my room.

I locked the door, closed the flimsy curtains and turned off the light. In darkness, I ate a tin of sardines with a loaf of stodgy white bread I'd bought in Arua the day before.

An hour later, the two men from the bar banged loudly on my door. 'Come drink beer,' they called. I lay in bed hoping my door would not collapse under the barrage but they soon gave up and returned to the party. The music played until the early hours, and then the drinkers banged on the tables for more.

*

It rained during the night, and I resigned myself to another day of falls in slippery red mud for the 240-kilometre ride to Epulu, where I would visit the Okapi Breeding and Research Station to see the rare and beautiful giraffe-like animals with the legs of zebras and the bodies of horses.

Before the ride to Epulu, I needed fuel, and to buy it I needed to buy nouveaux zaires. But this was no easy task. The garage selling petrol would accept dollars, but it would mean paying double the price compared to paying in nouveaux zaires. I was told by the garage owner that the bank was closed after a rush on its shipment of new currency, which had arrived from the capital Kinshasa by light plane the previous afternoon. Not enough of the new money had been printed and, understandably, people were in a panic. Most of the shops, run by Indian merchants, refused to accept the old currency from people desperate to convert their soon-to-be-worthless cash into non-perishable goods.

Indian shopkeepers are always after American dollars, I reasoned, and headed to one of the shops lining the muddy street where a crowd had gathered. Inside, a line of people ended where the Indian shopkeeper, a stout, middle-aged man, sat at a table. He was buried behind several stacks of old zaire notes. Still more were stacked on the floor beside and behind him. I joined the queue and stood behind a neatly dressed young African man in navy slacks and the whitest of shirts, which seemed out of place in all the mud that stained everything with a reddish hue.

'Mobutu extend the deadline. We have another day to spend these old zaires but this Indian man is greedy and sells his goods for high price,' he said as we watched an African woman, hands on her wide hips, arguing with the Indian shopkeeper.

'She is not happy about his prices but she has no choice,' he said.

'How will he get rid of all the old money? Will he get stuck with it?' I asked as I watched the woman reluctantly empty her handbag of a pile of crumbled notes in exchange for a few goods: several cakes of soap, a tin of cooking oil and a small sack of rice.

'There will be another plane from Kinshasa and he will change all that old money for nouveaux zaires,' he said, pointing to the stacks of cash piled around him.

Watching the chaos, I realised I was witnessing an economy in free fall. The Indian shopkeeper was obviously too busy to be interested in my five US$1 notes, which was all I wanted to change. Opposite was another Indian shop that was deserted of customers as it refused to accept old zaires. A portly Indian man with his arms folded across his large belly leaned casually against the open doorway, watching the mayhem across the road.

'He take big risk. Maybe the bank run out of nouveaux zaires and he is owner of many piles of old paper worth nothing,' he said as I walked up the three low steps to stand beside him.

'I need nouveaux zaires to buy petrol,' I said and held out my five one-dollar notes.

He reached into a trouser pocket to retrieve a wad of notes and unfurled a fifty.

'Thank you so much,' I said, understanding he was doing me a favour by giving double the official rate of five nouveaux zaires.

Inflation was already climbing on the nouveau zaire even before it had been officially introduced. When I produced the fifty at the petrol station, the man shook his head and told me he had no change. Mobutu had little faith in the new currency and only a limited number of small denomination notes had been printed, as he knew the new currency would devalue the moment it went into circulation.

The African man at the garage advised I go to Atul's, another Indian shop, where I could buy a voucher for the fuel using my dollars. Mr Atul sat at the back of his shop and looked worn out from many years struggling to run a business in Zaire. He was also having a quiet day, as he too refused to deal in the old currency. I handed over US$2 and was given a voucher for the petrol. He also did me a huge favour and exchanged my fifty nouveau zaire note for smaller denominations.

Two hours later, with a full tank of petrol, I was on my way, only to be stopped a few kilometres outside Bunia at a checkpoint manned by four soldiers armed with AK47 machine-guns.

'*Documentation*,' demanded one of them.

I handed over my passport and, much to my amazement, he handed it back. If he'd kept it, I would have had no choice but to either wait it out or give him 'dollar'.

'*Registration*,' he said.

The registration papers for the TT were hidden in the Pelican case, along with the US$2300 in travellers' cheques and cash. This was all locked to the bike and concealed inside a plastic fuel container strapped to the back rack. I had no intention of opening the case and revealing my hidden stash, so instead I pretended I didn't understand.

'Give dollar,' he said and stared at me with angry eyes.

'*Oui, oui,*' I said. Then I put the TT in gear and rode quickly through the barrier and down the road, leaving the soldiers to stare after me.

I'd been told that the soldiers' salaries were fixed at sixty nouveaux zaires per month, a token amount that nobody could survive on. Here in the eastern provinces, soldiers often went months without being paid. Bullets were expensive and scarce, and as the soldiers had to buy their own, it was unlikely they would shoot me. An AK47 and a uniform were persuasive enough to extract money from the vehicles that had no choice but to stop. Nobody wanted any trouble, least of all these groups of soldiers far from the control of Mobuto, who lived surrounded by luxury over 2000 kilometres away in Kinshasa. Shooting a tourist would bring all sorts of unwanted attention to their private extortion activities.

It was late afternoon when I reached Lolwa, a ramshackle village of mud-and-thatch huts surrounded by dense rainforest about halfway to Epulu. The Indian shopkeepers had warned me that the road beyond Lolwa deteriorated to truck-size bog-holes, and I thought it best I tackle these in the morning, in daylight. An English backpacker in Nairobi had also told me that I could camp on the sprawling lawns of the Lolwa mission, run by an American family, which was the only place to stay in this small roadside village.

I pulled up outside the mission's house, a quaint red-brick cottage, and an African man, the mission's gardener pointed to a nearby shed. A tall white man wearing dark-blue overalls was bent over the engine of an old

Land Rover. When he stood from tinkering under the bonnet there was no mistaking the thought behind his steely glare: *Not another bloody traveller to eat us out of house and home.*

'Can I camp here? I'll be gone first thing in the morning. I'll be no trouble. I have my own food,' I said, to reassure him as best I could that I had no intention of abusing his family's hospitality.

Without a word, he pointed with a grease-covered hand to where I could set up my tent and to the hole-in-the-ground toilet at the back of the garden. I saw no more of him or his wife, although two of their children, a girl and a boy in their early teens, came to visit me after I'd settled into my tent. Before I left early the next morning they returned with a hand of bananas and a freshly baked loaf of bread.

Just before reaching Mombasa, I was forced to stop, as a truck overloaded with goods secured under green canvas was stuck in a bog-hole bigger than it. The mud was almost dry, but a week ago it would have been one of the bigger bog-holes on the mud highway to Kisangani. While it was marked on the map as a main arterial road, it was actually no more than a single-lane dirt road fringed by a tunnel of green as it cut through endless, impenetrable rainforest.

To the locals and the soldiers, bog-holes were big business, and makeshift villages had grown next to them. A constant stream of trucks carrying all sorts of goods – food, consumables and fuel – travelled this road to reach Zaire's interior. During the wet season it took three weeks to travel the 630 kilometres from Komanda to Kisangani. A bogged truck needed manpower to dig it out and mamas to cook food. The driver and passengers were also at the mercy of the soldiers, who demanded they pay imaginary toll fees.

When I stopped, four soldiers with AK47s surrounded me and advised they'd help for 'dollar', but I simply told them I was in no hurry.

As we watched the truck slip and slide, its wheels spinning and motor revving, I ate a banana, offering the rest to the soldiers, who devoured the lot in seconds. They were hungry and when they asked for more food, I gave them the loaf of bread.

'*Fini*,' I said when they asked for more, and I prayed the truck would move quickly and let me pass so I could be away from the soldiers with their guns and wild eyes.

One of them started shouting, yelling a tirade of abuse in French. With a lurch, the truck was free of the mud and I got back on my motorcycle. The four soldiers jumped back as it roared to life. I opened the throttle and followed one of the truck's deep wheel ruts, the panniers scraping on the hard-packed mud as I left the soldiers to stare bewildered after me.

After Mombasa, I passed through another checkpoint before the soldiers, who were lounging on dried mounds of mud beside the road, had time to reach for their guns. The last seventy kilometres to Epulu were without incident, as the bog-holes were dry and smooth and I easily rode through one deep depression after another. It felt like I was riding over a series of low hills and gullies. Up and down I went, the TT's shock-absorber cushioning my ride.

As I reached the outskirts of Epulu, I rode past a long line of twelve trucks, each waiting its turn to pass the monster of all bog-holes. It was so big, it looked like it would never dry out. Each truck would drive in, get bogged, then get dug out by the locals. I rode to the front of the queue, where several drivers, a motley crew of Indian and African men, lounged on bits of canvas in the shade under a truck. They told me they'd been there for ten days waiting their turn. An equal number of trucks waited on the other side.

'Why don't you pay the locals to fix the road? Get them to fill it in with rocks?' I asked.

'Government's job,' said a middle-aged Indian man with a large belly, who reclined Buddha-like on his side.

Business thrived around this bog-hole. Women cooked food in blackened pots, kids sold cigarettes singly from the packet they carried, and men laboured with shovels, large sticks and bare hands.

My only chance to get around it was to ride on a walking path that skirted the enormous hole. About halfway along the path was a large pile of mud that blocked my way. I grabbed a stick and the bog-hole men offered to help, calling out 'give dollar' from where they were sitting on piles of dried mud.

'I can get through,' I yelled as I dug the stick into the pile of mud. One of the men threw me a shovel.

'*Merci*,' I said and pushed a great lump of it into the knee-deep, reddish-brown sludge beside the path.

Another man climbed down from the mud pile and took the shovel from me, moving the mud in a matter of minutes.

'You fall into the mud,' called the Indian man lying on his side in a tone of casual certainty for my fate.

Don't look at the hole, I repeated to myself as a mantra, and got back on the TT. I opened the throttle, using the bike's power to keep me steady on the narrow path. I reached the other side and stopped to wave farewell to the men. The African and Indian truck drivers had crawled out from the shade. Mamas and small children clapped loudly. The African bog-hole men cheered, a few pumped the air with fists.

'*Merci, merci*!' I shouted back.

Epulu was just around the next bend. Against what seemed insurmountable odds, I had made it. Alone, I had conquered the mud highway – and if I could do that, I reasoned, I was capable of anything.

11

FOREST PEOPLE
ZAIRE

The campsite operated by the Okapi Breeding and Research Station was nestled close to the banks of the Epulu River, which was still swollen and fast-flowing from the last of the wet-season rains. The neat lawn, picnic tables and iron-roof shelters with smooth cement floors seemed out of place in a world where progress struggled to penetrate the thick, dark, green rainforest that stretched across the heart of Africa. The campground was deserted of campers and I had my pick of spots, so I parked the TT under the shelter closest to the river and pitched my tent, feeling pleased I would be dry if it rained. The caretaker, a slim young African man neatly dressed in khaki, appeared from nowhere, and as I paid the small fee for camping he pointed to the river and simply said 'many crocodiles'.

A short stroll away, at the end of the campsite, was a small rectangular cement-block building. Inside were two cement laundry tubs, a flush toilet (of all things!) and a shower, where I washed off the day's mud under the cold water, which was refreshing and invigorating in the tropical heat. In the late afternoon I headed down the narrow path fringed with ferns and plants with large, dark-green leaves; a carpet of thick green moss covered the moist ground. The path led to a fenced compound where a dozen okapi stood alone, one per pen. Freaks of nature, these strange, solitary, antelope-like animals were partly why I'd taken this 400-kilometre

155

round-trip detour. The other reason was a week-long hike deep into the rainforest organised through the Okapi Breeding and Research Station.

The okapi had once freely roamed the nearly 63,000-square-kilometre Ituri Rainforest surrounding Epulu, but poaching and the tradition of pygmy men giving okapi skins to their brides had pushed this harmless, shy creature to near extinction. The research station's breeding and anti-poaching program, paid for with funds donated by UNESCO and by a good many zoos from around the world, was now the okapi's only hope of survival.

From their pens, these freakish beasts stared at me unfazed, their luxurious reddish-brown coats shimmering in the dappled sunlight that filtered through the forest canopy. I leaned on the fence and one of them slowly ambled towards me. I stared into its moist eyes, which glistened with my own reflection. We were two solitary beings living our purpose on this earth for a brief moment in time.

While I enjoyed the company of all the people I met, like the okapi I also enjoyed my solitude. Alone, I had no distractions to mask the growing influence of my intuition, which told me unequivocally that I was surrounded by a hidden energy as real as the radiation levels I had once monitored at the uranium mine in Kakadu. Solitude also gave me time to think about the coincidences and chance encounters that had been occurring with ever-increasing regularity the further I travelled. Since surviving Lake Turkana, when help had miraculously arrived to carry Sharif and me to safety, I no longer worried about the next hour, day, week or month. To be completely devoid of worry was liberating. I had been set free to drift where circumstance, combined with my own gut feeling, directed me. I lived completely in the now, as though there were no past and no future, and this detour to Epulu simply felt like the right thing to do.

I was about halfway to Kisangani, which was about as close to the middle of Africa as one could get. From Epulu the sensible thing to do would be to continue riding along the bog-hole highway to Kisangani, where I planned to take a barge down the Zaire River to Kinshasa to reach the west coast. But that would be far too easy, and would mean missing out on hiking the majestic Rwenzori Mountains that straddled the border of Zaire and Uganda. I was not in Africa simply to beeline from the southern tip to the northern-most point. So here I was in Epulu, and when it was time to move on I would ride halfway back along the same road to the village of Mambasa and then take a detour along a track to Beni, a reasonable-sized town where I could buy supplies for the Rwenzori hike.

*

At any one time, there are thousands of people travelling the world by motorcycle. It is the vehicle that carries us ordinary folk to extraordinary places so that we can explore those unknown frontiers. So when I returned to my tent to find two Germans travelling on mud-encrusted BMW R100GS's camped nearby, I was not at all surprised.

The two men in their mid-thirties – both tall, blond, lean and somewhat tired – had ridden down through Europe, North and West Africa, across the Central African Republic and into Zaire in only three months. They thought I was absolutely crazy to continue my travels into the interior, where there were armed rebels and Mobutu's unpaid soldiers, who all knew I carried cash that amounted to a small fortune to them. But despite these cold, hard facts, I refused to consider the danger. I refused to live in a world ruled by fear. Instead, I wanted to live in a world ruled by *ubuntu*.

'I'm loving every minute of it. The people, the forest, the mountains and even the desert. The freedom of motorcycling and the challenge. It's living life,' I babbled, unable to keep up with the excitement I felt for the Africa that had embraced me. 'Except the mud, I don't think much of that.'

The two men nodded in agreement, their heads and shoulders bent in defeat at the hands of a different Africa that they perceived as the enemy rather than a friend. 'We need a beach as fast as possible,' they chorused and looked at me as though I'd been exposed to too much African sun.

Later, over dinner and beers in a rectangular mud-and-thatch hut a short walk from the campsite, which was the only place serving food, I tried to convince them to spend the following day at Epulu. They needed time out to relax, sleep in, catch their breath and, by the look of their sweat-stained T-shirts, do some washing.

The Germans weren't the first motorcycle travellers I'd met who were rushing through Africa as though they just wanted to cross it off as a super-human feat of endurance. I was learning that Africa does not take too kindly to this sort of impatience. Because then what? Return to normal life – whatever that was meant to be?

I knew this ride through Africa would end all too soon for me. I knew it was a once-in-a-lifetime adventure, a rare opportunity to grow and learn things about myself that would be impossible under the crushing influence of Western social norms. No, I would not be rushing through Africa, where I'd discovered a completely different way of being. I would take my time and savour every moment of my journey, which was already nearly a year long.

As we ate our dinner of goat-meat stew and manioc (a thick porridge made from ground cassava), a tall, dark-haired, middle-aged American came over to us. Unshaven and dressed in khaki shorts and shirt, he had a commanding presence as he towered above us inside the cramped confines of the restaurant, with its low ceiling of forest timber and paraffin lamps hanging from its beams.

'Hi. I'm Leo,' he said and explained that he worked for a film company funded by a German wildlife group. It was his job to capture rare rainfor-est animals, mostly nocturnal ones, and film them in a specially constructed set designed to look like their natural habitat.

'So I expect you'll want to visit the pygmies,' Leo said between mouth-fuls of goat stew.

A visit to a pygmy camp was one of the highlights of the overland truck tours and was a profitable business for the pygmies of Epulu. But the thought of being hassled to death by four-foot people who looked at me with utter contempt held little appeal.

'I'd like to hike into the forest but I'd prefer to leave the pygmies in peace. I'm sure they've had enough of gawking tourists. Besides, I'll probably pass through a pygmy village on the ride from Mambasa to Beni,' I said, and explained that I intended to take this back road as a short cut to reach the Rwenzori Mountains.

'There's a pygmy camp about two days walk from Epulu. You'll be welcome there. They never see tourists so they'll be gawking at you,' he laughed. 'You should do it. The hike into the rainforest alone is well worth it. 'You won't get another opportunity like this. What do you say?' Leo asked raising a bushy black eyebrow questioningly.

'Okay. Sounds perfect,' I said and the Germans looked at me convinced I was, in fact, completely mad.

*

After leaving the TT in safe storage with Leo, I went to the ranger's office the next morning and organised a five-day walk for US$65. With my guide, Oscar, a quietly-spoken young African neatly dressed in khaki, two other local men who acted as porters and a pygmy man to lead the way, we set off, walking about ten kilometres back along the road towards Mambasa before turning into the thick, dark, green forest. We followed a faint path over moss-covered logs as black-and-white colobus monkeys played and chatted in the dense canopy above.

After a four-hour hike we arrived at a small clearing and a collection of dome huts made of bent saplings and covered with broad leaves. The pygmy group was an extended family of about twenty people. The men, women and older children glanced at us briefly when we entered the clearing then went back to their chores; the women busied themselves around the cooking fires while the men sat on mounds of nets made from bark rolled into string and twisted into rope. I assumed they were discussing the day's hunt – ten duikers (small forest antelopes) lay dead in a line on the ground beside the nets. The younger children stopped their chasing games and stared at us with wide eyes. The pygmies wore the bare minimum of threadbare clothes, stained the same reddish-brown as the forest floor. The men wore only shorts and the women wore a piece of cloth wrapped as a sarong.

We were not the only visitors. There was also a group of African traders from Epulu: a man and his wife, and another man with his two teenage daughters. Oscar explained they traded rice, cassava, sugar and salt for the duikers.

I followed Oscar to one of the dome huts, and asked for hot water to make coffee. We gave our gifts of salt, palm oil, sugar and tobacco to Zaire, the chief, as our payment to stay. Despite his small size, he had a commanding presence, leaving no doubt he was in charge. He accepted our gifts and called over to a woman to collect them. The gifts were all part of the fee I'd paid at the ranger's office earlier that morning. We sat on little stools made from vines and sticks and I made coffee as Zaire chatted with Oscar, laughing as he heard the latest gossip from Epulu.

'Tomorrow they take you on a hunt,' Oscar said as he spooned several scoops of sugar into his coffee. Zaire did the same.

Oscar told me that Zaire and his extended family would stay camped at this clearing for about three weeks, hunting the duiker until all within a several-kilometre radius had been caught. I asked Oscar if we had taken someone's hut, as I had brought my tent and could sleep in that. He told Zaire, who laughed.

'They like to sleep outside, around the fire on their nets or on a bed of leaves. If it rains, there are enough huts for everybody,' Oscar said.

Everything belonging to the pygmies, except the cooking pots, knives and their dirt-stained clothing, was made entirely from the forest.

One of the pygmy women retrieved a leaf-wrapped parcel from the coals and placed it on the ground near our feet. I thanked her and she smiled shyly. The little parcel contained duiker meat sprinkled with salt and chilli and as I ate the tender, juicy meat, the children watched me suspiciously. I felt like an intruder: an unwelcome visitor to their home deep in the rainforest. As I sat on the stool, I tried to look as inconspicuous as possible, writing my diary and practising French. Soon everybody forgot I was there, and I forgot about them.

'Where is the track to the creek?' I asked Oscar when he returned from chatting to the traders, who were still busy smoking the duiker meat on the opposite side of the clearing.

A number of tracks led from the dome huts into the thick forest and Oscar pointed to one of them. As I walked away from the camp, two of the pygmy girls aged about ten years joined me, running ahead to lead the way.

The creek was only about a hundred metres along a path that I could barely make out through the thick green foliage. I followed the girls down a steep bank and onto a flat rock, where I could splash my face and fill my water bottle. The girls filled their pots and sat beside me, dangling their feet in the cool running water. The creek was about five metres wide, and from the rock I had a clear view up and down its length. A dense wall, of dark-green trees, broad-leafed shrubs and ferns grew close to its banks. Moss-covered logs lay where the giant trees had fallen, vines dangled from where they were entwined above, and the shrill call of birds broke the calm silence.

One of the girls touched my arm and pointed. Further along the creek, a duiker drank. We watched this dainty creature until it sensed our presence and bounded away to disappear into the forest. The girls smiled and in that shared moment I no longer felt unwelcome.

When we returned, the same woman as before placed a pot of duiker stew and a bowl of rice at our feet and Oscar, the two porters and I ate as night fell quickly over the forest that encircled us like an impenetrable wall. Branches were thrown on the central fire, sparks flew up into the darkness, and Zaire and his extended family reclined comfortably on the piles of nets. Some of the men began jumping around animatedly. It did not matter that I did not know their language; their miming clearly told the story of the day's hunt. Zaire began to speak and the men fell quiet.

'What's going on?' I asked Oscar.

'Zaire will soon move the camp deeper into the forest. They have caught nearly all the duikers here. The ones they trapped today they walked a long way to find,' he said. 'The young men want to settle near Epulu like the other pygmies have done. They want to build huts and grow cassava. Moving further into the forest will mean the traders won't come, and they will have to go without salt, rice and cassava. They do not want to eat meat all the time. Near Epulu it is exciting. There are many different people.'

Zaire leaned back on the nets and listened to their argument, letting each man speak his turn. Then sitting upright, he spoke with a slow deliberateness that affirmed his authority.

'Zaire says it is better to stay in the forest. It will be the end of them if they move to Epulu,' Oscar said, translating.

As the chief, Zaire's decision was final. In a few days they would move the camp deeper into the forest.

Oscar explained that years ago there had not been the same demand for duikers, but with more people living in Epulu, including the many pygmies settled on its outskirts, there were many more people who wanted to eat duiker meat.

'Soon duikers will be scarce even this far from Epulu. But the forest is very big, so the pygmies have to make a choice. Either live deep within the forest or settle near places like Epulu,' he said.

'Everybody wants to be Westernised these days,' I commented. 'But it's not everything. It can be lonely and for those with no family, it can be a hard life with no money or support. Here they have each other. They have the forest,' I said, envious of their life and its eternal rhythm with the earth.

The chief stretched out on the net, his wife and children cuddled in next to him. The other families did the same and I moved back to my stool outside the dome hut. I offered Oscar and the porters cigarettes and brewed them coffee. We watched in silence as the embers of the fire faded to a faint glow. Slowly the murmurs of the pygmies ceased and I listened to the insect noises rising as a soft melody out of the surrounding forest.

*

The next morning a light drizzle fell from the grey clouds that hung heavy over the rainforest. Oscar, the two porters and I ate our breakfast of duiker stew and boiled cassava, watching the rain from where we sat inside the dome hut. In the afternoon it had stopped and we joined the pygmies on a hunt, but we didn't catch any duikers. On our return I helped the women pick bright orange mushrooms, which ordinarily I would have thought to be deadly poisonous, but when they were fried in palm oil and served with roasted duiker they gave the tender meat a delicious, spicy, slightly salty flavour. That night it rained heavily and drizzled for most of the following day, so we were forced to stay in the dome huts.

'We leave tomorrow?' Oscar asked, staring out at the rain that fell as a light mist.

The two porters looked at me expectantly.

'It's not much fun in the rain, is it,' I said, and they all nodded.

'They will hunt again in the morning. We go along. Then we leave?' Oscar asked and I agreed.

Only the elders and small children stayed behind at the camp while everyone else went on the hunt. Oscar and I followed the men, who carried the heavy rope nets on their heads and draped down their backs. Zaire carried a burning ember and, in the buttress roots of an enormous tree, a fire was lit as a ceremony to the spirits. The smoke from the burning leaves trailed up through the canopy as the men sat on their haunches watching it.

We walked in silence for about an hour, deep into the forest, and then Zaire indicated for the net to be strung out in a giant arch. Oscar and I hid behind a tree while the pygmy men did the same all along the length of the net, which stretched for over a hundred metres. The women and older children, who had silently walked ahead, now thrashed the ground with branches and yelled to scare any duikers into the net's arc. Only three duikers were caught, one near where Oscar and I were hiding. It was slaughtered by Zaire then quickly gutted, the contents squeezed out of its intestines and bowels; nothing was wasted. All was placed in a bag made of tightly woven vines. I asked Oscar about buying one of the duikers to take back to Leo to thank him for storing my motorcycle.

'What have you got to trade?' he asked.

I held up a plain faded black T-shirt, two packets of cigarettes and several safety pins, which were highly prized for digging jigger worms from bare feet.

Oscar took all of this to Zaire and a moment later returned with a still-warm duiker, which I wrapped in leaves and stuffed into my daypack.

Oscar took the bag from me and gave it to one of the porters, who had nothing to carry, as we'd given most of what we'd carried from Epulu to the chief.

'You have good life in the forest. Thank you for sharing it with me,' I said to Zaire. Oscar translated, and Zaire nodded, giving me a faint smile. I felt it as acknowledgement of a long-forgotten bond that joined us all as brothers and sisters.

It was late afternoon when we walked back into Epulu. I was totally exhausted and after buying beers in the village I headed down the path to Leo's thatched mud-brick hut and its menagerie of forest animals. He was busy with the afternoon's feeding and I helped collect snails from his vegetable garden to feed a baby potto, a nocturnal creature with soft brown fur and huge, sad eyes. Later, as Leo cooked duiker stew, I cuddled this adorable creature and it snuggled into my arms. The next day I would leave Epulu and ride to Mambasa to take a back road down to Beni.

'I've heard the bridge might be washed out,' Leo said with casual indifference as he skinned the duiker. Earlier, I'd skinned a viper snake from Leo's collection that had died the night before. I'd asked if I could have it, as I wanted to wrap its skin around the TT's handlebars near where I stored the *panga*.

'Go for it,' Leo had said shaking his head at my madness. But it was not such a silly thing to do, as the viper is Africa's most poisonous and feared of snakes. I reasoned that as I travelled into Africa's interior, where people were deeply superstitious, the sight of the viper skin would fill them with fear and respect for my courage, as they'd assume I'd killed it. The viper, along with the *panga*, would add to my aura of protection and the TT's aura of strength and indestructibility.

*

The following morning I rode away from Epulu and through the enormous bog-hole, which was now completely dry. All the trucks were gone, along with the men, women and children who'd buzzed around the bog-hole like bees drinking the abundant nectar of a huge flower. I reached Mambasa by lunch and stopped at a thatched mud-brick hut, the local restaurant.

Before I could get off the bike, two strong hands grabbed my shoulders and I turned to see Dave. Behind him were Eric and Rolf, the Canberra boys from Mama Roche's. We all grinned with delight.

'This is unbelievable,' we chorused. Each of the boys wrapped their strong arms around me in a bear-hug, repeatedly saying how worried they'd been for me travelling alone in Zaire. They were on their way to Kisangani, but had been in Mambasa for two days waiting for a lift. As we ate goat stew and manioc, often the only meal on the menu in these parts, we shared our tales of adventure since leaving Mama's a month ago.

'So what happened to climbing the Rwenzoris?' I asked.

'The soldiers have checkpoints all along the road to Mutwanga,' Eric said.

'It's too dangerous,' Rolf added.

'Don't take the road from Komanda to Beni,' Dave warned. 'The bloody soldiers will hassle you to death. We got a lift on a truck and at every checkpoint the soldiers demanded money and would hit anyone who refused with the butt of their guns. When a mama yelled at them, probably telling them to piss off, a soldier bashed her in the head. Blood ran down her face. They don't care if you're a woman,' he said and put his hand on my shoulder, gripping it tightly as if to make sure I understood the danger.

'I'm taking the short cut from here to Beni. There'll be no checkpoints,' I said.

'You're joking, aren't you? That's just a walking track,' Dave said.

'There'll be no soldiers. It'll be okay,' I replied, raising my voice to show them I knew what I was doing. I sounded impatient and I hoped I wasn't offending them, as I knew they were only concerned for my safety.

'Don't stay in the hotels in Beni. They've been taken over by the soldiers. They hang out there to get drunk and stoned,' Eric said. 'Ask for George, he's a Greek coffee merchant. We told him about you, and you can stay with him. He's expecting you.'

Over lunch, we talked about Mobuto's new money, and how everybody was in confusion and nobody knew the exchange rate. I told them of the campsite in Epulu and of my stay at the pygmy camp, but they said if they got a truck going all the way through to Kisangani they would not stop.

'It's all right for you on your motorbike. But without wheels, it's no fun hanging around in a village for days on end when you want to get moving,' Eric said.

'Will you still be in Kisangani on Christmas Day?' I asked in a pleading little-girl voice.

These three Australian boys were, at that moment, the closest thing to family I had in Africa and I hoped I would be with them on Christmas Day.

'Probably,' Rolf said and explained that they intended to buy a pirogue in Kisangani and paddle down the Zaire River for 1750 kilometres to Kinshasa.

With lunch over, we stood up and walked outside into the bright tropical sunshine, which beat down and burnt our fair skin. Each of them gave me a farewell hug, wrapping their arms around me as if the force of the hug would protect me long after we'd gone our separate ways.

'No matter what, do not stop at any roadblock. Keep riding. They won't shoot. They won't waste their bullets or don't have any,' Dave said with his arm around my shoulders as we walked over to the TT. 'You'll be okay. See you for Christmas. We'll have a few beers.'

I got back on the bike and rode out of Mambasa, leaving behind its sprawling collection of thatched mud-brick huts and the boys from Canberra with whom I shared such a strong bond of camaraderie. Their adventure in Africa, I imagined, was the grand finale of a long list of adventures they'd shared since childhood. I envied them, as I'd never experienced such friendship. My family had moved often during my childhood. My parents would buy a block of land, build a house, sell it and move on, using the profits to buy a bigger block of land and build a bigger house. It was a process that had an average turnaround of two years and meant that I had attended eight different schools, including three different high schools. It had been an interesting and varied life, but I also felt I'd missed out on those strong friendships that emerge out of a shared history.

In my search for the track to Beni, I followed a street that headed east. To confirm I was heading in the right direction, I stopped at a workshop and asked the African mechanic. He pointed to a man on a bicycle riding along a narrow path that disappeared into the thickness of the forest.

'Beni,' he said and gave me a wave, his hand held high as if sending forth well-wishes for the arduous journey ahead. Without a moment of hesitation, I, too, disappeared into the dark, impenetrable wall of trees.

12

WHERE GOD GOES TO GET AWAY FROM IT ALL
ZAIRE

'George not here, gone to Nairobi,' said the Greek man, with a sharpness intended to dismiss me. He looked to be about fifty and had sleek black hair flecked with grey and little patience for unannounced visitors. He glared at me for a brief second before returning to his paperwork, which was stacked in two neat piles on an oversized wooden desk, an antique imported from Europe. He was a coffee merchant, and in Beni, in the tropical highlands of eastern Zaire, coffee was big business. It was mid-afternoon and I stood before him in an enormous office, hoping none of the red mud on my jeans and boots would fall onto the gleaming polished floorboards.

From Mambasa, it had taken me the good part of two days to reach the quaint township of Beni with its red-brick bungalows. Thankfully the bridge had not been washed out as Leo had warned. The walking track that disappeared into the dense, dark-green rainforest had soon become a narrow two-wheeled road that was smooth and mostly dry. I'd pitched my tent the previous night at a pygmy village, where I'd indicated with my hands held against my tilted head that I needed somewhere to sleep. The day's ride to Beni had been pleasant and uneventful, some of it on wonderful smooth tarmac.

'I am a friend of Dave, Eric and Rolf, the Australians,' I said to the Greek man, hurriedly trying to explain why a mud-encrusted wild woman with matted hair who smelt of sweat was standing in his office.

'What do you want?' he asked as he shuffled a thick wad of papers.

'The Australian boys told George about me. They said it's not safe at the hotels with the soldiers,' I said.

He ignored me. I stood motionless for a few awkward seconds, regretting troubling him. 'Sorry to bother you,' I said finally.

He didn't look up and I was left to stare at the top of his head.

As I turned to leave, a tall, middle-aged Greek man with black, wavy hair bounded into the office with jovial good humour, in complete contrast to his business partner. 'Ah. Hello. You must be the Australian girl. The boys Dave, Eric and Rolf tell me about you. Come, you stay with me,' he said. 'I am Tarso.'

I followed Tarso's Land Rover as it chugged along the main street, pulling up outside a set of high steel gates, which were immediately opened by an elderly African man who walked with a stoop. Tarso directed me to park the TT close to the whitewashed brick house at the end of the gravel drive. Low cement stairs led to a wide veranda fringed by a two-metre-wide rose garden. Deep red, soft yellow and milky pink roses bloomed in all their glory as a striking display of colour against the backdrop of the house and its dazzlingly white plaster walls. This was the colonial Africa of a bygone era, where buildings had not turned to mud and dust and broken windows.

After leaving my muddy boots and jacket on the wide veranda, I was shown to a room with a bathroom next to it. Everything in the house was white: the tiles on the floor, the walls, the leather lounge, the guest room.

'Bath,' Tarso pointed and turned to leave.

I had expected a simple room or to pitch my tent on their lawn and be on my way the next morning.

Once I was spotlessly clean, I joined Tarso on the veranda for beers. He was sitting with another coffee dealer, who introduced himself as

Francis. He was a kindly Belgian man with thinning grey hair who shared the house with Tarso. I told them about my travels and my plans to trek the Rwenzoris, and that I'd leave in the morning.

'Why you want to go there? It is very dangerous. The rebels are in this area and the army has checkpoints all along the road to Mutwanga. You must not do this,' Tarso said with a frown that knitted his bushy black eyebrows together as one.

'I'd still like to give it a try,' I said quickly and realised I sounded naive in the face of such obvious dangers. 'The Rwenzoris are described as one of the most magnificent places on earth. I planned this hike long before I even came to Africa,' I said, trying to sound prepared and capable.

I had planned to spend one night in Beni, buy supplies, and then ride the forty kilometres to the Rwenzori Mountains, but I ended up staying three days at Tarso and Francis's insistence. My few items of clothing were washed, ironed and folded, and Tarso's gardener washed my motorcycle to the cleanest it had been since it was new. With the thick layer of mud removed, I changed the oil and serviced it, checking for any loose nuts and bolts and for any damage and emerging problems. The TT was in perfect order despite all I had asked of it.

As a guest of the Greeks, each evening was the same – an extravagant dinner at a Greek coffee-merchant's house set amongst serene gardens in a secure compound. All were as luxurious as each other.

'Do you do this every night?' I asked Francis, who, like myself, felt left out because he did not speak Greek.

'The coffee harvest has just finished. It has been a good year and they celebrate,' he said.

'It must have been a nightmare to do business with the old currency,' I said and he smiled at the memory.

'Before the nouveaux zaire we'd go to the villages with two trucks. One for the coffee beans and one full of money to pay the villagers,' he laughed. 'It became such a joke. We talked in tonnes of money.'

When I'd arrived in Zaire over a week ago, the rate was three nouveaux zaires to one dollar. While the bank rate had not changed, the black market rate was now 25 nouveaux zaires. Francis thought it would level out at 100 by Christmas, which was only two weeks away.

The Greeks had plenty of small denomination notes, and were only too happy to change money with me. Before it lost any value, I immediately spent it all on petrol, cigarettes, and food for the Rwenzori hike.

On my third day in Beni, I was sitting on Tarso's veranda writing in my diary and sipping strong black coffee, when Graham, the gangly New Zealander travelling on a Yamaha XT500, wandered through the gates. We'd met at Tiwi Beach during the weeks I'd meandered along Kenya's coast after Lake Turkana. He was on his way to see the gorillas at Rumangabo, then planned to cross Rwanda to Tanzania and ride back down to Cape Town. He'd been passing through Beni the previous day when the electrics on his motorcycle had failed, but he'd fixed the problem and would leave in the morning. He was staying at a local hotel and when the owner had told him about the girl on a motorbike he knew it was me.

'You are very lucky you're staying with the Greeks,' he said. 'Last night I was having dinner when the soldiers came into the hotel bar. They were drunk and stoned and demanded to see my documents and searched my pockets. The soldier in charge found my pepper spray. I thought for sure he would press the nozzle. He asked what it was, and I told him it was for asthma. *Demonstration*, he asked, and I just said *medication*, and pretended not to understand. Thankfully, they got bored. I hurried back to my room and locked the door,' Graham said, nervously combing long fingers through his honey-blond hair.

That night, Graham and I had a farewell dinner at the Hotel Beni in its luxurious dining room where a full set-menu of vegetable soup, roast chicken with all the trimmings and chocolate cake cost US$2 each. After days of speaking in broken English, it was good to talk without searching for the words. I told Graham of my plans to hike the Rwenzoris and asked if he would join me.

'I'd love to, but I've already extended my trip by a month. I've got to get home if I'm still to have a job. Be careful up there,' he said and reached across the table to squeeze my hand, which felt small and delicate in his. It was the first time in nearly a year that a man had touched me with what felt like affection and pangs of desire tingled inside me. I looked into his blue eyes but they were only filled with a genuine brotherly concern for my wellbeing.

'Don't worry,' I said. 'The Greeks are panic merchants.' I told him that I'd talked to a number of African shop owners, who'd advised me to pass through the checkpoints early in the morning. 'They'll still be asleep then,' I explained. 'The soldiers start drinking and smoking dope when they wake up about mid-morning, and continue until late into the night as they celebrate the day's takings.'

The Africans all warned me not to stop and not to pass in the afternoon, when I would not stand a chance of slipping through.

Graham left the next morning and I wished circumstances were different – that he could toss in his job. I never asked what he did. We embraced and he told me over and over to be careful. He was a practical man who operated on facts, while I travelled with an unwavering belief in positive outcomes, that things would always work out and there was no need to worry.

*

I left Beni early the following morning. I carried only what I needed: tent, sleeping bag, petrol stove, warm clothes and food, including several packets of dried curried soya mince I'd bought from a camping shop in Nairobi especially for the Rwenzori hike. In Beni I'd also purchased pasta, rice, peanuts, coffee, sugar, cocoa and milk powder. The daughter of one of the African shop owners gave me the gift of a kilogram bag of boiled sweets. The rest of my things I stored at Tarso's house.

On the forty-kilometre ride to Mutsora, a ranger station and village where I'd begin the Rwenzori hike, I easily passed through the first couple of checkpoints. The soldiers were still asleep and did not even stir as the

TT rumbled past. But as I approached a checkpoint before a bridge, I saw that a barrier made of logs and sticks lay across the road. Several soldiers lounged under a tree. I accelerated and as I sped past, I checked my mirror and saw them stagger to their feet and look down the road, confused at the thing that had just roared through.

The Mutsora ranger station looked deserted, but as I got off the bike a local man dressed in rags and in bare feet appeared from nowhere and indicated I follow him into the large rectangular stone building with a rusting corrugated-iron roof. It sat next to a stream that flowed from the mountains, which towered over the village.

'Yes. We can organise trek for you,' said the park conservator, a big man with a round black face and ready smile. 'I find the key,' he said, rummaging through the drawers of an enormous desk in his gloomy office that sat at the end of a long, dark corridor. It had been over a month since the last climb, but the conservator assured me there were no rebels in the area.

'With no tourists to ambush, there is no reason for the rebels to hike all the way up the mountain. They have gone to rob the tourists who climb the mountain from Uganda. Ah, here it is,' he said, and held up a large brass key to the climbing hut, which sat near the main building. I followed him and, once inside the mud-brick and thatch hut, he brushed aside the dust and cobwebs on the counter before opening the hiking register, a large leather-bound book with yellowed pages, and recorded my details. A five-day climb would cost US$75, of which US$55 was park fees, including two nights' camping at the ranger station – the night before and the night after the climb. The fee also included a guide and two porters. The conservator's nephew, who was studying park management, would also join us on the hike, which was a good thing, because he was the only one who could speak even a little English.

The Rwenzori mountain range, known as the 'mountains of the moon', borders Uganda and Zaire. It rises as a gentle slope from Uganda but it is a steep, almost vertical climb of 4500 metres to the summit hut on the Zaire side, providing the perfect conditions for dramatic changes in its alien-like vegetation. With the end of the wet season the rain had moved off to the east, and the thick, heavy clouds now hugged the slopes in Uganda, leaving the steep Zaire side cloud-free.

With the TT locked up in the ranger station's storeroom, the five of us left at daylight, quietly strolling through the village to reach the track to start our ascent. Markus, my guide, wore thongs and carried nothing except a wool blanket and jacket. The first porter, James, carried a cloth sack filled with dried fish and a ten-kilo bag of manioc. The second porter, Lardie, carried my Gearsack balanced on his head. It was laden with food, warm clothes and my sleeping bag. All three men, aged about thirty, were fit with sinewy muscles. I could see the hike would be an easy stroll for them. However, the conservator's nephew, Tombo, a slightly pudgy youth with black curly hair cropped close to frame a happy round face, would struggle along with myself to keep up. Tombo carried his own things in a daypack, and I carried my camera, water bottle and two hands of bananas.

We passed mud huts, small plots of cassava, coffee bushes, clumps of banana plants and mango trees heavy with ripe fruit. After the farms, the track narrowed and headed almost vertically up the mountain, which was overgrown with ferns and nettles.

On the lower slopes the vegetation was dense rainforest, and we hacked our way through the overgrown path, crossing mountain streams and passing giant wild banana plants and huge hardwoods with vines and moss hanging from the mist-shrouded branches. Tombo and I found the almost vertical track hard going and insisted we rest often. I was in no hurry, and sat on the edge of the path where an opening in the forest gave spectacular cloud-free views out over the forested plains below.

We arrived late afternoon at the first hut, Kalongi, at 2138 metres, and sat exhausted on the veranda. Lardie cooked a dinner of manioc with a sauce made from the dried fish and flavoured with orange fungi and bright-red chillies he'd picked during the hike. It was a tasty addition, Tombo assured me, but I declined, as even with the chillies it smelled slightly rotten, and was very much an acquired taste. Instead, I cooked my own dinner – a pot of curried soya mince and rice.

The porters only ate twice a day. It was always the same meal of manioc and dried fish, so the food I gave them was a very special treat, Tombo told me. Each morning I cooked a pot of porridge with sliced banana, milk powder, sugar and cinnamon, and made them all cups of steaming hot chocolate. At lunch we ate peanuts and sucked on boiled sweets.

The second day's walk to Mahungu hut, at 3310 metres, was an exhausting, almost vertical hike. In some places we had to climb up slippery rocks. At first the track was very overgrown, and we could not see it for the tangle of vines and stinging thistles, which Lardie hacked away with his *panga*.

We stopped for lunch near a shrine made of old twisted sticks that stood like a little tepee about a foot high on a windswept granite rock. Bits of grey lichen lay on the damp wood as though placed there by forest goblins. Old zaire notes and US bills in one- and five-dollar denominations littered the shrine, and more money was tied with bits of string to the sticks at the little entrance.

Like others before us, we gave our offerings – nouveaux zaires and a handful of sweets – to the mountain spirits. I asked the spirits to please keep the sun shining while we were on the mountain.

'Why doesn't someone take the money?' I asked Tombo.

'They would not dare. The money belongs to the God of the Mountain,' he said with deadly seriousness.

The last couple of hours to Mahungu we climbed over a tangle of twisted tree roots of giant heather. A thick blanket of moss covered the boggy ground and silver-grey lichen hung heavy from the branches.

My legs ached and I was totally exhausted by the time Tombo and I struggled up the last few steep metres to the hut. The others had arrived about half an hour ahead of us. We staggered inside and were welcomed by a warm fire made from the wood they'd collected on the trek. During the day I walked in canvas shoes, leggings and a short-sleeved shirt, but as the sun disappeared a cold wind blew, and the nights were freezing. We cooked our food and sat close to the fire to eat and then sipped hot chocolate. Tombo and the porters slept near the fire, as their few clothes and single blankets offered little warmth, while I slept on one of the bunk beds, snug in my feather-down sleeping bag.

On the hike to Kiondo hut the next morning, we climbed over more of the twisted roots, old and gnarled and covered in a thick blanket of bright-green moss. I half expected to see forest goblins and fairies around each bend of the boggy path. Instead, iridescent green chameleons sat motionless on the branches, watching us with their large rotating eyes.

After passing through this ancient enchanted forest, the track opened to clear views over the mountains and valleys below. We rested in warm sunshine on a thick carpet of greyish-green moss surrounded by giant lobelia, each long stalk blooming with tiny bright-blue flowers.

The last stretch, an almost vertical ascent to Kiondo hut (4300 metres), was by far the most difficult. The small stone hut perched on a barren ridge always seemed just out of our reach. The porters and guide walked ahead and an hour later Tombo and I stumbled through the door, my legs quivering like jelly.

In the last of the afternoon light and with a mug of steaming hot chocolate, I walked to the edge of the ridge and sat on a rocky outcrop. Before me stood the majestic snow-covered peaks of Margarita, Alexandra and Stanley; below were deep, dark lakes. Waterfalls cascaded hundreds of metres into the lower valleys. Misty clouds floated up, blown by the wind to cover me in a dense fog, and then were gone as quickly as they had appeared.

In a sudden moment of illumination, experienced as an intuitive tug in the pit of my stomach, I realised that the act of reaching the top was not about conquering but about communing – about being closer to something powerful. As I sat precariously on the rock, I understood why people search for spiritual solace at the top of mountains. Mountains, these highest of high places on the earth, are like magnets that not only draw us to them but also to other forces as well. Forces that flow around the earth as it orbits eternally around the sun. This understanding was palpable.

Travelling alone had afforded me the opportunity to become in tune with my intuition and it was now so much a habit that I never questioned it, never doubted it. I knew I had stumbled across a universal law, like gravity or the pull of the tides or the rotation of the earth. It was enormous and majestic, like the three giant mountain peaks that rose before me as three sentinels guarding the universe's greatest secret.

The mist suddenly lifted and long fingers of sunlight reached down to bathe the snow-capped mountain peaks in ethereal splendour. Then the light was gone and the clouds descended, along with a biting cold. I quickly retreated to the hut where the guys sat close to the fireplace, feeding it with the legs of a chair. The hut's furniture was the only fuel available, and the porters had smashed a chair into pieces to warm us and to cook our dinner.

I mixed a pot of packet tomato soup and made croutons by frying manioc rolled into little balls. The men spoke Swahili and as they talked amongst themselves I understood enough to know they were talking about me and the return to Matsora. Tombo translated and told me that only Lardie and I would go on to Moraine hut at the base of the mountain peaks, and the others would return to the first hut, where we would meet them the following afternoon. Markus did not want to go on to Moraine as he said the ropes were old and were probably broken.

'It is very dangerous. It has been a long time since anyone has climbed the mountain and he is not equipped. He wear only thongs, while Lardie has boots and warm clothings,' Tombo said as he held his blanket tightly around his shoulders. 'It is cold for us at night. We have only one blanket each, while you sleep warm in your sack,' he remarked as he tossed a chair leg onto the fire.

'No, it is too far to go in one day. You wait for us at the second hut,' I insisted.

Markus glared at me. I could not understand his role on this hike. So far Lardie had acted as my guide, as well as my porter, much more than Markus. Eventually, though, he agreed that they would wait for us at the second hut, as it was the rule that we all descend together, and it was espe-cially essential for me to descend with Markus, my nominated guide.

In the morning Tombo, Markus and James headed down the mountain while Lardie and I hiked to Moraine hut (4500 metres) and the snow line.

From Kiondo hut we descended a steep path towards Grey Lake, hang-ing onto the weathered ropes, which Lardie had inspected to make sure they would not snap under our weight. When we needed to traverse the edge of a cliff, we used the natural hand and foot holds on the bare rock rather than relying on the ropes, which were worn and frayed. I looked down to the valleys far below: a misplaced foot could be fatal. As a warn-ing, Lardie told me, in a mix of Swahili and English, that years ago a tourist had fallen on this section and broken his leg, so Lardie had had to carry him down the mountain to Matsora.

It was a clear morning, a rarity at high altitudes in the Rwenzoris. The sun warmed us, and I tied my jacket around my waist as we stood on the large, flat granite rocks fringing the icy lake; above, only the very top of Mount Stanley was shrouded in cloud. All around we had clear views of the rugged mountains set against a dark-blue sky. The lower slopes were covered with a fine dusting of snow from the previous night's fall.

We walked on, passing through a forest of giant tree groundsels that were upwards of eight metres tall. The Rwenzoris' rich volcanic soil and equatorial humidity, even at 4500 metres, provided optimum conditions for these alpine plants to reach dizzying heights.

We used the flattened tops of clumps of tough grass as stepping stones to cross the boggy ground. Crunching through snow that shimmered in the morning sun, we finally reached Moraine hut. Cold and solitary, it sat on a wind-blown outcrop. Next to the few names on the wall inside I scrawled mine in charcoal: 'Heather Ellis here 16/12/1993' and I drew a picture of the TT so it, too, would be immortalised in this magical land.

Cloud finally descended and Lardie and I quickly walked down the mountain in a fine mist of rain over slippery rocks, mud and a tangle of exposed tree roots. A fall would surely result in a broken or twisted ankle.

We reached the second hut late in the afternoon and found it deserted. Tombo had left a note on a scrap of paper. In big letters scrawled in charcoal were the words: 'Too cold here.' They had descended without me after all.

The walk to Matsora felt like the most difficult. The mountain was shrouded in thick cloud and the sunshine that had illuminated a magical fantasy world on the hike up was gone. There was nothing but greyness and mist and I felt the searing pain in my muscles with each step. Several times I slipped down the steep muddy track as I tried to keep up with Lardie, who forged ahead with great strides of his long legs.

We reached the bottom and Matsora Park Headquarters by late afternoon and I pitched my tent beside the creek that babbled down from the mountains. I looked up and felt truly blessed to have visited a place of such magnificent wonder, where God must surely go to get away from it all.

13

THE FIRST CHRISTMAS
ZAIRE

The morning after the hike down the Rwenzoris, I returned early to Beni, again riding through the roadblocks before the soldiers stirred from the previous night of alcohol- and cannabis-fuelled revelry. I arrived at Tarso's immaculate whitewashed house as he and Francis were eating breakfast on their veranda, which was filled with the perfume of a rose garden in full bloom. As I feasted on crusty bread rolls, cheeses and cold cuts washed down with freshly brewed coffee, my generous hosts told me that they had fully expected I would never return; that surely, I would come to some horrible end at the hands of the rebels on the mountain slopes.

'I am here. I survived and now I share your wonderful breakfast,' I gushed, grateful for the feast but also sounding a little like a prophet who had spent too much time meditating on a high mountain top – which I had.

I was learning there were two distinct versions of danger in Africa: the expatriate version and the African version. To the coffee merchants, Africa was a frightening, mercenary place fraught with risk, but the African people shared a different version with me. It was based on the reality of the current circumstances, not any perceived fears, and I chose to listen to their advice.

Before leaving Beni, Tarso and Francis insisted I visit their coffee factory where the beans, grown in the pristine equatorial conditions, were roasted and bagged. As well as half a kilogram of ground coffee, they gave me a handful of still-warm Arabica beans straight from the ovens and I sucked on these during the five-hour ride to Rumangabo. The caffeine gave me a pleasant buzz as I rode along the mostly smooth dirt road, winding my way past clusters of mud-and-thatch huts and crops of bananas and cassava growing in abundance in the rich volcanic soils.

I arrived at Rumangabo in the late afternoon, just before the park office closed, and arranged a visit for US$60 to a mountain gorilla group of about fifteen individuals that lived on the gentle slopes of the dormant Virungu volcano.

The next morning, with two guides and two armed guards, we hiked for about three hours until we came upon a twenty-metre-wide path of destruction – trampled bushes, felled saplings, trees ripped of branches, and huge piles of shit covered in tiny black flies. We then simply followed this path until, an hour later, we found the gorilla family feeding on the leafy vegetation in a small clearing deep within the thick forest.

Visits from tourists had, over the years, habituated the group to human contact, and when we found them they looked at us with disinterest as they munched on vegetation, groomed each other and played. It was midday and the troop had stopped to rest. They were quiet and I was told I could mingle amongst them but was to stay low, hunched over a bit, and not look at the dominant male silverback. Several of the troop mingled around me and at times brushed past me, their coarse black hair tingling the skin on my bare arms. A mother cradling her baby sat down beside me as juveniles played chasing games around us. I looked into her eyes, which shone with a loving tenderness as the infant clung to her. It was a shared moment of woman to woman: of mother to the mother I would later become. Keeping a protective watch, the proud silverback, massive and powerful with enormous thick arms, sat back on the thick vegetation and, in complete contentment, let out a loud fart.

I hoped the government realised mountain gorillas were far more valuable alive than dead, even just for the revenue earned from the tourist dollar. But Zaire was unsafe for tourists and was likely to remain so for many years. The gorillas lived on borrowed time. Farmers wanted to clear more land to grow coffee and poachers wanted the profits from gorilla meat or body parts used in traditional medicine and as grotesque souvenirs. Babies were the most prized and were sold to Zaire's elite, who could afford such expensive pets.

I left Rumangabo early the following morning for the seven-hour ride to Bukavu, most of which was on smooth, hard-packed dirt. I detoured around the roadblocks, as the soldiers were preoccupied with extracting payment from the vehicles that had been forced to stop. I passed makeshift barriers set up by teenage boys who demanded a few zaires from the drivers to move them. Trucks, of course, would go straight through, scattering the sticks and small trees felled with razor-sharp *pangas*. I rode past enterprising boys as young as six who stood beside potholes they had repaired, hoping grateful drivers would give them a tip. Most did. Where there were no potholes they dug new ones and then refilled them and waited with angelic faces for payment. I had just missed a fierce storm that had uprooted trees, and rode skidding and sliding through the mud, which covered the road like pea soup. But soon there were no more barriers and no more mud, and in the coolness of late afternoon I rode into Bukavu, a city of crumbling colonial brick buildings that sprawled over the valleys and low hills on the southern shores of Lake Kivu. I booked into the Hotel Metropole, where a room with a toilet, a deep bath and endless hot water cost US$4.

Before the ride into Zaire's interior, where telecommunications were non-existent, I needed to phone my parents. They were unlikely to hear from me for the next two, possibly three, months. Even in relatively modernised Bukavu there were no phones, so the next morning I rode across the border into Rwanda, where there was a phone at the post office in Gisuma. Down a line that crackled with static, I wished my parents a merry Christmas and advised them not to worry that there would be no letters from me until I reached Kinshasa. The call lasted a matter of minutes and cost US$15, but I could not afford more. I ended the call repeating that they were not to worry. I was okay.

In truth, I was more than okay. I felt invincible, as my confidence and physical strength had grown exponentially. My muscles were strong from the weeks of riding on roads that were a constant test of endurance. I felt so much a part of the TT that when I rode it, I somehow became one with it, as though flesh blended with metal at a level far beyond mere physical existence.

The next morning, before leaving Bukavu, I also posted a letter to my parents through the Anglican Mission. It would go on the African Inland Mission plane the next day to Nairobi. Since arriving in Africa, I had made a point of writing long, detailed accounts of my travels and posting these letters home every week without fail. I handed the letter to the minister, a no-nonsense, tall, silver-haired Australian in his late sixties.

'Thank you. It's for my parents. This will be the last I can send till I reach Kinshasa. I'll take a barge from Kisangani. I'm meeting some Australian friends there for Christmas,' I said, sounding upbeat at the thought of celebrating with the Canberra boys.

'You'll never make it in two days,' he said with a stern look that clearly said I was completely out of my depth, in a country that he considered had little compassion for single white females travelling alone. I just nodded, not wanting anything to burst my bubble of optimism.

I had to make it. In two days it would be Christmas and I was carrying a one-kilogram cheese I'd purchased for US$8 from a fromagerie in downtown Bukavu. Beer brewing, it seemed, was not the only skill the Belgians had left behind in Zaire. The cheese was pure luxury and was my Christmas present for Dave, Eric and Rolf.

The 700-kilometre highway from Bukavu to Kisangani cut a wide swathe through impenetrable rainforest. It had started as a joint aid project between the German and Chinese governments in the early 1980s. The Chinese started from Bukavu and the Germans from Kisangani, but when construction far exceeded budget the highway was never completed and several sections of it remained unfinished. Over the past ten years, lack of maintenance and heavy seasonal rain had riddled the tarmac with potholes, which I dodged as I passed through the dense rainforest and large stands of giant bamboo. But there was none of the slippery red mud I feared so much and I fell into a false sense of security. This is not so bad, I thought, and leaned back into the soft comfort of the Gearsack, fully expecting the ride to Kisangani to be an easy two days under a cloud-free blue sky.

As I neared a range of low hills, the road slowly climbed and here construction of the highway ended abruptly. I stopped where the tarmac gave way to thick mud. Recent rains and the passing of many trucks transporting goods to Kisangani had turned what lay before me into one almost continuous bog-hole. It might be an enduro rider's dream, but it was my worst nightmare.

I sat down on the edge of the tarmac, my boots resting in the mud, and lit a cigarette, mentally preparing myself for the struggle that lay ahead. We can do this, I said to reassure both myself and the TT. Riding up a hill on a road of thick, squashy, wet mud looked an impossible feat, but it was a feat purely in the physical sense. Experience had taught me that impossible feats were the norm on this ride through Africa. I thought back to the rocky gullies in the stone country of northern Kenya and the mud roads over the past two weeks in Zaire. The TT and I had tackled them all head on, and had made it through only because I'd refused to be overcome by weakness and fear. Instead, I'd believed I would make it, and I had. If I fell, well, events would unfold to help me on my way. This is how it always happened. Why should I doubt it would not be this way on the mud highway from hell?

Before tackling the mud, I topped up the bike's tank with petrol from an old five-litre plastic container a garage had given me in Bukavu. My ten-litre jerry was also full. I was carrying the extra fuel because the Australian minister had advised that it was unlikely I'd be able to buy any on the way. The bike's twenty-one-litre tank had a range of 400 kilometres, with fifty on reserve. If all went well, with the extra ten litres I would reach Kisangani on fumes late afternoon on Christmas Eve.

I started the bike and the sound of its engine, a deep rumble, echoed through the rainforest that lined the road as a solid wall of dark-green foliage. I put it in gear and as the thick enduro tyres hit the mud, it slid out of control, but I did not fall. I steered it up over the first section of the range, my arms tense as my muscles strained. When the road levelled, I rode on the hard-packed walking track that skirted a bog-hole. Here, too, Africa was one village, and when I did fall there was no shortage of people offering to help. The recent heavy rains at the end of the wet season meant that business for the bog-hole men, the women who cooked from blackened pots and the children who sold cigarettes was booming, when normally it would be very quiet. The African truck drivers, bored with being stuck for days, cheered me on as I rode through, laughing when I lost control and stood up covered in mud from head to toe.

As I'd bought all the fuel and food I needed for the two-day ride to Kisangani, and planned to camp that night at the Mission in Walikale, I only carried forty nouveaux zaire, about US$2. I also had five packets of cigarettes, which I gave to the guys who helped lift my motorcycle out of the mud. Cigarettes were a universally acknowledged way to say thank you. When I got to the last packet, I handed them out singly until all but two were left, and then I pleaded I was broke, which they accepted and *au revoir*'ed me on my way.

On one of the worst stretches of mud, I followed a path beside the road and over a narrow culvert reinforced with a few sticks, strong enough for people but not for my overloaded motorcycle. The sticks collapsed and the TT and I went tumbling down the muddy bank, about a five-metre drop. I came to a stop at the bottom and looked up to see the bike wedged between two piles of mud a few metres above me. It was upside down and I quickly scrambled up the steep bank to stop my precious fuel dripping from the hole in the petrol cap. The air-bleed hose had long since broken off. With my thumb over the hole, I could only call out and wait for help. It was not long before a group of three young men walking from one village to the next came by.

'*Aide moi!*' I called to them as they looked down at me with obvious surprise.

'*Bonjour madame*. You have problem?' the tallest of the three asked.

'*Oui, oui,*' I said. 'Please help me.'

'Ah, we must talk of some money,' said the second young man who stood beside him, arms folded across his broad chest.

I reached into my jacket pocket for my forty nouveaux zaires and held the wad of crumpled, muddy notes to an outstretched hand.

'No more. I'm sorry. Exchange rate no good. I go to Kisangani,' I said, hoping they understood there was no reason for me to carry more money than necessary, as it would instantly be devalued.

'It is not enough, but we help you anyway,' said the third man, and his two friends nodded. 'It is far to Kisangani. You will need it for food.'

The young men gave their help because I needed it. This was the African way I had come to expect. While at first I was often seen as business, an opportunity to make money, attitudes quickly changed when people realised how far I had travelled and how far I still had to go. This was often followed with the words 'Long journey. Much courage' and sighs of reverence for what my journey meant, both in hardship and in terms of a search of some greater, unspoken meaning. Their ways and words always empowered me, and the deeper I travelled into Africa the deeper was my admiration for their profound sense of what it means to be human. Africa was not so much an undeveloped world but one where people lived for today, for their family and friends, and showed a willingness to help a stranger lying under an upside-down motorcycle in the mud. This was *ubuntu*, I was coming to realise.

The three men climbed down the bank and together, with one mighty heave, upturned the TT and then hauled it back onto the road.

The fall had made me lose confidence. I would ride through one bog-hole only to be confronted by another around the next bend. I stopped often to rest my arms, which quivered like jelly from the strain.

Darkness settled over the rainforest with the closing force of a curtain dropping on a stage performance. One moment it was day and the next it was night, as I passed a cluster of crumbling mud-and-thatch huts built beside the muddy highway. An old man wearing dirt-stained, threadbare clothes sat listening to a radio as he reclined on a chair made from sticks and tied with vines. As I rumbled to a stop beside him, he raised his hand in a wave of welcome.

'*Dormir ici avec la moto?*' I asked, placing my hands together against my head to indicate that I wanted to sleep right there next to my bike. Right there in the mud.

He nodded his understanding and pointed to one of the huts.

'*Non, merci,*' I said, and looked up at the stars that shone in a clear night sky. It was a warm, humid night, and I was so exhausted that it felt like the mud caked on my jeans and jacket was the only thing holding me up. I reached into the Gearsack and pulled out the torch and then the groundsheet from one of the panniers and laid it down next to the bike. The old man called to a boy who stood in the doorway of a hut, watching mesmerised by this strange white woman on a motorcycle who had miraculously appeared out of nowhere. The boy carried over a chair. I pulled out two of the three small loaves of bread bought in Bukavu and gave these to the old man. He smiled a toothless grin and handed the loaves to the boy, who disappeared into one of the huts. The old man indicated I should sit with him. I carried over my petrol stove, water bottle, pot and things to make coffee. As I waited for the water to boil, I ate three bananas with the third tiny loaf of bread. The old man refused when I insisted he eat some too. Once the water had boiled, I poured two cups of sweet black coffee and offered the old man the last of my two cigarettes. I had the other, and under the clear night sky he tuned his radio to the BBC World Service.

'*Merci,*' I said and he nodded in reply. He was using his precious batteries for me, as the words from the British newsreader meant nothing to him. It was the first world news I had heard since leaving Kampala a lifetime ago. I can't remember what the news was about: a war here, fighting there. The world sounded like a dangerous and frightening place, but as we smoked the cigarettes and drank the coffee surrounded by the blackness of the forest, our world was one of peace and unity.

*

I awoke at daylight with aching muscles, wet and still exhausted. A fine mist of rain had fallen during the night and the groundsheet wrapped tightly around me had offered little protection. The people in the huts were still asleep and I pushed the bike down the road a short distance before starting it so I would not wake them.

People were only just stirring when I reached the small town of Walikale and, after a breakfast of warm *mandazis* (bite-sized fried dough balls) washed down with sweet black tea, I was on my way to Kisangani. At last, I'd left the mud behind. It was Christmas Eve and I was riding on a perfect tarmac road as good as any autobahn in Europe. At last, I'd reached the German section, where a wide swathe of tarmac cut through the thick forest. It must have been an insurmountable challenge for the engineers, but they'd overcome the difficulties and before me lay a truly great stretch of highway. I wanted to open the throttle, to sit back and cruise, but around each sweeping bend herds of goats rested on the tarmac or grazed on the grassy verge. All day, I saw only six vehicles, and I wondered why. Was the road washed out somewhere before Kisangani?

About a hundred kilometres from Kisangani the road deteriorated into a series of potholes and for thirty kilometres the tarmac was almost completely weathered. Without regular maintenance, in an environment of heavy rainfall, the forest eventually claims back its own.

My battle with the highway was nearly over though, and as I neared Kisangani the tarmac was littered with only a few potholes, which I easily dodged. I relaxed into the ride and was lost in my thoughts when I almost did not see the man waving frantically in front of me. Skidding to a stop, I narrowly missed hurtling down a drop of about twenty metres. The bridge had collapsed and most of the timber had been washed away in the torrential wet-season rains. This did not stop the trucks, which were detouring down the steep bank, across the narrow stream, now just a trickle, and up the steep bank on the other side. I rode to the bottom of the creek and was immediately surrounded by men eager to help push me and the bike up the walking track that skirted the steep wheel-rutted track.

'*Non merci, j'attends pour le camion*,' I said, preferring to wait until the truck in front reached the top of the bank. I needed speed to make it up the other side and could only do this by riding in one of the deep wheel ruts.

When the track was clear, I tried to start the bike, but the kick-starter was jammed. It had happened a few times over the past week and gently wiggling it usually made it move to the kick-start position.

'*Rapide, camion*,' the men yelled as I finally freed the kick-starter. I quickly accelerated across the stream and up a deep wheel rut, the panniers scraping on the mud sides. As I came hurtling onto the tarmac, the rear wheel still spinning, a driver was manoeuvring his truck for the steep descent. I was forced to skid, laying the bike on its side to avoid ploughing into the side of the truck. The driver braked hard and men came running to help. No damage was done, except that I would soon have a nice bruise running the length of my left leg.

It was a momentous occasion as I rode into Kisangani an hour later. I had made it to the heart of Africa. This sprawling city of bullet-riddled and derelict cement-block buildings sat near the equator, and it represented my halfway point. It was a significant milestone, as countless times during the planning I had stared at the name on my Michelin map. From an idea that had popped into my head nearly two years ago, I had single-handedly, one step at a time, made that idea a reality. As I rode along the wide boulevards, I swelled with pride over my achievement.

Kisangani had once been a prosperous city built by the Belgians. Live bands had once played at the colonial hotels, but the beautiful facades were now crumbling and bullet-riddled. The most recent damage had been done in the riots of 1991 when the soldiers went on a rampage in protest over unpaid wages. After several months with no money, in desperation, they had demanded the business people, mostly Greek and Lebanese diamond and gold buyers, pay them instead. A deadline was set, the business people refused to pay, the soldiers went berserk and most of the foreigners evacuated, flying by chartered light plane to Nairobi.

But the Greeks and Lebanese soon returned to buy diamonds and gold from the locals for a fraction of their real worth. I rode past a cafe that reminded me of Europe, but only a handful of men and women – a mix of Africans, Greeks and Lebanese, those with money – sat at the outdoor tables. It was Christmas Eve and the streets were almost deserted.

I found the Hotel Olympia and stopped outside the closed double steel gates. After the Belgians had left, the hotel had become popular with independent travellers and overland truck tours crossing Africa's dark centre. These days, with so much political unrest, few made it to Kisangani. A group of youths – the resident hustlers, moneychangers and guides – surrounded me.

'Ah, you Aussie. G'day mate,' one of them said as I took off my helmet. He was quick to identify the sticker of an Australian flag on the TT's petrol tank.

'Must have taken you a while to perfect that,' I said, quite impressed by his Australian accent.

'Many Aussies in trucks used to come here. I was their mate,' he said, emphasising 'mate' as though he'd just found a new one in me.

'Are the three Aussie fellas here?' I asked expectantly.

'Dave, Eric and Rolf? Nar, those blokes left a week ago. Eric, he go back to Nairobi. Dave and Rolf buy a pirogue and go to Kinshasa,' he said and traced the map on the side-cover of the bike with his index finger. 'Long journey,' he added. It was good to hear the Canberra boys had made it, but disappointing to learn I'd missed them.

'Any other travellers here?' I asked, hoping I would not be alone to celebrate Christmas, which was just another day for the Africans.

'Nar. Come inside. You need a cold beer,' he said and flicked a large piece of dried mud off the shoulder of my bike jacket.

'Great Christmas this will be,' I said, starting the TT as he opened the double steel gates. With the hustlers following, I rode to the back of the main building where a yard opened onto a garden bar with purple bougainvillaea hanging over the whitewashed brick walls. A cement path led to a rectangular block of six rooms and on the veranda sat a large woman drinking a beer, her buttocks overflowing from a chair that looked as though it might collapse at any moment. She was the mama and I asked about a room. She waved a chubby arm to the African barman and he ambled over to unlock a door. The room was large, dark and dingy. It had a double bed, an enormous bath and electricity, sometimes. To me, it was the ultimate in luxury and cost 80 nouveaux zaires per night, about US$1.

Before I unpacked the bike, I sat with a very cold Primus beer in the garden bar and was immediately joined by the hustlers.

'You see overland truck. It come this way?' one of them asked expectantly, holding his hands together as if in prayer.

'No. I see no overland truck. No other travellers. I'm sorry,' I said, apologising for the business they no longer had from the tourist dollar. If there was no fighting, if the world was a safe place, everyone would benefit. Many more of us would get to satisfy that innate human need to explore and, in so doing, support millions of people with the dollars we left behind for food, transport, accommodation and sight-seeing.

The hustlers inundated me with offers to change money, go on a trip to Stanley Falls up the river, buy ivory, buy diamonds, or buy clothing ingeniously made from cotton flour-sacks. Several letters of recommendation printed dubiously on overland tour company letterhead were placed on the table for me to inspect.

'See, I am recommended by Encounter,' said one youth. 'And I by Exodus,' said another.

I read the letters, which outlined how helpful, reliable, honest and trustworthy they all were.

'Change money?' a well-dressed man asked. His neat black slacks, lemon polo shirt and patent leather shoes seemed out of place in the centre of Africa, where it was mostly poverty, red mud and endless, dark-green forest.

Since leaving Bukavu two days earlier I'd had absolutely no idea of the exchange rate. 'How much for dollar?' I asked.

'Fifty nouveaux zaire,' he said. It was the same rate as two days ago, which was a long time under Zaire's rapid inflation.

'Do you think I am an idiot?' I said and placed my beer on the wrought-iron table a little too hard to emphasise my annoyance.

'No, no, I only joke. Seventy,' he said apologetically and patted me on the shoulder.

'Ninety and I change ten dollar,' I said to push him for a better rate. It was all a game and I enjoyed the haggling as much as he did.

'I give only seventy,' he said, with a determination that had me convinced; besides, I just wanted to eat, have a bath and sleep. I found out later that the real rate was, in fact, ninety.

I woke late morning on Christmas Day and consoled myself by cutting the one-kilo Edam cheese for my breakfast, eating several large wedges with a freshly baked baguette I'd bought at the nearby market. Without family and friends and any of the distractions of the commercial hype, for the first time in my life I thought about Jesus. After all, it was his birthday. He had been human, just like the rest of us, except for a series of unexplained miracles that may or may not have been embellished with the passing of time. I thought about all those chance encounters and uncanny coincidences that had become such a normal part of my journey, and about the growing connection I felt with everything – the people, the mountains, the forest, and even the TT, as if even it radiated a secret energy that I could feel but could not see. Was this the answer? Was Jesus simply in tune with this hidden mysterious energy that surrounds us all?

As I sat with a beer, pondering the true meaning of Christmas, I needn't have worried about spending the day alone. A young man of about thirty, with sandy-blond hair trimmed short and neat, hazel eyes and a cocky smile, walked into the garden bar. He pulled over a chair and sat down at my table. His skin was a deep golden brown against the whiteness of his T-shirt and he wore faded khaki shorts that were a mass of pockets and zips.

'Ah, *bon chance*, another traveller in town! I am Benwar,' he said with a thick French accent.

'Please, have some cheese,' I said and raised my hand to the barman, indicating to him to bring a beer.

'The local boys tell me about you and I come to meet this brave Australian girl on the large *moto*,' he said and cut off a wedge of cheese, popping it into his mouth with a look of sheer pleasure. 'I travel with my friend Mikail from Angola. We camp on the lawn of the Presbyterian minister's house. It overlooks the river.' He spoke with such infectious gaiety that I found myself smiling for no particular reason. 'It is a big *moto* for you. How do you manage in the mud?' he asked, gazing over at the TT parked outside my room.

'We do okay,' I said and he raised a questioning eyebrow before casting a quick look around the garden bar, as if half expecting to see a boyfriend, which would then explain everything.

'Where you *both* go from here?' he asked mischievously. He either understood the rider/*moto* bond or was playing along with this crazy Australian girl made delusional by Africa's equatorial heat.

'*We're* going to Kinshasa on the big timber barge,' I said, passing on what the boys who hung around the hotel had told me yesterday.

'We too go on this barge. It leave in four, maybe five, days,' he said. The beer arrived and between mouthfuls of cheese he told me his story.

'I am from Marseilles. I take a few months' leave from my job as a computer specialist to travel Africa,' he said. 'But I am not one of these, how you say, backpackers,' he quickly added so I would not mistake him for anything but a serious traveller.

As we drank our beer, Benwar explained that he had met Mikail in Nairobi. He was eighteen, from a small village in central Angola. He had fled his war-torn country for a better life, but had ended up on Nairobi's streets sniffing glue and living by his wits in a state of hopeless despair.

'I invite Mikail to travel with me through Zaire and we go down the river to Kinshasa then into Angola to Mikail's village. He has not seen his family for many months. We will travel to Namibia and I will sponsor Mikail so he can come back with me to France. It is good we are all on the barge together. It will be an exciting journey down the river,' he babbled with the enthusiasm of a small boy about to embark on a great adventure.

'How long does it take?' I asked, as everyone I spoke with gave a different response – maybe ten days, maybe fifteen, maybe a month.

'This is Africa. Who knows?' he replied with the same casual response I'd received from the locals.

'Do the soldiers visit you?' he asked. 'They stop me already, several times. They demand *passeport* then say I must pay fine to get it back. I have no choice but to pay. Bastards.'

'No. They don't bother me. Not yet anyway,' I replied.

'It is because you are a woman. To ask a woman for money is big loss of face,' Benwar said.

'Did you meet Dave, Eric and Rolf?' I asked, suddenly feeling chirpy. When I'd arrived in Kisangani, I had been so disappointed not to find them, but those feelings now seemed like a distant memory, even though it was less than twenty-four hours since I'd learnt I had missed the boys by a week.

'Yes, they leave quickly when the military threatened to shoot up the town if the business people did not pay them a Christmas bonus,' Benwar said and explained how the soldiers had gone months without receiving wages from Mobutu, and had once again demanded the business people pay them instead. A deadline was set, and if their demands were not met, they would open fire. It was no bluff; they'd done it only two years before.

'Fortunately, this time the business people learnt their lesson and paid them,' Benwar added, breathing an involuntary sigh of relief as he slumped back in his chair, his enthusiasm momentarily dampened by worry for what might have been.

'I need to buy a little petrol,' I said. The TT had beem on reserve for awhile and I estimated I could get another ten or so kilometres out of it.

'Ah, you must come with me to see the *précuré* at the Mission Catholique. He is a very kind old man,' Benwar said and raised a hand to signal the barman to bring two more beers.

*

The Mission Catholique was a collection of two-storey, red-brick buildings and a prestigious cathedral set in a secure compound that had a commanding view overlooking the mighty Zaire River.

Benwar was on first-name terms with the security guard, who quickly opened the ornate wrought-iron gate. With Benwar as my pillion, I rode under the brick arch and parked outside one of the buildings. The mission and its perfectly manicured lawns and flowerbeds looked decidedly out of place in a city in decay, fringed on all sides by an endless, impenetrable rainforest. Benwar pushed opened a heavy timber door and I followed him along a maze of corridors to the *précuré*'s office, which opened to a large arched courtyard and a lawn clipped as short and smooth as any golf green.

The *précuré* was a jolly old man with white hair and a stoop, and he welcomed Benwar like a son. They went through the formalities of greeting and he offered us each a beer from the small fridge next to his desk. Benwar picked up the remote control for the television and the screen flashed to life. I was mesmerised by the scenes of a world far away. Benwar was like a mischievous child and began flipping through the channels while he pointed to the satellite dish outside rotating from one side of its arc to the other as it searched for a signal.

'Unbelievable, hey, French television here in the middle of the jungle,' Benwar said. 'He is not allowed to sell petrol, but he will see what he can do,' he added, and smiled to reassure me it would be arranged.

The *précuré* wrote a note and handed it to Benwar. We finished our beers and thanked him for his generosity. We walked back along the corridors and once we emerged into the hot sunshine, I pushed the TT to a nearby workshop where an African man pumped about ten litres of fuel from a large drum into the bike's tank. It was more than I needed, as I would hardly be riding anywhere until I reached Kinshasa, but Benwar insisted and told the man to keep pumping.

Benwar and I both needed to change more money and it seemed the best place to do this was at the Hotel Kisangani, a short ride from the Mission Catholique. The African diamond buyers had set up residence in this derelict hotel, which had once been the social hub of Kisangani. We sat at a timber bar that ran almost the length of the enormous ballroom. I looked up at the ornate plaster now riddled with bullet holes.

'It must have been a wonderful time when the Belgians danced and the bands played,' I said, imagining the bygone era of prosperity.

'Look at this,' he said and opened the photo album lying on the bar.

I slowly turned the pages, transported to a time when Kisangani was a fashionable and exotic place.

We changed money with one of the diamond buyers. The rate was now 120 nouveaux zaires to the dollar. It would soon be dark, and I gave Benwar a lift back to the Presbyterian minister's house, running over a chicken on the way.

'The owner will find me. I will have to pay. The police and everybody will be in on the act. I will be fined for everything from reckless driving to not stopping at the scene of a crime. I will have to pay compensation to the owner, plus bogus administration costs,' I said when Benwar insisted I keep going.

'It is no problem. The owner of the chicken has more than a motorcycle to worry about,' he said as I rode slowly along the rough dirt track to the minister's house.

Benwar's tent was on the gently sloping lawn overlooking the river and as I approached, Mikail emerged to welcome me with a warm smile. With his tight black curls trimmed to a flat top and zigzags shaved on both sides, he looked like a trendy American teenager and quite out of place among the Zairean boys of the same age.

'So what problem does the chicken owner have?' I asked Benwar, once we'd stopped.

'Someone has a pet leopard and cannot afford to feed it, so every night the owner lets it out, and it feeds itself on the neighbours' chickens and goats,' he explained.

'It goes back to its cage by choice?' I asked in disbelief.

'Yes, of course. It has been raised from a cub and knows nothing else. The cage is its home,' he said.

'But, surely his neighbours must know. A leopard is not an easy thing to hide,' I said.

'Yes, they do, but the leopard is a symbol of power. It's the symbol of Mobutu, and they are afraid to kill it.'

*

My Zairean visa was due to expire in two days, and so for two hours I sat patiently in the foyer of a once-ornate Belgian mansion that was now the immigration headquarters. The clerk had assured me my month's extension would be ready within an hour. But in the tropical heat, I lost my patience and demanded to see the Commissioner of Immigration immediately.

The clerk, with nothing better to do, stood and led me up the wide staircase to a waiting room, where I was seated on a Louis-style chair covered in faded red velvet. After a few minutes, I was summoned into the plush, air-conditioned commissioner's office. He was wearing dark tailored trousers, a starched white business shirt and polished black leather shoes, and he extended a manicured hand as he rose from behind an antique desk. A photo of Mobutu adorned the wall behind him.

'*Bonjour madame*,' he said, and indicated I should sit. 'I hope you enjoy your holiday in beautiful Zaire.'

'Yes. Zaire is a wonderful place. It is a great country,' I said and handed him my passport. He called to a clerk, who immediately entered the room and took it away. As I waited for the visa extension, I told the commissioner about my travels through Zaire. He was the epitome of gentlemanly good manners and within minutes my passport was returned with the visa in place. It cost the equivalent of US$5, and the commissioner assured me any additional extensions would not be a problem. 'Madame, you are most welcome in Zaire,' he said as I thanked him and then quickly left.

The next morning, Benwar and Mikail arrived as I was servicing the TT. With the engine cold, I checked the valve clearances, which, as usual, needed no adjustment. I greased the swing arm and cleaned the air filter.

I also removed the kick-starter, but nothing seemed broken. I replaced it and hoped it would stop sticking.

'We go buy our tickets for the barge. Rumour is the price will double tomorrow. It is chaos at the docks. It is best you come with us,' Benwar advised.

'Okay,' I said as I wiped the grease from my hands with a rag.

'The journey down this river will be a big adventure. It is real Africa,' Benwar added.

Real Africa. It seemed an elusive state, one that had compelled many a traveller to journey to Africa. While I too had come here in search of a grand adventure, my journey had also evolved into a search for an elusive greater meaning, one that was slowing revealing itself to me.

Stopping to snorkel the Ningaloo Reef, off the coast of Western Australia

Myles at Emmanuel's Campsite, Cape Maclear, Malawi

Mama Roche with Frank, a 4x4 overlander from Germany, at her campsite in Nairobi, Kenya

Me and Kaoru from Japan with her Suzuki FX200 at Fisherman's Camp, Lake Naivasha, Kenya

Kadil (left in checked shirt), Sharif (wearing a keffiyeh), and Abdersak (third from right) outside the Cold Drink Hotel, Loiyangalani, Kenya

Chief Zaire's pygmy group in the Ituri Rainforest near Epulu, Zaire

The TT on the 'mud highway' between
Bukavu and Kisangani, Zaire

The 'floating village' – the flotilla of barges on
the Zaire River. I am camped on the barge on
the left

Donenglish, me, Chokie, Adidas and another boy at the front of the 'floating village' as it nears Kinshasa, Zaire

Sunset over the Zaire River

Crossing the Ntem River from Gabon to Cameroon

On the road to Busua Beach, Ghana

Market day in Bankass, Mali

Repairing a puncture in Mauritania.
Notice the bald Michelin desert tyre

Stopping for fuel near Nouakchott, Mauritania

The TT is loaded on a cargo ship bound for Antwerp, Belgium after 'our' journey ends in Nouadhibou, Mauritania

14

THE FLOATING VILLAGE
ZAIRE

The Zaire River, also known as the Congo, is 4700 kilometres long and, in places, a staggering 220 metres deep and up to thirteen kilometres wide. My voyage from Kisangani to Kinshasa would cover 1750 kilometres of this mighty river, the world's second largest after the Amazon. This giant artery flows in a wide brown arc from the mountains of the East African Rift to the Atlantic Ocean. In a country with few roads and highways, the river is the only means to transport goods – and people – from Kisangani in the centre to the capital Kinshasa in the west. Several hundred people were now crowded on the docks in a last-minute attempt to buy passage on an enormous flotilla of barges before the scheduled departure the following morning.

Benwar, Mikail and I fought our way through this crowd to reach the ticket office. People were camped outside the gates with their belongings and goods, waiting to board and get the best spots on the decks to trade, which would mean more customers and greater profits. For most passengers, this journey was business, and it wasn't the first time they had been down the river selling and trading their goods with the river people.

We made it to the ticket counter just as the clerk pulled down the shutter. I was grateful Benwar could speak French as he begged the man to stay open a moment longer.

'*Non cabine,*' the clerk said and Benwar insisted we were happy to sleep on deck.

'*Non possible,*' he said, but Benwar demanded to see his superior.

The clerk pointed to the main office that sat above the ticket booth, only too happy to palm us off to a higher official, and we bounded up the stairs. Our demands worked and my ticket on one of the world's most exciting river journeys cost the equivalent of US$8 for me and the TT.

'We leave tomorrow morning at ten. We must be on the barge by nine. It is very lucky we are here when this timber barge is leaving. Only once a year does a flotilla of barges this big go down the river,' Benwar said as we walked back to my hotel.

*

The hotel guard banged on my door at daylight as I'd asked. I wanted to be on the docks by seven to load my bike before the crowds arrived and well before departure at ten. But I was not the only one planning to beat the rush, and long before I reached the gates I had to weave through hundreds of people as I slowly rode towards the river. A mass of bodies stood outside the locked gates and armed soldiers stood at the turnstiles. Benwar and Mikail were there beside them, pressed against the wire-mesh fence.

'Eda. *Rapide*, you must hurry. We go through. The soldiers will unlock the gate so you can load the *moto*!' Benwar yelled over the hum of voices.

As I slowly idled forward the crowd reluctantly moved aside, then rushed to fill the gap behind me. Everyone was desperate to be first on the barges and claim the best spots. Once we were through the gate the docks were mostly deserted, except for a few dock workers who stood near the rusted bulk of a crane as it loaded the last bags of dried cassava into the holds.

'They will let the crowds through any minute. Quick, we must find a good position before the chaos,' Benwar said with nervous excitement and called out to the men to help us load the TT.

The barges were a juggernaut of twelve rusting river barges, each about fifty metres long. This flotilla was tied together, and pushed by an ageing tugboat. It had been commissioned by a French timber company to transport stacks of enormous logs cut from the Congo Basin, the world's second-largest patch of rainforest after the Amazon. Hundreds of logs were stacked up to five high on the decks. The logs were stamped, indicating the trees had been felled with permits, as illegal logging was widespread in Zaire. It was a practice that saw, with each passing year, the earth losing a little more of its lungs.

On the journey downriver, the barges would continue to load more produce: bags of rice, peanuts, maize and dried cassava, which was later ground to a white powder to make manioc. On our departure there were about two thousand passengers on board, and I was told this number would double by the time we reached Kinshasa.

Schedules for the barges moving up and down the river were spasmodic; loading cargo and regular breakdowns determined travelling time. At best it was two weeks for the 1750-kilometre journey, but often it took a month. I wondered about Dave and Rolf in their pirogue and where they might be at that moment as they floated on the strong current downriver.

With the help of the dock workers, we wheeled the TT across a narrow plank of wood and manoeuvred it to a clear spot on the front of a barge in the centre of the flotilla. We all agreed this would be a good spot, and quickly set up our tents. Then the gates were opened and a mass of people ran towards the barges, swarming over the decks to stake their claim. By ten a.m., all were settled and ready for departure, but the juggernaut did not move.

'Maybe this afternoon,' Benwar said when he returned from speaking to the captain.

We had no choice but to wait there in the hot sun all that day, and half of the next, as thieves would ransack our things the moment we turned our backs. At last, after nearly two days, the pusher's engines fired, sounding as though thunder gurgled under us, and the captain gave the horn a long and mighty blast. A deafening cheer rose from the passengers and the 'floating village' moved forward for the slow chug downriver.

Away from the dock there was slightly less risk of thieves, but one of us had to always remain with our tents. With Mikail taking first watch,

Benwar and I walked along the decks single file, skirting past the people, to watch our departure from the roof of the bridge. Hundreds of people perched on the stacks of enormous logs. Others rested under sheets of blue plastic, canvas and lengths of coloured cloth strung up as shade from the intense tropical sun. We moved downriver to the steady pounding of manioc leaves and plantains as the women prepared the next meal for their families or food to sell from makeshift stalls.

Benwar, Mikail and I were the only tourists on the barges, and somewhat of a novelty. A group of teenage boys sat perched on the back of the barge tied to the front of ours and taunted Mikail, who did his best to ignore them.

'Fuck off, you little bastards!' Benwar yelled. 'They tease Mikail. They say he is our *petit*, our small boy. They call him a black slave. Our little monkey,' Benwar said, translating the boy's taunts.

For our meals, we purchased fish or lumps of goat or pork meat from the river people who rowed over on pirogues carved from forest trees. The river was their lifeline. They sold dried and fresh fish, huge river eels, smoked bushmeat, butchered monkeys, live crocodiles, giant forest snails, baskets of fat wood-grubs and many other exotic foods, alive and dead, collected from the forest and the river. These foods, purchased by the people on the barges, would be sold at much higher prices in Kinshasa. The floating village was also a floating market, selling salt, soap, cloth, cigarettes and medicines to the villagers who lived along the river. Everybody, it seemed, was buying or selling something. For many of the people on the barges, this was their way of life. With the profit from the fresh produce, they purchased Western goods to sell to the river people on the return trip to Kisangani.

Our closest neighbour, a large woman, was a veteran trader. With her son, a gangly youth, and her older sister, a thin sickly woman, they had staked a claim next to us, which was on the corner, a thoroughfare for customers and those wanting to trade bush meat and dried fish.

Street kids who'd sneaked on board in Kisangani survived by doing odd jobs such as shelling peanuts or peeling dried manioc in return for a free meal. We quickly befriended our neighbours, as together we were a more powerful force to keep the thieves at bay.

Our drinking water came from my ten-litre container, which I'd filled in Kisangani and would refill again when we reached Bumba in two days' time. But to wash our dishes, we formed a partnership with our neighbours to haul the murky brown water from the river. Mama had a tin, but no rope. I had a rope but no tin. Benwar told me this was a very good partnership, as Mama was a shrewd and wealthy trader, respected by the other barge people. Befriending her meant we would be treated with an equal amount of respect, and her son would always watch our belongings, leaving the three of us free to explore and experience life on the floating village.

Trading was always brisk, with haggling intense between the barge people and the river people in their pirogues. The traders tried their best to delay the deal, knowing the further the barge travelled downriver, the cheaper the price of the produce. The current was strong, and it was hard work to paddle back to their cluster of huts.

Benwar, Mikail and I returned to our tents with the ingredients for lunch: several giant forest snails, a monkey's arm, plantains, cassava and a bunch of freshly picked cassava leaves, all purchased for the equivalent of less than US$1. Benwar gave the monkey arm to our neighbour and paid her to cook it into a stew. I told Benwar of my reservations about its purchase, but he replied that it was already dead.

The boys who teased Mikail watched our every move as we prepared our feast. I lit my petrol stove and over the next two hours we boiled plantains, fried cassava chips and stir-fried manioc leaves in palm oil. Benwar boiled the snails and I braved tasting a morsel of the tough, rubbery flesh seasoned with chilli. It was a feast filled with nutrients as pure as the untouched forest from where it had come.

We arrived at Bumba on New Year's Eve.

'*Bon chance*. We have beers, music and dancing to celebrate,' I said to Benwar and Mikail from where we sat perched high on the logs stacked near our tents. It was a sentiment we shared with our fellow passengers, and an air of intense excitement settled over the juggernaut as it manoeuvred against the dock.

Unbelievably, in deepest Africa, we were not the only Western travellers in town. Once we had docked, the local boys told Mikail about some tourists on motorbikes and in a pirogue, and I knew it had to be Rolf and Dave. After paying our neighbour's son US$1, a generous fee, to guard our tents and gear, we rushed to their hotel and found them drinking at the bar. I squealed in delight as I hugged them both.

'We got here two days ago and sold our pirogue. We got ten bucks,' Rolf said and I was puzzled as to why they were turning back.

'It's been an amazing adventure. But the next 1400 kilometres and three weeks will be just the same. It is a very long river,' Dave said in answer to my questioning look.

Four young men, two Japanese and two Swiss, sat together at another table staring shell-shocked at their half-drunk bottles of Primus.

'Ah, don't worry about those guys. They're just a bit Africa'd out,' Dave said and handed me an ice-cold beer.

The four motorcycle travellers looked to be in their mid-twenties. The Japanese rode Honda XR250s, while the Swiss were each on BMW R80GSs.

I insisted they join us and we put some tables together, but they hardly spoke as we chatted excitedly about our experiences on the river and ate a meal of pan-fried fish, plantain chips and salad. With the meal finished they returned to their rooms, declining our offer to celebrate New Year's Eve in a local bar filled with people dancing to the beat of Zairoise music.

With each passing day in Africa, I felt more and more elated about all I was experiencing and I found it hard to understand that it was not the same for others. I, too, had dealt with my share of corrupt officials, thieves, bad roads and people who were not always friendly – although most were. But I did not succumb to negativity. Instead, Africa had taught me resilience and to always expect a positive outcome even in times when it appeared doubtful. I believed my experience was borne out of a deep respect for the African people. It was an energy that radiated from me and was returned with equal vigour from those I met. As we drank and danced, I celebrated all that was good in life well into the early hours of 1994.

Late afternoon on New Year's Day, Rolf, Dave and the four motorcycle travellers left on a barge to Kisangani. The Canberra boys would return to Nairobi, then home to Australia. Through a strange turn of events, our paths had crossed often as we travelled through Africa but this would be the last time and it was a sad farewell.

'Time for sundowners,' I said to Benwar and Mikail, as the barge carrying Dave and Rolf disappeared around a wide bend.

We walked down the narrow plank onto a barge moored to the dock, selling cold Primus from an esky filled with ice. As we reclined on bamboo chairs, I inhaled deeply the oxygen-rich air pumped out by the foliage of a billion trees. Men in their pirogues floated past, silhouetted by a huge red sun, the scene tinged a deep orange as the last rays filtered through a thick haze that hung over the endless forest.

I would be alone again the following day, as Benwar and Mikail were also leaving, on a barge that would only take five days to reach Kinshasa. They did not have the luxury of time for the slow chug as I did. In a month Benwar had to return to France and his job, and he still needed to travel through Angola to Mikail's village and then on to Namibia, where they would arrange Mikail's immigration papers.

'Come with us?' Mikail asked.

'No. I'll be right. I like life on the river,' I said, though I was sad to lose their company. But the TT was now hemmed in by stacks of smoked monkey, bags of peanuts, dried cassava and all the other produce Mama had purchased from the river people. It would be impossible to move. And besides, I had no pressing need to rush or be anywhere else at any particular time. It was of no real concern to me when the journey on this mighty river in the heart of Africa would end.

*

The next morning, Benwar, Mikail and I embraced and then I was on my own. Mama wasted no time in filling the space they left behind with more hessian bags filled with dried cassava and bundles of smoked monkey purchased from the Bumba market.

I fell into the predictable routine of barge life, and one day drifted into the next as the barges continued to load cargo. Like the rest of the passengers, I didn't worry when we would leave Bumba. Now that I was alone, I ate all my meals with Chokie, Adidas and Donenglish, the hip young teenagers who had teased Mikail. I'd purchase fresh fish or a lump of meat, ignoring what it might be, and they would cook it into a stew on my petrol stove. Together we ate with our fingers; I was grateful for their cooking and they for the chance to eat an abundance of fish and meat.

They were travelling to Kinshasa, where they hoped for a miracle – a place at a mission school. They understood the power of education, how it could lift them out of poverty. Adidas and Donenglish were the chosen ones, and their families had paid their fare and some living expenses to reach Kinshasa. Chokie was a street kid from Kisangani who had sneaked on board. I learnt all this as they practised their English and I my French. In Kisangani, I'd asked Benwar about the schools, as all the ones I'd passed were derelict, with broken windows and rusted sheets of iron. Apparently Mobuto had ruled that education was no longer necessary and refused to pay the teachers. They'd gone months without pay but eventually they, too, needed to survive.

After five days, loading was complete and the floating village heaved away from the docks at Bumba and into the fast flow of the murky river, which was now nearly five kilometres wide. With meat and fish so cheap and so abundant, everybody ate well and a sense of deep contentment settled over the floating village, as it seemed life on the river was one continuous feast. I was now the only white person on board, and as we slowly moved down the river, I became part of this village without walls. I wandered about the barges to calls of 'Bonjour, Miss Eda' or 'Bonjour, Miss Tourist'. Mamas would invite me to sample their cooking, and husbands insisted I join them to drink the local gin, *kassee*. I'd feign a sore belly (which I often did have).

Two days later we reached Lisala, and immediately people came onto the barges selling twenty-litre plastic jerries of home-brewed alcohol of dubious purity. Someone wired a ghetto-blaster to a truck battery, and the barges rocked to the beat of Zairoise music. After two days we moved on, but the party lasted another four days until the *kassee* was gone.

A group of soldiers had taken over the roofed top deck of the barge adjoining mine. It was a good position to catch the cool breeze. They spent their days and evenings drinking and smoking cannabis, while their women screamed and scratched at each other during frequent fights. Occasionally, the soldiers would hassle me about taking photos, but the passengers yelled at them to leave me alone.

It was always interesting to see what the villagers were selling from their pirogues. Baby monkeys sat traumatised, grey parrots looked up quizzically from their little bamboo cages and metre-long crocodiles were tightly bound with vines. But mostly it was stack upon stack of smoked fish and bush meat.

About three thousand people, hundreds of goats, countless chickens and ducks, and even a few pigs were now crowded on the decks. There was only one toilet and washroom, which was also used to store the captain's metre-long monitor lizard in a bamboo cage. The indignant lizard was destined for the dinner table of some well-to-do African in Kinshasa. It was the ideal spot for the lizard, as the washroom was continually flooded and slime grew an inch thick on the walls. There was a continual queue for the toilet, which was understandable considering the toilet-to-passenger ratio. When I had to use the toilet, I was given special treatment and pushed to the front of the queue. At first, I was prepared to wait my turn, but when I was struck down with diarrhoea I appreciated the preferential treatment.

Only once did I use the shower, a rusty pipe protruding from the slime-covered wall. Instead, I preferred the cleaner option and, in my swimsuit,

I joined the children who played under the spray from a hose that continually pumped water from the river on the back deck of the tugboat.

With my bike and tent, my neighbours told me I was taking up far too much space for one person. I agreed, and a single mother and her four young children aged from five to sixteen moved in to share the shade under my groundsheet. Edith was a slim woman who looked much older than her thirty-two years, but while she appeared tired from the effort of providing for her brood, she was resourceful and was quick to grasp an opportunity. Seeing how well the three boys ate, Edith also offered to cook for me, and I now bought meat or fish for seven people, all for not much more than US$2 a day.

I also befriended Marceline, a bubbly young mother of twenty-five who was travelling with her loving husband, a two-year-old girl with a mass of little short plaits and a six-month-old baby boy. Marceline ran a stall selling salt, soap, cigarettes, *mandazis* and plates of stew cooked in large fire-blackened pots. Together with her husband, who traded with the river people to buy smoked fish and bush meat, theirs was a profitable business, with produce stacked nearly two metres high. This was their fifth trip on the river and would be their last, as once they reached Kinshasa they would have enough money to open a small restaurant.

Marceline spoke a little English and as I nursed her baby she chatted excitedly about their business plans and the new life they would lead in the city of opportunity. As I sat with her, I realised that her life had a quality far greater than what money could provide. With a husband who constantly and spontaneously hugged and kissed her and their two adorable children, they had a life filled with love and happiness.

'You're so lucky,' I often said to her and she'd smile back knowingly. Here was a woman in one of Africa's poorest countries who was a mother, a wife and business owner. She had it all, more than most women – regardless of race, colour or wealth.

Space was now at a premium on the barges. My bike and tent were surrounded by produce, and I had to climb over bags of dried manioc and bundles of smoked fish and bush meat just to leave and return from my wanderings. Edith and her children were all employed by Mama, my neighbour, to shell peanuts. But in the heat of the afternoon, the children would lie under the shade with me as a tangle of limbs. We would play snap with my playing cards, eat juicy pineapples or chew on sticks of sugarcane, spitting the pulp over the side. When we'd docked in Lisala I'd bought a bundle of sugarcane for them, as it was the Zairean equivalent of a big bag of sweets.

Each morning someone would ask for my binoculars and my pocket-sized photo album with photos of my family and life in Australia. The binoculars and album would be passed around the passengers, who got hours of entertainment looking at the photos, scrutinising each one and asking for an explanation. With the binoculars, they would sit high up on the stacks of wood and watch the villages on the shore, growing very excited when another barge approached. Everybody would stand and wave to the people on the barge who waved back. At first, I was worried the binoculars would be stolen.

'They would not dare,' Marceline assured me. 'They fear the captain. If there is any trouble these people are locked away and put off at the next town.'

For a few days the barges travelled very close to the bank, and I gazed in awe at the thick green forest, which was mirrored in the calm waters of the river as we floated by. In some places, grass-roofed huts were dotted along the bank. I was sitting with Eric, a boy of sixteen who spoke good English and was on his way to stay with his uncle, an Anglican minister, in Kinshasa. He would go to high school and hoped to eventually attend university to study medicine.

'What a peaceful, carefree life the villagers must lead,' I said as we glided past a very narrow pirogue paddled by a boy aged about five years. His baby sister, no more than a toddler, stood precariously balanced, staring mesmerised at the juggernaut. On shore a man, who I assumed was their father, reclined in a chair made of bamboo and vines.

'Here in the forest with family and friends, they have no worries about money. There is plenty of fresh food and pure, clean air. Life would be so uncomplicated,' I said and imagined myself living on the river with children and a husband, like Marceline's, who adored me.

'Ah, but what about the *mostiques*, the malaria, getting sick and having no doctor, and all the babies who die,' Eric said, bursting the bubble of my naive idealism. 'It is a tough life living in the forest.'

The juggernaut of barges stopped each night, held firm against the current by thick ropes tied to the trees lining the riverbank. Since the barges formed such a huge mass, and with so many sandbars, which shifted continuously with the fast flow of the current, it was too dangerous to move at night. But nobody slept, as close to the riverbank the mosquitoes buzzed incessantly, gorging on our blood as they bit into every inch of exposed flesh.

We arrived at Mbandaka, the halfway point to Kinshasa, late one afternoon and everybody was excited about the chance to get off for a stroll. We'd be docked for two days to load yet more cargo. I joined a diamond dealer and his girlfriend, whom I'd first met at the Hotel Olympia in Kisangani, and we headed to a nearby bar for cold beers. The best part, though, was that the bar had a porcelain squat toilet, gloriously clean compared to the slime-covered washroom and toilet on the barges.

Mbandaka had once been a prosperous town with fashionable shops, restaurants and cafes lining the wide, tree-lined boulevards, but like all the other towns along the river, post-colonial disintegration had seen it fall to ruin. When the Belgians left, so too did the money and sugar-cane farming; the town's sugar mill was now a rusting hulk. But it should not have been this way, as Zaire was rich in minerals and the possibilities for commercial agriculture in the well-watered, fertile soils were endless. The Zairean people were angry and dissatisfied; I heard many complaints about Mobuto's corruption, thievery and abuse of their beloved country. With an estimated personal fortune of US$5 billion, how could a leader not spend even a small portion of his vast wealth on his country's infrastructure – on schools, hospitals and roads?

It was a hot, humid night in Mbandaka and a storm gathered in the distance. From where I sat on one of the giant logs near my tent, I watched the lightning fork in spectacular flashes from sky to earth. Later the stillness and humidity finally gave way to heavy rain. My tent was anything but waterproof, but I was still much better off than most, who only had the shelter of a piece of cloth.

I awoke the following morning to a commotion at the front of the barges. One man had taken advantage of the rain and stolen a goat. He was tightly bound and surrounded by the passengers, all intent on humiliating him. They laughed at him and called him a goat. People poked him with sticks and others flogged him with lengths of thick rope.

'Miss Tourist!' the people called to me and pushed me to the front of the crowd.

'You hit,' a man said and forced a stick into my hands.

'*Non,*' I said and walked away.

The police arrived about an hour later and took the thief. They would show no mercy and probably beat him to within an inch of his life.

'It must be this way,' Marceline said to me later, and I understood that in a country with little law and order, the alternative would be anarchy.

While still docked in Mbandaka, I had taken a liking to the little parcels of fermented manioc sold each afternoon by kids who carried trays of it balanced on their heads. It was wrapped, while still warm, in banana leaves and so was the ideal breeding ground for bacteria, but this did not occur to me – until I came down with dysentery. I treated myself with a course of Flagyl, but it took me three days to recover and I was grateful for the toilet at the bar and my preferential treatment to use the slime-covered washroom on the barges when I could not make it.

My neighbours on the floating village insisted I eat dried caterpillars, as these were the Zairean equivalent to vitamin pills and a cure for a multitude of ailments. When I thought about it, it made perfect sense, as the caterpillars, having fed on the forest, would be packed with nutrients of the purest form. But I felt too sick and nearly vomited when a handful were offered to me.

We left Mbandaka with more passengers, more goats, and even more cargo. Every inch of space was taken; people slept in every nook and cranny amongst the wood, and sat lined up along the giant logs. A pungent smell of pigs, goats and fish hung over the barges.

Fights, mostly amongst the women, broke out often. Everybody stood and watched this spectacle of screaming, scratching and hair-pulling – a few moments later they would be friends, as it seemed nobody held a grudge.

A few days later a solemn mood descended on the barges; the voyage was taking longer than anticipated. Some people had run out of money, others were getting very sick. A baby died, and a boy of ten years lay gravely ill with dysentery. I offered him my last course of Flagyl.

'No, you keep it. You may need it. He already has medication from the doctor,' Eric said.

Instead, I gave the boy's parents a packet of dextrose tablets and some effervescent mineral salts. I was pleased to see that he was a little better the next day. Word then spread that I had medicine and a girl with conjuncti-vitis so bad she could not open her eyes was brought to me. I gave her mother a tube of ointment to treat the infection and some salt and Eric explained to her how she must bathe her daughter's eyes and apply the ointment.

As we neared Kinshasa the forests gave way to low hills and flat lands covered with golden grass that waved in the breeze. I sat on one of the steel rope pillars at the front of the fleet of barges, enjoying the novelty of gaz-ing out over wide open spaces again after nearly two months of dense, dark green. The river was now choppy and water washed onto the decks. At my feet, several metre-long crocodiles sat facing the spray, opening their jaws as wide as the vines that bound them would allow. As I walked back to my tent, people stopped me to wish me well on my journey, as the following day the barges would dock in Kinshasa and we might not get a chance to say a last goodbye. I would miss the floating village and its people who, over the past twenty-three days, had treated me as one of their own.

15

A CITY IN DECAY
ZAIRE

A thunderstorm brewed behind us as the last rays of the afternoon sun pierced through the clouds to reflect off the cluster of Kinshasa's high-rise buildings. I stood on the roof of the bridge with Eric, Chokie, Adidas and Donenglish to watch our approach to this modern city within a primitive land. Opposite, across the wide brown river, was Brazzaville, the capital of Congo. We passed half-sunken barges and tugs; hundreds of wrecks littered the riverbank, rusting hulks of the bygone colonial era when the river was once busy with traffic.

As we neared the city, motorised pirogues and boats, which operated as water taxis, ferried those passengers who could afford it, along with all their river produce – pigs, goats, chickens, ducks and bundles of smoked monkey and dried fish – off the barges. It was quite clear, as the juggernaut manoeuvred against the dock, that this additional expense of doing business on the river was an absolute necessity. More than a thousand people stood waiting and the imminent expectation of a grab for booty was palpable with each closing metre. The captain had assured me it was safe to sleep on the barges, as I did not want to ride the streets of one of the world's most dangerous cities at night. But I quickly realised this was not such a smart idea. Seeing that bedlam was about to erupt, I rushed down from the bridge intent on quickly packing my tent and belongings.

'Eda, you must pack your things and leave. You must not stay here tonight. The *voleurs* will come, knock you on the head and take everything, including your *moto*,' one of my neighbours, the moneychanger, called as I arrived breathless at my tent.

As I began packing my things, the thieves gathered as though ready to pounce. They sat on the logs and stared greedily at me. Even as the floating village was being tied to the docks, these men jumped across the gap. They were desperate men with sinewy, muscle-wasted bodies, near-starvation driving out most, if not all, of their compassion. They watched me with eyes crazed with hunger and there was no doubt I would be ripped apart for my possessions, which represented an absolute fortune to them.

'Eda, I must take a sick boy to hospital. Do not move from your *moto*. I come back then you come with me and stay at my uncle's house,' Eric said in quick, nervous sentences as he emerged from the seething mass on the barges.

'Okay. I'll wait for you. Thank you,' I said, my hands shaking as I fumbled to push my kitchen into one pannier and my bedroom into another, a task that ordinarily needed careful attention for it all to fit neatly into the limited space.

'You must watch your things. These men are very bad thieves of the worst kind,' Eric warned as he pointed at the men perched on the logs. Their piercing black eyes glinted with an evil I had never seen before in the people of Africa.

Eric disappeared into the crowd that now swarmed over the barges, either to offer their labour or to take whatever produce they could the moment someone turned their backs. Street kids ran off in all directions with smoked carcasses of monkey or bundles of dried fish tucked under their arms. I'd packed all but the tent, and went to dismantle it when I realised the thieves had slashed the back panel and my Gore-Tex motorcycle jacket, which contained a pocket camera and address book, was gone.

'Twenty dollar for my jacket!' I shouted to the men on the logs and in one smooth movement they gave chase like a flock of seagulls taking flight for a morsel of food.

The jacket could be replaced but the film in my camera – all the photos taken on the mud highway to Kisangani – and the addresses in the notebook could not. I would never know if Kaoru, the Japanese girl I'd met in Kenya, had made it. I would never be able to send the postcard to the Canberra boys when I reached Morocco. Or visit Ronnie in Scotland or Martin in Germany or Philippe and Yvan in Switzerland. I would no longer be able to keep my promise to send the photos I'd taken of those families who'd given me a free meal and a place to sleep.

The captain was told of the theft and as I stood cursing my stupidity, a soldier armed with an AK47 appeared beside me. My neighbour, the moneychanger, told me as he was leaving the barges that the captain had paid the soldier to ensure I would be safe until I left the docks.

'Thank you,' I said to the soldier, wanting to embrace him. He offered a cigarette and then grabbed two bottles of soft drink from a passing vendor.

'*Non* money, *avec le* jacket,' I said.

'*Non problème*,' he replied and smiled with a relaxed self-confidence that must only come when armed with a machine gun, with several bullet belts draped across your chest.

Three men who offered their labour to unload cargo helped me wheel the bike off the barges and across a narrow plank to the dock. Not once did they ask for payment.

In darkness, and surrounded by a seething mass of bodies on the dock, I waited for Eric to return. The soldier stood immovable beside me.

'Eda, Eda,' I heard and peered into the darkness to see Eric push his way through the crowd, which I estimated to number close to two thousand people.

As I wheeled the bike forward, Eric walked beside me while the soldier walked behind to ensure nothing was stolen, yelling at the crowd to stand back. When we reached the gates, I thanked the soldier and Eric waved down a taxi. Behind us trailed several relatives, an old man and two women with three small children. They had travelled with Eric from Kisangani and they all piled into the car for the short distance to his uncle's house.

'This boy will lead you,' Eric said as he pulled a boy aged about ten years at random from the crowd that surrounded us. He then got into the taxi, which disappeared into Kinshasa's dark streets.

As I slowly followed the boy, dodging the potholes and open drains lining the main road, a black Mercedes appeared out of the darkness and glided to a stop beside me.

'What you doing? Where you going?' the driver, a dark-haired, olive-skinned man, called out through the open window.

As I stopped, a crowd of about twenty gathered and pressed close around me.

'I'm going to the Anglican minister's house,' I shouted, to be heard over the din, and the man, aged about thirty, shook his head in disbelief that I would be so crazy to be alone at night in Kinshasa.

'This is very bad area. Come, you stay with my friends. Much safer,' he said.

'First I must tell my friend Eric,' I replied. 'It is not far.' The dark stranger agreed and drove slowly behind as I followed the boy who jogged ahead. He turned down a narrow street littered with rubbish to stop outside a square cement house with a flat tin roof.

'Be careful of the Lebanese,' Eric said as I explained about the man in the Mercedes and my change of plans for my first night in Kinshasa.

'You will make a great doctor. Believe it and it will happen. Thank you for everything,' I said and we embraced with the emotion of two old friends, even though we'd only shared a river journey of less than a month.

As I followed the tail-lights of the Mercedes that bounced over the potholes, I said a silent prayer of thanks for yet another turn of good fortune.

The black Mercedes pulled into the driveway leading to a house behind a high brick wall and heavy steel gates. A small and elderly African man, who looked much too frail to handle such a heavy gate, pushed it open and, once we were inside, easily pushed it closed. I rode the TT into a garage and the stranger ushered me into the house, where I was greeted by his three friends, all Lebanese men in their thirties. Ahmed (the driver of the Mercedes), Salim, Hussin and Hakim insisted I make myself at home. I was given the guest room with adjoining ensuite. It was absolute luxury after the slime-covered washroom and toilet I'd used on the barges for the past month. 'You stay as long as you want,' Salim said when I told them I would move to the Protestant Mission in the morning.

The men, who were casually dressed in board shorts and T-shirts, had lived in Kinshasa for two years. They hated every moment living in this modern city in decay and described their lives as akin to being in prison. But Kinshasa was good business and time spent there meant they could set themselves up when they returned to Lebanon to marry and start a family.

'We only stay a few years. Save our money, then we leave. We just put up with this life for now,' Hakim said and I nodded, thinking of the years I'd put in at the uranium mine and of the diamond miners in South Africa, who worked just enough to make a quality life. It all sounded so familiar. Hakim was a hairdresser for the expats, while Ahmed, Hussin and Salim imported all manner of consumables. As they explained, importing goods into a country that manufactured nothing and had a population of around forty million was lucrative.

The next morning, I rode into Kinshasa's city centre to apply for a visa for Congo and Gabon. The high-rise buildings that lined the main boulevard gave the city an air of prosperity but a few streets back from this facade lay the encroaching shantytown of Kinshasa proper. The streets were a mass of potholes, with one so large it had swallowed a car. The shops lining the main boulevard were mostly bare of the Western goods that they advertised in their windows, and armed guards stood outside the few Western restaurants, which were mostly deserted.

I rode through the city centre and out along the leafy avenues fringing the river in search of the British Embassy. I hoped to convince the consul to issue a letter of recommendation, a requirement for the visa for Congo, which was gripped by civil war. When I had told the Lebanese about my plans to ride through Congo, they'd advised the fighting was only in the west outside of Brazzaville and I would be okay as long as I avoided the highway leading to the coast. I passed private mansions and foreign embassies of every nationality, surrounded by high walls, electric fences and security surveillance. Protected, the expats were imprisoned in their mansions with manicured gardens, tennis courts, swimming pools and superb river views.

'Where did you come from? How did you get here?' asked the British clerk from behind inch-thick bullet-proof glass when I presented myself at the British Embassy, a whitewashed colonial mansion in a quiet, leafy street.

'I came down the river from Kisangani. I would like a letter of recommendation to go to Congo,' I asked.

'What! They're having a bloody civil war over there. Every night we see the flashes of mortar blasts. You have got to be joking if you think the British government will recommend you to go there,' said the young man, who'd gone red in the face as he shouted through the glass.

'Well, what do I do?' I shouted back. 'Go see the Canadians. They're responsible for you Australians,' he said and then, in complete contrast, wished me luck as I turned to leave.

As I walked back to my bike, I passed the embassy workshop and asked the English mechanic if he would drill out a bolt that attached the clutch pedal to the frame. It had snapped when I had over-tightened it in Kisangani. It was a simple task for him with his fully equipped workshop, and while he worked I asked about life as an expat in Kinshasa.

'We make the most of it,' he said in casual acceptance, and went on to describe a routine of tennis, embassy parties and daytrips in speedboats to a private island out in the middle of the mighty Zaire River.

The Canadian consul was housed at the American Embassy and, after passing through several security checkpoints to gain access to the fortified building, I was allowed to wait in the air-conditioned lounge for the Canadian official to return from lunch. It was a short wait and when he returned a few moments later I was ushered into his office. He was a tired, grey-haired man with the look of someone passing time before retirement.

'Please sit down,' he said. 'How can I help you?'

'I need a letter of recommendation to get a visa to cross Congo. I am travelling from south to north Africa on a motorcycle,' I said and suddenly realised how crazy this must sound.

'The civil war is being fought west of Brazzaville. You need to avoid the highway heading towards the coast,' he said, repeating what the Lebanese had told me, which also reassured me it was not unfeasible I travel through Congo.

'So things are not as bad as they say?' I asked, seeking reassurance that the civil war was just a few skirmishes by the rebels. My travels in Zaire had taught me that perceived dangers were often not actual dangers – either that, or I'd just had an exceptional run of good luck.

'There is no fighting in the city. Come back Monday. The letter will be ready then,' he said. It was Friday and, if all went well, I would be issued with the Congo and Gabon visas on Monday morning in time to board the ferry to Brazzaville that would leave late that afternoon.

After my experience on the river, the generous hospitality of the Lebanese was not wasted on me. I was treated like a family member – a sister, perhaps – who'd arrived unexpectedly for a brief visit all the way from Lebanon. I needed these days of rest and the delicious Lebanese food to regain my strength for the ride ahead into Congo and north to West Africa. I think the Lebanese knew this too; they often told me how brave I was and that very few people have the courage to live their dream.

'We want to help you. This is the least we can do,' Salim said when I thanked them yet again for their hospitality shown to a complete stranger, a stray they had rescued from Kinshasa's dark and dangerous streets.

As the Lebanese went about their business, by day I wandered the stalls of Kinshasa's main market, the Grand Marché, just a few blocks from their house. I hoped my Gore-Tex jacket with my address book still in a pocket would miraculously appear here and I could buy it back, no questions asked. I described my jacket to one of the stallholders selling second-hand clothing shipped as an aid donation from Europe. I asked if he would put the word out that I was willing to pay US$20 for its return. But nothing came of it. Finally, I accepted that it was gone and bought a navy Burberry trench coat for US$2.

Compared to the river, food was expensive – nearly ten times the price at the market, which was alive with colour and variety, and was always a hive of activity. From each foray I would return loaded with lettuce, tomatoes, cucumbers and avocados to make a salad to go with our evening meal of barbecued goat or chicken delicately flavoured with garlic, lemon and spices.

Kinshasa had once been the live music capital of Africa, but bands rarely played at the hotels and bars throughout the city now, as people were too afraid to go out at night. It was Saturday night, though, and the Lebanese wanted to take me to a nightclub. I dressed in my 'going out' clothes – my blue sweatshirt and black leggings – and put on a splash of eyeliner, mascara and lipstick, something I had not done since Nairobi when I'd gone clubbing with some backpackers staying at Mama Roche's. As my black canvas shoes had finally disintegrated on the barges and I'd thrown them into the river, my only footwear (other than a pair of thongs) was my steel-cap work boots.

Even though my clothes were faded and I wore grubby boots, I thought I looked passable for a night out, but the Lebanese saw things differently and insisted I looked 'too sexy'.

'You've got to be kidding,' I said, looking down at myself.

'You look too good and we do not want anyone to come near you. It would mean trouble for us,' Salim said.

Reluctantly, I changed into my faded, oil-stained jeans with rips in both knees, which hung off me like an old sack. Then we all piled into the sleek black Mercedes for the short drive to the nightclub. Even though it was just one block from their house, it was still too dangerous to walk. Armed soldiers stood at the entrance and the Lebanese paid them to guard the car.

The nightclub's clientele were mostly middle-aged Lebanese businessmen, and all the women, beautiful girls aged no more than twenty, were prostitutes. I was mesmerised by their dark-skinned beauty and perfect bodies with long slender legs as they danced to the catchy beat of Zairoise music.

'Do you want to know their secret?' Hussin whispered, when I commented to their sveltness. 'HIV,' he said, before I could even hazard a guess. 'It keeps them slim.'

'Don't they know about the dangers of unprotected sex?' I asked as I watched one of the girls dance. She was wearing a cropped lime-green top and hot-pink mini-skirt. Her outfit emphasised her breasts and every curve of her beautiful sleek body, and hid not an inch of her long legs. She had a sweet, innocent face and as if she sensed us watching her, flashed us a look with her dark almond eyes. Since I'd been in Zaire, I'd never once seen anything like the billboards in Uganda and Kenya that warned of HIV/AIDS.

'Yes, they know about HIV, but this is Africa. If they don't die of AIDS, they will die of something. HIV is not the worst that can happen. And besides, not everyone with HIV dies of AIDS,' Hussin said and raised his hand to the girl in the pink skirt. With several strides of her long legs, she slipped in beside Hussin to join us on the plush velvet couch, where she whispered into his ear and giggled demurely at his reply.

As I watched the girls dance with the middle-aged Lebanese, through air thick with cigarette smoke and sexual tension, I thought of my own sexuality and how it had been suppressed without conscious thought. I still did not think about sex, there was not even the slightest stirring of desire, and I still had not had a period since leaving Australia nearly a year ago. I reasoned it was probably because I had more important things to occupy my mind and body – things like survival. I was grateful for this celibacy and wore it like a protective cloak that would shield me from any risk of HIV. But HIV was something you did not see. It was not spoken of, and so it was forgotten. If they were infected with the virus, these beautiful girls would also be forgotten when their bodies could no longer fight it. When their beauty was gone, and they began to wither, they would be cast aside, shunned, to waste away until death took them.

This night out was to celebrate my farewell as I'd leave Kinshasa on Monday, but an air of melancholy settled over me as I thought of Africa's savagery. Beauty and death co-existed here, but I was yet to experience evil. So far, Africa had given me all I needed even before the desire had been expressed. Would my run of good fortune come to an end? How long could it last? What fate awaited me when I rode through Congo and its civil war?

To banish these negative thoughts, I reminded myself that events on my ride had always unfolded in my favour; there was no reason this would not continue. My attitude was now so much a habit that I rarely questioned it. I reasoned that I had two choices: I could expect good things to come my way or I could expect bad things. As each took the same amount of thought, the choice was simple. And so far this choice had not failed me.

PART THREE

CONGO TO MAURITANIA

16

THOU SHALT ALSO DECREE A THING...
CONGO

With the TT packed the night before, I was ready to leave by eight a.m. Monday morning so I could be at the Gabon Embassy at nine a.m. The Lebanese treated me to a delicious breakfast of a doughy bun stuffed with cheese, baked and then drenched in sugar syrup, all washed down with strong black coffee. It was a breakfast loaded with calories and would sustain me for most of the day.

We embraced and I professed my gratitude for their hospitality, to the point of almost embarrassing them. At first, the generosity of the Lebanese had made me feel uncomfortable because it was all too much and nothing was expected of me in return. I didn't dare speak of my concerns for fear of offending them, so I just accepted their magnanimousness for what it was – kindness in its purest form, shown to another who needed it. They all told me repeatedly to take care when crossing Congo and I repeatedly reassured them I would be fine. These weren't just empty words said for their benefit. 'I'll be okay. Don't worry. The Canadian consulate would not have issued the letter of recommendation if it was not safe to go there,' I said.

This seemed to reassure them and then I was gone, riding off towards the Gabon Embassy to collect my passport with a three-day transit visa affixed for US$16. Next, I collected my letter from the Canadians and then headed to the Congo Embassy to be issued with a three-day transit visa for US$50 on the spot.

By midday I'd boarded the ferry, which was already filled with passengers, produce and an assortment of cars and vans covered in dents and varying degrees of rust. My fare was equivalent to a few US dollars and the ferry would depart when full. I was told this would be late afternoon, maybe five p.m. I parked the TT beside a barely drivable white Ford Transit van belonging to a Congolese trader, a rather large, jovial man. He sold goods purchased in Kinshasa for a handsome profit in Brazzaville and his good fortune was a direct by-product of the civil war, which raged west of the city. He told me that rebel forces loyal to former Congolese prime minister Bernard Kolélas had blockaded the main road and rail-line leading to the coast and the sea port of Pointe-Noire.

'This is very good for me,' he said and beamed a wide grin, his round face shiny and dotted with beads of sweat from the tropical heat. Imported food, particularly flour, now mostly came across river from Kinshasa.

'Just how dangerous is it over there?' I asked, as he was the first person I'd spoken to with first-hand experience of the situation rather than hearsay reports.

'The government troops control the city. It is safe,' he said and slid open the side door of his van to reveal stacks of boxes, sacks of flour and trays of fresh baguettes, as Brazzaville's bakers had long since run out of flour. He reached in and grabbed two sticks of crusty bread and passed one to me. 'Fighting is west of the city. You stay away from this highway and you have *non problème*.'

'So how do I reach Gabon if I can't go this way?' I asked, unfolding my map to show him that the only road to Gabon was on the main highway west.

'Take the road north to Lekana and you will find a road crossing to Gabon,' he said and pointed to my map, where no road was marked.

Seeing my doubtful look, he hastened to reassure me. 'There is a road. You will see,' he said, dusting bits of bread crust from his shirt, the buttons straining across his round belly.

As we neared the opposite riverbank, he asked where I planned to stay in Brazzaville.

'I'm not sure,' I said as I leaned over the rails to get a glimpse of the city, its high-rise buildings shimmering with flashes of light as the late afternoon sun reflected off glass and metal. 'Do you know of a hotel that is not too expensive?' I'd already read in the Congo section of my Lonely Planet *Africa* guidebook, a mere seven pages, that a grubby room would cost me upwards of US$30.

'You go to the Sisters' Residence of the Mission Catholique. You will be safe there. The sisters will look after you,' he said and nodded to emphasise that his recommendation was a good choice for a girl alone in Africa.

I agreed, reasoning that due to the civil war it would be okay for me to turn up unannounced on their doorstep, even though they did not usually offer accommodation to passing foreign tourists.

'The docks here are full of thieves. The soldiers will try to give you problem. When you go to immigration, I watch your *moto*. Then you watch my van,' he said as the ferry manoeuvred against the dock. 'See this door. It not lock,' he said and demonstrated how easy it would be for the thieves to help themselves to the goods inside. 'My wife wait for me on the dock, but the thieves take no notice of her.'

As I rode off the ferry following the Congolese trader, a crowd of men, just as desperate as those I'd seen on the docks at Kinshasa, closed in on me. The Congolese trader waved them away with his chubby arms and then stood guard over the TT as I rushed to immigration. A moment later I returned, my passport and carnet stamped, and stood watch over the van while his slender young wife sat inside with the window tightly closed.

'Quick. We go and leave these thieves!' the Congolese trader shouted as he pushed his way through the crowd of men who stood in a tight semi-circle staring at me. The double steel gates of the dock area were opened, and I followed the van out into the city of Brazzaville.

For a city supposedly gripped by civil war it looked quiet, orderly and, unlike many of the African cities I'd seen, very modern. High-rise buildings, Western-style shops containing expensive European goods, trendy boutiques and a small supermarket that would not have looked out of place in France lined the wide boulevards. I passed a bar that was filled with customers: both Congolese and European expats sat at the outdoor tables enjoying a late-afternoon drink with friends. Once we were well away from the docks, the van stopped and I pulled up beside it.

'*Bon chance* for your journey,' said the Congolese trader, and gave me directions to the Sisters' Residence of the Mission Catholique before driving off.

As if I was expected, a Congolese man, bent and hunched, appeared from nowhere to unlock the wrought-iron gates when I pulled up outside the mission. Once opened, I rode into the secure compound of the Sisters' Residence, which sat on a low hill overlooking the city centre. It was a large double-storey, red-brick building. I walked through the arched entrance to the foyer, which opened to a perfectly manicured lawn. I was greeted by one of the sisters, a European woman aged about fifty. I asked if I could camp there for the night and, without speaking, she indicated I follow her to the second floor. I grabbed a few things, locked all my bags, and then left the TT where I'd parked it, knowing it would be safe in the mission's secure compound. As I trailed behind her up the stairs, I told her of my plans to ride on a minor road north to Lekana to reach Gabon.

'I do not know of this road, but you must avoid the roads west,' she said with a heavy French accent and stopped at a door halfway down the corridor.

'Yes. I have been warned,' I said.

'I come back for you for dinner. You can wash there,' she said and pointed to the bathroom at the end of the corridor before disappearing back down the stairs.

I opened the door to a neat little room with a clear view out over Brazzaville. Once I'd showered, the sister returned and I followed her to the dining room and sat down to a dinner of chicken stew and rice. The sisters asked me about my travels and shook their heads in disbelief when I recounted my trip down the Zaire River on the 'floating village'. The sister who had greeted me earlier told me again to avoid all roads heading west.

'It is too dangerous. The rebels control these roads. All are blockaded,' she said, her eyes wide as if to emphasise the danger.

Later, as I lay in the dark on a narrow wrought-iron bed on top of crisp white sheets under a mosquito net, protected from the hungry swarms that buzzed incessantly around me, I pondered my departure from Brazzaville the following day. Were things as bad as the sisters and the British clerk in Kinshasa had suggested? Before drifting off to sleep, I reassured myself with the words of the Congolese trader that there was a road north into Gabon from Lekana.

In the tropical heat, I tossed and turned all night and was awake at daylight. I packed the TT and then waited on the steps outside until one of the sisters appeared, the same one who'd greeted me when I arrived.

'Thank you for the room and meal. Please, I want to make a donation for my stay,' I said and handed her US$10.

'No. You will need it. You have a long journey,' she replied, raising her hand as I offered her the note. 'Stay off the roads to the west,' she repeated with the sternness of a schoolmarm, and I assured her I would.

Before leaving the city, I rode to the defunct Brazzaville Zoo close to the city centre, which Leo, the dark-haired American I'd met in Epulu, had told me I simply must visit. The zoo was used to house orphaned gorillas in a rehabilitation program funded by a wealthy British conservationist. The only animals kept at the zoo were about thirty gorillas – from babies in nappies to young adults. They'd been orphaned as a result of poachers trapping the babies to sell to wealthy Africans. An entire gorilla group would be killed to get one baby, as all fought to the death to protect their youngest member. The baby gorillas had been confiscated by park rangers and, understandably, had arrived traumatised after witnessing the slaughter of their families.

As I pulled up, a Congolese carer approached and said that yes, it was okay for me to be there, and I joined three other Congolese carers, who sat on a large, round cement platform.

One of the carers told me the gorillas would all eventually be reintroduced to the wild, placed in small, isolated areas of rainforests such as the Lefini Reserve in northern Congo. I told them about Leo, who would be based at Lefini to monitor the successful reintroduction of the gorillas into their new environment.

The orphans were let out of their cages and, like toddlers, ran towards us to launch themselves into our laps. As I cuddled a gorilla baby, it looked at me with moist eyes and I thought of the pain it had endured at the hands of humans. After cuddles, the babies joined the juveniles and, under the watch of the carers, were allowed to play in the trees within the zoo's compound.

Before leaving, I asked the carers about the best way to leave Brazzaville. Go north, they said and I smiled because this backed up everything the Congolese trader had said.

So north I went and by mid-morning I'd reached the outskirts and the first checkpoint.

'*Bonjour madame. Passeport*,' said a soldier dressed in full battle fatigues and armed with an AK47.

'You voyage from Australia?' he asked in a perplexed tone as he flicked through each page of my passport.

'*Oui*,' I said, and pointed to the world map on the side-cover of my bike.

'*Madame*, in Africa on *la moto*. Very dangerous,' he said.

'So far *non problème*,' I said as he scrutinised my passport.

'*Non problème*, you go,' the soldier said when he turned the last page.

'The road north is good?' I asked.

'*Oui, non difficile*,' he replied with such casual indifference that any remaining worries about a rebel ambush were finally gone.

As I headed north, I rode on smooth black tarmac and passed a landscape of rolling hills covered in golden grass that shimmered in the gentle breeze, but within a few kilometres of the checkpoint the tarmac deteriorated to a two-wheeled track that cut across an undulating plain of sandy loam. In the late afternoon, I rode exhausted into the village of Djambala and looked for a hotel, but the town was a military post and the gendarme directed me to the Sisters' Residence of the Mission Catholique. At the mission, I asked the sister, a middle-aged French woman who came to the gate, if they knew of a hotel, even though I'd just been told there was none.

'*Non hôtel*,' she said and opened the gate to their compound.

Since arriving in Zaire, other than the floating village, I had mostly moved from one protected mission and enclave of expats to another, and I was beginning to feel a barrier had arisen between me and Africa. The connection I'd made with the people of the floating village seemed a distant memory and I yearned to make such a connection again.

'I am happy to camp,' I said, feeling every bit the freeloader for my intrusion.

'The *voleurs* are many,' she said and pointed to a storage shed. 'The *moto* will be safe there.'

After locking the TT in the shed and retrieving a towel, toiletry bag and clean clothes, I followed her to the nearby low-set, cement-block building with a rusting tin roof and wide veranda. She stopped outside a door and opened it to reveal a simple room furnished with a small desk and a single bed with a mosquito net suspended above it.

I later joined the mission sisters, four French women, for a dinner of fried chicken, boiled potatoes and green beans freshly picked from the mission garden. They spoke only a few words of English, but I understood that their role was to provide religious instruction, education and basic healthcare to the villagers, especially the women, as medical services were often male-dominated. While church missions in equatorial Africa were a relic of colonial domination, the missionaries I'd met in Zaire and now Congo all seemed committed to improving the lives of the people in their communities. I wondered what would become of the sisters, though, as they were all aged in their late fifties, I guessed, and one looked to be in her late sixties. Would they live out their days here? Who would look after them?

'This is our home and the people need us,' replied one sister, who could speak a little bit more English than the others, when I asked how they managed.

They had made a life-long commitment to the villagers, to the Catholic faith, and to each other – and they seemed happy with their choice. Happier, I imagined, than they would be living alone as spinsters in some nondescript French city apartment.

I asked about the mysterious road to Gabon from Lekana not marked on any map and was told the father at the Lekana Mission was Nigerian and he would know of this back road, if it existed. As a Nigerian, he would also be fluent in English.

With the meal over, I excused myself, apologising that I needed to sleep. The day had been hot and humid, and I had struggled with the bike on the sandy track. Having not ridden any distance for over a month, I was exhausted.

*

I reached Lekana, a village of ramshackle corrugated-iron buildings and mud huts, after an easy thirty-kilometre ride on a relatively hard-packed dirt road. I rode along the potholed main street of red dirt and stopped to ask a man for directions to the Mission Catholique. It was Sunday, mid-morning, and mass had just ended.

Lekana, and especially the Lekana Catholic Mission, was a little piece of paradise hidden away in the far reaches of equatorial Africa. It was a collection of colonial red-brick buildings, neat lawns with tree-lined paths, and small paddocks where black-faced, woolly sheep grazed on lush green grass. The founding missionaries had planted an orchard of fruit trees and an extensive vegetable garden.

I parked near the church and waited for the father to be free. He was standing on the wide steps leading to the arched entrance of the church while his congregation filed out. He was a gentle man, seemingly at peace with the world, and gave his time freely to each man, woman and child. When the last person walked away, he came over and introduced himself

232

as Father John. He was of slight build and I estimated his age at around forty. I asked him about the road to Lekoni in Gabon.

'It is Sunday. You just rest today. We will make some enquiries tomorrow,' he said with such serenity that I nodded obediently.

'Come, I will show you to your room, and then we will have lunch,' he said and I followed, wheeling my bike behind him down the path that led to a cluster of three red-brick buildings that faced onto a secluded lawn fringed with flowering shrubs. Nestled amongst this central garden was a small statue of the Virgin Mary nursing baby Jesus. 'You must stay here tonight and leave in the morning,' Father John insisted. While I was eager to be on the road again, leaving in the afternoon would mean sleeping out on the plains alone, where I would be more exposed to harm, so I agreed to stay.

After I'd stored the TT in a shed, I walked with Father John down the tree-lined path to another red-brick building for lunch and he told me of the road, a narrow two-wheel track that crossed the Lekana plains to reach Lekoni in Gabon.

'Usually this is a much-travelled short cut to Brazzaville from Gabon but with the civil war, few vehicles now travel this way,' he said.

When we reached the quaint little building, he opened the door to reveal a large table covered in linen fringed with delicate white lace and set with polished silver.

'Please, come sit. We serve lunch,' he smiled holding the door open for me.

I sat down with the six Congolese mission staff and after prayers of thanks, a large plate with roast lamb and all the trimmings was brought out. I could not believe my eyes – or my nose. Here I was in the far reaches of Africa, about as far as one could get from civilisation, and I was about to eat the most succulent roast lamb served with fresh mint sauce, baby peas, crispy roast potatoes, sweet potatoes and even parsnips.

After this feast, I spent the afternoon in my room, which was simply furnished with a single wrought-iron bed and a side table with a dog-eared copy of the Bible on it. On the floating village I had given Eric my only novel, *Papillon* by Henri Charrière, and had not had a chance to find another, so I began to read the Bible.

I later joined Father John for supper by the faint light of a paraffin lamp but it seemed the day ended early at the mission, and when supper finished he said goodnight, so I went back to my room to read a few more pages of the Bible by candlelight. I imagined Father John was probably doing the same.

*

I was packed and ready early the next morning and I thanked Father John for his kind hospitality, before riding to the immigration post on the outskirts of the village. But my expectation of an early start soon ended when the immigration official advised I could not pass alone. It was too dangerous and I would have to wait and travel with another vehicle.

I sat down in the shade and leaned against the wall of his mud-and-thatch hut and waited. An hour passed and then another but no vehicle came. By midday, Father John arrived on his little Yamaha 125cc motorcycle, checking to see if I was still there, as he'd mentioned the immigration official might insist I wait to accompany a vehicle.

'It is pointless you wait any longer,' he said. 'If there is a vehicle, it would only pass in the morning. It is lunch,' he said. So I got back on the TT and followed him to the mission.

One day drifted into the next. Each morning, I waited at the immigration post and by lunch time Father John would come for me and I would enjoy another gastronomic delight: fried chicken, chips and garden salad, lamb chops or stew delicately flavoured with fresh herbs. In the afternoons I helped pick beans, tomatoes and carrots from the vegetable garden for our evening meal. Or I would watch the boys from the village skilfully play soccer on the grounds beside the mission. In the evening, I'd join Father John for a supper of vegetable stew, and by the soft light of a paraffin lamp our conversations always turned to God. With nothing else to read and nothing else to do, I spent long hours with the Bible.

'It's an interesting story. Jesus was a remarkable man with ideas ahead of his time,' I said when Father John asked what I thought of it.

'Jesus taught us how to see beyond ourselves and our own needs,' he said and looked at me intently, waiting for my reply.

'What of those people who do not know of Christianity? Who have never heard of God but they still know kindness? They still welcome a stranger,' I commented.

'All people are good. It is circumstances that change what is deep within us,' he replied. 'The Bible contains the threads that hold the fabric of society together. It gives meaning and purpose to our lives. God gives us faith to believe in something beyond our existence here on earth,' Father John said and looked at me with downcast eyes, as if in humble gratitude at the presence of God.

As we sat at the little wooden table, the light from the lamp bathed the room in a soft glow that made me feel that time was no longer important; that somehow, we had risen above the physical world and were about to grasp the true meaning of humanity's existence.

'I've never had the opportunity to read the Bible until now,' I said. 'But I can relate to the words: *Thou shalt also decree a thing, and it shall be established unto thee.* My journey has shown me not to doubt, but to trust. I believe no harm will come to me and so far it hasn't. It is as though all I have wished for has come true and those words seem to explain my own experiences,' I continued, as I tried to understand my emerging faith as a kind of energy that can influence our lives if we choose to acknowledge it. Father John called this God but I interpreted it as something else, although it was, in fact, the very same thing.

'*And so it was established unto thee and the light shall shine upon thy ways,*' he replied, speaking the words of the scripture with a familiarity that came from years of devotion. 'It is as it reads and God is with you in all that you desire that is good for the benefit of all.'

'The benefit of all?' I asked. 'I'm not sure how riding a motorcycle across Africa is of any benefit to anybody but myself,' I said and thought of the shallowness of my life before this journey. Back then, my life was devoid of any thoughts of spirituality; but the more I travelled in Africa, the more frequent chance encounters and coincidences were – too frequent to be explained as just random occurrences. My mind searched for an explanation.

'I can see you search for meaning. God sees this too, and it shall come to pass,' Father John said with an air of reverence. He settled his eyes upon me, waiting for my reply, but I just felt rather silly trying to explain something that was still beyond my understanding.

*

On the afternoon of the fourth day a white Toyota 4×4 utility arrived from Gabon. The driver brought wheat flour to be sold to the surrounding villages and mission and the following morning the 4×4 would return to Gabon, loaded with ground cassava and passengers.

Father John insisted I eat a big breakfast of four fried eggs and tomatoes before leaving. He refused the US$20 donation I offered to pay for my board and meals. 'You have a long journey and you will need all your money,' he said, the words all too familiar.

Father John rode with me to the immigration post. My passport and carnet were stamped and the immigration official told the driver he was responsible for my safety until I reached Lekoni, about a hundred kilometres along a two-wheeled track over undulating grassy plains.

'The track is very sandy. I have asked the driver to carry your bags so your motorbike is not so heavy and he has agreed,' said Father John. I removed the panniers, Gearsack, tent, my spare fuel and water container from the bike, but left the Pelican case hidden inside the plastic jerry and covered with hessian locked to the pannier frame. I could not risk it going missing.

'Thank you for everything,' I said, and held out my hand.

'May God bless you,' Father John said and shook my hand with a grip that carried the strength of his blessing for the ride ahead.

The driver was ready to leave. I waved goodbye and then followed the 4×4, overloaded with bags of cassava and people, along the narrow, overgrown track to Lekoni. I rode with a sense of great expectation because, after four days in Lekana and nearly a month on the floating village, it felt good to be moving forward into the great unknown.

17

A FRIEND OF ALL THE WORLD
CONGO TO GABON

Even with most of my gear stripped off the TT, it was difficult to ride in the deep wheel ruts of the sandy track. As I crossed the undulating plains to Lekoni, I lost count of the number of times I fell. I'd ride only a few hundred metres, my arms tense as I tried to keep the front wheel steady, before I'd lose control and tumble into the soft sand. Exhausted after one such fall, I left the bike on its side where it had fallen on a low rise and stood to admire the infinite expanse of the plains. The knee-high grass shimmered like golden green velvet as it moved in a cool breeze that carried the scent of rain. Herds of cattle by the thousand could graze here or wheat could be grown, but there was nothing. Not yet.

I imagined that Zaire and Congo, all of sub-Saharan Africa, would be a starving world's breadbasket in a thousand, a hundred years – maybe even sooner. The forests and plains would be gone, farmed to feed an over-populated world.

Since leaving Lekana that morning, I had ridden a hard eighty kilometres over the past eight hours. My arms ached and as I rested, I watched a late-afternoon storm loom on the eastern horizon. The clouds were dark and rumbled with thunder and flashes of lightning. Wind blew through my sweat-matted hair and, a moment later, heavy drops splashed my face as the storm passed over me.

As darkness fell, we were still about twenty kilometres from Lekoni. I continued riding as long as I could with the faint light of the bike's six-volt headlight, until it was almost impossible to steer in the narrow ruts that coursed through the deep sand. After dropping the TT and being too exhausted to lift it, I sat and waited for the Toyota, which was a few kilometres behind. When it reached me, I told the driver I could ride no further and would sleep here and continue to Lekoni at first light. 'You go ahead. I will take my gear now,' I said to him.

He looked at me, horrified. 'No. You must not stay here. There are wild animals. They will eat you,' he said and reminded me that we were in convoy and needed to travel together as the captain of the Congo Gendarmerie in Lekana had instructed.

Like many of the Africans I'd met, he believed that the African bush was teeming with lions ready to eat any human stupid enough to roam into the wild alone. In fact, there were few lions – or any 'wild animals' for that matter – living in areas outside wildlife reserves, as they'd long since fallen victim to poachers and villagers wanting to rid their farmland of any threat.

'My headlight is very faint and I cannot see. I cannot ride any further. You go on. I will be okay,' I said, shouting to be heard above the engine noise of the Toyota.

'We stay,' the driver shouted back, then informed his passengers of this sudden change of plan. Angry words were exchanged and I felt their eyes burn into me as they reluctantly began to prepare themselves to spend the night on the open plains.

After eating two tins of sardines and the baguette given to me by Father John, I lay my groundsheet and sleeping bag beside the TT, crawled into it and fell into an exhausted sleep. But in the early hours, I was woken by the light of a torch shone directly in my face.

'We go. We cannot sleep!' the 4×4 driver yelled down at me.

'What time is it?' I asked, shielding my eyes from the bright light.

'It is one a.m.,' he replied.

'I'll see you in Lekoni,' I said, crawling out of my sleeping bag to retrieve my gear from the vehicle.

My panniers, Gearsack, spare fuel and water containers were thrown down and I sat watching the 4×4 until its lights disappeared and the plains were silent and dark. I felt alone in this great expanse of blackness and began to regret my decision to stay. I crawled back into my sleeping bag and huddled close to the TT.

Despite my common sense telling me there was nothing to fear, I woke at daylight from a troubled sleep filled with dreams of wild animals roaming the plains in search of an easy meal. After fitting the panniers and packing my things, I rode across the last of the plains, which ended a few kilometres further on, the track disappearing into thick woodland. Over the next five hours I struggled to ride less than twenty kilometres over a series of steep, sandy gullies. It was impossible to ride through these with the TT fully loaded so at each one I unloaded the panniers, the Gearsack and my half-empty ten-litre container of water to carry to the other side and then returned for the bike. It was a long, slow and exhausting process that was repeated several times. At one point, lathered in sweat, I fell down under the weight of my bags and sat, unable to move. I had not eaten since the sardines and bread, but then I remembered the large tin of peaches stored forgotten in the bottom of a pannier. I'd carried the peaches all the way from Nairobi as I'd vowed, after near starvation in the desert of Lake Turkana, to always carry emergency food which was only to be opened in dire need. My heavy tin of peaches was probably not the best choice, and much lighter protein-rich nut bars would have sustained me for longer, but I figured 'emergency food' would likely also mean 'last meal food' and if this was the case it had to be something I would enjoy.

I retrieved the peaches and my tin-opener, cracked open the tin and drank the sweet juice before gorging on the peaches. The sugar coursed through my veins like the most potent drug. I stood up and, like a madwoman with super-human strength, trudged up the gully lugging my gear, then trudged back for the bike. I crossed three more gullies like this and finally arrived, exhausted, at Lekoni at eleven a.m.

'We worry for you. We not think you make it over the gullies. You very strong woman,' said the Congolese driver as I pulled up beside him.

They were still waiting for their documents to be stamped by immigration and customs. Some did not have visas and the cargo needed to be valued and the appropriate customs fee negotiated. I faced no such delay and, after downing two bottles of warm Coke and eating several bananas purchased from the stalls selling not much else, I was soon cruising along the glorious smooth black tarmac to Franceville, a two-hour ride to the west. The road was perfection compared to what I had just endured and I opened the throttle in sheer exhilaration. The TT responded and leapt forward as giddy as a colt given the chance of a good gallop. After riding it through so much sand and mostly in first gear, I worried I'd done irreparable damage by overheating the engine or wearing out the clutch plates, but it was just as strong and reliable as always. I'd asked so much of this motorcycle and it had never once failed me. The TT's big bore single-cylinder engine echoed loud and thumping as I rode down a tunnel of green through the thick tropical rainforest.

As I neared Franceville, I rode past small villages of cement-block houses with corrugated-iron roofs. Gabon was one of the wealthiest countries in sub-Saharan Africa, rich in oil and minerals, especially manganese, and Franceville was a busy town that sprawled over the surrounding green hills and valleys cleared of the thick forest that bordered it. It owed its prosperity to the nearby manganese and uranium mines and had a significant French and American expatriate community. There was also a training centre for American Peace Corps volunteers, funded by the US government for university students who volunteered on development projects in Central and West Africa. I was soon to learn there was also a multi-million-dollar primate research institute, the Centre de Primatologie, focused on finding a cure for malaria and HIV.

As I rode into the city centre, an open-top jeep driven by a handsome blond American pulled up beside me. The driver's name was Chris and he was a science student on sabbatical at the primate institute. He insisted I stay at the institute's guest quarters, a modern two-bedroom unit reserved for visiting scientists. I followed him and when he unlocked the door, he told me to make myself at home and then was gone. The unit was well stocked with Western food, as though a scientist was expected to arrive that very day. A crusty baguette lay on the bench and fresh fruit filled a large bowl. I drooled as I opened the fridge to find several different cheeses, ham, juicy ripe tomatoes, milk, yoghurt and jars of mustards and mayonnaise. I opened the pantry; it too was well stocked with crackers, sweet biscuits, packets of cereal, coffee, every kind of tea imaginable, and neat rows of tinned food including, of all things, a large tin of peaches. I grinned and reached for it with both hands. 'Thank you,' I said aloud, to show my gratitude for how quickly my 'emergency food' had been replaced after I'd eaten it only a few hours earlier. As I carried my precious gift to my Gearsack, I reassured myself by remembering that Chris had said to make myself at home.

The unit was also furnished with a washing machine and dryer, and had a deep bath with an abundant supply of toiletries and fluffy white towels. As I soaked in the tub, I ran my entire wardrobe through the washing machine and later tumble-dried it. Wrapped in a fluffy robe, I made a snack, or rather a meal, out of just about every item in the fridge, starting with the bread, cheese, ham and tomatoes, and ending with fruit and yoghurt, finally washing it all down with freshly brewed coffee. A few hours later, Chris returned in his open-top jeep and we joined a group of his friends for beers and pizza at an outdoor cafe in downtown Franceville.

As we chatted and I sang for my supper by entertaining them with stories of my travels, I felt mildly annoyed that I had been entrapped by these expats. Although I was grateful for their hospitality and for a belly full of pizza on top of my earlier feast, a part of me secretly resented them for separating me from Africa. But exhaustion from nearly two days of hard riding left me powerless to complain and I offered little resistance.

*

Before leaving the next morning, I rode out to the primate research institute, a gleaming building of glass and cement and big-budget spending (it
was jointly funded by the Gabon government and the World Bank). Chris
was not there, as he had errands in town, but he had arranged with his
colleague, Pierre, one of the institute's veterinarians, to give me a guided
tour. I pulled up outside the double glass doors and called to a dark-haired
man heading towards the entrance. It was Pierre, and after introductions
I followed him to the laboratory while he told me that most of the primates housed at the institute, mainly gorillas and chimpanzees, had been
confiscated from poachers.

At the back of the main building the Gabonese staff were busy loading
a trailer with bunches of bananas, pineapples, tomatoes and leafy vegetation for the morning feed. We walked down the wide cement drive to
where the gorillas and chimps were kept in large heavy-duty steel-barred
enclosures with bare cement floors. These creatures were merely existing,
living in frustration and anger after years of caged confinement. The first
enclosure housed a large silverback gorilla. As we approached he charged
at us, throwing tomatoes, bananas and assorted fruit, leftovers from yesterday's dinner now gone rotten. His cage was large enough for him to run,
but it was still a cage.

'They are very ferocious,' Pierre warned and he stopped just out of
range of the rotten fruit hurtling towards us. The silverback charged again,
screaming and snarling with absolute hatred.

'It's terrible for them to live in these cages. Isn't there any way they
can be reintroduced to a game reserve?' I asked, shocked by the gorilla's
deprivation.

'No, not the gorillas and chimps,' Pierre replied as he dodged a low-
flying banana that was thrown with calculated precision. 'But we have
several acres of forest that is fenced and the mandrills have freedom to roam
and forage there. But we still must feed them. You will see later,' he said and
walked past the cage to reach the next enclosure housing the chimpanzees.

A few old tyres hung on ropes from the wire-mesh roof and there was a raised cement platform for them to sit and groom each other. Opposite were the rhesus macaque monkeys, who weren't so privileged. They had been imported from Asia ten years prior and were housed, one per tiny cage, in a row about ten metres long and stacked three high.

'These monkeys were imported for HIV and malaria research because physiologically they are closer to humans than Africa's primates,' Pierre said, as I stood motionless and stared into the monkeys' sad eyes while they watched me as if pleading with me to end their misery. It was as though they were silently calling out, 'Please release us. Please end our suffering.'

I felt crushed by the pain that permeated through the institute as though it were embedded in the cement, like the build-up of a bad smell. There was no denying the negative energy that flowed from these monkeys trapped forever in row upon row of little cages.

'Come. I show you the hospital,' Pierre called and I quickly followed, feeling ashamed that by doing nothing, I, too, was part of this cruelty.

'The rhesus monkeys used to be kept here,' Pierre said as we walked down the long dark corridor towards the operating theatres. 'Their cages were facing each other, so in frustration they would self-mutilate. They chewed their arms and hands. At least now they can look at the chimps and have sunlight,' he said, sensing my sadness.

The hospital had two operating theatres but they were only used to fit IUDs in the female chimps, as more primates were the last thing the institute needed.

My tour ended with the morning feeding of the mandrills, who lived a relatively natural life in a few acres of forest surrounded by a high wire-mesh fence. A troop of about sixty eagerly waited for us, and once the bins were emptied of bananas and old bread they rushed over and greedily grabbed the food. Each filled their mouths with five or more bananas. The yellow bananas against their bright blue faces made them look like performing clowns, but life for these little fellows could not have been more serious.

By mid-morning, I was riding away from Franceville and the primates caged in their living hell, heading north to reach Cameroon before my three-day transit visa expired. Each day I rode as far as I could before finding a local hotel before nightfall. I reached Lastoursville one night and Mitzic the next. On the second day, I crossed the equator for the seventh time since arriving in Africa, but this was the first time I noticed, because there was a sign telling me so. The road was well-graded, with the thick forest hugging its edge. I passed small villages and roadside stalls selling dead monkeys or small forest antelope impaled on long sticks, the contents of their stomachs swollen as their bodies fermented in the hot tropical sun. I stopped at these roadside stalls to refuel with petrol hand-pumped from old drums. The drivers of logging trucks frequently pulled in for beers and a meal of antelope stew and rice and insisted I join them.

To cross into Cameroon, I travelled on a minor road that ran close to the border between Gabon and Equatorial Guinea. According to my map there was a ferry operating at the Ntem River just over the Cameroon border.

At the Cameroon immigration post a few kilometres from the river, I was asked why I did not have a visa. I explained, very politely, that I had been advised by the Cameroon Embassy in Kinshasa that I could get the visa at the border.

'This is not so,' said the immigration official, a large man who puffed out his chest with importance in his sweat-stained military uniform. 'You must have visa.'

'What do I do?' I pleaded and felt like bursting into tears right there in front of him. I'd started the day with a headache that had worsened since leaving Mitzic that morning and my head now throbbed with intense pain.

'I talk to the commander,' the official said and sighed as he walked out from behind the counter and headed to the thatched hut opposite.

'You can go, but you must get visa in Ebolowa,' he said when he returned a few minutes later. 'How you cross the river to Ambam?' he asked with a quizzical look as he handed me my passport.

'The ferry,' I said with a shrug as I turned to leave, and the official just shook his head and laughed.

The ferry across the Ntem River was a few kilometres further along a narrow dirt road from the border post. When I reached the riverbank, the road disappeared suddenly into the murky brown river and I quickly understood the official's laughter. The river was wide, about a hundred metres, and fast flowing. Resting derelict at its edge, half-submerged and surrounded by reeds and water lilies, was the ferry. It must have been this way for quite some time – several years by the look of the rust.

But the ferry's breakdown had not stopped the flow of people and their goods. Along the riverbank was a long row of tiny wooden boats made of what looked like rather thin plywood roughly tacked together with little nails. My head ached like it was being squeezed in a vice; I felt weak and had begun to shiver. With the boat boys smiling expectantly for my business, I stood at the river's edge and shuddered at the thought of the TT in one of those flimsy boats.

'Is very safe,' said a confident teenager manning the boat closest to where I was standing on the riverbank.

'How much?' I asked, my brow knitted with worry.

'*Huit mille*,' he replied. It was 8000 CFA, about US$15 – way too much.

'How much do they charge for a Coke?' I asked. I'd parked the TT next to one of the stalls overlooking the river that sold warm beers, soft-drinks, snacks and cigarettes. Several of the boys called out *cent cinquante* and looked at me puzzled as to why I'd enquired. A Coke would cost me 150 CFA, and from the little pouch attached to my belt I pulled out 2500 CFA (about US$4) and held the crumpled notes in my outstretched hand.

'After paying for the Coke, this is all the money I have until I change my travellers' cheques in Yaoundé,' I said with casual indifference. It was the sort of indifference that comes from too many months dealing with the best of Africa's hustlers.

'It is not enough. *Cinq mille* [5000 CFA] is lowest price,' the boys called to me, united in their determination for a better deal.

'I will be up there drinking my Coke,' I said and pointed to the stall.

I actually did have a few more CFAs, but I would need this for food and fuel. I also knew the boat boys would drop their price. As I sat drinking my warm Coke, I counted thirty boats waiting for business and I was the only customer.

But I had a new problem to contend with. The immigration official monitoring goods and people crossing the river had spotted me. He marched over and in rapid French demanded I follow him to his office.

'I don't speak French,' I apologised, but understood full well the meaning of his babbling.

'Come to office. Check *passeport*,' he demanded.

'How far to your office?' I asked, and swallowed the last of the warm Coke.

'Over hill,' he replied.

'It is too far. I ride my *moto*. I meet you there,' I said and stood to leave, showing complete compliance with his authority.

As I walked over to the TT, one of the boat boys approached me.

'Quick, we go,' he said quietly.

'For 2500 CFA?' I asked, unable to hide my disbelief.

'Yes. We go now,' he said and moved to help me push the TT down the steep bank.

In the unstable little boat, I reasoned it would be safer to lay the bike on its side; no, I was told, it was better to stand it up. The bike was lifted onto the flimsy boat, called *Rodeo*, and one of the boys sat astride it to hold it stable while the other rowed. I was rowed across the river in another boat, my heart in my mouth the whole time as I watched the water lap only inches from its beam.

'*Non rapide*,' I shouted to the boy rowing the boat with my bike.

'*Non problème, non problème!*' he yelled back as his friend sat grinning on the TT, pretending to ride it.

'*Merci*,' I sighed when the boats finally hit the muddy bank. I hugged all three boys, who were a little embarrassed by my sudden show of affection.

'*Pardon*, what is *L'ami de tout le monde?*' I asked and pointed to the boat called *Rodeo,* which had the words roughly painted along its length.

'Ah, it is friend of all the world,' he said, beaming a wide smile.

'I like that,' I said.

'Yes, that is me. I am friend of all the world. Africa is friend of all the world,' he laughed and held up his hands, spreading his arms wide as if to embrace all of humanity.

'If only everybody were friend of all the world,' I said and rode off to leave the last of the great rainforests of equatorial Africa behind.

18

THE THROWBACK
CAMEROON

At the river crossing the previous day, when my head had pounded with such intensity I thought it might split in two, I had dismissed the possibility that it was a symptom of malaria. I reasoned it could not be. I had never once missed my weekly Lariam pill, which I took as a malaria prophylactic. It must be something else; after all, headache and fever were also the symptoms of many other illnesses – most likely some virus or bacteria I'd picked up from the forests in Zaire, Congo or Gabon. The hot, humid equatorial climate of Central Africa was the perfect breeding ground for all life, great and microscopic. For the past two months, I'd been swimming in a sea of microorganisms and a few malignant ones, I suspected, now thrived within my warm, nutrient-rich body. Since leaving the floating village, I also had not been able to shake off intermittent diarrhoea, and it suddenly occurred to me that the Lariam could have passed through my gut, unabsorbed.

As I rode into Ebolowa in near darkness, weak and feverish, I now feared the worst, but I had no medication to treat malaria other than Lariam. I'd given most of my medications, including all the Halfan and Fansidar I carried, to the sick passengers on the floating village, and I had neglected to re-stock my first-aid kit in Kinshasa. It was an understandable oversight on my part, as I had fallen into a false sense of security and assumed the Lariam was protecting me.

With no energy to find the immigration office for the Cameroon visa (I figured it would be closed anyway), I searched for a pharmacy and a place to sleep, but the shops were closed and there was nothing that resembled a local hotel. As I passed Ebolowa's sprawling Catholic Mission, I succumbed to the easy option and pulled up outside its double steel gates.

'What you want?' a voice boomed from behind the thick steel when I banged on the gates.

'Please, can I stay here?' I pleaded. I did not have the energy to travel further. Now, more than ever, I needed the comfort and security that was assured behind the mission's high brick walls topped with broken glass and razor wire.

'Tourist, you go. Find hotel,' he bellowed back. Cameroon was a popular destination with North American and European backpackers, and I suspected I was not the first foreigner to knock on their gate.

'Please, speak to the sister,' I pleaded again but there was no reply. As I leaned my head in defeat against the hard steel, I heard the jangle of keys as he walked away.

A moment later, the surly guard opened the gates. One of the sisters, a kindly middle-aged French woman, was standing beside him. She ushered me inside and I followed her to a whitewashed cement-block building where she unlocked a door to a guest room simply furnished with a desk, a wardrobe and a single bed with a mosquito net suspended above it.

'Thank you,' I said. 'This is most kind.'

'Please, leave your things. It is time for dinner,' she replied, her strong French accent tinged with annoyance at my unexpected arrival during the evening meal.

'Thank you but I am not hungry. I am feeling a little unwell and need to rest,' I said, wiping beads of sweat from my forehead.

'Do you need a doctor?' she asked, her look of annoyance changing to concern.

'No, I will be fine. I have taken medication,' I lied, as I did not want to be a further burden on the mission's gracious hospitality.

'Very well,' she said with a frown and turned to leave.

I quickly opened my toiletries bag and retrieved the pack of Lariam. The instructions to treat mild to moderate malaria stated I was to take five tablets, but warned that Lariam would be ineffective if I'd been using it as a prophylactic. I popped the five pills in my mouth and washed them down with a swig of water. If this dose of Lariam didn't work, I reasoned, I'd find a pharmacy in the morning.

I took off my dirty clothes and, despite the humidity, put on my leggings and long-sleeve shirt and found two spare blankets in the cupboard. Even under three blankets I shivered, but by morning the fever had broken and my headache was only a mild throb. The Lariam had worked.

I packed, then went in search of the sister to offer a donation of US$10 for my stay, which she refused. I declined her offer of breakfast as I felt like I'd probably throw up and I also wanted to reach Yaoundé, Cameroon's capital, as quickly as possible.

As I rode away from Ebolowa, I did not give another thought to finding a pharmacy or the immigration post. My only concern was the letters from home that waited inside Yaoundé's main post office.

It was an easy two-hour ride on smooth tarmac, and by mid-morning I rode into Yaoundé, a city of cement-block buildings and French colonial architecture, built on wealth from the oil that lay off the nation's coast. I pulled up outside the main post office, parking the TT near the street vendors who lined the pavement. I asked an old man selling sliced pineapple if he would watch my motorcycle and when he smiled in toothless agreement, I bounded up the low steps and ran across the wide expanse of polished floor to arrive breathless at the Post Restante counter. It had been more than three months since I'd received news from home.

I blurted out my name to the Cameroonian woman behind the counter and she handed me a thick envelope. I ripped it open. A padded envelope contained a set of front brake pads and a whole bundle of letters. While I was there, I also posted the long letter I'd penned to my parents during my stay at the Lekana Mission. I added a few more words advising I was now in Cameroon and all was well, that I loved them and not to worry, and that I would write again soon.

I resisted opening even one of my precious letters until I reached the Foyer International, a student hostel in a leafy park on the outskirts of the city. It was listed in my guidebook as being popular with overland travellers. I pulled up at a grand, old colonial red-brick house shaded by large leafy trees, but it was disappointingly empty. In fact, I was the only guest, and I was shown to the women's dormitory, where a bed cost 2000 CFA (US$3.50).

Only once I had showered and was seated on the veranda with a ham and salad baguette, the ingredients purchased from a city supermarket stocked full of imported food, did I open my letters. With my baguette on one side and my mug of tea on the other, I relaxed in a comfy lounge chair, the floral fabric worn and frayed, and read each letter, savouring every word of news from family and friends.

But as I read about their lives thousands of kilometers away, I wondered how I would fit back into that life: what would happen to me when my travels were over? I had no set time limit, but I would arrive home at some point in the distant future. Reading the letters was the first time I'd given any thought to my post-travelling life. Through habit, I was living completely in the moment and did not worry about what may or may not happen tomorrow or the day after that. I now accepted that everything would work out. It was then that I had the sudden realisation that this newly developed mindset need not be cast aside when my travels came to an end. I would simply begin a new chapter of this journey called life. I leaned back into the chair and smiled as I was filled with an overwhelming sense of expectation about all that lay ahead. I embraced this insight as openly as I had embraced all my experiences in Africa – all those that were good as well as those that had been tests of endurance.

*

Overnight, my headache returned and by morning, as I shivered with fever, I knew I needed urgent medical help. My symptoms were much worse than the two bouts of malaria I'd suffered in Kenya. I had heard stories often enough of backpackers dying from cerebral malaria, mistaking their symptoms for a hangover until it was too late and they were found dead in their sleeping bags. As I travelled through Africa, I had developed a relaxed attitude to my health simply because I had rarely been sick. I gave little thought to what I ate from the blackened pots or to the unhygienic conditions in which food may have been prepared by street vendors. I lived as the Africans did. I never bought bottled water; I always filled my water bottle from a tap, drum or creek – whatever was available. This is what everyone else did and I had mostly remained in good health. I felt my body was better for it and my immune system had grown stronger with Africa coursing through my veins.

Just before leaving Australia, I'd spent two weeks visiting my parents on their banana farm in far north Queensland. On my last night there, I sat outside on the patio drinking beers with my father.

'You'll do okay in Africa. You're strong. A lot stronger than you know,' my father said, and with his words the soft hum of insects and the call of frogs seemed to reach a crescendo in the darkness of the warm tropical night.

The meaty fingers of his large, hairy hand gripped the stubby cooler around his beer. He had farmer's hands, made tough and calloused from years on the land, the skin stained red by the rich volcanic soils.

'I'm prepared for this trip. I've been getting fit. Going to the gym and learning how to fix my bike. I know I'll be okay,' I said to reassure him, because I knew secretly he was worried.

'You are my daughter and that makes you the kin of Neanderthal man,' he said and sat back smiling proudly, clasping his oversized hands behind his mostly bald head, which was tanned a dark brown.

'What?' I asked. After a few beers, my father liked to discuss the meaning of life and other such philosophical matters, but this was the first time I'd heard him allude to the Ellis family having heritage that dated back 40,000 years to when Neanderthals hunted bison, wild horses and deer across northern Europe and Britain, including Wales, where my father had grown up.

'Look at me. Look at these arms. Look at this hair. I am a throwback,' he said, pulling at the mat of hair tinged red that covered his thick forearms, the skin baked to a leather toughness by years under a tropical sun.

'And I have the tooth to prove it,' he said and opened his mouth to show a large gap in the row of molars along his bottom jaw.

'So where's this tooth?' I asked, daring him to prove his theory.

'It has only one root. Not two like normal teeth. It's very rare, so the dentist asked to keep it,' he replied.

The more I pondered my family heritage, the more his theory made sense. My father was short, stocky and rather hairy. His head was large for his small stature. His forearms were thick and his shoulders broad. I had often witnessed him complete great feats of strength for his size. In the faint light cast through the kitchen window, I could actually see the Neanderthal in him, now that he'd mentioned his prehistoric origins. If he was a throwback, with more than just a hint of Neanderthal genes than the rest of the human race, that meant I was too. I had the same stocky legs (an Ellis family trait), although not as short as his, and some of his hairiness. My forearms were quite thick and my shoulders a little too broad. Even as a child, I was unusually strong for a girl.

'This is something to be proud of,' he said, deadly serious.

'But it's not something I'm going to announce to the world,' I joked, then flexed the muscles of my left forearm to feel the strength that lay under the skin.

'Neanderthals were stronger, lived longer and could resist disease better than homo sapiens,' he said, as though we were a different species.

I later read more about the physical traits of Neanderthals. My father was right. The human race would be much stronger and more disease-free if Homo sapiens, as they'd migrated into northern Europe, had interbred with more of the Neanderthals, instead of slaughtering them to extinction as some evolutionary anthropologists have theorised.

I sat on the edge of my bed, trying to muster all the strength of my Neanderthal genes so that I could stagger from the women's dormitory to the veranda, where I could hear the voices of the two Cameroonian youths, the hostel's caretakers. Holding myself up, and walking with one hand on the wall, I reached the veranda, where they lounged on the steps in the warm morning sun.

'I have malaria. Where is the nearest pharmacy?' I asked and flopped down beside them for fear I may pass out at any moment.

'Not opened. Today is Youth Day. It is holiday,' said the first young man.

'You look very sick. We take you to mission hospital. It is not far,' said the second and they both put their arms around me to walk me there through the park.

I had to wait nearly an hour before the doctor would see me. My head pounded and sweat ran down my face and saturated my shirt as my body struggled to fight the malaria parasite that was rapidly multiplying inside me.

'I am taking Lariam. I need Halfan or Fansidar,' I told the doctor when I was finally called into his office; but neither of these medications was stocked in the hospital pharmacy and instead, he gave me a packet of paracetamol.

'This is no good,' I said to the doctor.

'I am sorry. We have nothing else here,' he said apologetically and asked the nurse to send in the next patient, a mother with a small baby who had not stopped crying since arriving a few minutes after me.

'I'll go back to the hostel. Maybe another traveller has arrived and they will have something,' I said to the two youths who waited for me outside the doctor's office.

They helped me walk back to the Foyer. As we approached the steps, I saw that a freckle-faced young man with thinning brown hair sat drinking a beer on the veranda.

'Hi. I'm Gary,' he chirped. 'You don't look so good.'

'Do you have any Halfan or Fansidar?' I asked, collapsing on the lounge beside him.

'Yes, Fansidar,' he said and rushed off to retrieve it from his backpack.

The drug had an immediate effect. Two hours later the fever broke and as I lay soaked in sweat, Gary told me about his travels through North and West Africa.

He was from Canada and had 'defected' from his overland truck tour a few weeks ago. 'Defected' was the term commonly used to describe the hardy individuals who abandoned these tours in favour of independent travel.

'From Cameroon, I'll cross Central African Republic, Zaire and then on to Uganda and Kenya,' he said rapidly, barely able to contain his excitement.

'I'm so glad to be away from that truck. It was terrible. You sit in the back of it all day. We pass straight through villages where the children throw stones at us. We have to camp away from the road. Well away from any people. It is not the way to experience Africa,' he said, and I nodded lethargically from where I lay on the couch.

'But that's the way it is with overland trucks. The locals hate them because they stop at their villages and buy everything from the market, pushing up the prices,' I said, recalling one of my many conversations with Eric on the floating village on how best to defeat poverty in Africa. I believed that budget travellers had much to contribute to village economies but Eric disagreed, pointing out the anger and intense dislike the overland truck tours caused.

'Every meal they cook is the same: rice and vegetables. On my own, I am free. I can eat African food,' Gary said. 'And they form little groups and argue with each other all the time. The couples bicker non-stop.'

'An overland truck tour is not for everybody,' I said, noticing that my headache was now just a mild ache.

'It was my worst nightmare,' he said and picked up my empty glass to refill it from the kitchen sink.

During the night I woke with a dry cough that wracked my weak body, and by morning my torso was covered in an itchy rash. I asked Gary for the Fansidar packet and read the side-effects listed in the enclosed leaflet. A cough and rash indicated a severe allergic reaction to the sulphur-based drug, and if this happened, the drug was not to be used again. For the next three nights, I hardly slept as I coughed and scratched. On the fourth day, the cough was gone and the mass of angry red welts covering my back and stomach had calmed to a faint pink. I felt strong enough to ride into the city, to the Nigerian Embassy. The two-week visa would cost 6500 CFA (US$13), and I was told by the sullen clerk to collect my passport in two days.

I used this time to rest and to service the TT. I cursed myself when I found one of the hoses from the air box had disconnected. The hose had probably come off when I'd dropped the bike while riding in the sand as I crossed from Congo to Gabon hundreds of kilometres back. The inside of the air-filter was covered with grass seeds and grit. Dust had sucked straight through the top of the carburettor and into the engine. I felt like crying. I had been so diligent, bordering on obsessive, and had cleaned and oiled the air-filter daily, as well as changed the engine oil more often than I needed to, to prevent the premature wearing of engine parts. Days of hard riding through equatorial Africa, coupled with the intermittent diarrhoea I could not shake off, had weakened me and I'd become careless. It would have been a simple job to check the bike in Franceville. This lack of attention had almost certainly shortened its life. The only thing I could do was change the oil. Fortunately, I had collected four litres from the Mobil depot in Yaoundé the previous day.

'I'm sorry,' I said and patted the TT in apology. This motorcycle had always given me constant reliability that seemed to defy the laws of basic mechanics. If I were to believe my intuition the same way I did when deciding what road to take or whether a person was good or intended me harm, then the explanation for its reliability lay at a very deep level – far beyond the sum of its parts, down to the deepest level of all, where trillions of atoms vibrate in perfect harmony to the ever-so-slight frequency generated by my own positively charged thoughts of devotion.

On the morning of the second day, I collected my Nigerian visa and rode away from Yaoundé towards northern Cameroon. But I did not have the same feeling of anticipation about the journey as I had had in Zaire and Congo, or during my sprint through Gabon. I still felt weak and the TT was not its usual self. Instead of a steady deep rumble, it coughed and spluttered as the last of the dirt and grass seeds worked through the carburettor. Several times, I drained the float bowl and gave the carburettor a good knock with my hammer to dislodge any particles that had partially blocked the jets.

I rode past Mount Cameroon, shrouded in cloud, and on to Kumba, where the smooth tarmac ended abruptly to become a rough dirt road full of potholes and covered in fine red dust. I rode almost non-stop each day, riding until dark, and slept at local hotels.

At Foumban I rested for a day, to visit the city's fourteenth-century royal palace. Despite Foumban being one of Cameroon's major tourist attractions and a centre of traditional African art, it was unusually empty of foreigners. As I wandered the corridors of the deserted palace and its rooms of artefacts and ornate gowns, brittle and yellowed with age, I questioned why I had not ridden directly west into Nigeria. I'd have been nearly across it by now rather than doing this ride into the hot, dry lands of northern Cameroon – a 3000-kilometre detour. But then, if I were to take the shortest way, what was the point of riding through Africa at all?

One late afternoon, I rode into Tibati, a small village on the road leading north. Dust swirled around me as overcrowded Peugeot 504 station wagons, used as local taxis, and heavily laden trucks rumbled past. I was covered in a thick layer of red dust, my sweat turning it to red mud that ran down my cheeks. Before I checked into a local hotel, I refuelled and topped up the oil. The TT's oil consumption had settled at one litre every 800 kilometres. While compression was still good, I feared oil consumption was likely to increase and I was glad that Mobil had numerous depots throughout West Africa.

I'd gone all day without eating. While on the bike, I gave little thought to food and it was only when I stopped that hunger pains forced me to search for a meal. I was still suffering from bouts of diarrhoea, which I'd not been able to shake since Zaire. Outside the hotel, by the faint glow of coals burning in an oil drum cut in half sideways, a man sold roasted meat on sticks.

'Yuck, liver,' I said in disgust as I bit into the strip of meat woven onto a stick. I gave it to a boy aged about ten who stood close beside me.

I pointed to the larger strips of meat, which looked like steak. I took a big bite, anticipating juicy tender beef, but it too was liver. I ate it anyway, thinking the iron would do me good, but then wondered if it was full of tapeworm eggs or some other parasite. The thought turned my stomach and I no longer felt like a beer so I drank a Coke instead; at least it was cold.

Was I Africa'd out? Where had my enthusiasm gone? I just wanted to retreat from Africa. I reasoned that my low mood was due to the last few days of hard riding. I was still weak from the malaria, and the diarrhoea had gotten steadily worse. It was only natural that I was not feeling full of life. This ride north had become an ordeal, a test of endurance, and I prayed for tarmac, for relief from the dust, potholes and bone-shaking corrugations.

My wish came the next day, when the dirt ended and I rode on 300 kilometres of new tarmac to Garoua. I arrived just before nightfall at the Hotel Salem and negotiated a room for 1500 CFA (US$2). I removed the panniers so the TT could be pushed through the narrow doorway to reach the back courtyard and the guest rooms.

'Can you help me, please?' I asked the four Cameroonian men in their early twenties who were lounging with lethargic disinterest on a thread-bare couch.

'Ah, we are very weak. It is Ramadan and we have not eaten all day,' said the one who looked to be the eldest of the four.

'I, too, am very weak,' I replied, and leaned against the wall to rest before struggling to carry my panniers through to my room.

When I returned for the TT, the four men were standing next to it, ready to lift it up the two low steps and push it down the corridor to the courtyard adjoining my room.

My room was small, clean, and had electricity, but it backed onto the open-air shower and toilet, which was just a hole in the cement floor. At least it was washed clean and the thick cement walls stopped the foul odour emanating from this gigantic pit of shit.

The night was hot and it was a pleasure to stand motionless under the cold shower. As the water washed away the dust and fatigue, I looked up at the clear night sky filled with a billion bright stars, the call to prayer resonating in the distance.

After a meal of fried goat meat and rice, I lay on my bed and was asleep before my head hit the pillow.

But in the early hours, I awoke with stomach pains, and at daylight I was shitting blood and mucus. In Yaoundé, I had restocked my first-aid kit with Halfan, antibiotic powder, surgical spirit, bandaids, bandages and Fasigyn, an antibiotic to treat intestinal bacterial infections. The pharmacy did not have Flagyl, but I was told Fasigyn would also treat dysentery and Giardia. I rested during the day but was still shitting mucus and blood by evening. This was worse than Giardia. I flipped through the pages of my guidebook and discovered that it was inadvisable to eat the local peanut butter sold in little dollops at market stalls. While on the floating village, I had filled an old coffee tin with this homemade peanut butter and wantonly consumed it. In the hot African sun the spread, probably ground in the most unhygienic of conditions, was the perfect breeding ground for amoebic bacteria.

I took two Fasigyn pills, which I hoped would be enough to kill whatever I had ingested, and retired to my room to write my diary, but movement soon caught my eye. I watched in disgust as one of the largest cockroaches I'd ever seen, a beast of a thing as big as my thumb, and then another, emerged from a hole in the floor. Just a few came at first, then more followed. I quickly swatted these, but my room backed onto the hole-in-the-ground toilet and sat on top of a pit of filth that harboured a whole civilisation of the things. I shivered as I thought of the cockroaches crawling around my room and over me the previous night.

I had been exhausted and must have slept through their night-time forays into my space.

The closest thing I had to cockroach killer was engine oil so I poured a little of this down the hole. A swarm rushed out and I swatted them all. I poured more oil down the hole and stuffed it with toilet paper to stop the second wave. After I swept the dead cockroaches into a pile and deposited them outside my front door, I spent a restless night filled with nightmares about cockroaches crawling into my every orifice. When one landed on me, I sat bolt upright and screamed. I spent the rest of the night awake, sorting my gear, cleaning out my bags and scraping off the red dirt caked to the leather panniers.

At daylight, I washed the TT and noticed two cracks in the pannier frame. It was not the first time the welding had cracked. Fixing it was a simple job of unbolting the frame from the bike. As the town stirred, I rode off to find a local welder and was back at the hotel as its adjoining restaurant opened for breakfast. My appetite had returned; the Fasigyn had worked. After a breakfast of omelette, bread and sweet black tea, I said goodbye to the four men who'd helped me when I arrived. Two sat on the front step and the other two lounged on the couch at reception.

'We hope you had a pleasant stay at Hotel Salem,' said one of the men seated on the couch.

'You have a big problem with cockroaches. I have never seen so many,' I said, unable to forget my nightmare experience.

'They will not bite,' laughed the man beside him but I just shuddered.

I moved on, glad to leave the Hotel Salem and its enormous population of cockroaches, and set out for Rhumsiki, arriving late that afternoon. I rode through its village of mud-and-thatch huts to the nearby lookout, to view the lunar landscape of the Rhumsiki volcanic plugs, one of Cameroon's most popular tourist attractions. The sun cast a hazy, red glow over these tall volcanic formations, which dotted the wide brown valley. The West African trade winds, the Harmattan, blew hot, dusty air down from the Sahara all the way to the Gulf of Guinea in West Africa.

It was a mystical scene and a just reward for the hard ride north. Alone at the lookout, I sat mesmerised. What drove the power of the Harmattan winds, I wondered? What forces could carry tonnes of dust over thousands of miles? I wondered how far the particles of dust blown onto my face had travelled.

My solitude lasted only minutes until a group of youths, who'd started their chase when I rode through their village, reached the lookout. Breathless and sweaty, they clambered up the steps to the low cement platform where I was sitting.

'Unbelievable. Doesn't that just take your breath away?' I said as they sat down beside me.

'You go on hike?' they puffed.

'No. I must find somewhere to stay. It will soon be dark,' I said and took one last look before heading back to the TT.

'Tomorrow then,' they chorused.

'No. To sit here is enough for me,' I said and they looked at me with the sad eyes of a litter of puppies denied a tasty scrap of meat. The chance of business would soon slip away.

I did not fancy a night in Rhumsiki village with all its resident hustlers. With two hours of daylight left, I'd keep riding until something else turned up.

'You can stay at my uncle's village,' said a boy on a rusty bicycle who'd been the first of the horde to reach the lookout.

'Lead the way,' I smiled knowingly. Somewhere to sleep always materialised. It had become such a regular occurrence that I never doubted it would.

I followed the boy, and after three kilometres we left the dirt road where a goat track led to a collection of mud huts with tall conical-shaped thatched roofs surrounded by a high mud-brick wall.

I greeted the boy's uncle and was invited into the compound. Pushing the TT through the narrow entrance, I was shown a windowless mud hut, the air inside thick with dust and smelling of dried cow shit. I declined in favour of my tent. For the hut and dinner, I was told it would cost 2000 CFA (US$3.50) and I gave the boy 500 CFA for his effort.

After washing the dust from my face with water from my ten-litre container, I poured the rest into a large clay pot and the elderly thin woman bent over the fire nodded her thanks. I could easily get more water tomorrow, while all their water had to be carried by the women and girls in containers balanced on their heads for several kilometres. I then sat down at the cooking fire with half a dozen grubby kids and we watched as the elderly woman stirred stiff millet porridge and green lumpy slime – a highly nutritious sauce made from the leaves of the baobab tree. When the meal was served, I could not eat the sauce, as it tasted like rotten muck. The kids laughed hysterically when I screwed up my face after scooping it into my mouth with some of the millet porridge.

The following morning I travelled on a back road over the dry rocky hills to reach the Nigerian border. I stopped several times to photograph the groups of tall conical-roofed huts and was almost immediately surrounded by hordes of children, their bellies swollen from malnutrition. Holding out their grubby hands, they looked at me with eyes that were red and watery from the constant irritation of dust. It was mango season across the Sahel and I'd bought four large peach-coloured mangoes from a village I'd passed through earlier. I gave the fruit to the children, who gave them to the older girls, who quickly carried them back to their hut.

'*Donnez cadeau? Donnez bonbon?*' they asked nervously, their hands held out in anticipation.

'I'm sorry. *Cadeau fini,*' I said, feeling helpless as I had no more food to give and did not carry sweets as gifts. Although the children's view of the white man or woman as the bearer of Bics and *bonbons* had been firmly established years ago, I did not want to contribute to perpetuating this view. I got back on my bike. I was only a few kilometres from the Nigerian border town of Banki and I rode towards it, a little nervous. I'd been frequently warned by other travellers of Nigeria's lawlessness – of how it discarded its dead on the roadside and in its rivers to float grey and swollen towards the ocean. But my more immediate concern was getting through Nigerian customs without a valid *carnet de passage*. I had chosen not to pay the more expensive bond to underwrite the cost of the 400 per cent import duty this nation of oil required – the only such country to do so on my travels. The Nigerian officials would be well aware of this detail and I would either have to pay a huge amount of 'dash', which I could not afford, or I would be refused entry. It would require great stealth and cunning on my part to outwit them.

19

LAND OF OIL
NIGERIA

Late in the afternoon, I rode through the border town of Banki, a collection of dilapidated corrugated-iron huts and dust-covered cement buildings. It sat on a flat expanse of desert dotted with thorny trees. The ramshackle market was busy with traders. Overloaded trucks belched black smoke and dented Peugeot station wagons used as taxis arrived and departed, spewing passengers and their belongings onto the town's dusty streets.

Banki was also a popular border crossing for the overland truck tours from London, but none passed through that afternoon. When my documents were stamped at Cameroon customs and immigration, not an eyebrow was raised over the absence of a visa. Further up the road, at the Nigerian immigration post, the official in military fatigues was just as polite as he stamped my passport without question.

'Have a good holiday in our beautiful Nigeria. Customs is over there,' said the young man, pointing to the small, dust-covered cement-block hut with a flat corrugated-iron roof.

As I walked slowly towards the TT, I did a quick calculation as to how much 'dash' I could afford. This would be my point of negotiation when Nigerian customs discovered my carnet was not valid. I had about US$1600 left from the money I'd withdrawn through American Express in Kampala. Only half was in cash, and I could not afford to pay the hundreds they would surely demand. I decided that my only choice was to take my chances.

I quickly put on my helmet, fumbling nervously as I did up the strap. I slipped on my gloves, torn and faded from more than a year in Africa, and thanked God when the TT spluttered to life with the first kick. As I rode slowly away from Banki, I kept one eye on the customs office reflected in my mirror and the other on the potholes that littered the road. There were no frantic waves for me to stop. I did not want a bullet in my back if they mistook me for a terrorist instead of a street-smart traveller. If I was pulled over, I would plead ignorant. But I was not stopped and I soon reached the smooth tarmac for the 120-kilometre ride to Maiduguri.

Gary, the Canadian backpacker in Yaoundé, had warned me about the number of police and military checkpoints on Nigeria's roads. Like their counterparts in Zaire, Nigerian police and soldiers also subsidised their meagre wages with money from passing motorists and the occasional tourist, whose fine, of course, increased accordingly to their nationality, as one must be cashed up in order to travel so far from home. I passed three checkpoints before I reached Bama, seventy kilometres from Banki. I rode straight through each one, as nobody attempted to stop me and I was not about to volunteer. Each time, I looked in my mirror but the soldiers did not move from where they lazed in the shade of a spindly tree beside the road. Maybe it was just too hot for them to bother.

I avoided another military checkpoint at the junction for Bama, even though I stopped at a deserted garage opposite as I needed to refuel. A boy came out to the bowser but waved me on, shaking his head to indicate there was no petrol and pointing up the road, indicating I'd find petrol at the next garage. Nigeria had vast oil reserves, and in partnership with American oil companies had drilled the offshore fields since the early 1960s. The oil reserves were still substantial, but due to a lack of specialised equipment and expertise to refine the oil, nearly all of Nigeria's crude was sold on the world market. The Nigerian government then had to import most of its petrol and diesel, selling it to its people at a highly subsidised rate. Even with petrol shortages, though, the black market price was still only ten naira, about six cents, per litre.

A few kilometres up the road, I reached the next garage and, as the TT was being refuelled from a hand-pumped drum, a beat-up Toyota pickup filled with armed soldiers in military fatigues stopped in a cloud of dust beside me.

'Travel documents!' boomed the sergeant. Four Nigerian soldiers sat perched in the back clutching machine-guns. The sergeant fumed with rage and I quickly handed over my passport.

'You have been to South Africa!' he yelled as he flicked through the pages. He obviously had not heard apartheid was over.

'You come back with us. We search your bags. You must be hiding something. You did not stop at the checkpoint,' he barked as beads of sweat covered his shiny forehead and his military fatigues strained under the pressure of an overweight body that must have been lean and strong when the uniform was first issued to him.

The teenage boys who sold petrol from the drums stood back and watched in respectful silence while the sergeant continued to exert his authority. After I'd paid the boy for the fuel, I had no choice but to follow.

'Sit here,' the sergeant pointed as he walked towards a mud-brick hut after I'd followed the pickup to the military checkpoint at Bama junction. I sat on the edge of the woven straw mat with a group of armed soldiers sprawled in the shade under a scraggly tree. A moment later I was summoned.

'Why did you not stop?' the captain demanded, the additional badges and bling on his uniform leaving me in no doubt of his authority.

'I have just arrived in Nigeria. I did not see the checkpoint. I was day-dreaming. In a world of my own. I am very sorry,' I said, and hoped my torrent of excuses and pleading tone would convince him.

'Your journey is long. Australia, it is very far,' he said as he continued to study the visas and entry and exit stamps of all the countries in Africa I'd passed through. As he browsed the pages of my passport, I professed how good it was to be in Nigeria, with so many friendly English-speaking people, and how much I was looking forward to travelling this beautiful country and trying all the delicious Nigerian food I'd heard so much about.

'We wish you well on your journey. You go,' he said, handing back my passport.

As I rode away, the captain and his men stood outside the hut and waved me on with vigour filled with good wishes. I could not believe my luck.

I rode on through a flat expanse of desert. After the first hundred kilometres on the endless stretch of black tarmac, I was bored. It was only the speed of the occasional car or truck dangerously overtaking me that kept me alert for the ride to Kano, 700 kilometres to the north-west. Other motorcycle travellers had warned me about the dangers of travelling on Nigeria's roads. The 504 Peugeot taxis, crammed with passengers, had an average speed of 140 kilometres per hour. Suspect brakes and balding tyres meant accidents were a common sight and I passed several upturned wrecks, rusted and burnt out, a pertinent reminder of this ever-present danger.

I had decided to ride the additional 700 kilometres to Kano, instead of heading south from the junction at Bama, as I reasoned that since I was this far north it would be a shame not to visit this ancient desert city with its impressive Kurmi Market, one of the largest markets in Africa. I also wanted to buy trade beads. Many of these had been made in Venice as early as the fifteenth century. Shiploads of them had been sent to Africa to buy slaves, ivory and gold. I was especially interested in the chevron beads made from layers of red, blue and white Venetian glass. I'd seen them in Nairobi but the price of US$25 to US$50 per bead made them a souvenir I could not afford. I hoped that in Kano the prices would be cheaper.

I passed through Maiduguri late afternoon and refuelled, but I kept going as I had no desire to sleep in any of the grubby hotels in that dust-covered city. I travelled a further fifty kilometres in the last of the day's light and stopped where a collection of mud-and-thatch huts lined the road near a radio tower enclosed by a high mesh and barbed-wire fence.

Children barely dressed in dirty rags ran to greet me. A boy aged about twelve could speak some English and, on my behalf, asked the old man, the caretaker of the radio tower, if I could sleep there. The boy asked if I wanted to eat. They would cook a chicken. I thanked him and handed the old man 100 naira, which he refused.

'Is it not enough?' I asked, perplexed. The money was equivalent to two dollars and a high price to pay for a scrawny African chicken.

'No money,' the boy said and I understood that I was their guest. But later I secretly gave the 100 naira to the old man, who accepted it graciously.

The gates to the radio tower were unlocked, and I parked the TT inside the fence at the back of the square brick hut, where it would be out of sight of passing traffic. Unlocking the instrument room, the old man indicated I could sleep inside. He flicked a switch and smiled, showing a mouth mostly devoid of teeth. It was like the ancient world meeting the modern as the room suddenly filled with the bright glow of fluorescent light. Out here, in the middle of the desert, I would have light to write in my diary.

After a quick wash using my own water, I headed to the thatched huts, my plate in hand, to wait with the half-dozen children for dinner, the aroma of frying chicken making my mouth water.

'We bring for you,' the boy told me when I'd sat down on the dirt, the children staring wide-eyed at this strange white woman who'd ridden into their lives on a monster of a motorcycle.

'No, I would like to eat with all of you,' I said and he fetched a low stool made of sticks and woven bark.

About ten minutes later, the old man summoned me with a wave to come inside the cooking hut. The mama placed three bowls on a straw mat on the hardened earth floor. She indicated I eat. I passed on the green slime made from the leaves of the baobab tree, and with my hand, I took a scoop of the heavy millet porridge and selected three small pieces of the scrawny chicken, but I could easily have eaten it all. The children sat patiently outside; they would get the leftovers. When I'd ridden through Maiduguri earlier, I'd passed stalls of freshly butchered meat and now wished I'd bought some; we would all have been feasting on meat tonight. Next time I would make sure I had more than a loaf of bread, sugar, tea and rice to share with people who had nothing but gave their hospitality so freely to a passing traveller.

It was hot and stuffy in the radio tower's instrument room, so I slept outside next to the TT, cooled by a whisper of breeze. But stomach cramps kept me awake, and in the early hours I was shitting blood and mucus again. The amoebic bacteria had re-colonised my intestines. I immediately began my last course of Fasigyn.

*

After thanking the old man with a firm handshake and warm smile, I rode west at daylight the next morning. The sun filled the horizon like an immense golden orb rising out of the Sahel. The morning was cool, and it was a relief to ride the first few hours without the unbearable heat. I stopped in Potiskum and attracted a crowd of about a hundred people, mostly children. They surrounded the TT and stared through the fine wire mesh covering the door and windows of a small restaurant where I ate a breakfast of two hard-boiled eggs and white stodgy bread, clenching my bottom for fear the food would pass straight through me. I refuelled, as this was the last petrol stop until I reached Kano, 300 kilometres along a straight stretch of black tarmac. The temperature would soon reach over forty degrees Celsius and there would be no Cokes, not even warm ones.

Every kilometre passed agonisingly slowly. Each stretch of ten felt like it took ages to clock over. From mid-morning, the heat rising from the hot asphalt forced me to stop often to drink from my water bottle. The water was so hot I could have brewed tea. Like a mirage emerging out of the desert in the intense heat of mid-afternoon, Kano finally appeared on the horizon.

Before riding to the Kano Tourist Camp on the outskirts of the city, I needed more medication. The Fasigyn was not enough against this hardiest of bacteria and I hoped I'd be able to buy Flagyl. All kinds of prescription drugs could be purchased at the roadside kiosk and as another painful spasm tore at my gut, I leaned against the counter that faced the dusty street. I was given a blank look when I asked for Flagyl and wrote it in large neat letters. I could only assume the drug was sold under a different label in Nigeria. I was asked to describe my poo.

'It's got pus and blood in it,' I said and the shopkeeper gave me a packet of white pills in nondescript packaging for 70 naira (US$1.50).

Ten minutes later I pulled up at the Kano Tourist Camp, where a dorm bed cost the equivalent of US$1, and was told that another tourist on a motorcycle had arrived the previous day. What good luck, I thought, as I carried my panniers and Gearsack into the large louvered dormitory, and was greeted by a handsome, broad-shouldered, sandy-haired man with hazel-green eyes and an easy nature. We introduced ourselves and vigorously shook hands as neither of us had seen another motorcycle traveller for some months. In fact, I was the first Peter had met. He was from New Zealand, about the same age as me, and had ridden down through Tunisia and Algeria from London on a Yamaha XT600. We spoke nonstop about our travels, our voices blending as a hum under the ceiling fan that whirred above, cooling us with its light breeze.

After I'd unpacked my things and showered, I joined Peter in the lounge and we continued our tales of adventure. He had left his job with the New Zealand police force and was riding to South Africa, where he hoped to join the South African police.

'I want some excitement in my life,' he said, his eyes sparkling with an awareness that life holds so much more when it is embraced with full force.

'You will certainly get it in South Africa,' I said, unable to take my eyes from the TV, which was playing a re-run of *Home and Away*. It had been months since I'd seen television and while I normally had no interest in this internationally popular Australian soapie, in Nigeria I was mesmerised.

'You know,' Peter whispered, leaning close, suddenly making me notice the muscles of his tanned arms and broad chest through the thinness of his white T-shirt, 'people who travel on motorbikes, especially through Africa and on their own, are social misfits.'

'I've never really thought of myself as a social misfit, whatever that may be,' I said. 'I've always done my own thing, but I can't see any harm in that.'

I enjoyed Peter's stories, told with wit, of his adventures fraught with danger and corruption. He'd learnt the hard way, and when he'd first arrived in Africa he'd lost more than US$500 to unscrupulous border officials and moneychangers in Algeria and Niger.

Peter was certainly a little eccentric and very funny as well. I had not laughed with such carefree abandon for a long time and I realised I was very attracted to him. It was a strange feeling that had crept up on me unawares.

But this feeling did not linger, and in any case he represented something of far more immediate importance to my journey: he was a skilled motorcycle mechanic. With his help, I changed the clutch plates, but an adjustment was all that was really needed. I'd been carrying a spare set provided by Yamaha Australia and was glad to rid myself of the weight from the bottom of a pannier.

As we chatted, the TT unceremoniously laid on its side in the courtyard, I again felt physical desire for Peter. I had not had sex since leaving Kakadu over a year ago, but Peter stirred a warm responsiveness in me. With our shoulders almost touching, I breathed in the possibilities carried by his scent. Why not drop everything and suggest we ride together to South Africa? Maybe he was the reason I'd felt compelled to take this 3000-kilometre detour north? Maybe greater forces were at play to bring us together. What would he say?

But, like me, Peter was on his own journey of discovery. And he seemed just as determined as me to see it through to the end, no matter what.

'All done,' he said, oblivious to my thoughts as he tightened the last bolt on the engine case.

*

The white pills, Nigeria's equivalent to Flagyl, had killed the amoebic bacteria in my gut but I was still weak and needed another day's rest before the two-day ride to Nigeria's coast.

Peter and I spent this day in Kano seeing the tourist sites – the famous indigo dye pits, the labyrinth of the Kurmi Market with row upon row of stalls selling trade beads. I'd read that the African traders had barrel-loads of these old beads, but to control the price they only released small amounts at a time to the markets. Even here, they wanted US$20 per chevron bead. That was twenty nights' accommodation, or food and fuel for a week.

Without privacy in the dormitory Peter and I shared, I never got a chance to take the sexual energy I felt towards him any further and we said goodbye at daylight the next morning. As we embraced, we promised to stay in touch.

I rode south on a road that cut a straight black line through a desert still cooled by the last of the night air. Ahead was 1000 kilometres, two days of hard riding, to reach the coast. To break the monotony, I travelled on a minor dirt road for some of the way but headed back to the main highway after a clash with an angry mob in a small village. I'd taken a wrong turn and stopped to ask directions from a group of teenage boys, but they and several men had surrounded me and the anger in their eyes had told me to get out. Fortunately, the engine was still running and I was able to leave in a roar of stones and dust thrown up by the TTs knobby rear tyre when hands tried to pull me from the bike. I was grateful for its power, as a lesser motorcycle would not have had the strength to escape. The warm and gracious hospitality of the Islamic north was gone.

A third of Nigerians are Christians, mostly living in the populated south. Halfway to the coast, I spent the night in the grounds of a church, sleeping under a mango tree on my groundsheet, next to the TT. There was no hotel or mission in the town and a group of Nigerian teenagers had advised I would be safe at the church. But my intuition, like a gut-wrenching ache, warned me of their menace and I spent a sleepless night fearing I'd be bumped on the head and robbed of everything.

As I neared Nigeria's coast, it was good to ride on smooth tarmac once again through the lush dark green of tropical Africa. I stopped to refuel in Ikom and checked my map. Just over two weeks earlier, I had passed through Mamfe across the border in Cameroon. I could have ridden just over 100 kilometres to reach this very same spot where I now waited in the queue at the petrol station. Instead, for reasons I could not explain, I had chosen to take a 3000-kilometre detour, as though distance, time and wear-and-tear on the TT were irrelevant to my decision. This ill-conceived ride north had left me filthy, tired and rundown, and the bike in need of a new chain and sprockets. For this reason I now headed to the town of Eket on the coast. Leo and Myles, the two Australian motorcycle travellers I'd met in Malawi, had pointed out the possible places throughout Africa where I might get spares for the TT or help with mechanical repairs. At the time I had not taken much notice, but I was now grateful they had penned on my map next to Eket: 'expats/bikes'.

I had also redirected any letters that might arrive in Yaoundé to Eket, but there was only one letter from my aunt in England, advising me that my ten rolls of undeveloped slide film posted from Cameroon had arrived. What a relief it was learning this parcel had made it.

'Are you going to the Mobil terminal?' asked the well-dressed Nigerian man in dark slacks and white starched collared shirt. He'd approached me as I was standing outside the small iron-clad Eket post office reading the letter from my aunt.

'What Mobil terminal?' I asked, puzzled. Leo and Myles had never mentioned anything about a Mobil terminal.

'Out at QIT,' he replied and pointed to the Mobil sticker on the TT.

Even though I had a letter of introduction from Mobil Australia, I only ever presented it at Mobil depots to receive a four-litre bottle or two of Mobil 1 fully synthetic engine oil and as much petrol as I could carry, topping up the TT's tank and my spare ten-litre jerry.

I was unsure what to expect as I rode down the narrow tarmac road towards the sprawling Mobil terminal. But I knew the moment I passed through security and rode towards the mass of stainless-steel pipes and tanks that I would momentarily leave Africa.

'You look like you need a rest. We'll book you into the Mobil staff house for a week,' said a senior manager, a grey-haired American who towered above me as he read my letter from Mobil Australia. As I stood in the pristine neatness of the reception area, I vigorously nodded my thanks, feeling like a character straight from the pages of Charles Dickens. My hair was matted with dirt and the faded navy Burberry trench was covered in dust. I'm sure I stank of sweat. Since leaving Kano two days earlier I had not washed, and the previous night I'd slept in the dirt. For the past two days, I'd mostly lived on warm Coke and Nigeria's stodgy white bread, a legacy of the former British colonialists. And I was still weak from the amoebic bacteria that had lived in my intestines for nearly two months.

After being introduced to the motorcycle enthusiasts that made up some of Mobil management, I was taken to the Bristow helicopter hangar and workshops.

'Ah, heaven for the TT,' I said as I walked into the enormous modern hangar with its shiny grey floor that was so clean I would happily eat my dinner off it. As I followed the Mobil staffer, both the Nigerian workers and the white expat pilots and mechanics stared at me as though I was the strangest thing they'd ever seen.

The expats were a mix of English and Scottish men. I was still having problems with the TT's carburettor; the whole thing needed a good clean out. I asked the stout, grey-haired Scotsman, the chief mechanic, if I could use his workshop and was told to bring my motorcycle in the morning.

As I followed the car ferrying the pilots to the Mobil guesthouse in Eket, I said a prayer of thanks for this most recent twist of fate. The guesthouse was a whitewashed colonial building surrounded by clipped lawns and an immaculate garden that bloomed with purple bougainvillea. I was given an air-conditioned room with ensuite.

'Dinner is at six,' the Nigerian housekeeper told me and I was left alone in absolute luxury that seemed so unreal I was afraid to move in case it all vanished just as miraculously as it had appeared.

After a very long bath, I joined two middle-aged Scotsmen watching TV in the lounge. They were deep-sea divers employed by the contractor Sea Weld Engineering and they were at the end of a string of twelve-hour shifts. The following day they would return to Britain for their swing off.

'Aye, ya one crazy lassie to travel Africa,' said the ginger-haired man, the younger of the two, who introduced himself as Keith.

'How da ya get on with the roadblocks? Any problems?' asked Brian, the second man, who had thinning brown hair and looked to be in his mid-forties.

'No, I never stop, I just ride through,' I said and helped myself to another chocolate biscuit as the two Scots looked at me in disbelief.

'Dinna ya know, an English guy got shot dead for runnin' a police checkpoint just the other day. The bullet went right through the back of his head. Twas a shame,' Keith said. 'The bastards are allowed to shoot anybody who does not stop.'

'Bloody hell, I'll be stopping from now on,' I said and sat back on the lounge, silently thanking whatever it was that was keeping me safe, for what must have been the millionth time.

'When will you be back?' I asked.

'Next week,' Keith replied.

'Can I ask a big favour? Can you bring me a chain and sprockets?' I asked.

'Aye, there's a Yamaha dealer in Aberdeen. It'll be naw problem,' Keith said.

'I'll meet you at Lagos airport before you fly back to Eket,' I added, thankful that sourcing my new spares would be a trouble-free process.

After dinner, I joined the Scots and we walked over to the Mobil staff bar in the same fenced compound as the guesthouse. Here I met a few of the helicopter pilots. All, at one stage or another, had done their time in the North Sea oil fields. After the wind, cold and poor visibility of Scotland, Eket was a holiday camp for the pilots, who ferried oil workers to and from the nearby offshore drilling platforms in year-round perfect weather. One of the pilots, was a clean-cut, dark-haired Australian in his mid-thirties. His name was Mike and he was a motorcyclist. We hit it off immediately.

'It's amazing what you've done. Millions dream of doing such a trip, but most never do it,' he gushed and I was a little embarrassed, as I didn't feel like anybody special.

'I'm just an ordinary girl riding a motorcycle through Africa. Lots of people are out there doing it,' I said, which was true. Lots of people were travelling the world by motorcycle; lots of women too – although I'd only come across one, Kaoru, the Japanese girl I'd met at Lake Naivasha in Kenya. I hoped she was okay. I hoped she'd made it on to South Africa and up through Namibia to Angola and Zaire. I would never know, as her address was gone along with my motorcycle jacket, stolen in Kinshasa.

'It takes a lot of guts to do it, though,' Mike said, not deterred.

'But anyone *can* do it,' I shot back. 'I reckon you just have to take that first step and then once you're on the road, it's easy. Everything falls into place. Travelling Africa has made me realise that I can do whatever I want to do, but it couldn't happen until I made the first move. After that, momentum takes care of the rest,' I said, trying to explain what it was that had propelled me to come this far; to leave the security of my home, my family and friends and a well-paid job in northern Australia.

'That's the hard part. Most people give up on their dream. They never even take that first step. They always find excuses not to,' said Mike, signalling to the barman to bring two more beers. 'I was in a dead-end, boring job in Australia in a factory. I didn't do that well at school, but one day I got this idea that I wanted to fly helicopters. Everyone thought I was mad. They put me down. Told me I couldn't do it. But I worked long hours to save the money for the lessons. I studied hard and in the end I passed the tests. I received my licence and landed a job with Bristow. I haven't looked back,' said Mike, nodding in complete agreement with my views.

'You know, the thing is, when you make that first move, it's like something steps in beside you and helps you. It's like all these chance encounters and coincidences start happening. There have been so many times on this ride when everything was about to turn to shit, but then something right out of the blue happened to help me,' I said, trying to explain what I now accepted as completely normal.

'I've also learnt to trust my intuition,' I continued, 'because I'd get a feeling that I should go this way or that way and this gut feeling has never been wrong.'

*

The next morning I was at the helicopter hangar early. The grey-haired Scottish mechanic led me to an air-conditioned workshop and I was given a bench with a set of precision tools to dismantle the TT's carburettor. I cleaned every tiny piece, refitted it, and once the bike had cooled began the process of checking the valve tappets. But the exhaust-valve adjuster caps felt like they were moulded to the engine and I did not have the strength to undo them. I asked one of the Nigerian trade assistants to help me. I assumed he'd know to undo the cap in an anti-clockwise direction, so I didn't bother to supervise him, but when I heard the snap, I knew immediately what had gone wrong.

'Oh shit,' I said, then looked at the Nigerian, who had a very worried look and handed me the spanner.

'Bloody hell,' I said.

'Problem?' he asked.

'Yes, big problem,' I replied. 'But don't worry. It is not your fault.'

'Oh good. I must go,' he said, and before I had a chance to say another word, he turned and walked with long strides out of the hangar. I undid the second valve cap, which was not as tight, and checked the tappets. Neither the intake nor the exhaust needed any adjustment and I cursed myself for messing with them in the first place. As the manual instructed, I'd checked the valve tappets about every 10,000 kilometres but they'd only ever needed slight adjustments.

After I'd told the Scottish head mechanic what had happened, he used metal glue to repair the cap and secured it to the engine with silica and wire.

'We'll fax Keith. He can bring back a new one. Aye, this will get you to Lagos,' he said.

As I waited for my spares, I spent my days lazing around the pool at the Mobil staff bar, where all food and drinks were free; but even cold beers, steak sandwiches and ice-cream got boring after four days so I hitched a ride with Mike in his helicopter for a tour of an oil rig.

I moved on from Eket the next day, a Sunday, riding to Abraka, where I planned to spend the night. It was about halfway to Lagos, which would mean I'd avoid entering Nigeria's notorious capital after dark. Keith would fly in to Lagos airport on Tuesday afternoon and I'd collect my spares from him before he boarded his flight to Eket.

Even though I'd regained my health and a little weight, I'd lost some of my confidence as I rode west towards Lagos. I even questioned my reasons for riding a motorcycle alone through Africa. Many of the Mobil staff had repeatedly asked me: 'Why are you doing this? You might get killed. Aren't you afraid?'

I did not know how to answer their questions as I'd never given these concerns much thought. But their worry for my welfare now cast a shadow over my blind faith. However, as the TT rumbled west on smooth black tarmac, the thump of its single-cylinder big-bore engine sounded strong and reassuring. Even though I was risking my life and the road I travelled was often rough, tiresome and discouraging, I would not give up. I did not want to give up. I opened the throttle and the TT responded. It did not want to give up either.

Several times after leaving Eket, I was forced to ride around logs strewn across the road as makeshift roadblocks by armed men from the nearby villages. The area I was driving to was home to a large expatriate community working for the oil companies and any expat driving at night would be held up at gunpoint. There were also numerous police and military roadblocks. I fully intended to stop, but I was always waved through. Over the last eighty kilometres to Abraka I passed five roadblocks, but I was a small fish compared to the steady stream of expats heading to the Abraka Hotel for Sunday lunch. It was halfway to Lagos and an Austrian couple travelling in a Land Rover who I'd met at Mama Roche's in Nairobi had recommended I stay there. They'd described it as a serene place set in a forest with a white sandy beach and crystal-clear spring-fed pools – paradise.

I turned off the main tarmac road and followed a dirt track where a sign indicated the direction to Abraka Town. After following the track through dense forest for about five kilometres, I came to a collection of huts. Ten or more late-model cars – BMWs, Peugeots and Mercedes – lined the track near a corrugated-iron-clad hut.

'What do you want?' asked a thickly set Nigerian man, his biceps straining under the thin cotton of a dirty and ripped T-shirt of a nondescript colour.

'Where is the Abraka Hotel?' I asked.

'Back down the road,' he replied.

'What, you mean the track to the left, just there?' I asked, and pointed to where the track led from the huts into the forest.

'No, back to the road,' he shouted angrily.

Three men came out from the hut and walked towards us. They were also dressed in rags. Two men followed behind them, but these men wore tailored pants, collared shirts and highly polished black leather shoes. Then it dawned on me: I had ridden into a hideout of stolen cars.

I put the TT in gear, quickly turned and accelerated before those in charge might think I would blow their cover. I am sure discussions were held as to whether or not to put a bullet in me as I sped away.

The Abraka Hotel was only another five kilometres along the main tarmac road, and then about two kilometres along a track clearly marked with signs directing the way. I could not believe I'd missed it earlier.

It was hot and humid, and my only thought was to swim in the crystal-clear pools. With my bathers and towel, I headed to the back of the hotel and the white sandy beach.

My first impression was of a beach resort in Kenya. Fat white men and stunning African women in brightly coloured one-pieces and floral bikinis frolicked in the water. Waiters, neatly dressed in long black shorts and white T-shirts, carried trays of beers and fancy cocktails to the guests, who sat under thatched sun-shelters. Reggae music played through the loud-speakers and the aroma of barbecuing meat filled the air.

I placed my things on a sun-lounge shaded by a thatched shelter and headed to the women's toilets to change into my navy one-piece swimsuit. That first dive was pure heaven. Taking huge gulps of air, I swam under-water for as long as I could, as though I'd morphed into a river otter. With each dive, it felt like the spring-fed pools with their pure white sand and pale aqua water held some kind of magical power. I emerged refreshed and energised to doze on a sun-lounge, undisturbed except by the waiter who brought me the cold Coke and hamburger I ordered for lunch.

At five p.m., to avoid the risk of armed holdup if caught out after dark, all the expats packed and left for their compounds in Warri and Port Harcourt. Not one of them had spoken to me all afternoon, they had just stolen the occasional glance as though I were a homeless person, a hobo, to be avoided. I waited for the rush to be over and then returned to the TT. A group of Nigerian drivers were gathered around it, and when I reached them they all asked questions about my journey.

'Where you stay tonight?' one of them asked.

'I was thinking about here,' I said.

'No, it is very expensive. You must come with us to Sapele. I will talk to my master,' he insisted. 'Master', I knew, was the term Nigerians used to refer to their employer. 'We are waiting for them. Shortly, they be here,' he said.

The 'masters' soon arrived, a group of four German men, all about thirtyish. They introduced themselves, telling me that they were also motorcyclists, and had toured Europe, Morocco and Algeria. They invited me to stay with them.

'See, they are good men,' one of the drivers whispered once I'd accepted their offer.

The Germans lived in a double-storey brick townhouse in a secure compound in Sapele, and worked as electricians refurbishing an old power station. I was shown to a spare room and after a shower, I joined them on the balcony for beers and a meal of barbecued steak and salad. As we chatted long into the night about our motorcycle adventures, I felt grateful for this camaraderie and shared appreciation for life on the road.

*

As I rode into Lagos the next day – on three occasions coming very close to having a head-on collision on the road from Sapele to Benin City – I was anxious and a little scared about what I'd find. Everything I'd heard and read about this sprawling city of nearly ten million people made it sound like I was about to ride to my death. If the speeding traffic didn't kill me, the armed robbers would.

Originally I'd had no intention of visiting Lagos, but I needed the spares that Keith would bring from Scotland. Despite Lagos's bad reputation for everything – traffic congestion, the odd decomposing body in the harbour and aggressive, unfriendly people – on first appearances, it was nothing like the horror stories I'd heard. The glass panelling of modern high-rise buildings reflected the hot afternoon sun, and a four-lane highway led into the city. I followed the signs to Ikoyi Island, the road taking me over the newly constructed Third Axial Bridge. It afforded sweeping views over central Lagos, and then, amongst all the glitter, I could see the squatter camps and people living in squalor under the flyovers.

Once I reached Ikoyi, I also reached the traffic congestion and the pollution from the engines of more than a million vehicles. I weaved past queues of double-parked cars that had been waiting for hours, even days, at the few service stations lucky enough to have fuel. I thanked my good luck, and Mobil Eket, for the slip of paper in my pocket that said I was booked into the Mobil guesthouse for a week. God help me if I had to stay in a local hotel in downtown Lagos, which would be both expensive and dangerous.

Ikoyi Island was the Beverly Hills of Lagos with its shady, tree-lined avenues and grand colonial houses hidden behind high-security fences. It was a world away from the potholed streets, traffic congestion and open bubbling black sewers that was Lagos proper. I headed over the lagoon and onto Victoria Island, where the ultra-modern building of Mobil House sat. After a brief meeting with Mobil management, my arrival was phoned through to the guesthouse.

Once again I was housed in absolute luxury. I showered, then headed to the lounge for pre-dinner drinks and watched the world fall apart on CNN. The news reports from Africa were far removed from my reality. Just before dinner, the Mobil contractors and those employees in transit to Eket arrived and I sat with three American men contracted to install Mobil's computer systems. It was all very comfortable, but I looked forward to the next evening when I would collect my parts from Keith at the airport, and be on my way back into the thick of things. For the past week I had been living in a world that was so detached from the rest of Africa it was as though I was not even there.

*

I recognised the ginger-haired Keith instantly when he came through the international arrivals gate of Lagos airport.

'I could naw get the cap,' he told me as I walked with him towards the terminal for his flight to Eket.

'I might be able to get one from the auto spares market,' I said and handed him 100 English pounds for the chain and sprockets. When I'd arrived in Lagos, the Nigerian staff at the Mobil guesthouse had told me I could get whatever parts I needed for my motorcycle at the sprawling Lapido auto spares market.

'I hope bringing the spares didn't cause you too much trouble with customs,' I said as an apology, as I knew he'd paid 'dash' to the officials.

'Naw,' he lied.

I thanked Keith and quickly left, as I had the use of a car and driver from Mobil management and I wanted to get back to Ikoyi. It would take two hours or more to get through the late-afternoon traffic. When I opened the package while sitting in the back of the sleek, air-conditioned Mercedes, I realised at first glance that the sprockets were not compatible with the TT and the chain was too short. It was not Keith's fault; I should have ordered the spares from Yamaha Australia while I was in Eket. By air courier, although expensive, the spares would have arrived within a week.

First thing the next morning, I rode out to the auto spares market but could not find the valve cap, so I faxed Yamaha Australia with a list of the spares and my credit card number. As well as the exhaust valve cap, I ordered a carburettor float bowl O-ring as the one on the bike had flattened and was leaking. Also a fifty-tooth rear sprocket, a fourteen-tooth front, and four oil filters.

For the chain I phoned Mike in Eket, asking if I could swap the one from Britain with his spare. No problem, he said, telling me it would be on the next flight to Lagos. I was impatient to get moving again, and tried consoling myself that it was only a matter of waiting for the parts to arrive. No more than a week, I was assured when I phoned Yamaha.

The expats looked after me well, taking me to their hangouts: the Lagos Yacht Club; Coco and Fekki's, bars that overlooked the lagoon; embassy social nights; the markets; various restaurants; and afternoon drinks at luxury hotels such as the Federal Palace and Eko Meridien. On Sundays we went to Eleki Beach, where vendors wandered past the bars selling everything an expat might desire – if they did not have it you only had to ask. With money anything was possible.

I spent most of my days with three university students whose parents lived as expats in Lagos. The students were on a semester break from their studies in Britain. I met them at the Lagos Yacht Club and would join them sailing a dinghy, the strong winds carrying us at speed up and down the lagoon. For my thirtieth birthday, they took me to the renowned Lagos night spot the Shrine, to see Fela Anikulapo Kuti. Fela, who died in 1997, was the pioneer of Afrobeat music and spoke up against human rights abuses and political injustices. He was Nigeria's most famous musician and his words criticised government policy, only adding to his notoriety amongst the downtrodden masses.

It was midnight when we walked down Pepu Street in Ikeja, past the stalls selling marijuana, beer and spicy grilled meat, and into the large corrugated-iron shed that was the Shrine. We waited, drank a few beers, smoked a few joints, and waited another couple of hours. Finally, at four a.m., Fela staggered onto the stage holding a cigar-sized joint, with much cheering from his adoring fans. He could hardly stand and mumbled and slurred his way through the lyrics of his famous songs. The crowd, out of respect, watched, listened and cheered, but after an hour Fela called it a night.

I was thirty years old – a third of my life lived. It was a turning point, a significant milestone, and it seemed fitting that I celebrate the occasion at the Shrine and in the presence of the great Fela. In only a year, I had grown from having about as much spiritual depth as the muddy puddles on the potholed street outside to knowing there was something truly great influencing our lives. For a brief moment, through the haze of pungent smoke, I understood how it all worked: we were part of a vast pool of energy that ebbed and flowed in response to our thoughts, working with us to make our dreams come true.

'Yes, that is it!' I shouted, but my words were lost in the calls from the crowd for Fela. When I tried to explore the concept further, when I questioned it and tried to make sense of it, it was gone, lost in the haze that circulated inside the Shrine's cavernous interior.

'Fela, Fela, Fela!' shouted the crowd, their voices rising in a deafening crescendo.

*

As I waited for the spares to arrive by air courier from Australia, I lodged my visa applications for Burkina Faso, Benin and Ghana. On the day I came to collect my Benin visa, I sat on a wooden bench outside the steel gates, waiting for the embassy to open after lunch. I felt a little depressed, as I'd been languishing in Lagos for nearly two weeks. I had phoned Yamaha Australia the previous day and been assured the spares had been shipped and would arrive any day.

At first, I'd enjoyed the expat lifestyle and Mobil's generous hospitality, but I craved being back on the road again – to be back in the real Africa. I also felt I had outworn my welcome with Mobil, although the expats assured me that the expense was just a tiny drop in the very large Mobil ocean. They also reminded me of the good PR Mobil had received through the articles about me published in Nigeria's leading national newspapers and read by millions: the *Guardian*, *Sunday Times*, *Sunday Tribune* and *National Concord*. The journalists' stories had been filled with praise for the support Mobil had provided and had embellished to the extreme my comments about the Nigerian people and all the help and hospitality I'd received from them.

I'd also learnt that my father had had a heart attack in late January. I discovered this when I first arrived in Lagos and phoned my parents. My father assured me he was fine and back at work growing bananas, but he no longer cut the heavy bunches, some of which weighed up to a hundred kilograms. He'd employed a fit young man to do all the heavy work and he mostly stayed in the shed de-handing the bunches. His heart attack had been caused by a rapid heartbeat, which was now controlled with medication. But what if he had died? He would have been long buried by the time I learnt of his passing. These thoughts played on my mind for days and made me realise the full impact of my isolation from my family. I'd last phoned my parents in Rwanda, which was over three months ago. When the Nigerian journalists had interviewed me, they were horrified I'd visited Rwanda. 'This is a very dangerous country,' they'd said, just days before the Rwandan genocide erupted on 7 April 1994; the Hutu majority slaughtered nearly one million Tutsi people over the next hundred days.

I scratched the ground absently with a stick, making patterns in the dirt. An old Nigerian man in ragged shorts and shirt, his skin wrinkled and his bony, calloused feet in sandals made from car tyres, shuffled over from a nearby roadside stall. He sat beside me on the narrow bench and mumbled some words in his language.

'What?' I asked, deep in melancholy, as if the dark cloud that had settled over Africa as blood soaked into Rwanda's soil had settled over me, too. The old man giggled, a few drops of saliva wetting his lips as he smiled a toothless grin.

'It means a snake can't swallow a crab,' said the Nigerian man selling drinks and cigarettes from the stall, and chuckled at the cleverness of the African saying. 'You are the crab and nothing can swallow you. You also have a hard shell and nothing can get through to hurt you,' he added.

I looked at the old man and smiled in understanding. Yes, I suppose I was like a crab and had managed to scurry away from danger many times. But I was struck by a further meaning. Perhaps the snake doesn't want to swallow the crab, but instead respects its hard shell and audaciousness, just as the crab respects the power and strength of the snake. This seemed a more apt meaning for me, and for the relationship I'd formed with Africa.

*

Finally, after three weeks in Lagos, late one afternoon I received a phone call from Mobil management to say that a package from Yamaha had arrived and would be delivered to the guesthouse shortly. It arrived after dark, so I was up at daylight, fitting the sprockets and chain and the new exhaust valve cap; then I packed the TT and ate a very large full English breakfast, my plate loaded with crispy bacon, fried eggs, mushrooms, grilled tomato and hash browns. I phoned Mobil management to thank them for their hospitality. I thanked all the Nigerian staff at the Mobil guesthouse for looking after me, and by eleven a.m. I was riding away from Lagos. I rode over the long, sweeping Third Axial Bridge, towards Benin and back into Africa proper.

20

A TRIBAL CLASH
TOGO TO GHANA

To cross into Benin and then Togo, the neighbouring countries which occupy two strips of land wedged between Nigeria and Ghana, I chose Pobè, a small immigration post about a hundred kilometres north of the busy Trans-West African Coastal highway border crossing at Seme Border. With a carnet not valid for Nigeria and my fourteen-day visa expired by nearly three weeks, I knew I would be forced to pay much 'dash' to the notoriously corrupt Nigerian immigration and customs officials.

Fortunately, at Pobè, the immigration official, a young man neatly dressed in new military fatigues, did not notice my very poor attempt at forging the expiry date on my Nigerian visa. I'd bought the ink pad and date stamp in Nairobi after the Austrian who'd sold me the tent and petrol stove at Mama Roche's advised that this was an absolute necessity, as delays were an inevitable part of a ride through Africa.

'You must see customs before you cross,' the Nigerian official said and pointed to the iron-clad shack across the potholed tarmac.

'Yes, of course,' I said and smiled my thanks as he handed back my passport. With my carnet tucked under my arm, I headed for the customs hut opposite, hoping this official would be just as polite and kind – even more so if he should notice that Nigeria was not listed on my carnet.

When I reached the open doorway, I found the customs official shirtless and snoring, his rather large hairy belly rising and falling as he slept on a dirty foam mattress on a rusty spring bed. An empty bottle of the local gin lay on the floor. I stepped silently into the shack, counted slowly to sixty, then walked with casual confidence back to the TT, hoping I had not raised the suspicions of the immigration official, who was still standing in the doorway of his hut opposite.

'I hope you had a pleasant stay in Nigeria?' he called.

'Yes. It was very pleasant. Thank you. Goodbye,' I called back as I fumbled nervously with my helmet strap and then pulled on my gloves.

As I disappeared down the road, I glanced in my mirror. The fresh, as-yet-uncorrupted official gave me a wave before retreating into his hut. I opened the throttle and the TT leapt forward as if in celebration of our freedom. There'd be no need for dodgy date stamps, no need to sweet-talk my way out of paying 'dash' to corrupt officials, and no need to dodge roadblocks or even the stray bullet. Ahead was an easy two-hour ride back towards the coast on smooth tarmac. It was Friday and my destination for the weekend was Alice's Place, a small campsite on the outskirts of Togo's capital Lomé near the Ghanaian border. The motorcycle travellers at Mama Roche's had told me about the Swiss lady, Alice, and her shady campsite and thatched bar. It was popular with motorcycle and 4×4 over-landers from the UK and Europe, and I was looking forward to sharing a few beers and swapping tales of adventure. Mobil Nigeria did not import Mobil 1 but they'd phoned Mobil Togo and I would collect eight litres from the Mobil depot in Lomé on Monday morning. I needed this oil for the ride into North Africa. I also needed a *laissez-passer*, a permit issued by Togo immigration in Lomé, which would give me permission to pass into Ghana, as the border was officially closed due to tribal clashes in the north.

To reach Burkina Faso, I would need to ride north, but I'd been assured by the Ghanaian embassy official in Lagos that the army had control of the area and peace had returned.

I rode into Alice's Place late in the afternoon. But there were no motorcycle travellers, no overlanders, not even a lone backpacker. The grounds were clean, relatively secure and a roughly painted sign pointed to the beach.

Disappointed, I walked into the thatched bar to pay the small fee to pitch my tent and buy a cold beer. I expected to meet Alice and envisioned her as another Mama Roche, but Alice was away for the weekend and a broad-shouldered Togolese man in a Hawaiian shirt placed a cold beer on the bar. The only guests were four middle-aged German men at a table covered with empty beer bottles.

'Sit. Drink beer!' boomed a tall, thin, bearded man with lank dark hair that coiled to his shoulders.

With beer in hand, I walked over and sat at their table, and the bearded man cleared a few of the empty bottles aside to make room.

'Thank you. So where are all the travellers?' I asked, my disappointment sounding all too pitiful in the company of the Germans, who had the shifty eyes of men whose business was in shady dealings.

'Us. We are the travellers,' he bellowed and stretched his long arms as though embracing his friends and laughed.

'You are Australian. Australians are good. Drink much beer,' he said on hearing my accent, then raised his hand to the barman to bring another round.

'So Australian lady, where you go from Togo?' he asked.

'Through Ghana to Mauritania and then Morocco,' I said with certainty, but inside I was a bundle of nerves with little confidence for the ride ahead. There was a lot of desert and drifting Saharan dunes to ride through before I reached Morocco. It was the end of my first day back on the road, my first day back in Africa after three weeks of expats telling me how dangerous Africa was. Three weeks of watching news reports of wars, murders and disasters on CNN that implied anyone who ventured outside their lounge room must have a death wish. Over those three weeks, it was as though I'd been brainwashed and a battle raged inside me. One voice reassured me of the kindness of strangers and reminded me that things had always worked out, while the other filled my head with taunts of all the things that could go wrong. It taunted doubly louder with the knowledge that I would soon ride through an area of burnt-out villages where people had slaughtered each other with machetes.

But I reminded myself of the reassuring words of the official at the Ghanaian Embassy in Lagos. Yes, I would take this back road. I would find a village where I could safely pitch my tent with the permission of the headman, whose authority would protect me. This back road would take me back into Africa.

The Germans told me the days of there being many travellers at Alice's were over. The risk of armed hold-up made the route down from Algeria across the Sahara too dangerous and only the hardiest of individuals took this overland route. These days, most took the alternative route from Morocco to Mauritania, but this too was fraught with risk. The border was officially closed due to the long-running Western Sahara conflict over disputed lands. The desert crossing over sand dunes was also reported to be mined, and the only way to cross was with a military-escorted convoy of trucks carrying goods from Morocco. I'd already decided Algeria was not an option for me. While I had not heard about the bandits, it would be irresponsible to travel alone for seven days across a desert of shifting sand dunes. 'It is much better you fly to Europe or take ship,' said the bearded German, and his three friends chirped, '*Ja, ja.*'

'We are car salesmen,' he said, when I asked what they were doing in Togo. He told me they bought used Peugeot 504 sedans and station wagons in France and shipped them to Togo to sell to the Nigerians who worshipped this French car for its reliability and longevity even under the harshest of African road conditions. 'It is very hard to kill this car,' he said. 'I see you also beat Africa. It not kill you. You tough Australian lady,' he laughed and patted me on the back in beer-fuelled merriment.

'For many years, we drive down from Europe through Algeria with our cars but today is dangerous. Bandits hold up travellers and take everything. Just leave you in your underwears. You smart not to go through

Algeria. We don't take this chance anymore. Now we put our Peugeots in containers and ship to Lomé. Much safer and better, but we have problem with our Togolese buyer. He did a deal with customs and we must pay dollar or they will confiscate our cars so we wait here for three weeks to negotiate price. Welcome to business in Africa,' he laughed.

I spent the weekend drinking beers with the Germans, swimming in an aqua-blue sea and generally lazing around the shaded, sandy campsite of Alice's Place. On Monday, I collected the eight litres of Mobil 1 and, after a two-hour wait in the hot sun outside the immigration office in Lomé, was issued with a *laissez-passer*, the permit to cross into Ghana.

I rode into Ghana's capital, Accra, in the late afternoon. As with most capital cities in Africa, I was only there to get the visas I needed to cross into the next country or two. In Accra, I would get the visa for Mali issued in twenty-four hours for US$20. My guidebook recommended the cheapest places to stay were the YMCA (men only) and YWCA (women only) near the city centre.

The guard unlocked the gate and directed me to the women's dormitory, a large double-storey cement-block building set in a securely fenced compound. A plump Ghanaian woman, the caretaker, was sitting on the front step and struggled to stand as I approached. She waddled down the dark hallway and I followed her to a four-bed dorm, where a petite blond American lay on a bottom bunk reading a novel. Her name was Kelly and she told me she was a Peace Corps volunteer on a short break from volunteering with a community north of Accra.

The other dormitories were overcrowded with young women from all over West and North Africa. They were students on university scholarships funded by a plethora of international aid organisations. The toilets were overflowing, the plumbing leaked, and lacy underwear hung from every available space. The evening was hot and humid, and mosquitoes buzzed around us incessantly. To escape the hot, stuffy room, Kelly and I sat on the front step with two young women from Sudan who were waiting for their boyfriends to collect them for a night out dancing. They were dressed in tight blue jeans and snug-fitting singlets, their breasts round and perky in push-up bras. They were stunningly beautiful. Both were on scholarships studying English and commerce at the University of Ghana.

'Life is good in Accra. We never want to go back to Sudan,' said the one in a bright-pink singlet when I asked about her job prospects in war-torn Sudan.

'Here we go out every night dancing. The men, they love us,' said the second, her skin a luminous black against the white of her ribbed cotton top. 'It is so much fun being here. You two should come with us to Piccadilly Circle. The band is good,' she said, her dark almond eyes sparkling with all that was exciting in life. We agreed to meet them later. It was only nine p.m., and it would be midnight before the crowd filled the open-air nightclub.

We danced under the stars to the sounds of African rhythms mixed with jazz. At dawn I was still on a high from the shared energy generated by all who filled that dance floor and could not sleep, so I ordered a breakfast of sweet milky coffee, thick slices of white bread spread liberally with margarine and two fried eggs from a street vendor outside the hostel's gates. I showered and then packed the TT and rode out to the Malian Embassy to collect my passport when it opened at nine a.m. I'd lodged my visa application when I'd arrived in Accra the previous afternoon.

An hour later I was riding west on smooth tarmac lined with tall coconut palms, a white sandy beach on one side and tropical rainforest on the other. I only planned to travel about 250 kilometres to Busua Beach, but on the way I detoured to the slave port of Cape Coast and its notorious castle, built by Swedish traders around 1650. It had first been used for trade in timber and gold but had later become the 'gate of no return' in the trans-Atlantic slave trade to the Americas and the Caribbean. Alone, I walked the castle's battlements and dark dungeons. I looked down into the deep pits where thousands of West Africans had once been kept chained and then branded before being loaded into the cramped and inhumane conditions of the slave ships. Rising from the dark earth floor was a mild stench. It hinted of a hundred years of human excrement and suffering. The stone walls were covered in scratches where the people, enslaved into misery, had left their immortal mark with nails worn until bleeding.

Upstairs was the governor's offices and sleeping quarters, cooled by a sea breeze. I wondered if the moans of his captives had ever pulled at his conscience; or perhaps he'd been impervious to the suffering as he sat in velvet-covered luxury sipping tea from fine china.

*

I planned to stay at Busua Beach for a few days as once I headed north, I would leave the coast and, soon after, Africa. My ride was nearly over and I wanted to drag it out and savour every last moment before it came to its end. Through my travels and through her people, Africa had led me down a path of awakening that hinted at something greater than mere day-to-day existence. It had been a slow unfolding of awareness, as though Africa was my mentor, the keeper of all knowledge and wisdom, and little by little she had revealed small snippets of what I needed to know.

As I neared Busua, the tarmac deteriorated to a sandy track that hugged the coast. By the late afternoon I'd arrived at the Busua Pleasure Beach Hotel, where camping was the standard fee of US$1 per night (about 800 cedis). I was the only guest and pitched my tent under a shady tree, where I had uninterrupted views of the sea and was lulled to sleep by the gentle sound of rolling surf washing over the golden sand.

I camped there for four days but it could have been four weeks, as I fell into a void where time seemed to stand still. I walked for hours along the beach, deep in thought as I tried to understand my journey and what it meant, if it meant anything at all. I questioned my theories about synchronicity – all those chance encounters and coincidences that had happened with such regularity. Maybe this is just what happens when you travel, because you are moving through so many experiences? Of course such things will happen, because life is no longer curtailed by routine.

Each morning and afternoon I flopped and wallowed in the surf, absorbing every ounce of goodness that comes from the sea, hoping it would bring me peace. Late in the afternoon I walked the few hundred metres along the beach carrying my blackened cooking pot, which doubled as my eating bowl, to Busua village, to buy dinner of fish and rice from one of the mamas. It was also the time of day when the fishermen returned to shore in their brightly painted boats, their sails fluttering in the wind. I'd sit on the hull of an upturned dinghy with a group of children and watch the boats ride in over the surf, while others were pushed out over the waves to fish during the night. The day's catch – tuna, shark and black marlin – were laid on the sand in a neat line and would be shared equally amongst the fishermen's wives. It was an exciting time and the entire village came to help.

'Why you not have husband?' asked a boy of about twelve years perched on the hull of the upturned boat beside me.

'I have not met the right man. I have not yet fallen in love. Maybe one day I will be so lucky,' I said, amused.

'How old are you?' the boy on my left asked, joining the conversation.

'Thirty years. I've just had my birthday in Lagos,' I replied, and they both looked at me horrified.

'Oh, it is so terrible. You are not yet married. You not have baby. Soon you will be too old,' he said with genuine concern for my happiness. 'I will marry you,' he offered and crossed his arms with a firm shrug that hinted he would one day be a strong, considerate and handsome man.

'It is very kind of you, but I am not ready for a husband. I must complete my journey first. Then, if God wishes, I will have a husband and a baby, or maybe two or three,' I said, and realised the boys might be right. I was thirty years old and if I was to find a husband and have children, I had better be quick about it, as my fertility would soon start to decline.

But while it was true that I didn't have endless years, I was also not ready to start a family. After Africa, my intention was to work in London as a motorcycle courier for six months or so. I needed to top up my travelling funds before the ride home through Russia and along the Silk Road down through China and then South East Asia. I had a vague idea of the route I'd take home and, just as Africa had beckoned me, so too did Russia. My intention to work as a motorcycle courier was as much a part of my motorcycle ride as my travels through Africa. Without the TT, the magic we shared would be gone and there would be no journey.

'Well, if you change your mind, I am a good fisherman. I can look after you,' he said, sitting straight and proud with all the confidence of youth.

*

After a restless night caused by strong winds that blew in across the sea and shook my tent, I woke early the next morning and packed the TT. It was time to move on.

I followed the back roads to Yeji, from where I'd cross Lake Volta and head into the tribal lands, where the fighting between the Togolese and Ghanaian villagers had just ended. As I neared Lake Volta, two Ghanaian men at a petrol station where I refuelled assured me peace had returned. The tribal clashes had occurred after a Togolese tribe crossed into Ghana, settled on some land and successfully farmed it. The Ghanaians, a happy-go-lucky friendly people, did not mind – not until they realised the Togolese were doing so well. They demanded the Togolese share the profits; after all, it was their land. The Togolese refused and defended their hard work with machetes. Eventually the Ghanaian army was called in to stop the massacre by the more warlike invaders who were better equipped and stronger fighters than the Ghanaians. Countless villages were burnt and thousands of people displaced. Yeji, a sprawling fishing village on the shores of the receding Lake Volta, was now bursting with refugees.

I pulled up outside a crumbling, low-set cement-block building, the Volta Lake Hotel, where I got a room for 3000 cedis (US$3). After showering, I carried my cooking pot to a nearby street vendor and bought my dinner of *fufu* and goat-meat stew with a hot spicy sauce, and with a cold beer I sat on the front step. In the coolness of late afternoon, it seemed that all of Yeji was on promenade on its dusty main street. When I finished eating, I idly watched the parade of couples, families and groups of men and women ambling along the dusty road while I waited until eight p.m., when the hotel, operating as the local cinema, would screen *Terminator* in its courtyard. As I sat on the step, I was soon joined by a soldier, a broad-shouldered young sergeant. He and his men had just returned from the north.

'We are here to give the people confidence so they will return to their land,' he said, his military uniform dusty and sweat-stained from his peace-keeping duties. 'I show you some photos,' he said and handed me a photo of a mutilated body and then another, explaining each as he passed them on. 'And this one. This is the leader of the Togo tribe. A bad man. He was a big trouble-maker.'

I held the photo, mesmerised. It was of the sergeant standing over the body of the Togolese leader, whose sprawled bare legs appeared to have been cut with a machete. His head was being held back for the photo and his eyes were open and bulged. The man had been dead for some time as his body was bloated and dried blood was caked to his matted hair and face. It looked like he had been beaten to death. At first I could not look at the photo, it revolted me, but then I stared fascinated, studying every detail.

'I kill him,' he said, smiling with obvious pride. 'We sleep together tonight?' he added in the same breath, as he'd misinterpreted my fascination as admiration for his fighting prowess.

'No, I don't think so,' I said and handed back the photo.

'I just ask, that is all,' he said. 'And here. These are my children and this is my wife,' he continued, and handed me the last of the photos from the same envelope as the snapshots of the mutilated bodies.

'You have beautiful children and a beautiful wife,' I said.

'Yes, I am lucky man. Life has been good to me.'

'The movie is starting,' I said and stood up.

'I go to drink some beers with my men,' he said and held out his hand. His grip was firm and I wished him and his men all the best with bringing peace to the region. I watched him walk down the street and into a bar busy with drinkers that spilled outside. For a moment, I thought of joining him, as drinking beers with the soldiers and learning more about Ghana interested me more than *Terminator*. But being a single woman alone in a bar full of men and booze was scary, no matter what country I was in. The safer option was a movie in the hotel courtyard, which was mostly filled with teenage boys and girls.

*

The next morning, the ferry docked on the opposite side of the lake and I rode into a war zone. Soldiers armed with AK47s stood guard and checked the passengers for hidden weapons. I began to doubt whether it was as safe as the locals in Yeji had assured me, but the soldiers waved me forward, until I was stopped a little further on.

'What is this? You carry gun!' the soldier yelled, poking at my tent with his rifle.

'It is my tent,' I said, and began untying it from where it lay across the handlebars.

'No problem,' he said.

'Everything is safe?' I asked, nervous about the scene that looked to be anything but safe.

'Yes. The trouble is finished,' he said 'You go.'

I rode on over a potholed two-wheeled track through dry bushland and past deserted villages, now burnt and ransacked. It was the same until just before Tamale, Ghana's largest northern town. Here the road widened but soon deteriorated into a series of deep corrugations and potholes all the way to the border where I crossed into Burkina Faso. I was now back in Francophone Africa and heading towards its capital, Ouagadougou.

21

AN UNGUARDED MOMENT
BURKINA FASO TO MALI

I crossed Burkina Faso, sleeping just one night at a backpacker hostel in central Ouagadougou, the nation's capital and a hub of African jazz. I was sorely disappointed there were no other travellers to invite me to join them to see the musicians play in the bars a short walk from the hostel. As a single woman, I dared not go alone. Instead, I settled for a beer in the hostel's lounge. The only other foreign guests were a couple in their late twenties in matching hiking sandals, cargo shorts and dark-coloured T-shirts.

'We see your motorbike. You travel alone. Is this not dangerous?' the woman asked when I approached them.

'What you do when you break down?' asked the man. They were German and had arrived at the hostel at the same time as me. I felt they were not asking me questions but rather passing judgement: was I a mad woman or some vagrant equally at home in Africa as living on the streets of Berlin or Munich or Frankfurt?

'No, I haven't had any problems. The people are always good to me,' I said and waited for their invitation to join them, but instead I found myself looking at the tops of their downturned heads. Their brown hair was cropped short, as if they'd decided this was more practical for Africa. I recalled I'd once thought this too; I'd had my hair cut short on the cargo ship before it had docked in Durban. As the couple studied their map, they exchanged a few quietly spoken words in German. I took the hint, turned and retreated to a table in the far corner.

As I sat with my beer and map, I calculated distances for the next day's ride to Bankass, across the border in Mali. It was a small market town and the economic centre for the Dogon people, who have resisted outside influence for centuries and instead choose to live as one with the earth in their mud-hut villages built at the base of Bandiagara Escarpment. This 120-kilometre-long, red sandstone cliff reaches up to 500 metres high, and was a four-hour ride away. I would need to leave early to beat the heat.

I felt a slight twinge of loneliness as I sat in the lounge, the Germans at one end and I at the other. At first, I was confused as to why they didn't accept me the way the people of Africa accepted me. But I'd forgotten the social rules of conformity based on material gain – rules I'd soon ride into when I reached Europe. I was on the last leg of my ride through Africa and these next two months were precious. I was aware that I might not have another opportunity to live so close to the earth: to sleep on the ground, to cook my food on an open fire, and to be alone with its vast expanse when I stopped to contemplate its beauty. Travelling Africa had been like one long camping trip, which had connected me to the ebb and flow of the earth – to its sunrises and sunsets. It was as though I bathed in the earth's energy every hour of every day. Its electromagnetic field flowed through me, unhindered by any barrier such as cement or walls or all the noise that comes with the technological world. But I'd soon be returning to this world – my world. What would I do in that world? I knew I could never entirely give up the freedom I'd found in Africa.

*

The further north I rode, the hotter and drier the Sahel became. It was about noon as I neared Bankass, riding on a two-wheeled track packed hard by the wheels of carts pulled by donkeys. It was market day and I passed tribespeople perched on their carts, overloaded with produce bought or to be sold in Bankass. Distracted by the colourful parade, I did not see a large pothole and hit it hard. While I narrowly avoided a crash, the impact cracked the pannier frame, but I was not too concerned as the crack in the glob of rusted weld could easily be re-welded again. This would be the sixth time.

At midday, I walked into the shaded coolness of Ben's Bar and Hotel, an ageing and dust-encrusted cement-block building with large open windows and wide veranda. It was the only hotel in Bankass and as I walked into the bar, I was followed by several young men. Dressed in the street clothes of American youth they chorused, 'You want tour guide?' Bankass was a starting point for tourists to visit the nearest Dogon village, Ende, twelve kilometres along a sandy track at the base of the cliffs.

Ben, a thick-set middle-aged Malian man, sat at the bar. I ordered a beer and asked if the town had a welder.

'Of course. You leave your bags here. It will all be safe,' he said with exuberant optimism that made me feel most welcome. 'No cost,' he said when I asked.

I found a welder near the market, which was bursting with colour. Women – dressed in indigo wraps, colourful beads and large gold earrings – dominated trading, while the men, with calabashes of millet beer, discussed the latest gossip while sitting in groups in the shade around the few scraggly trees. Juicy, ripe mangoes spilled from tilted carts; bright red chillies, spices, onions and brown nuts were laid on straw mats in neat little piles. Of all the markets I'd seen in Africa, none were as alive with tribal life as this one.

Once the pannier frame was repaired, instead of fitting it back on the bike, I left it with most of my gear at Ben's and negotiated a deal with one of the Malian boys who touted for my business to be my tour guide. Several young men hovered close and repeated the same words: 'I speak good English.' One was more persistent and pushed his way to the front to stand beside me.

'I am Pulla,' he said. He was a slender boy aged about seventeen and, as my pillion, would not make the bike too heavy to ride over the sandy track. Pulla was more desperate in his persistence to be my guide than the rest and I'm sure there was a good reason he needed the money. It likely involved a sick relative or paying for an education, or perhaps simply funding his worship of 'the look' with a new pair of brand-name trainers or T-shirt. Since arriving in West Africa, I'd often questioned these young men as to why, when they came into some money, they spent it all on clothes and shoes and did not save a little for their bellies beyond that first big meal. Their reply was always: 'The look is everything' and 'Tomorrow is too far away'.

I knew I could ride to the Dogon villages without a guide and pay the chief myself. But Ben told me the Dogon did not speak English well enough to explain their animist culture. So I appointed Pulla to be my guide for three days. Pulla's fee started out at 50,000 CFA (US$100), but after a brief negotiation we agreed on 10,000 CFA.

With supplies of rice, sugar, tea and vegetables from the market, we reached Ende, the closest village to Bankass, about twenty minutes later. When I turned off the TT's engine, I began asking Pulla questions.

'*Quoi?*' Pulla asked and stared at me blankly as I pointed to the multi-storey mud houses and granaries built amongst the rocks at the base of the cliff. Pulla had skilfully duped me and knew very little English beyond the basic questions about a trip to the Dogon area. All were questions he'd been asked many times before, but any deviation from these and he was on unknown ground.

Several boys stood admiring the TT, and I noticed that the bike and all of us were tinged with the same reflected reddish-brown hue as the cliffs rising tall above us.

'You can't speak English,' I hissed at Pulla, annoyed I would learn nothing of the Dogon people.

'I speak good English,' Pulla said, indignant that I doubted his ability.

'I just want to get out of here. How far can I go before it gets too sandy?' I asked as I scanned Ben's roughly drawn map. The children, sensing I was about to leave, began chanting, '*Donnez cadeau, donnez bonbon.*'

'Here. This village will do. We stop in Yabatalu,' I said and then kick-started the bike, the children jumping back as its deep rumble echoed off the escarpment.

The track to Yabatalu was an easy ride of about eight kilometres over sand packed hard by the wheels of carts and many bare feet. As soon as we arrived, hordes of children barely dressed in dirty rags swarmed down from their mud huts built at the base of the rocky cliff.

'*Donnez bonbon*,' they chanted and I quickly untied the Gearsack from the back of the TT and followed Pulla to the chief's hut, the children trailing behind without let-up in their chants. The Dogon people endured hordes of tourists who flocked to see one of the world's oldest cultures, and the children's chants, while unbearable, were understandable.

'*Moto* is okay,' Pulla had assured me when I protested about leaving it in the open for the night. But I had no choice, as it was impossible to ride or even push it any further to be closer to the dozen huts clustered amongst the slabs of rock at the base of the cliffs.

I was introduced to the chief, a wrinkled little old man in bare feet, threadbare shorts and a T-shirt that was once, long long ago, white. He barely reached my shoulders and smiled a wide, toothless grin at this appearance of 'business'. He beckoned me inside his hut to inspect his collection of Dogon masks, statues and brass figurines neatly laid out for sale on a woven grass mat. I was reminded of the tourist dollar and the part it plays in supporting families and providing opportunities. I'd listened to many an idealised debate from travellers about tourists corrupting the culture of ancient people and the tackiness of our visits. But why deny these people an income that may also help preserve their culture rather than destroy it?

'I'm not buying souvenir. No money and no space on *moto*,' I said and glanced down at the TT parked alone and vulnerable at the base of the cliffs. The old man nodded and I asked Pulla to explain that I'd like to climb to the rocks above the village to watch the sun sink as a giant orange orb beyond the endless sandy plains.

'*Non problème*,' Pulla said and led me along a path to where we could

climb to several large slabs of red sandstone. Only a few of the older children trailed behind and when we reached our vantage point, I gave them
my binoculars, which stopped their chants immediately. Intrigued, they
spied on their families in the village below as I gazed out over the dry plains
that six months prior had grown crops of millet and sorghum. In July, the
rains would return and the cycle of growth and harvest would continue.

As I looked down at the huts and watched the women pound millet
for the evening meal, I felt the same twinge of envy at their lifestyle that I
had felt when I'd visited the pygmy tribe deep in the forest near Epulu: a
yearning for a life linked so closely to the earth and its seasons.

Was it harder to leave the land the closer we lived to it? Maybe when
we moved away from tilling the soil, distance and disconnection weakened
our bond until we no longer felt, so therefore we no longer cared? But
while I idealised the Dogon lifestyle, I could not forget the bitter looks
cast my way from the adults and older children when I'd arrived.

'There's resentment here,' I said.

'*Quoi?*' Pulla asked, puzzled.

'The tourists come here with all their money and pass through the villages handing out Bics and *bonbons*. They take photos like visiting a zoo
and then they leave,' I said.

'What you say?' Pulla asked.

'So this is eco-tourism,' I said.

'Yes, tourists, many come,' Pulla said and smiled. He knew this word
well. 'Dogon make much money from tourist.'

'You might be right, but they still don't like us being here,' I said and
thought of how my tourist dollar was as much a part of the Dogon economy as the produce traded at the Bankass market.

Pulla and I were given space to sleep within the mud-walled courtyard
of the chief's tiny hut and in exchange I gave him our payment of rice,
sugar and tea. I washed my face and hands and cooked our own meal of
rice, packet soup and vegetables. Later, I lay listening to the beat of drums
from neighbouring villages echo off the escarpment.

I woke early and told Pulla I wanted to return to Bankass. I thanked the chief and apologised for my intrusion into his home and village.

We rode into Bankass mid-morning and after I'd refitted the pannier-frame and packed the TT, Ben offered a room where I could shower and then invited me to lunch with his family and friends. Later, I'd ride the 165 kilometres to Djenné, a town made of mud on the Niger.

'I am sorry you not have a good visit to the Dogon villages,' Ben said when I sat down at the large table.

'It was my own fault,' I said as a plate of goat-meat stew and rice was placed before me.

'Why did you choose Pulla as your guide? He cannot even speak English,' said the well-dressed Malian man sitting opposite Ben.

'He is a very smart guide,' I said to the man who introduced himself as Muhammad. He was about forty with rich, coffee-brown skin. I noticed the way his muscles strained under his dark-grey polo shirt.

'Pulla is from Mopti. If you want to see smart guides, go there,' Muhammad laughed and his whole face lit up with a cheeky grin that made me smile. He told me he also worked as a tour guide for those tourists who wanted to gain a deeper insight into the Dogon culture. I understood this to mean those that were cashed-up, compared to the backpackers that were Pulla's usual customers.

'I think I'll keep away from Mopti. I'm going to Djenné now,' I said and thought how lucky I was to be sitting here in Bankass, freshly showered and fed and amongst people who offered their hospitality so openly.

'There is a good market in Djenné,' Muhammad said.

'But it is on Monday and today is Wednesday. Maybe it is too long for me to wait,' I said and calculated the cost. This part of West Africa was a little more expensive than what I was used to and I was down to just under US$1000. I could not access more cash until I reached the next American Express office in Morocco. If anything should happen, $1000 would not buy a great deal.

'No, Djenné will hold you. It is good to spend some time there. Don't be in too much hurry,' Muhammad said and continued to stare at me as though our paths had crossed at some distant point in the past.

'I will see,' I lied, as it was unlikely I would stop travelling for five days.

By mid-afternoon I was riding away from Bankass, and after eighty kilometres of smooth, hard-packed dirt, I reached freshly laid tarmac. Sixty kilometres further, I took the turn-off to Djenné, a town built from mud, with no electricity and no traffic. As I rode under a mud-walled arch, I felt as if I was riding back in time.

Djenné was founded in the ninth century. It was once on the trans-Saharan trade route and was famous for its mud mosque and colourful Monday market, which I'd already heard much about. The town sat on an island on the now-dry Niger River Delta and I arrived as the afternoon sun was beginning to bathe the ancient town in a brown-orange haze. I found the camping ground and parked the bike under the shade of a large, leafy tree. Nearby was a mud-brick building, the restaurant that also doubled as the living area for the manager and his extended family, who had recently stirred from their afternoon nap. Thin mattresses covered the length of the wide veranda.

'Welcome,' the manager called as I stood in the doorway watching as the women and older children began rolling up the mattresses with deft precision.

'Can I camp out there?' I asked and pointed to where I'd parked the TT under the tree.

'*Non problème*, 1500 CFA (US$3),' he said from where he still lay on his side on a mattress in baggy khaki pants and long-flowing, white cotton shirt.

It was not long before word travelled that a tourist was in town and numerous young men, the tour guides, all in their late teens and twenties, filtered through the gates of the camping ground.

'I am just here to relax, I don't want to go anywhere or look at anything,' I told each as they pestered me. The moment I'd ridden into Djenné, this ancient mud town untouched by civilisation had won my heart and

I'd made up my mind to stay for the famous Monday market.

On my second night I was visited by Tim, a Peace Corps volunteer. He was a freckled-faced, sandy-haired American with an agricultural degree who was helping communities improve crop yields. Each evening we sat at one of the stalls near the mud mosque, where the mamas cooked up the evening meal. This was Mali's equivalent of fast food. After buying a bowl of street food, usually a stew of goat meat, guinea fowl or chicken served with rice, we would sit with the boys who had neither family nor home. Dressed in no more than dirty rags, these were the marabout children, all boys, aged from about eight to twelve years, and they stood around us with their empty calabash bowls. They had been sent by their parents from distant villages to Djenné to learn the Koran under the tutelage of a marabout, a Muslim religious teacher. It was considered an honour to study in Djenné, but only the tuition was provided free by the mosque. To eat they had to beg, and Tim and I bought extra pieces of meat to drop in their bowls.

Each evening ended with a walk along the labyrinth of dark, narrow streets and past the flat-top mud houses where everyone slept to escape the heat. Robed figures brushed past us, and in the flickering light of an oil lamp a few men sat drinking tea around the stalls that mostly sold cigarettes, tea and sugar wrapped in small parcels. In this very Muslim town, Tim knew the secret place to drink millet beer. He led me to a place, hidden behind mud walls, where we drank from the same calabash with several Malian men and women who had not fully converted to Islam, or who'd chosen to put their faith aside during the dark of the night.

*

On Monday the quiet mud town of Djenné came alive with people from the surrounding villages. Women dressed in their best multi-coloured robes, their wealth displayed in heavy gold earrings that hung from stretched lobes. The area in front of the mosque was crowded with produce, including mangoes and spices. People stood in groups to chat, catching up on the latest gossip, while the donkeys, untethered from their carts, stood around the perimeter and swished their tails at the flies. Monday was also when the tour groups from Bamako, on their way to see the Dogon villages, descended on the market. They stopped only briefly, long enough for the passengers to have a quick walk, take a few photos, and then they were gone. I got the distinct feeling the market people resented this invasion on their life as the tourists, oblivious to the unwelcoming stares, happily clicked away with their cameras. The children, on the other hand, thought the arrival of the tourist groups a wonderful thing. Conditioned from years of tourists giving bonbons, Bics and coins, they pestered the tour groups, following them everywhere around the market.

Later that night, I came down with a fever and headache. It felt like another attack of malaria, and while it was probably something else, I treated it with Halfan just in case. I had stopped taking Lariam as a malaria prophylactic when I had left Ghana, as I had reasoned that I no longer needed to worry about malaria in the dry north of Mali. But I'd forgotten about the Niger River and its abundant mosquitoes. I'd only thought about minimising the risk of side-effects from Lariam, especially the hallucinations. The last thing I needed as I travelled alone was to lose my mind.

By the following morning the fever had subsided and I recommenced my weekly dose of Lariam. I felt weak and washed out but I packed to leave as I could not afford to stop moving. Stopping meant more money for accommodation and food. And in places like Djenné, stopping also meant the temptation to buy souvenirs. I'd spent US$80 on hand-dyed mudcloth and a mask embossed in metal. Even though I had no money for curios, my journey would soon end and I wanted a little of Africa to fuel my memories into the future.

*

Instead of the featureless tarmac road, I followed the back roads to Bamako, riding to Segou across the flat dusty plains of the Niger River Delta. I lost my way at the first turn, as a myriad of dirt tracks criss-crossed each other out over the plains, but it didn't matter. Mud villages, small versions of Djenné, all with the same-styled Islamic mud mosque, were scattered over this area, and I passed through them with frequent regularity.

By late afternoon I was still fifty kilometres from Segou and the tarmac road that would take me to Bamako. When it was time to stop I rode into a small village, and asked permission to camp.

'*Non problème*,' said my host and introduced himself as Adama. Like most people along the delta he was a Muslim and wore a *boubou*, a long tunic of cool, white cotton. In my jeans and navy trench, buttoned to my neck and falling to my knees, my outfit more than met Muslim dress standards. It completely covered my womanly shape and no doubt brought me greater acceptance when I appeared out of nowhere on a strictly Muslim doorstep. Covering my body in such a way was not planned. Like everything else about my journey it had fallen into place as naturally as day turning to night. After my motorcycle jacket had been stolen in Kinshasa, the trench had been the only suitable jacket I could find. It was the perfect outfit for Muslim Africa.

With a wave of his hand, Adama indicated I follow him into the low, mud-walled compound of his house, where I was seated on a low stool; but a moment later an elderly man, the chief, arrived and I stood as was expected in the presence of the headman. I was formally welcomed to Kelli. I was now a guest and under his protection.

In all the villages I'd ridden through on the dry Niger delta, flocks of guinea fowl roamed the dusty streets, and Kelli was no exception. I asked about buying one for dinner by pointing to one of the birds. Adama nodded his understanding and I followed him. A moment later we stood outside a mud hut. It seemed that all the guinea fowl, of which there were hundreds, belonged to this one old man. He scratched the figure of 700 in the sand, and I handed over the money (about US$2.50). Several minutes later the bird was dropped at my feet.

'Is possible to *cuisine?*' I asked, picking up the dead bird.

Adama laughed and took it from me, giving it to his wife to cook. In the faint moonlight we all ate the stewed pieces of guinea fowl, which were tough, but the dark game meat was absolutely delicious.

I'd filled my ten-litre water container in Djenné, just in case I broke down on the hot, dry plains.

'*D'eau,*' Adama pointed as I filled my water bottle from the container.

'Djenné *d'eau,*' I replied, and filled a cup and offered it to him, oblivious to my insulting insinuation that Djenné water was so much better that I had insisted on carrying ten litres of it.

'Djenné, Djenné,' he said, in a tone that indicated he'd heard enough about Djenné and refused to drink the water.

Djenné got all the attention while the rest of the villages along the Niger delta were forgotten. He pointed to my green water bottle, which I was about to fill from the ten-litre container, and indicated I give it to him. It was passed to his son, a boy aged about eight years, and a moment later he returned with it filled from a large clay pot.

'*Eau de Kelli,*' he said proudly, and handed me the bottle.

I took a sip and swallowed. '*Excellent. Eau de Kelli très bon,*' I said and we all broke into fits of laughter, not just over our joke about Djenné's water but over a sense of belonging and unity, and that life was good and all was right with the world.

*

I rode into the city of Bamako during the late-afternoon rush hour. All roads were chaotic with buses, pickups, sedans and hundreds of mopeds. I asked a young Malian man riding a little 125cc motorcycle for directions to the Catholic mission, as this was listed as a cheaper alternative to many of the budget hotels listed in my guidebook. It was on a pot-holed back street near the city centre. Behind the wrought-iron fence it was very quaint, secure and also still too expensive, at 4000 CFA (US$15) per night.

'Is there something cheaper?' I asked the Malian motorcyclist. It was Wednesday and I expected to be in Bamako for at least a few days, as I needed a visa for Mauritania and new tyres for the TT.

'*Le Maison des Jeunes*,' the young man suggested, and I followed him, dodging potholes and weaving my way through the traffic and crowded streets.

The Maison des Jeunes was a hostel for university students from all over Mali. An old multi-storey building, its dusty pink paint flaking and faded, it overlooked the Niger River. Set in an area shaded by leafy trees, its tranquillity was deceptive, and I was warned by the Malian motorcyclist that the thieves were very bad.

'Do not walk alone at night,' he said before speeding off into the chaotic traffic.

I chose to sleep next to my bike on the large cement area at the front of the hostel. It was cooler, and it was safer that I stay near the TT, as there was no place to secure it away from the thieves. This area was also well lit by floodlights, and the hostel administrator assured me I would be safe.

'Rambo will look after you,' he said, and he called to the tall hulk of a Malian youth carrying a case of beer to the small open-air bar.

Rambo smiled a wide childlike grin, showing a mouth full of oversized crooked teeth, but I knew that if anybody attempted to harm me, he would rip both their arms and legs off with his massive bare hands. I also paid the watchman 500 CFA per night to keep a close eye on me and the TT during the dark early hours. He assured me he did not fall asleep.

Camping was 1000 CFA per night, mozzie net supplied, which was an absolute necessity, I realised, when I woke the next morning to the sight of mosquitoes, their blood-enlarged abdomens bright red in the morning sun, resting only inches from my face on the *inside* of the mozzie net. As I'd only just recommenced taking Lariam it was too early for it to offer any protection, and I resigned myself to the fact that I would probably suffer another malaria attack in the next week or so.

I rode to the Mauritanian Embassy on the outskirts of Bamako first thing with the expectation that I'd be issued with the visa the following day and be on my way on Saturday.

'Closed Friday. Come back Monday. Collect passport then,' said the embassy official when I handed over my passport and 11,500 CFA for the visa.

When I arrived back at the Maison des Jeunes, the hustlers and would-be tour guides were waiting. Word had spread that a new tourist was in town.

'I don't want to go to Dogon country, I don't want a tour of Bamako,' I replied to their persistent demands.

'Don't stay here,' I was told repeatedly. 'Come stay in my home. You don't have to pay. We look after you,' they chorused.

'I don't think so,' I replied.

These guys had perfected hustling to a fine art and didn't invite travellers to stay with them out of kindness. The situation would begin with a display of generosity, and then, once they had won my confidence, there would be subtle requests for small amounts of money: 'Oh, loan me 1000 CFA to buy some rice.' The traveller would feel obliged to pay; after all, the family had given them food and somewhere to stay. The guys would get bolder, and ask for more and more money, such as for a sick relative who needed medicine. I'd heard many stories of how even the most hardened of travellers had been conned.

Since I was stuck in Bamako for the next few days, I serviced the bike – cleaned the air filter and replaced the decompression cable, which had broken that morning. Once that was done, I rode off down a back street in search of a welder to repair a small hole in the muffler.

Both the front and rear tyres were getting worn. The front looked like it would make it to Morocco but I doubted the rear, the Michelin Desert, would last the distance. Tyres and most other spares for Yamaha XT, Honda XL and BMW GS motorcycles were all readily available from the auto spares market in Bamako. I saw a hardly worn rear Michelin Desert but, like most of the rear tyres, it was a 17-inch. I needed an 18-inch, which was a pity, because that one was only US$20. It had probably found its way to Bamako after a Paris–Dakar Rally.

I inspected my rear tyre again and as I pondered whether to risk it and end my search, one of the hustlers, a gorilla-sized man in his late twenties, came up and introduced himself as Tarzan.

'You want tyre. My friend has tyre,' he said. I looked up from where I was sitting next to the TT and thought, why not? If it was the right size he would get a commission from the tyre-seller and I would get my tyre, so I had nothing to lose.

'It must be 18-inch,' I said, handing him the piece of paper with the tyre dimensions.

My intuition warned me I was making a mistake, but I ignored it. I chose instead to believe that deep down all people are good; a naive attitude in the dog-eat-dog world of a city, and Bamako was no exception. People need money just to survive. Most, especially the hustlers, did not have the security net of their families looking after them. Many of the young men had come from smaller towns and villages to the city, where there was the opportunity to make money from tourists. The rewards were high. In places like Bamako they could make more money in one day from some gullible tourist than they ever dreamed possible, much more than they could herding their families' goats or tilling the fields to grow millet.

'Come, I find tyre,' Tarzan told me the next morning and I sat behind him on his moped as he sped through the morning traffic.

'Tyre,' he said and pointed to the stack outside a motorcycle repair and parts shop not far from the hostel. It was the same row of shops I'd visited the day before.

'I have already looked here. They are not the right size. Forget it,' I said, and asked him to take me back to the hostel.

'You pay me 2500 CFA (US$5),' he demanded when he stopped outside the Maison des Jeunes.

'What for?' I asked, not believing his outrageous demand for money. 'Just for taking me five minutes away and the tyre was not the right one?' I said, then turned and walked back to the TT.

He followed, then stood glaring at me as I sat on the low brick wall beside my bike. I had just created an enemy. I was worried and this meanest of hustlers knew it. I offered him 500 CFA, which he refused. Three of the young guys who no longer pestered me but would often stop to chat came over when they saw I was being hassled.

'Is problem?' asked Alex, the shortest of the three, and I explained the story of Tarzan and his unreasonable demand.

'He is bad man,' Alex whispered.

'He is trying to frighten me to pay him some money,' I replied, more as a plea to them to suggest what I should do.

Just at that moment, Muhammad, who I'd met in Bankass at Ben's Bar, walked past on his way to the administrator's office.

'I see you made it to Bamako, but it looks like you have problem,' he said, and then listened to Alex as he repeated the story.

'I was here to see a friend but I think you should leave with me now,' Muhammad insisted with a firmness that was in complete contrast to his light-hearted greeting just seconds before.

'No, I will be all right. I'm not going to let that ape frighten me away. Besides, I quite like staying here,' I replied. Even though I could not completely relax, I did like staying at the Maison des Jeunes. Each afternoon, the students had band practice, cold beers were served in the bar, and there was always the opportunity to talk to the students, who were keen to practise their English.

'I know an American girl. She lives in a house over the river with her Malian boyfriend. It will be no problem for you to stay there,' he insisted more vehemently.

I looked around as I considered Muhammad's offer. The hustlers now surrounded me and were arguing about something. Tarzan continued to give me threatening looks, and Alex, seeing I was about to leave, now asked for money.

'I do not even have any money to buy food,' he said, his hands cupped, and I slipped him 500 CFA from the few notes stuffed into the pouch on my belt, hoping that the other hustlers hadn't seen.

'Okay, I will have a look,' I said to Muhammad and quickly packed my things, stuffing everything into the panniers and Gearsack.

'Ah, that is good. If you knew what they were saying you would not spend one more second here,' Muhammad said.

'Why, what is going on?' I asked.

'We will speak of this later. Now we must leave,' he said. When I was ready he hailed a taxi and I followed, crossing the Niger to arrive at a low-set, blue cement house on a dusty suburban street.

The American girl, Karen, was tanned and slender with a mop of short, honey-blond curls. She had once worked as a Peace Corps volunteer in Mopti, where she'd met Jake, her Malian boyfriend. They both welcomed me to their house, which was a sanctuary compared to what I'd just left behind at the Maison des Jeunes. It was Sunday afternoon and they sat drinking beers and smoking joints with three other young Malian men in the cool of the shaded front veranda. Once Muhammad had helped me push the TT inside to the front room, we joined them.

'You know that big guy was going to torch you and your motorbike if you didn't pay him,' Karen said.

'Bloody hell,' I replied, shocked to learn of my close call. I'd been completely oblivious and I shuddered with what might have happened if Muhammad hadn't been there at that very moment to avert imminent disaster.

'Yeah, while you were sleeping, he threatened to douse you with petrol and then throw a match on you. You are very lucky Muhammad came by when he did,' she said.

The afternoon turned to evening. Malian men came and went. Some would arrive with crates of beer and when it ran out, Jake sent out for more. Food arrived too: plates of fried chicken and rice ordered from a street vendor down the road. The beer was cold, the people good company and for both Karen's and my benefit, the conversation was in English. Travelling alone, I was always careful about having my wits about me, as the risk to my personal safety was an ever-present threat. But with Muhammad, Karen and Jake I felt safe; I could relax, I could let my guard down.

As the night wore on, Jake's Malian friends left and Karen and Jake called it a night. Muhammad and I moved out to the courtyard at the back of the house. A gnarled creeper covered the nearby brick wall, where the faint moonlight cast soft shadows through the spindly branches of a tree, its trunk twisted with age.

As though we were old friends who'd met up after a very long absence, we'd talked and laughed all afternoon and now late into the evening. It was not often that I had the opportunity to communicate so easily and learn so much. Many times my lack of French kept me isolated from the people I met and so I bombarded Muhammad, who spoke perfect English, with many questions about life in Mali. Then our conversation turned to Mali's women, as their world was closed to me unlike the worlds of women elsewhere in Africa, where women had often spoken to me openly about their lives.

'In Mali, in all of Africa, poverty forces a woman to have sex to win favours, gifts and to be cared for, while a man has sex for his own pleasure,' he said and exhaled a long trail of pungent smoke. 'Here in Mali, women are still circumcised. Some old woman with a kitchen knife cuts out the clitoris of the young girls just before they flower. A woman who has been cut may never feel the pleasure of orgasm. Sex may also be painful, but she will endure the pain so she can receive favours,' he said.

'Even in Mali, people live in modern times. Don't they realise circumcision is so barbaric, so completely unnecessary?' I said horrified by the pain these women must endure.

'I will never marry a woman who has been cut. I will marry a Western woman. They know the pleasure of sex,' he said with firm conviction.

'But surely there are Malian women who have not been circumcised?' I asked.

'Not very many. The religious leaders are very strong, and know all the young girls who are to be circumcised,' he said. 'Even the educated women have this done to their daughters, and they have been cut themselves. You would think they would know better. They know the pain that it will cause their daughters to feel,' he said and reached into the bowl to roll another joint.

'What about condoms?' I asked, curious about whether or not the warnings about HIV had any impact.

'Wives have no choice. And the poor African does not worry about using a condom. He knows he will eventually die of something. He only thinks of today, tomorrow is too far away,' he said, and I thought of all the times I had heard these words.

'I see you do not think of tomorrow either,' Muhammad continued. 'This is good as you are free to learn from every experience that comes your way. People forget we are all going to die. Instead they worry about the future, which is pointless. Worry takes much thought and keeps you trapped from what is really going on,' he said and I nodded in agreement. 'I see you have learnt this. Africa has taught you well, but you have been up for too long and now it is your turn to come down. Be careful, don't make the fall too hard.'

I wondered why he should say such a thing. Was it just plain good luck and not synchronicity, influenced by my own thoughts, that had kept me safe for so long?

'I'll be all right,' I said, ignoring his ominous predictions.

'No, you must come down. Otherwise you cannot go up any higher. You will learn from the bad times which are coming for you,' he prophesied through glazed eyes.

'I need to sleep now,' I said and stood up, holding the back of the chair to steady myself. I didn't know what time it was but the sun would soon rise and after all the beers and dope, I suddenly felt very green.

I staggered toward, the room that Karen had showed me earlier. Inside I fell onto the couch and kicked off my boots. I decided I needed to listen to Pink Floyd's *The Dark Side of the Moon*. I often listened to it before going to sleep and the tape was always in my walkman. I fumbled with the earphones and a moment later the lyrics from 'Great Gig in the Sky' filled my head. The words about dying, about not being frightened, about how we all die some time, seemed strangely reassuring at that very moment, as though life and death were one and the same. As the vocals rose to a crescendo – a struggle against death – the room began to spin and a wave of nausea washed over me.

Hands reached for me in the darkness. I sat up. It was Muhammad. 'Please, I must sleep,' I said and dragged my sleeping bag and walkman to lie on the thin foam mattress on the floor. Muhammad followed, his hands expertly trying to unzip my jeans. The vocals were falling now, into acceptance as though letting go of the struggle with death.

I moved back to the couch, leaving both my sleeping bag and walkman on the floor. Muhammad followed, his mouth reaching for mine with a persistence meant to wear me down.

'I'm feeling sick,' I said and pushed him away, moving back to the floor, where the room began to spin. I lay on my back and then on my side and warm, smooth hands reached under my shirt and stroked my skin, which tingled to the touch. While my head screamed no, my body responded and I felt a warm, swollen responsiveness between my legs.

'Relax and I will bring you pleasure,' he crooned in my ear.

No, this cannot be, I thought, but I had no control. The alcohol and marijuana had dulled my mind, had taken away all my defences, and now my body ruled this moment in the darkness. All that mattered was an all-consuming need to have sex, to reach climax. For more than a year, I'd had no sexual desire but it now poured forth as though it had been held back by a dam that had suddenly burst. I was as pliable as soft putty in his hands and Muhammad knew it.

'You've got to use a condom,' I whispered, but it was a feeble attempt at using protection as neither of us had a condom, and as our sexual desire reached fever-pitch, neither of us cared. A moment later our naked bodies were entwined and wave after wave of pleasure washed over me as I reached orgasm again and again. Exhausted, we lay naked together as the first rays of dawn penetrated the thin curtains.

I woke a few hours later and Muhammad was gone. I quickly dressed, trying to ignore what had happened. Trying to ignore that I'd had unprotected sex in Africa. How could I have been so stupid? I cursed myself for letting my guard down and for getting drunk and stoned, a deadly combination that had left me defenceless. I quickly packed my things as if leaving would allow me to ride away from the experience as though it had never happened.

'Where do you go from here?' Karen asked, handing me a cup of sweet milky coffee as I stumbled, bleary-eyed, into the kitchen.

'I'll collect my visa for Mauritania and then I'd like to find a village on the Niger before crossing the border. When I leave Mali that'll be the end of the Africa I've come to know. I want to spend some time saying goodbye,' I said, trying to sound cheerful in my attempt to push all thoughts of the deadly consequences of my carelessness out of my mind. As if my denial alone would protect me from harm. I'd escaped death in Africa before, I reasoned, and I would escape it again.

'You've been in Africa far too long. It has gotten into your soul,' Karen said, but her words were like a faint muffled sound heard through the thick fog of regret. My heart beat loudly as I battled with what had happened and what it may mean, but the damage was done and I cursed my body again for its betrayal.

'Here. What do you know about this village?' I asked, my finger landing randomly on Nyamina on my map. It was on the banks of the Niger River.

'I have never heard of it. Muhammad would know. It's strange he left so early without saying goodbye. Jake might know,' she said and called out to him on the front veranda.

'Nyamina is a special place. You choose a good village,' Jake said when we both sat down with him to drink our coffee. 'It is an important Muslim town, and you will be there for Tabaski, the festival after Ramadan. All over the world, Muslim families will slaughter a white ram to honour the day when God tested Abraham's faith and asked him to sacrifice his first-born son, Ishmael, but gave him a lamb instead,' he said.

'Tabaski brings with it the opportunity of second chances,' he added, and I hoped my visit to Nyamina would be my second chance. I would pray to Allah, to all the gods, to the universal energy. But I feared Muhammad's prophecy was right and I would soon come down from the high I'd lived for the past year.

'In Nyamina, Tabaski will be very good,' Jake said. 'You will be made most welcome. You can trust the people in Nyamina, but as you head north be careful. From now on you will meet the young men trying for a new life in Europe. They have come from all over West Africa, and by the time they reach Mauritania and Morocco their money is nearly finished, and they live by their wits. They will see you and they will steal from you. Be very careful. Trust nobody,' Jake warned.

I heard his warning, but I felt I had no more to lose, as I feared I'd already lost everything. What further harm could come to me?

'Thank you,' I said and handed Karen 5000 CFA for my stay. I collected my passport with the Mauritanian visa and rode away from Bamako, my head consumed by thoughts of my one unguarded moment. The damage had been done so what was the point of worrying? Instead, I chose denial.

Nyamina was only 160 kilometres from Bamako, and I relaxed into the easy ride, leaving the tarmac a few kilometres north of Koulikoro. At first, the dirt road was graded smooth, but I was soon following the rough dirt track for most of the eighty kilometres to the village. In the dry season it was an easy ride, but I could see from the large potholes and deep wheel ruts that the road would be almost impassable after the rains. It was market day, and in the coolness of late afternoon I passed donkey carts loaded with people and their purchases as they returned to their villages dotted all along the banks of the Niger.

Just before nightfall I rode into the sleepy village of Nyamina. A few people wandered about the streets, which were lined with flat-roofed mud houses. They stopped to stare at me in disbelief, as though the arrival of a traveller on a motorcycle was something they'd never seen. I asked a group of teenage boys for directions to the camping ground and they ran ahead into a mud-wall compound built on the high banks of the almost-dry Niger River.

'*Le campement?*' I asked the robed man who came to greet me.

'*Oui.* Your home,' he said.

When I asked how much it was to camp, he looked at me horrified. '*Non* money,' he said, and led me to a low, rectangular, mud-brick building of three partially completed rooms with a wide, cement, open patio.

I parked the TT next to it under the shade of a stunted tree, and a mattress was brought over from the main house. Another man and a woman brought over a basin of water, a chair and table, then a lantern. After I washed, a bowl of rice and meat appeared. I was a total stranger, and they were showering me with hospitality. If one of them were to arrive unannounced on the doorstep of a family in the Western world, would they be shown the same kindness? I could not help thinking there must be a catch.

'Sit,' the man said. 'I am Momadou. That is my wife, Madam, our friend, Muhammad, and my children, Tabu and Upa. Why you come to Nyamina?' he asked.

'It is a silly reason, but I have come to say goodbye to Africa. From here I go north to Mauritania. Then the Africa I have come to love will be behind me.'

'I see you are sad to leave,' he said, and handed me a small glass of sweet black tea flavoured with mint.

The following morning it was Tabaski. I wandered the streets, passing men and women dressed in their best boubou outfits of bright, shimmering colours intricately embroidered with gold for the day of celebration. I walked into the compound of Momadou's house just as he was leading the family's prized white ram to the side of the building. This ram had been well cared for, fed on grain and hand-picked shoots of tender grass. For the past year he'd been kept spotlessly white. The following year's Tabaski ram, still a lamb, walked behind, but soon lost interest and returned to forage near the front of the house. A shallow hole was dug, the ram was laid down and with one swift movement his throat was cut. Blood, bright and frothy, flowed from him. His nerves twitched as the last signs of life drained out with the blood that soaked into the sandy ground. The dead ram was hung from a nearby tree, the skin carefully removed. This would be cured and later used as a special prayer mat. The ram was gutted, the liver, kidneys and testicles removed. These were the first to go on the coals.

'Come, sit,' Momadou said and I sat on a stool around the small fire with the family and was offered pieces of grilled testicles.

All day the elaborately dressed people of Nyamina filtered into the compound, giving greetings for Tabaski. They stopped for a few minutes to gorge on the grilled meat of the ram.

*

I left West Africa at the windswept frontier town of Nara on the Mali border, where a small collection of dilapidated cement and corrugated-iron-roofed buildings sat on a flat expanse of barren land. I arrived late in the afternoon, having left Nyamina that morning. The border was closed so I would cross into Mauritania, and North Africa, the following day.

I found a place to sleep at the contractors' compound at the border crossing. It also operated as the camping ground and for 1000 CFA I was given a wrought-iron bed with a thin foam mattress placed on the open cement courtyard beside the three resident Malian road-works contractors. As I unpacked my gear a violent sandstorm blew over us, passing as quickly as it had appeared.

'Is that normal?' I asked, shaking sand from my hair.

'Only in the afternoon. In the evening, the stars will be bright,' said the Malian man sitting on the bed beside me smoking a cigarette.

At the Malian Customs Office the following morning, overloaded trucks and Toyota 4×4s were parked outside, the drivers and passengers lazing in the shade of their vehicles.

'Take me with you,' a young man called as I walked towards customs. He was sitting with several young African men, their clothes dirty and their skin pale with dust. These were the first of the trail of illegal immigrants heading to Europe.

'Sorry, no room,' I called back.

Once my documents were stamped I rode into the hot, dry nothing-ness that was the edge of the Sahara. The track was sandy, but I didn't find it difficult, and when I reached the top of a low ridge of broken sandstone I stopped and turned off the engine. In the immense silence, I looked back over the vast dry plains. I looked south out over Africa and thought of all I had been through. Everything had always worked in my favour. I could not believe it was all simply good luck or random occurrences. There had to be an explanation – a reason I had met all those people at just the right time and with such regularity. And while I sensed the hint of a dark cloud of foreboding looming in the distance, I knew whatever happened, I would survive. Africa had taught me that.

22

THE VISION
MAURITANIA

The Mauritanian border post of Adel Bagrou was a collection of flat-roofed, mud-brick structures on a vast expanse of nothingness – desert that stretched in every direction. It was late May, the start of the hottest time of year in this part of North Africa. Midday temperatures hovered at a scorching forty-five degrees Celsius.

As the TT rumbled to a stop, three elderly Arab men in blue robes and black headscarves glanced at me with disinterest from where they were sitting under the shade of a few sheets of rusted corrugated-iron that were leaning against the mud-brick wall of the immigration post. Behind an imaginary line a few metres from the TT, several grubby kids with sand-matted hair stared with dark doe eyes. I took off my helmet.

'*Ish tah ree*,' I faltered, attempting words of greeting in Hassaniya, the Arabic dialect spoken in Mauritania and the Western Sahara. A few broke into smiles, highlighting the delicate beauty of their light-brown skin and fine features.

'Tourist, come,' boomed the immigration official in faded military uniform from where he stood leaning against the doorway.

'Long journey,' he said as he slowly flipped through the pages of my passport.

'I am nearly at the end,' I said.

'Route to Nema, much sand. You have water?' he asked as he stamped my passport and carnet.

'Yes,' I said and nodded as I knew what lay ahead – 300 kilometres of sandy track to reach the tarmac, and the beginning of the potholed highway that cut across 1000 kilometres of sand-dunes to Nouakchott, Mauritania's coastal capital.

I rode on and an hour later, as the sun reached its zenith, I breathed a sigh of relief as I approached another cluster of flat-roofed, mud-brick buildings shimmering in the heat haze. I could not ride any further. I risked overheating not only myself but also the TT.

The gendarme, a middle-aged man in military uniform, heard my approach and as I pulled up beside him, I fought off dizziness brought on by the intense heat.

'You rest. *Beaucoup soleil*,' he said.

Several children watched me nervously. The older girls pulled at their hair and pointed to mine. It was only then that I realised I must cover my hair. I pulled a faded length of black cloth from the side pocket of the Gearsack. It usually doubled as both sheet and sarong, and now I draped it over my head before following the gendarme to his office and into an open courtyard with wide eaves that provided ample shade.

'Sit,' said the gendarme and pointed to the bare cement floor swept clean of sand. Exhausted, I leaned against the cool brick wall. The gendarme brewed tea and a girl aged about ten in a faded floral frock and bare feet, who I assumed was his daughter, placed a jug of water and a bowl on the floor near me. She returned a moment later with a bowl of oil-drenched rice with a few token pieces of gristly meat.

'You eat,' the gendarme said.

After washing my hands, I rolled small balls of the sticky rice with my fingers as he pushed most of the meat to my side, insisting I eat more.

'*Non, merci*,' I said and the bowl was taken away. I then did what the gendarme and the others, I expected, were doing in another room. In the heat and after a belly full of food, I leaned back against the wall and soon fell asleep. The gendarme rested against the wall opposite.

In the late afternoon I moved on, reaching the highway two hours later. I passed through the village of Timbadgha, a collection of flat-roofed buildings covered in drifts of fine red sand. Children outnumbered the adults by about five to one and some threw stones at me as I rode past. The women wore wraps of long lengths of soft, flowing cotton in bright blue or orange or green or pink and the few men wore blue or white robes that resembled long robes. I slowed, looking for somewhere to stay. In these small towns there were no hotels. Those passing through slept outside on carpets rolled out each evening in front of the roadside cafes. But it was still too early, so I kept riding, hoping to find a place to rest away from the promenade of people who wandered the main street and the children who pelted stones. I reached the outskirts of the township and pulled up at a well. It was busy with boys filling large drums to be hauled by donkey cart back to Timbadgha. A herd of about a hundred camels stood waiting to drink from a long trough, which was being filled by a man using a hand pump. There was only room for about twenty camels to drink at a time, and several herdsmen kept the others back, beating those that did not wait their turn with sticks.

I needed water, and this also looked to be my only opportunity to wash off the day's accumulation of dust and sand. I held up my water bottle to the closest herdsman and he nodded, pointing at the trough with his stick. I knelt down and splashed my dust-covered face. Undeterred, the camels beside me continued to suck water through hairy lips.

'You stay in Timbadgha tonight?' asked a youth filling a drum, who I guessed was aged about fifteen.

'Yes, I look for a place,' I said.

'You stay there,' he said, pointing to a mud-brick house on a low, sandy rise overlooking the well. 'Women own well.'

I nodded. By now it was almost dark and it seemed safe to sleep under the stars next to the TT on the soft, red desert sand. I got back on the bike and rode up the low rise.

Three very obese women and two equally plump teenage girls reclined on red velvet-covered mattresses and large cushions on the cement patio at the front of their little mud-brick house. In the late afternoon it was a good vantage point from which to watch the goings on at their well. This routine had probably gone on for generations. The patio was also where they would sleep under the stars, cooled by a gentle breeze blown across the desert.

The women were of Mauritania's largest ethnic group, the Bidan, the light-skinned elite of the Mauritanian Moors. They were draped in the finest of bright-coloured fabrics and their hands and feet were covered with intricate designs in henna. As the owners of the well, they were exceedingly rich by Mauritanian standards, so could afford to fatten themselves up to the maximum of desirability. In Mauritania, a fat woman is considered beautiful because it shows evidence of great wealth.

As I approached they did not move but continued to recline on their sides. An elderly African woman fussed over them and two African youths busied themselves nearby.

The younger of the three Bidan women, who I guessed to be about twenty-five, could speak a little English, and I asked if it was possible to sleep within the safety of their fenced compound.

'You welcome. Sit,' she replied with a wave of her chubby arm and I sat down on a corner of a mattress opposite.

The women and girls each drank from large calabash bowls filled with about three litres of camels' milk. The younger woman called out a few words to the two African youths. A few moments later they returned from the house with a red velvet-covered foam mattress, and then a calabash of camels' milk was placed beside me where I now lay on my side as the Bidan women did.

'Drink,' she told me, and I took a swallow of the warm milk. It was light and tasted like skimmed cows' milk, and was surprisingly refreshing.

The younger woman was jovial and full of energy. Her eyes sparkled and she took great delight in teasing the two teenage girls, who I presumed were her sisters, and ordering the African boys to run after her every whim.

'Are any of you married?' I asked, curious as to why there were so many women and no men in the household.

'*Non*,' she laughed. 'I am divorced. My mother divorced. Her sister divorced. Is good to be divorced, but I marry again. Maybe divorce again,' she said, smiling mischievously.

'It is normal for a woman to divorce so many times?' I asked, a little confused by the matriarchal power of these Bidan women in a country dominated by Islam.

'Oh yes. In Mauritania, the husband, he give many gold. The woman get to keep when she divorce,' she said and giggled.

'Why you not have husband? I know, you too skinny,' she said, and broke into fits of laughter, which made her whole body wobble like a huge plate of jelly.

'Here, we see if you will have husband,' she said, and called to the elderly African woman who was supervising the two youths in preparing the evening meal. She came over and squatted beside us, taking a handful of cowrie shells from a leather pouch that hung around her neck. She gently shook them like dice in her cupped hands and then cast the shells onto one of the mattresses.

I wondered how the shells had arrived here in the desert so far from the coast; probably they were brought by Arab merchants crossing the desert on camels along the trade routes. Cowrie shells, sometimes called money shells, mostly came from the Indian Ocean, from the Maldives, and were first brought to Africa by Arab traders in the fourteenth century to buy slaves from coastal West African tribes.

The other women leaned close as the old woman studied the shells that lay scattered in a random pattern on the mattress. They then went into a lengthy discussion as to what the placement of the shells revealed. A few moments later the old woman stopped poking at the shells and lifted her head, smiling a toothless grin at me.

'Ah, you are very lucky,' the young Mauritanian woman interpreted. 'You will have a very good husband. He love you very much. You will have three children. Twin boys and one girl,' she said, smiling at my good fortune.

'What about the more immediate future? What about my journey?' I asked.

The old woman cast the shells again and a deep frown creased her forehead as she poked at each one. She said a few curt words to the young woman who translated.

'Your journey will be safe but you must take care or you will become sick,' said the young Bidan woman as she gazed over to where the meal was being prepared, no longer interested in what the future held for me.

'What do you mean?' I said quickly. My heart pounded and I could feel sweat blistering on my forehead. I noticed that my hands were shaking.

'Do not worry. She says you will live a long and happy life,' she added after the old woman spoke a few words to her, but I sensed these words were said to reassure me instead of reading what the placement of the shells actually revealed.

'It is all true. You will see,' she said, sensing my doubt. 'We now eat,' she said and the old woman returned the shells to her pouch and then yelled a few words to the two youths. They appeared a moment later with an ornate silver bowl and jug for us to wash our hands. This was followed by a large tray piled with oil-saturated rice and bite-sized pieces of chicken.

*

As I finished packing to leave the next morning, a sandstorm blew in from the north. The mattresses were moved from the patio and the Bidan women rested out of the wind and stinging sand within the confines of their thick mud-brick house. I stood in the doorway, my black headscarf tightly wrapped to keep out the sand, and thanked the women for their hospitality.

'No, you must stay. It is not good to travel in storm,' the young Bidan woman said, looking at me horrified that I would even consider riding in such conditions.

I'd thought the storm would soon die down, but as I rode along the tarmac covered with drifts of fine sand, it only intensified. The wind nearly blew the bike off the road and the sand blinded me, even with the visor down and the black cloth wrapped tightly around my face under the helmet. Visibility was down to several metres and I was nearly out of fuel. I switched the TT to reserve and prayed that I would soon reach a village. I needed somewhere to shelter out of the wind and sand while I poured the petrol into the tank from my ten-litre jerry.

Up ahead, I could make out a cluster of square mud-brick buildings, which looked deserted. Some were half-buried in sand from the Sahara, which was steadily encroaching southward. I pulled up beside one of the houses, sheltering from the wind, and was about to refill the tank when two Bidan girls, aged about ten with sand-matted hair, bare feet and wearing faded floral dresses, appeared beside me. They insisted I follow them to one of the mud-brick huts. The entrance was draped with an old rug to stop the sand blown by the howling wind. Inside, several women, two old men and quite a few children of various ages were sitting on a worn carpet. None were fat, so I gathered they were poor, somehow eking out an existence in the desert. With the endless drought, no decent rain had fallen for twenty years and most of the livestock in these villages and small townships had perished long ago. All the able-bodied men, forced by necessity, had left to work in Nouakchott, and sent their meagre earnings back to their families. This was the same story for all the desert towns.

A metal stand filled with glowing coals heated a small teapot, and a glass of sweet black tea was poured and handed to me.

'*Shukran*,' I said and quickly sipped the tea, handing back the small glass as was the local way. As I waited for the storm to subside, I entertained the Mauritanians with photos of my family and of Australia, and an hour later, after I refuelled, I continued on my way to Ayoun al Atrous, the next township lining the highway.

*

'Where you come from?' called a male voice in a French accent when I pulled up in Ayoun outside the gendarmes' office. I had been on my way to ask them if I could sleep there for the night. I stopped and turned and saw a tall young man with short dark hair and a long thin face crawl out from under a faded and tattered length of canvas set up as a large tent to provide shade beside the gendarmes' office.

'I am Alfredo. I am from France,' said the dark-haired young man in baggy hippy trousers. 'I stay here to buy trade beads. I hitch a lift from Kiffa and tomorrow I hitch to Néma. It is no problem for you to stay here. The gendarmes are good men.'

After I'd spoken to the gendarmes, I joined Alfredo under the shade of the canvas and sat cross-legged on a handwoven carpet sipping sweet mint tea.

'It has been many weeks since I see another traveller,' he said. 'I am motorcyclist too. I ride Honda XL600 from Paris and sell it in Dakar for good price. Then I go to the desert villages to buy trade beads. I will sell these in the street markets of Paris.'

'I'd like to buy some chevron beads but I can't afford twenty dollars for one bead,' I said.

'Yes, in West Africa they ask too much for chevrons. The tourists push up the price. Here in Mauritania, you can buy chevrons much cheaper. No tourists come here. Later we go in town. There is lady selling beads. You pay maybe five dollar for one chevron,' he said and from a small cloth bag he poured a handful of multi-coloured glass beads onto the old carpet, including a few of the red, blue and white patterned chevrons. 'I buy these from her. They are beautiful, yes? The chevron was made in Venice and was highly prized by the chiefs and kings of West and Central Africa. Shiploads of chevron beads came to Africa to trade for slaves, gold and ivory.'

As we sipped tea and rested in the shade, Alfredo talked enthusiastically about Africa's trade beads. But after weeks of visiting the more remote desert villages and spending hours conversing with the women, he'd also developed a passion to protect the Mauritanian culture that was intricately linked to another kind of trade bead: the very old and unique beads made by the women of Mauritania's desert tribes. 'These can be four and five hundred years old,' Alfredo said. 'The oldest are more than eight hundred years. Most were made by women in the Kiffa area. They would sit for hours as they finely crushed coloured glass, then blended it with their spit, and spent even more hours creating intricate patterns before the bead was fired. The patterns have different meanings and each bead has a story. A family will keep several of these old beads and will only sell one in an emergency. One very wealthy family in Nouakchott sold just one bead to hire a helicopter to search for their son lost in the desert,' Alfredo explained.

'That one bead must have been worth thousands, but they're just bits of coloured glass,' I remarked, showing my complete ignorance of the culture of the desert people.

'No, not to the Mauritanians. The women will sit for hours sipping tea and discussing just one bead. How it has passed through different families. How it was sold when this child got sick or during a drought to buy food or for this wedding. Each time a bead is sold, its story grows and is intricately woven with many other stories. Without these beads, the old women cannot pass the family history to their daughters and the stories will be lost forever,' he said, his eyes filling with sadness.

'It is a crime that the foreign collectors want to take them away from Mauritania. What about you? Do you buy these beads?' I asked.

'I will buy the new beads, yes. These beads are still made by the nomadic women in the Kiffa area today and provide an income in a desert where there is nothing. This is good as the women can sell their art and make some money. But I will not buy the old Kiffa beads, even if I could afford one. These hold the stories. It should be illegal to take these away from Mauritania, but if a collector comes, the women will sell the old beads. Nothing can be done. Money is money,' he said.

With Alfredo translating, I later asked the gendarmes about travelling to Chinguetti via Tidjikja. Rather than ride directly to Nouakchott, I wanted to ride the long way to this ancient oasis town, famous as a medieval trading centre on the trans-Sahara trade route that dated back to the thirteenth century. As I would not dare travel across this vast stretch of dunes on my own, I asked about my chances of riding with another vehicle.

'You will not do this ride at this time of year. It is too hot,' Alfredo said, translating the comments from the gendarme, who looked at me horrified that I would even consider such a thing. 'But if you insist, you must wait in Moudjeria and go with a truck or 4×4,' he said. 'There is a French road crew building a road to Tidjikja from Moudjeria. They will help you.'

In the cool of the late afternoon, Alfredo took me to the lady selling the more common Venetian glass trade beads. I bought three chevrons and several little round beads made from ebony wood and inlaid with silver, all for 2000 ouguiya (about US$13). I made a necklace out of the beads and whenever I wore it, I felt a strange kind of power, as though the beads had travelled on a much longer journey than I ever would.

*

It was mid-morning as I neared Moudjeria. I stopped the bike when I reached the end of the graded dirt road that became two faint tyre tracks disappearing into a barrier of dunes. A sign in Arabic and French told me the Mauritanian government, with support from the World Bank, had allocated US$20 million to construct the road, but it ended here and it was still another eight kilometres of fine Sahara sand to Moudjeria. The purpose of the road was to link Tidjikja, an important date-growing area with a population of six thousand, to the highway. Once finished, it would go up over the Tagant Plateau and across fourteen kilometres of dunes to the date plantations.

In the mid-afternoon heat, riding over the dunes at speed so I would not sink into the soft sand was exhausting and I was at the point of passing out as I thundered into Moudjeria, which was half-buried by the Sahara. A line of dunes slowly crept towards it on one side while the Tagant Plateau rose as a sheer wall of steel-grey rock on the other. Flat-roofed houses made of mud-brick lined the streets, which were deserted, as the residents napped during the heat of the day. Some had heard my approach and stood in their doorways to stare in disbelief as I passed. When I reached the end of the town just before the dirt road climbed up to the plateau, I was waved down by a gendarme, a neatly dressed young man in military uniform.

'I don't think I will be riding to Tidjikja and Chinguetti,' I said as I stood beside the TT and gulped the last of my water.

'Not possible for you to go that way this time of year. Is very hot,' he said. 'Is better you leave the *moto* and go in truck. You wait for maybe one or two days. You are welcome to stay here,' he said and reached to take my empty water bottle, which he refilled at a tap just inside the mud-brick-walled gendarmes' compound. The tap was near a line of young eucalypts that reminded me of home. I pushed the TT inside and laid my groundsheet in the shade cast by the slender young gums.

There was no need to set up my tent, as in the desert there was no chance of rain. The tap inside the gendarmes' compound was also the only water supply for nearby residents. There were only a few water taps on the pipes that carried water from the spring at the base of the cliffs below the plateau. In the early part of the century, the French colonialists had installed an underground plumbing system, although, as the gendarme told me, it was in desperate need of urgent repair.

Over the next three days, as I waited for a truck to arrive, a steady stream of women and older children filled their containers at the tap, then balanced them on their heads to carry back to their homes. The younger children always waited outside and pelted me with stones, thrown through the open entrance and over the mud-brick wall. I refused to move from the only shaded area inside the compound, and chased and yelled at them to leave me alone. But instead of deterring them, I only encouraged them. I was their new game in a desert town where very little ever happened. Eventually, the gendarmes chased them away and I was left in peace.

In the late afternoon, as the heat left the day, the town came alive. Women in brightly coloured wraps and a few elderly men in white or blue ankle-length shirts wandered the main street. Children played chasing games, and the nomads returned with their goats and camels to water them after a day of grazing on desert shrubs and coarse grasses.

Each evening, the gendarme on duty spread a woven straw mat on the sand outside the compound. He brewed tea as we settled in to watch the afternoon promenade. Three plump Bidan girls in their late teens joined us. One of the girls could speak a little English. Her name was Farook and with my few words of French we chatted about her life in Moudjeria. Only a third of Moudjeria's 3000 residents still lived in the township. These comprised mostly women, children and old men, who sat out their lives in the unbearable heat. They subsisted on relief food and what few goods they could afford to buy with money sent to them by the men working in Nouakchott.

'How did the people survive before relief food?' I asked, as the present drought was by no means the worst.

'Even when all the animals die, there are usually still some dates, but when the drought is very long, the people turn to eating small lizards and even cockroaches. And in the most remote villages, there were rumours of cannibalism,' she whispered, leaning close to me.

'When the people talk of the past, they do not speak of the year, but of the drought. Each has a name and all the people know it, even the smallest child,' the gendarme added.

In the last of the daylight, one of the girls left and soon returned with a tray of oil-soaked rice with a few pieces of gristly meat scattered on top. The meat was tough and tasted like dirty socks, and I asked Farook what it was.

'*Chameau* [camel],' she said and giggled when I pulled a face.

On one of these evenings as we sat watching the promenade, the Bidan girls offered to dye my feet and hands with henna, something usually done before marriage or for a very special occasion.

'We are bored. We want to do this,' they chorused and I agreed.

The next day, I awoke with a slight headache and felt lethargic. I put this down to the heat, but by the afternoon there was no mistaking the symptoms of malaria. I shivered with fever and my head pounded. I had stopped taking Lariam as a prophylactic the day I left Bamako, two weeks earlier. I hadn't restocked with Halfan, after taking my last pills in Djenné, as I'd reasoned I would no longer need it in North Africa. But I had forgotten about the blood-engorged mosquitos on the inside of the mozzie net in Bamako. Fortunately, I still had several packets of Lariam and swallowed five pills, hoping it would kill the malaria parasite. For the next three days and nights I lay under the shade of the slender gums, weak with fever and frequent bouts of diarrhoea.

During this time two trucks arrived heading for the oasis town of Tidjikja, but I was too weak and reluctantly declined the trip across the desert.

As I recovered from the malaria, I craved fresh food. Since leaving Bamako, I had eaten only rice, meat and white bread. It was a diet totally lacking in vitamins and I became obsessed with images of freshly squeezed orange juice and steamed broccoli that floated before my eyes like a mirage rising out of the desert. The inside of my mouth was ulcerating, and my tastebuds were swollen and bleeding on my tongue. I had scurvy.

The few shops in town only sold bags of rice, flour, small packets of custard-cream biscuits, long-life milk and tinned sardines. There was not even any Laughing Cow processed cheese, which was often my staple snack food in Africa. In one shop, sitting covered in dust on a back shelf, I found a lone tin of mixed vegetables. It was all that remained of a relief food shipment sent as a gift from Saudi Arabia. I quickly carried my precious find back to the gendarmes' compound. My appetite had returned and I was ravenously hungry. But when I opened my prized tin, the vegetables were soaked in palm oil, no doubt to boost the calorie count, and the thought of eating any of it turned my stomach.

I was still weak, and knew it would be impossible for me to ride back over the dunes to reach the highway to Nouakchott. I had no choice but to wait for a truck to carry me and the TT to the tarmac. I'd now given up entirely on the idea of visiting the desert oasis towns of Tidjikja and Chinguetti. Instead, I would ride the easy way along the highway to Nouakchott.

Late the following afternoon, a smartly dressed man in his early thirties, wearing jeans and checked collared shirt, wandered into the gendarmes' compound. With his round glasses, neatly trimmed moustache and receding black hair he looked scholarly, and he spoke perfect English. He told me he was from Algeria and worked as a civil engineer employed by the French road construction firm to build the road to Tidjikja.

'I am Mounir. I live with three Mauritanians who also build the road. I come to invite you to dinner,' he said, the last rays of the sun glinting off his glasses.

Cooled by the gentle desert breeze, we walked the short distance to his house, with its open cement courtyard surrounded on two sides by arched walls, the rendered mud-brick highlighted in peach hues.

His friends lounged on mattresses sipping sweet mint tea from small glasses and I was welcomed as a special guest. An old woman brought over a tray of fresh green dates, the first of the crop from Tidjikja.

'Eat. The dates are good,' Mounir said, passing me a glass of tea.

'It is difficult. My mouth is sore,' I said and opened my mouth to show my tongue with its swollen and bleeding tastebuds.

'Ah, you need to drink camels' milk,' he said, and called to the old woman who shuffled over to inspect my mouth. She tut-tutted and a moment later returned with a bottle of purple antiseptic to swab the sores. Mounir also sent a boy to bring me a calabash bowl of camels' milk.

'This is scurvy,' I said. 'Do the children suffer from this?'

'Only sometimes, when they do not drink camels' milk,' he said and I cupped the calabash with both hands, gulping several mouthfuls.

I passed on the meal of rice and meat placed on the carpet before us where we lounged on foam mattresses and cushions, just like the Bidan women did at the well. Not only was my mouth too sore to eat, but I could not eat with my right hand as the henna had not completely dried. The day before, hearing I was up and about, the Bidan girls had come for me. After finishing their intricate designs, they insisted I was not to wash this hand for two days. And eating with my left hand was strictly forbidden as it was for lowly matters such as washing myself after using the toilet.

'So what you do now?' asked Mounir, enquiring about my revised travel plans, as he had heard the reports of the sick white girl on a motorcycle camped at the gendarmes' compound. I was likely to have been the hot topic of conversion within the town, as the gendarmes were very concerned about me and had sent for a doctor, but he'd only had Chloroquine. This less potent anti-malarial drug would be ineffective, as I had already taken a course of Lariam. It was just a matter of waiting for my body to win the battle with this particular malaria infection.

The malaria parasite seemed to evolve differently depending on where it originated. For me, each malaria attack and recovery time was different. The Kenyan malaria was quite mild compared to the strain I was infected with in Zaire. This most recent infection, picked up in Bamako or earlier in Djenné, was different again. It was not as vicious but I suffered a slow, lingering battle that raged inside me. Instead of the Chloroquine, I'd accepted the doctor's offer of a free packet of paracetamol, as I'd given all my supply of two packets to the gendarmes when I'd first arrived to treat their frequent headaches caused by drinking too much tea.

'I'm waiting for a truck to carry me and my motorcycle over the dunes to the highway. I am still too weak to ride through the sand,' I said.

'I think you have a long wait, maybe five days,' Mounir replied.

'Five days,' I said, as if it were a prison sentence.

'It is not so bad in Moudjeria,' he said, and looked over at his friends, who just laughed.

At the end of each day, when no truck arrived, I sat with the Bidan girls and gendarme on duty and sipped sweet tea as we watched the afternoon's promenade. Later, Mounir would come to invite me for dinner.

I assured him and his friends, as we sat outside on a worn carpet and cushions cooled by the evening breeze, that my left hand was clean, but even so I could feel their disgust. Out of respect, I let the old woman roll and squash the rice and meat together, but only for a few portions. I felt queasy about eating food so intimately handled by another. And out of respect for the Bidan girls, I could not destroy their art. They'd spent four hours cutting strips of elastoplast, sticking it on my hand and both feet in intricate designs, and then applying henna, which would be quickly dissolved by the goat fat covering my fingers if I ate with my right hand.

'Thank you, and goodbye if a truck comes tomorrow and I do not see you again,' I would say each evening before I returned to the gendarmes' compound after dinner. These were relaxing days and, although I was impatient to leave, I needed this time to recover. As the days passed, I felt my strength slowly return.

On my last evening in Moudjeria, after dinner with Mounir and his friends, I walked back to the gendarmes' compound by the light of the full moon, carrying my thongs so I could feel the softness of the fine sand under my bare feet. I'd read that the full moon is a time when the universal energy is in perfect planetary alignment, a time like no other, when your dreams would come true. I only wished to be doing exactly what I was doing at that very moment. I felt in complete balance – at one with myself and the world. It was a surreal feeling, as though time did not matter.

As I reached the compound, which sat in a depression in the shadow of the steel-grey cliffs, the air was still and hot and the only sounds were the occasional bleating of a goat or the bellow of a camel. By day the cliffs absorbed the hot sun and by night they radiated it out. It was several degrees hotter than in Mounir's raised cement courtyard and I lay sweating on top of my sleeping bag. I looked up through the leaves of the slender gums to gaze mesmerised at a billion stars until my eyes grew heavy.

In the blackness behind my lids, a rainbow of swirling colour suddenly appeared as an intense burst of light. I opened my eyes wide, and it stopped. What the fuck, I thought. I closed them again and the swirling mass of colour and light returned. My heart raced and I forced myself to keep my eyes closed. The burst of light settled and I looked into a mass of twirling colour as though I were looking through a window into another dimension. Scared, I opened my eyes and sat bolt upright.

Was it a hallucination, one of the most common side effects from long-term use of Lariam? But I'd stopped taking this drug as a malaria prophylactic over two weeks earlier. Maybe the five pills I'd taken to treat the latest bout was more than my body – or my mind for that matter – could handle. Or was I experiencing a divine revelation? Was this God? Or was it the mysterious hidden energy revealing itself to me at last? I lay back down and slowly closed my eyes and the movement of bright colours in circular patterns returned. It was like I had my own private showing of the aurora borealis but condensed into spectacular bursts of colour. Every part of me said this was real. After travelling alone for so long, I was used to relying on my intuition without question. What I was seeing confirmed all that I had awakened to on my journey. This moment was bringing everything together and it now all made sense. My experiences of good fortune were not random. All those coincidences and chance encounters had meaning. Greater forces were within my reach. I only had to believe.

But as I embraced the vision and looked deeper and deeper into it, an image of a person slowly emerged. It was a body lying in a coffin lined with white satin. My immediate thought was of my father. My eyes sprang open in horror. I dared not close them again. Could he have had another heart attack? The thought upset me and I felt my eyes fill with tears. All night I sat wide awake, leaning against one of the slender gums, waiting for daylight to approach.

At sunrise I waited patiently on the front steps of the gendarmerie for the two officers on duty; I would ask them if I could call home and reverse the charge.

'Telephone?' I asked when they finally arrived at the compound.

'*Non*. In Nouakchott,' said one of the gendarmes and looked at me questioningly.

'I must go to Nouakchott to phone my father,' I asked. 'I think he has died. I must know,' I explained.

The two gendarmes looked at each other and then back at me, convinced I was completely mad.

I sat in the compound all day, hoping for a truck to arrive from Tidjikja on its way to Nouakchott. Each minute felt like an hour, but by late afternoon my wish was answered.

'*Camion, camion!*' the children called as they came running into the compound.

Yes, a truck was slowly making its way down from the plataeu and it soon drove into town and stopped outside one of the roadside stores. The driver, a plump, middle-aged Mauritanian man, climbed from the cab of the rusting ten-tonne truck. Even before I reached it, I could see its high wooden boxed tray was fully loaded. I asked the driver if he would take me and my motorcycle over the dunes to the main road.

'10,000 ouguiya [US$66],' he said, spat on the ground, and headed into the store.

It was his first price. I was a tourist, so of course it was grossly inflated.

'I have only 3000 ouguiya [US$20]. Please take me as far as you can for this?' I pleaded, holding up the notes.

'We go *cinq minute*,' he said, snatching the notes from my hand.

I ran into the gendarmerie and asked the two men on duty to help me quickly lift the TT onto the truck loaded with empty LPG cylinders. I climbed onto the truck. Perched on top of gas cylinders were the passengers: five obese Mauritanian women and their bundles of luggage; an old man with a goat, its legs trussed together; and three young soldiers in faded fatigues. There was also a spare truck tyre.

The women looked at me with contempt, the soldiers sat on the truck's roof smoking cigarettes. It was obvious nobody was going to give up their comfortable position to make room for my motorcycle. The ideal spot to lay the TT was on the spare truck tyre, as this would cushion it from any damage. Nobody was sitting on the tyre, but I needed to move it slightly towards the back of the truck. I asked the women to move aside. They just sat and continued to stare at me. I was running out of time, and in desperation I picked up the tyre, surprising even myself, and moved it. My show of brute strength got everybody's attention. The women moved and the soldiers offered their help. Using my ropes, the bike was hoisted up on the truck and securely tied down just as the driver waddled out from the store. He spat out a large glob of phlegm, climbed into the cab, started the engine and with a crunching of gears, drove away from Moudjeria, not once checking to see if all his passengers were on board. I waved goodbye to the two gendarmes, who stood and waved back. 'Thank you. Say goodbye to Mounir,' I called and they nodded. Soon the desert town where I had spent over a week faded into the bleakness of undulating sand as the truck carried me over the barrier of dunes towards the highway to Nouakchott.

Around a hundred kilometres from the city, the driver stopped, got out of the cab, lit a cigarette, took a deep drag and yelled, 'You finish here!'

'*What?* We are nearly in Nouakchott. What difference will it make?' I wailed, not believing he was serious.

'Pay more money!' he yelled back.

'You bastard,' I mumbled, but his behaviour was an exercise in saving face. I'd asked him to take me as far as 3000 ouguiya would, even though he'd quoted 10,000 as the price to Nouakchott. So he'd decided that here, where a few flat-roofed mud-brick huts lined the tarmac as it cut through the Sahara, was the 3000 ouguiya drop-off point. Actually, I had done rather well, having only expected to be taken over the dunes, just before the highway at Sangrafa, and was not overly concerned about unloading the TT where he had stopped. The night before I'd also been treated to a meal of camel meat and rice shared from a communal platter, and later we'd all slept under the stars on carpets rolled out on the sand in front of a roadside cafe in a small village. The other passengers did not share my casual acceptance of the driver's decision, and argued strongly for him to take me all the way to Nouakchott. It was now mid-morning and the sun was already hot. It would take ten minutes or so to unload the bike and in the meantime they would have to endure the heat when we were all keen to get to Nouakchott without delay.

The driver would not be persuaded, and headed to a nearby hut to drink tea. The unloading of my motorcycle was none of his concern.

The road improved slightly as I neared Nouakchott. It also became busier, and I was soon riding through the city's shantytown outskirts. Here the sand lay in drifts against the mud-brick houses with flat tin roofs, the Sahara – an enormous, relentless, creeping thing – only a short distance away.

Nouakchott was a new city, built in 1960. It was created as the capital after Mauritania gained independence from France. Since the drought, the surrounding shantytown had grown due to the mass exodus of nomads and able-bodied men from the desert towns. The city centre of square, cement buildings looked characterless and uninteresting, and it appeared deserted compared to the bustling, fringe-dwelling community of robed nomads.

I headed for the post office to phone home and was relieved to learn that my father was fit and healthy. After a quick chat reassuring my parents I was fine, I said goodbye. This brief call cost US$40. With my money running low and no means of getting any more until I reached the next American Express office in Morocco, I could not afford to talk for longer.

The post office was a clean, modern building, and I felt out of place and self-conscious, even more so when I realised the three backpackers queuing at the counter were staring at me, open-mouthed.

After paying for my call, I went outside, and as I readied to leave, I caught a glimpse of my reflection in the building's tinted windows.

In the dusty, navy trench and oil-stained, ripped jeans and with the faded black cloth covering my head, I looked every bit the wild Tuareg nomad blown in from the desert. No wonder the backpackers had stared at me, I thought as I scoffed four of the oranges I had bought from the nearby stall and packed the extras into the Gearsack to eat later.

I glanced at my reflection again. What had happened to me? Had I travelled alone for so long that the last semblance of civilised, modern woman had fallen away in the desert from where I'd just come, blown from my skin by the hot, dry winds? Had I become a wild thing: a primitive being operating on pure instinct? I got back on the TT and slowly rumbled out of the city, along its wide boulevards and back into the desert where I felt I belonged.

23

UBUNTU
MAURITANIA

It was noon, the sun at its zenith. I should have waited rather than ride in the hottest part of the day. The temperature hovered at forty-five degrees Celsius, but I wanted to move on from Nouakchott and its sprawl of featureless, flat-roofed cement buildings. The tarmac was good for a while, but it soon deteriorated into potholes.

After about a hundred kilometres, when I could stand the heat no longer, I stopped at a rusted corrugated-iron shelter set back a little from the road. A pale-green, beat-up Peugeot 504 sedan was parked in the shade. The driver and passengers lay on mats and an old Bedford truck, more rust than red paint, was parked nearby. A few blue-robed men sat in its shade sipping tea. We exchanged nods of welcome and then I, too, dozed until late afternoon, when I continued on my way to ride on across the flat stretch of desert. Here the dunes had receded, and the landscape became an endless expanse of hard stony plains, its barrenness broken by the occasional scraggly shrub.

The highway gradually deteriorated from potholes to deep, bone-rattling corrugations. When the road lost all trace of black tarmac, I gave up on the highway and, like every other vehicle, followed one of the many dirt tracks that bordered it.

The sun had dropped below the horizon when I rode into the mining town of Akjoujt, another 150 kilometres along the potholed and corrugated highway. It was another collection of cement and corrugated-iron buildings, covered in a layer of fine red dust. On the far outskirts, I could see the outline of the crushing plant. I'd been told by more than one motorcycle traveller about the Australian copper mine operated by Gryphon Minerals and that I'd get a bed and free meal when I passed through. For the past two weeks I'd only washed out of a bucket, and I longed for the luxury of a decent shower. I craved good food. I was Australian. I'd once worked in the mining industry. These were the excuses I toyed with to justify my reasons for being another of the many travellers who imposed on Gryphon's generous hospitality.

Of course they won't mind, I thought as I rode through the dusty streets towards the mine workers' fenced compound.

'Can I camp here for the night?' I hesitantly asked the Mauritanian security guard when I pulled up at the wire-mesh gate.

The guard looked at me with annoyance, his bushy black eyebrows knitted in a frown. He grunted something unintelligible and walked away, returning with a burly man in khaki work shorts, thongs and a blue singlet pulled tight over his paunch. He looked a little pissed off, as I'd probably interrupted his dinner.

'You're an Aussie. Well, come on in then. We'll find you a *donga*,' he said, a smile breaking across his unshaven face, which a moment before had been stern.

'I worked at the Ranger mine in the Territory,' I said to further justify that I was not just another freeloader; that I was, in fact, a fellow mine worker – a comrade.

I rode away from Akjoujt early the next morning blissfully clean and well-fed. But my departure was not early enough for me to be able to thank and say goodbye to the mine workers before they left the compound for yet another shift at the mine.

With only 180 kilometres to Atar, my planned destination for the day, I was in no hurry and settled into what at first appeared to be a smooth, easy day's ride. The tyre tracks I followed across the stony plains began to move further away from the broken tarmac – all that remained of the road. As I left the plains behind, the landscape gradually changed to fine red sand and low dunes. I picked what looked to be the most recent tyre tracks and followed these north. *Please God, don't let me drop the bike*, I repeated. If I stopped in the sand, I would be stuck. Without the momentum of speed, the TT would sink, and without help I would not have the strength to push it out. More tyre tracks criss-crossed the pair I followed, and progressively they all became faint until the tracks disappeared completely. With endless drifts of sand, the scene was all the same, and I had left the badly corrugated main road ages ago. Now I had no idea if I was going in the right direction.

Fear welled inside me, as I imagined I was riding into the desert and soon I would be lost forever. I kept going at speed, as fast acceleration would keep the TT from sinking, but as I circled a low dune I cried out with joy when I saw two faint tyre tracks. Soon more became visible, all leading back to run parallel with the remnants of the tarmac. I rode up onto it gladly, no longer caring if I was rattled apart by corrugations as I headed to Atar.

*

I estimated I had about one more hour of daylight as I stood drinking a cold Coke outside one of the many general stores that lined the large open triangle area of central Atar. The square and its featureless cement buildings were stained a dirty brown by the dust blown in from the desert and sad, scrawny goats chewed on bits of paper lying on the dusty street. Old men in ragged robes watched me suspiciously from where they were sitting in small groups, and several boys pestered me by chanting '*Donnez cadeau*'.

'Ah, piss off, will ya,' I said to them, unable to tolerate their chants even for a moment.

I was at the end of Africa. I was tired. I looked down at the boys who surrounded me. Their hair was matted with dirt, their clothes grubby, and their dark almond eyes teary from constant irritation by the sand and dust. Had I become so hardened by so many months on the road that I no longer felt any empathy for these poor little buggers who lived wretched lives in these desert towns? The drought had not only taken their parents' wealth – their goats and camels – it had also taken their culture, their traditions, and now they were left with nothing.

'I'm sorry,' I said, more for the lifestyle that the drought had denied them, than as an apology for not giving them a gift.

'*Cadeaux fini. Voyage in Afrique très long,*' I said, and pointed to the map drawn on the side cover of the bike.

They all gathered to look. A small boy of about seven traced with his finger the route scratched into the plastic. I only drank a little of the Coke, and then I gave him the bottle. He quickly gulped a few mouthfuls before it was snatched by an older boy and then by another, until a moment later it was finished.

It was about eighty kilometres to Chinguetti. The storekeeper told me the road was good, so I left the dusty desert town of Atar behind, heading for this holy Muslim town on top of the Adrar Plateau. I would get my ancient desert town experience after all.

The road headed up through the Amogar Pass, a canyon of deep ravines and ragged cliffs. The narrow, rocky track had been blasted out of the sheer cliffs. The steep drop-offs were only a few feet from my tyres as the TT rumbled over the sharp rocks. When the track levelled, I stopped and gazed out over the canyon of deep gorges washed in the shades of rich reds and browns as the sun sank below a hidden horizon.

The sun had just set when I rode into Chinguetti, the half-buried town of crumbling mud-brick buildings. In a shadowy blackness, the encroaching dunes loomed large on its outskirts, where drifts lay up against the houses. I rode through deep sand and stopped near one of the flat-roofed buildings in the main streets where I leaned the TT against a brick wall as the sand was too soft to support the bike just on its side-stand. A man carrying a lantern approached.

'Come, I help you with the *moto*. Inside, there is a European woman. You are welcome to stay,' he said.

'Thank you,' I replied with a smile of gratitude and together we pushed the TT over the fine sand and through a narrow opening in the brick wall to the safety of a compound. Inside was a low-set plastered-brick house. Four obese Bidan women reclined on mattresses placed on carpets spread outside on the sand. The area was lit by several oil lamps that cast a soft light. With them was the European woman. She was middle-aged with pale skin and frizzy auburn hair and beamed a welcoming smile from a round face.

'Hi, I'm Anna,' she said, extending her hand towards me as she stood up. 'And this is Ba, my driver. He heard your motorbike.'

'Heather. I'm from Australia,' I said shaking her hand and nodding my thanks to the unassuming Mauritanian man, aged about thirty, who stood beside me.

'Please, you stay here with us. Your journey has been long,' she said.

'Thank you,' I said and sat down. A glass of mint tea was offered.

Laid out on the carpet at Anna's feet were an assortment of silver bracelets, necklaces and earrings embossed in ebony wood, and several rugs made from finely woven camel hair in striking geometric designs. Like the Kiffa beads, the crafts were another strand that strengthened the intricate web of Mauritania's desert culture.

'I am from GTZ in Germany helping these women. We fund their cooperative, the Project Promotion Feminine,' she said. GTZ was an international aid agency.

'Chinguetti can no longer support its people. There are four thousand here but most of the men who can work have left for Nouakchott and Nouadhibou. Through the cooperative, the women develop art and craft so they no longer just sit in their crumbling mud-brick houses waiting for the Sahara to cover them,' she said. 'They have already found buyers in Nouakchott for their art and we hope to sell in Europe and America, too.'

A large bowl of dried dates sat on the carpet between the mattresses, and the Bidan women insisted I eat. Then trays of rice and goat meat were served by two middle-aged African women. We washed our hands with water poured into a bowl from an ornate silver jug.

'These women are very wealthy. They own most of the date palms in Chinguetti,' Anna whispered as we ate. I asked about the African servants, who'd I'd read in my guidebook were actually treated more like slaves.

'They are not slaves,' she said indignantly. 'They are free to leave, but what is for them if they go? A life of poverty in the city, of discrimination and abuse. Here they are treated like one of the family. This is their home,' she added, a little angry I'd formed judgement without understanding the ebb and flow of life in this desert country.

I asked about the road to Ouadane, as I was thinking about visiting the ancient oasis town. Like Chinguetti, it was once a prosperous caravan centre on the great trade route from Europe.

'There is much sand. It is very bad. You will not make it on your motor-bike,' Anna said. Her words instantly dismissed this fleeting thought. Besides, I doubted the TT would make it: since leaving Nouakchott, it sounded tired and worn out. The timing chain inside the engine was loose, and being at the end of its automatic adjustment, I could not tighten it. I did not carry a spare, and even if I did, delving into the bowels of the TT's engine was way beyond my mechanical ability.

The float in the carburettor was also sticking, but there was no place free of sand to pull it apart as I'd done in the Mobil workshop in Nigeria. Instead, I would free it by reaching for my hammer and giving it a few good taps while still riding. It worked and the TT ran without problems for another few hours, until I needed to tap it again.

Everyone was awake early the next morning, and the mattresses and carpets were carried into the house. The Bidan women beckoned me to follow and, with Anna, I went inside.

The house was a labyrinth of bare rooms. In the central room, the carpets were spread out on the bare stone floor and the velvet-covered mattresses were laid on top, against the walls. The soft morning light filtered through a high window that ran almost the length of the back wall. One African woman poured tea, while another brought in a tray of freshly baked baguettes and a large bowl of dried dates.

'Ba and I leave Chinguetti this afternoon for Atar. Please, you must travel with us. The Amogar Pass is dangerous. You must not travel down alone. What if you should fall?' Anna asked with concern. 'Ba has spoken to me, and he is very worried, insisting I make you travel with us.'

'From here, I plan to ride to Choum and take the train to Nouadhibou, but I will pass through Atar again, so yes I will travel with you,' I replied.

'It is settled then. We will leave together, and you will stay with us in Atar. Ba will be happy. He would not have given me a moment's peace if you did not join us.'

I excused myself and Anna explained to the Bidan women that I wanted to look around Chinguetti while the morning was still cool.

Chinguetti had once been a major town on the camel caravan salt trade route that came down from the north across the desert to West Africa. It was an important Muslim town, the seventh holy city of Islam, and was once the gathering point for pilgrimages to Mecca.

The town was littered with the remnants of crumbling mosques and the sand lay in drifts against the old stone walls. I walked past the main mosque, which dominated the old quarter, the Ksar, and soon reached the outskirts. I climbed a high dune where, unnoticed, I looked out over the town. It appeared to be cut in half by the encroaching sand, and many of the old stone buildings now lay in ruins. In a few more years these would be buried by the dunes that towered like a wall of pale red sand behind them.

An old man on a camel led his small herd across this void, past the deserted houses on the outskirts and into the desert. He would return in the late afternoon after grazing his camels on the plateau. I watched as two young girls drew water from the well below me. A low fenced wall of stones had been erected to protect a few date palms planted beside the well, but the dune I was sitting on already covered one side of the wall and was moving towards the palms. It was only a matter of time, months perhaps, before it would also cover the well. I left Chinguetti with Anna and her driver Ba in the coolness of late afternoon. As I crossed the deep red sand and the stony plateau, and headed down the Amogar Pass to Atar, they followed behind in their white Toyota 4×4. I spent the night with them at the GTZ guesthouse and left the next morning for Choum. As I refuelled, Anna and Ba stood with me.

'Do you have ropes to tie your motorbike on the train?' Anna asked. 'Ba says the train moves a lot. It is very rough.'

'I have some. They will be okay,' I said. I had one length of rope which was strong enough to secure the TT on the train, I reasoned.

Ba walked to their Toyota parked nearby and returned with a roll of three-inch white webbing.

'Here. He says you must take some of this. It is very strong,' Anna said and uncoiled about four metres.

'That is your tow rope. You must not shorten it.'

Anna and Ba ignored my protests, cut it and rolled up the webbing, handing it to me. 'You must take care. It is very dangerous for a woman on her own in Africa,' Anna said with genuine concern.

'I will be all right. I promise. I have made it this far,' I said.

'Here, take this. You will not find much food after leaving Atar,' she said and handed me two packets of custard-cream biscuits and two cartons of long-life milk.

I hugged them both and they hugged me back as though we were old friends rather than two people I'd known for only a day.

I rode on a dirt track that cut across the sand and low dunes to Choum. As the sun heated the day, hot winds blew across the desert and it took all my strength to hold the TT steady and follow the long, straight track that seemed like it would never end. It was only 120 kilometres, but when I reached the few dilapidated tin shacks that lined the railway-track my spirits soared. I stopped at the first small tin shack, where a gendarme leaned against the door waiting for me.

'I am here for the train,' I shouted, struggling to be heard over the blowing wind as I handed him my passport. He glanced at me briefly and without a word handed it back and retreated to his hut out of the wind and stinging sand. I rode on to another tin shack nearby, where a group of people sat huddled on old carpets. I parked the TT beside the shack and several grubby children crowded around me, pulling at my coat and trying to push the bike over.

'Bugger off!' I yelled and threw up my arms to chase them away.

'Come over here,' a voice called above the noise of rattling tin flapping in the howling wind.

I wrapped the black cloth covering my head a little tighter to protect my face from the sand, and turned to look into the smiling black face of a young man, his T-shirt tight over his muscled shoulders.

'Go away!' he shouted at the children.

'Push your motorbike over there. It is better under that shelter,' he said and pointed to the nearby shack next to the one I was standing under.

'I am Mustafa. I am from Ghana and this is my friend Dionigi. He is from Nigeria. We are musicians and we go to Europe,' he said when we reached the shack. They both stood straight and tall, as though they knew for sure all their dreams would come true.

Mustafa, smaller and leaner than his friend but just as strong, helped me push the TT a little further under the shelter and out of the wind. I retrieved a carton of long-life milk and a packet of sweet biscuits from my Gearsack. As we shared the biscuits and milk, drinking it straight from the carton, they told me about their journey from Accra. They'd hitched lifts in trucks, but found it very difficult in Mauritania because they were black and the people treated them badly. But their journey was nearly over, and once they reached Nouadhibou they would sneak aboard a cargo ship bound for Europe.

'So what is the story with this train?' I asked, curious as to how I would get my motorcycle on top of a three-metre-high iron-ore wagon as the train travelled from the mine in Zouérat for the 600-kilometre journey to the port in Nouadhibou.

'For us it is easy. We just jump on. But you will need help to lift your motorbike. We will help but it will not be enough,' Mustafa said.

'How much for the ticket?' I asked.

'Ticket? The train is free,' Dionigi smiled mischievously.

'Not for me, I will buy a ticket. That way the train crew will help me,' I said.

'Maybe,' he said, unconvinced by my confidence.

'Later, I go with you to the station master,' Mustafa added, a little more upbeat for my benefit.

'The train passes late in the afternoon, at six,' Dionigi said.

I looked out from where we sat sheltered from the wind and sand under the tin shack. Clumps of dried shrub rolled past, blown by the wind, and a donkey stood in the hot sun as though it had given up on life's struggle.

'Four more hours in this godforsaken place,' I said. The boys had a watch and I could see it was only two p.m.

'Yes. Welcome to the end of the world,' Mustafa said and patted me on the back. 'You will survive. You've come this far. Only another twelve hours and you will be in Nouadhibou. You will see the blue ocean and eat fish, and life will be good once more.'

I stood up, stretched, and then untied my ten-litre plastic water container from the back rack of the TT. I would need to fix it somehow for the train ride across the desert. Several days ago, it had come loose and for a short distance dragged on the ground, wearing a hole in the bottom.

'Give to me. I fix,' Mustafa said as he watched me inspect the damage. 'Give me your knife, some plastic bag and a lighter.'

I watched as the two of them ingeniously bonded the plastic and repaired the hole with the heated blade of my pocket knife. Afterwards, I filled it with water from the well near the shack and it did not leak one drop.

As it neared six p.m., several Mauritanian men who'd been sitting with us under the shelter gathered their things and headed to the train track. They were probably on their way to search for work in Nouadhibou. Dionigi left with them to wait for the train while Mustafa, who spoke French, came with me to translate to the station master that I needed help to load my motorcycle. I paid the 2000 ouguiya (US$13) fare, and was assured this fee also included loading and unloading in Nouadhibou.

There was a cement platform near the train track and this looked the obvious place to load the TT. Mustafa came with me and asked the few teenage boys who were lingering around the platform if the train stopped there. The boys only teased Mustafa, and he soon lost his patience with them.

'I will be happy when I leave this terrible country and these terrible people,' he said.

'Look, the train is coming,' I said. In the distance was a faint trail of dust as the nearly three-kilometre-long line of wagons loaded with iron-ore slowly approached us.

'Quick. We must go to where Dionigi is waiting,' Mustafa said, urging me to start the TT so I could take him back to his friend.

We reached the others as the train came fully into view. As it pulled up there was a mad scramble as about fifty people rushed to climb on the wagons.

'We must go, the train will leave soon,' Mustafa said.

'Please help me!' I shouted in sheer desperation to four Mauritanian men standing along the edge of the track.

'No, the train is leaving. Do not try!' Dionigi called from where he was standing on top of a wagon.

The train had stopped for only a few minutes and now it lunged forward.

'Good journey!' they yelled, and I waved back.

I watched the last of the wagons disappear into the desert. It was almost dark and I slowly walked back to the TT and sat dejected on the dusty ground beside the tracks.

'*Le train pour Nouadhibou*,' a voice above me boomed. I had not heard anyone approach, and looked up to see a tall, solidly built Mauritanian youth aged about eighteen, dressed in a ragged shirt and torn, faded jeans too short for his long legs. Overly large feet in worn leather sandals protruded from the frayed ends.

I stood and looked into his slightly deformed face, which smiled at some secret joke.

'*What?*' I asked.

'Nouadhibou,' he replied, and pointed to the three wagons on a rail siding.

I rode over to the wagons and the Mauritanian followed behind, taking great strides with his long legs.

Two were iron-ore wagons, loaded with bags of rice, and the third was a flat-top stacked with crates of soft-drink. All of this had been trucked from Nouakchott, where the ship unloaded the relief food and where the fizzy drink was bottled. An old man was sitting on the ground, in the process of brewing tea. He and the young man were the caretakers of the rice and soft-drink.

'When does it leave?' I asked.

'*À minuit,*' the tall Mauritanian replied, a grin breaking across his face.

'Midnight!' I shouted with joy. I felt like hugging him.

'*Oui,*' he replied, and handed me the glass of tea the old man had poured.

The only place for the TT was on top of the wagons loaded with the rice, a distance of over three metres from the ground beside the raised tracks. Even though the tall Mauritanian looked as strong as an ox, with only the three of us it would be impossible to hoist 200 kilograms of loaded bike up that high.

It was dark, and I paced frantically beside the wagons. The old man and his helper watched me curiously from where they sat next to the wagon loaded with crates of soft-drink. As I turned, I saw two sets of lights approach along the tracks from the direction of the town. One belonged to a train engine, the other a vehicle, and it was purely a coincidence that they were approaching me at the same time. The vehicle was in front and I ran out to stop it. I hoped the driver could understand my broken French as I explained I needed help to lift my motorcycle onto the wagon. The tall Mauritanian appeared beside me and leaned over my shoulder. He explained my predicament.

As the train engine approached, I rushed over and stood on the tracks, waving and jumping for it to stop. It ground to a halt and I climbed up the steps to speak to the driver. I showed him my ticket, pointing to my motorcycle, the wagon and saying 'Nouadhibou'. I was desperate; this was my only chance of loading the TT – if I missed this opportunity, I envisioned days of waiting in this hot, dusty void.

With the help of the three men from the pickup, the driver of the train engine and the tall Mauritanian, the TT was hoisted onto the loaded wagon. I said a silent thank you to Anna and Ba for the length of webbing. My ropes would never have been strong enough. My motorcycle was laid in a depression on top of the canvas covering the sacks of rice. After tying it down, I was confident it would be secure for the rough ride across the desert to Nouadhibou.

It was not until nearly two a.m. that the second iron-ore train from the mine at Zouerat arrived. The three wagons were hitched to the rear of its long line and, in the early hours of the morning, it lurched forward to begin rattling and banging its way towards the coast.

On top of the loaded wagon, I huddled into the depression near the bike, hanging on for dear life as the wagon swayed and rocked violently. My trench coat gave some protection from the dust blown up by the wheels as the train coursed through the sand partially covering the tracks.

At dawn, I peered out through the black cloth covering my head to see the long trail of wagons, a straight line cutting across the desert. The train was the only sign of civilisation on the endless drifts of sand.

Occasionally we passed the tents of nomads; a few camels stood nearby, and robed men stared at us solemnly as we rattled past. I wondered how these people survived in the barrenness of the desert, as it seemed devoid of all life. Not even a spindly shrub could be seen.

The train ground to a halt at a collection of tin shacks that bordered one side of the track. I took advantage of the break to pee, quickly climbing down from the wagon and squatting with my trench coat flared out for privacy.

By mid-afternoon, we could see the ocean as we followed the narrow finger of land, the Cape Blanc peninsula, to the rail terminal on the outskirts of Nouadhibou.

Once we arrived, our three wagons were unhooked and then pushed by an engine to an insignificant rail siding away from the main track. The iron-ore wagons were taken to the port, where the ore would be loaded onto the waiting ships. As the engine was unhooked, I ran to it and climbed up to speak to the driver, but he did not speak English and ignored me when I showed him my ticket, which I'd been assured included unloading the TT. With our three wagons uncoupled, the engine reversed, gaining speed. I had no choice but to jump or be carried far away.

I ran back to the wagons, to the tall Mauritanian and old man who, like me, were covered in a fine layer of pale ivory-ochre dust. They were sitting in the shade of the soft-drink wagon, brewing tea. An hour went by and then another and no help came. It was only mid-morning, but I resigned myself to spending the night at the rail siding and climbed back on the wagon that held my bike. The Mauritanians were sitting on the crates of soft-drink, as if guarding them from hordes of thieves. I had shared the last of my biscuits with the two men that morning as it seemed they had no food. I was now hungry, but I could not risk leaving my motorcycle and all my possessions in search of a meal. We were still a long way from Nouadhibou. I scanned the area with my binoculars. There was nothing like a stall selling something to eat, but beyond the rail siding, within an area fenced with high wire mesh, a crane began unloading scrap metal from a truck. I ran over and stood clutching the wire-mesh fence. I called out and spoke in my best French.

'*Mille ouguiya pour décharger la moto*,' I said, offering about US$7 – all the cash I had – and pointed to the crane.

'*Non*,' they replied and returned to their work.

'How much then?' I asked. The words were universally understood, regardless of language, but the men ignored me.

I turned and walked slowly back to the wagons, accepting my fate of spending another day forgotten at the rail siding.

I climbed up on the wagons and lay down, covering myself with my old navy trench for shade.

'Come,' I heard from below and looked down to see the four men from the fenced area. It must have been their mid-morning break.

They ignored my protests as they dragged the TT from the top of the wagon and lowered it to the ground with a thump. The pannier frame was cracked in several places, but they demanded I pay them 4000 ouguiya, about US$25. I pointed to the damage they had done to the TT and showed them my ticket, telling them that unloading was included in the price. The tall Mauritanian stood beside me and it sounded like he told them to 'bugger off'. They looked at me, ranting and raving, and then at him, and realised it was pointless to argue with a crazy white woman and an oversized Mauritanian.

With the panniers and my belongings packed on the TT, I rode along the smooth tarmac into Nouadhibou, revelling in the freedom of moving again. But it was short-lived, as I soon reached the outskirts of this sprawling desert town that attracted the nomads like moths to a single bright light. I passed through a shantytown of tin shacks and then the fish-processing and refrigeration plants, surrounded by high wire-mesh security fences. In the distance, I could see the docks were busy with ships. Off-duty crewmen wandered the dusty streets. Thin goats, forsaken donkeys, women in brightly coloured wraps and blue-robed men mingled against a backdrop of pale sand.

My first priority was to repair the cracked pannier frame. There was no welding workshop, so I stopped at a fish-processing plant. As I asked the security guard at the gate about a welder, a man arrived in a taxi, a rusted, beat-up white Peugeot 504 sedan.

'Yes, we can weld your motorbike,' he said, and a moment later I was following Ahmed from Libya through the gates.

The pannier frame was cracked in four places and the muffler clamp was also broken. As I inspected the TT for damage, I also discovered the rubber around one of the two connectors from the carburettor to the engine had separated from the metal. The welding of the frame and replacing the clamp was a simple job, but the damaged connector was a detrimental blow.

Fine red desert sand had been sucked directly into the engine for God knows how long. But it did not matter: the damage was done, and I had not even noticed. I hadn't even known to check this for damage.

'Is problem?' Ahmed asked as I silently cursed my negligence.

'Yes,' I said.

'We fix. We use glue,' he said to cheer me up.

'No, the damage is done. It can't be fixed,' I said.

Ahmed helped me remove the pannier frame, and in no time it was welded and refitted back to the bike.

'You must stay with my friend. He is old man. A teacher from Syria,' he said. 'I go back to ship tonight, but it is no problem for you to stay with him. Two boys, my cousins from Libya, stay with him also. They speak English.'

I looked at him.

'Do not worry. They are good boys. You will be okay,' he said as he read my thoughts.

Ahmed hailed a taxi, and I followed him to a street a few back from the main road in the town centre.

The cement passageway to the central courtyard of the Syrian's house was too narrow for the TT, but by loosening the handlebars and twisting them, the bike could fit through. As Ahmed had assured me, the grey-haired Syrian teacher and his two Libyan cousins were the epitome of politeness, and they welcomed me into their home. I was shown the shower and after I'd washed off the dust, we shared a meal of pan-fried fish, salad, rice and pita bread. We lounged in the courtyard on soft cushions, around plates of food on the carpet, and between mouthfuls I told them about my journey on the train from Choum – and that I had hardly eaten for two days. They nodded and insisted I eat more.

As we ate, I asked my hosts if any trucks crossed the disputed land between Mauritania and Morocco. The border had been officially closed for years because of the war between Morocco and the Polisario (the rebel army of the Western Sahara independence movement). The Western Sahara had once been a Spanish colony, and when Spain withdrew, it divided the stretch of desert between Morocco and Mauritania. The Mauritanians already had enough desert and didn't want more. They were also reluctant to fight an expensive war with the Polisario. The Polisario and the Moroccans, however, had been fighting over the land ever since.

My hosts advised me that the overland crossing to Morocco was open and convoys guided by the military were making it over the disputed land, but that it was dangerous, as the dunes were mined.

'You cannot ride alone over the dunes,' Ahmed said.

'I will not ride my motorcycle. It would not make it through the sand. I was hoping for a convoy. To get a lift with a truck that could carry me and my bike to the tarmac in Morocco. It would be easy riding then,' I said, hoping the TT's engine would last until I reached Marrakesh and a motorcycle mechanic.

'It would be very expensive to go by truck. It is better you take a ship from here to Europe. There is a German ship. It leaves for Antwerp tomorrow,' Ahmed said.

'But if I do this I will not reach the top of Africa,' I said. All of a sudden, I realised my journey had come to an end. It was an abrupt and unceremonious ending, and I looked down as my eyes welled with tears and sadness filled my heart.

'You have done a special thing to travel Africa on your motorbike alone, and you made it. You have come further than most. I think you have found what you searched for,' Ahmed said and smiled at my puzzled look, as though he understood the meaning behind my journey.

'I can't believe it is over,' I said and looked up at the night sky filled with stars that shone down with a bright, almost ethereal glow. There was a long silence, my hosts respecting the moment as I reflected on my journey. I had come such a long way – 42,000 kilometres and nineteen countries in fifteen months – through sand and mud, and roads littered with potholes and rocks, through forests and up mountains, through a civil war and road blocks controlled by rebels armed with AK47s. I'd nearly died several times, but I'd always survived. And the African people had always embraced me, as though they understood innately the meaning behind my journey. I knew then that the desire to explore – to have an adventure, to find out what was really out there – is what makes us human, and is as integral to our evolution as new discoveries in technology, medicine and in all the other sciences.

'We are glad you decide to go on the German ship,' Ahmed whispered, gently bringing me out of my inner reflection.

'It looks like I have no choice,' I said. But I knew it was the right, the only, choice for me. 'I still can't believe it is over,' I repeated. 'What now?' While the next stage of my journey was yet to unfold, the German cargo ship being there, at the very moment I needed it, did not surprise me. It was just another in a very long line of happy coincidences. Even so, I said a silent prayer of gratitude, as I had always done for everything fortuitous that had come my way.

*

The next morning, I caught a taxi to the customs and immigration office in the city centre and after my passport and carnet were stamped, I packed my things for the short ride to the docks. I just assumed the Germans would give me and the TT passage.

My hosts helped me manoeuvre the bike down the narrow passageway from the courtyard of their house, and after tightening the handlebars, I was ready to leave.

Ahmed came back from his ship and I thanked him, his two Libyan cousins and the Syrian teacher for their kindness and hospitality. I'd met these men just the day before, but they'd treated me as though I were a dear friend. It was the same human kindness that had been shown to me throughout Africa, a sign of a bond that I had come to expect with all I met. And as we said goodbye, I suddenly thought of the words of the South African woman at the hostel in Cape Town: 'You will find the way of *ubuntu* as you travel Africa'.

I kick-started the TT. It spluttered to life with a forlorn rumble, as if terminally wounded at the end of this great crusade of ours but determined it would not give up until I was safe. I slowly nursed it along the sandy street as I rode towards the docks, but after just a hundred metres there was a loud crunch. The TT backfired, its engine spluttered, it hung on, the wheels kept turning, and then I hit the kill switch and ended its pain.

'What is wrong?' Ahmed yelled breathlessly as he and his two cousins ran towards me.

'I'd say the timing chain finally snapped,' I replied.

'Is your motorbike finished?' he asked with genuine concern.

I nodded. 'It is until I reach a mechanic in Europe. It is *bon chance* I'm taking this ship and am not riding across the desert.'

'You are blessed,' he replied. 'Allah is with you.'

As I sat on the TT for the last time in Africa, I could not believe that luck alone had caused it to stop at the moment when I was safe. The chain could just as easily have snapped in the desert when I was at my most vulnerable. But the TT had held on until the end, when its job was done and this ride was over. Despite all I'd asked of it, this motorcycle had never let me down. It was my dear friend and we had shared many adventures on our long and arduous journey. I rested my hands on its petrol tank as if pouring into it all my gratitude for its strength and reliability. I closed my eyes and imagined its trillions of atoms vibrating in harmony, devoid of friction and tension as it basked in the glow of my adoration.

A German man with wispy blond hair and a boyish face, who I guessed was about thirty, stood watching our approach as the Libyans helped me push the TT along the docks. I thanked Ahmed and his two cousins and we shook hands again to say goodbye. Then I walked up the gangway to speak with the German who was supervising the loading of scrap metal into the ship's hold. I asked about passage to Antwerp and he looked at me with disbelief in his clear blue eyes. I was then led to the bridge and the captain. The voyage would take ten days and the fare was US$20 per day to cover food – the fee was later waived, as the captain told me I was still a long way from home and I would need all my money.

The crane was lowered and the TT was hoisted onto the deck and then wheeled into a shipping container. To protect it from the moist, salt-laden air, I liberally sprayed it with a can of water-displacing spray and covered it in a sheet of clear plastic given to me by the chief engineer. Although the TT was beat-up, rusty and broken, it was not finished. I would have it repaired for the ride home to Australia. Before the holds were bolted shut, the crew searched the ship for stowaways. I thought of Mustafa and Dionigi, as this was how they hoped to make it to Europe.

I stood on the bow, the thick ropes were untied and we slowly pulled away from the docks. The beginning of my journey, on another ship, seemed so long ago. Then I'd been a naive young girl who'd never really considered what could go wrong. When I'd started my travels through Africa, I'd thought nothing of the meaning of chance encounters and coincidences. I was ignorant of the subtle promptings of intuition. But in Africa, I'd found meaning behind these sensations that pulled at my awareness. Everything had always worked in my favour and there was no reason to doubt it would not always be this way as I embarked on the next stage of my adventure. An unwavering faith burnt inside me and it would carry me through the bad times, whenever they might come.

The ship turned and moved into the open sea. I breathed in the salt air. 'Goodbye Africa! Thank you!' I shouted into the wind. The coast slowly disappeared and then was gone.

Africa and its people had looked out for me. I had only ever experienced their kindness and hospitality; even those who may have intended harm did not hurt me. Africa had shown me *ubuntu*.

AFTERWORD

After the German cargo ship docked in Antwerp and the TT was rebuilt in Germany (the excessive consumption of oil was due to a misalignment of the piston rings), I headed to London where I worked as a motorcycle courier for twelve months. But then, as I was about to embark on the second leg of my world motorcycle journey, which would take me to Moscow for the winter to study Russian, my plans abruptly changed. A three-month Russian visa required an HIV test. And on a grey, drizzly September day in 1995 at a suburban medical clinic in outer London, I was diagnosed with HIV.

It doesn't matter how I got it. What matters is how I survived. How my parents embraced me despite my fears they would reject me. How it took me twenty years to find the courage to overcome my fear of stigma to write this book – and to include this truth.

When I was diagnosed in 1995, I was given five years to live, and I realised I did not want what had been revealed to me on my journey to die with me. I felt something akin to an evolutionary duty to share the experiences that had so irrevocably changed me. I wanted to shout to all the world: 'Look, here is the evidence. I had an idea – a dream. I believed in it, I took that first step, and then everything fell into place. There is something out there helping us. It is true. This is what can happen.'

Following my diagnosis, I wrote the first draft of this book over six months in 1996, but like most first drafts, it failed to attract a publisher. I then packed the TT and rode home for one last adventure. That ride also became a search for salvation. While on the road in Africa I had been protected from harm, and I reasoned that my only hope in a world where there was none would be to go back on the road again. I arrived in Hanoi in a state of near-death from AIDS and immediately caught a flight to Australia. I was put in hospital and treated with a cocktail of protease inhibitors, a new generation of recently discovered HIV medicines that came just in time for me, though sadly not for the millions who died before this discovery. Even with this new treatment over a million people a year, most in Africa, still die from AIDS. Economics, politics, distance from medical clinics, drug-resistant strains of HIV, late-stage diagnosis, and stigma are mostly to blame – but none of these should be impossible to overcome.

Deep down, at my lowest point, when the doctors thought I was too far gone for the medications to work, something reassured me that I would not die. I remembered the mantra I'd come to know so well in Africa: *Things always worked out, so why should this time be any different?* Thanks to the medication, the virus was suppressed to undetectable levels and today I am one of sixteen million people who are able to access this life-saving treatment. But this is still less than half the thirty-seven million people living with HIV globally. For a long time, like many of the millions living with HIV, I also lived with fear of stigma. HIV was my dark secret, so dark that it almost crushed my yearning to share with the world what I had discovered in Africa.

But over those twenty years I also lived many other chapters of my life. I went to university and studied journalism. I got married and we created three gorgeous boys free of HIV, although sadly the marriage did not last. My fear of stigma remained – no longer for myself, but for our children. I did not want them to suffer rejection because of me.

Silence only fuels the spread of HIV and perpetuates stigma. It fuels fear of shame, disapproval, rejection and isolation from families and communities. All these things are not *ubuntu*. While *ubuntu* is a Bantu word, there are many words throughout Africa, and indeed throughout the world, that mean the same thing. When someone is kind to others, shows compassion, helps them in whatever capacity they can – they have *ubuntu*. I believe that if we all follow this one simple way of being, so much more will open to us. It is then just a matter of being aware of the ever-so-subtle prompting of our intuition to take advantage of those opportunities that are presented to us.

PLANNING TO GO

For those planning their own motorcycle journey, a full list of the equipment I carried on my travels through Africa is listed at www.heather-ellis.com.

RIDERS FOR HEALTH

The motorcycle is the perfect vehicle to deliver life-giving health services to remote communities in developing countries.

To help deliver health services to people in remote communities in Africa, including antiretroviral medications for those living with HIV, please support Riders for Health.

www.riders.org

ACKNOWLEDGEMENTS

The kindness of strangers ran deep during my travels through Africa, and they all helped write this book. Their conversations and their insights are the nuts and bolts of this story and I am humbly grateful to them all.

While that first draft languished on various computers over twenty years, it was never forgotten. In 2013, when I sat down to write this book, warts and all, several people were invaluable to me. Firstly, I thank my mother, Kitty Ellis, for her unwavering encouragement for a story that had to be told. Thank you to Annette Berning for her excitability, laughter, deep discussion and sometimes tears on listening to me read those parts for which I needed a sounding board. To Kerrie Hall, with whom I studied journalism at James Cook University in Cairns from 1998 to 2000, for always cheering me on and especially for her feedback on those early chapters. To Karen Forman for her 'just do it' attitude in bringing this book to life. Thank you my three beautiful friends. I love you dearly.

To freelance editor Nadine Davidoff for her manuscript assessment and structural expertise which pulled this story together and brought out its spark, and for unwittingly becoming my writing teacher at a time I desperately needed it. I am so grateful I found you. To Karen Le Rossignol for her continued faith in me as my lecturer as I studied the Master of Arts (creative enterprise) at Deakin University in Melbourne while writing this book. And to Cheryl Strayed (author of *Wild*), and my fellow ten talented writers at the Mont Blanc Writing Workshop in Chamonix, France. While I workshopped the sequel to this book during those ten days, the skills I gained in the craft of writing memoir were subsequently used to help further polish the final draft of *Ubuntu*. Before then I had worked in isolation as a writer and Mont Blanc was a revelation, taking me to that next level where the sky is now the limit. Thank you to Alison Boughey and Suzanne Lau Gooey from Positive Women Victoria and Daniel Brace from Living Positive Victoria both for your encouragement and for organising support with the cost of getting to Chamonix.

To those people who I met on my journey through Africa and then found twenty years later, thank you for allowing me to use your names and confirming my recollection of events and conversations. Thank you to Rolf, Anders Knigge, Gladis Johansson, Leo Baker, Myles and Atsuko Nott, Martin Steiner and Mounir Benseddik. And thank you to all those people I could not locate. I pray through this book you will find me – especially Kaoru, Anna, and the Canberra boys, Dave, Eric and Rolf. Thank you also to 'Dan' who unwittingly helped me find courage in the early days of this journey. To paleoanthropologist Dr Craig Feibel for confirming my research and my intuitive thoughts on how our ancestors could, in all likelihood, have evolved. To Bernd Tesch, who collects long-distance motorcycle travellers (he has the world's largest collection of books penned by motorcycle travellers and has held a world motorcycle travellers gathering every years since 1977), for always asking me, since 1998, when he could buy my book.

To all the team at Black Inc.: Jeanne Ryckmans for her words 'Straight up, I'm hooked', in her email in response to my submission. What more can an emerging writer ask from a publisher? And to Samantha Forge for her editorial expertise, which added that extra shine.

To Andrew Case from Mobil Australia for being my champion in providing the letter of introduction, which furnished me with many tanks of petrol and litres of Mobil 1 oil from Mobil depots throughout Africa.

Thank you to all the Mobil staff at those depots. And a special thank you also to Mobil Nigeria for your gracious hospitality in Eket and in Lagos. Thank you again to Andrew Case who arranged for Mobil Australia to pay for the repairs to the TT at Straubel Motorsport in Hameln, Germany. Chance put my beloved TT into the expert hands of Manfred Straubel, a former European enduro motorcycle champion and one of the world's most experienced and knowledgeable mechanics for the TT600. Thank you also to Yamaha Australia for giving me all the spare parts I requested and to Tsubaki Australia for the four motorcycle chains.

And finally, to the people of Africa who were my greatest inspiration to write this book. You are so special. The spirit of *ubuntu* runs deep within you.

CPSIA information can be obtained
at www.ICGtesting.com
Printed in the USA
BVHW060236070519
547457BV00018B/2046/P